The UN Association–USA

For Edie al Joe,
with many thanks
for all that you
do. Ed Elmendorf
2/28/2018

THE UN Association–USA

A Little Known History of Advocacy and Action

James Wurst

with contributions by
Tino Calabia, Doug Garr,
Jeffrey Laurenti, and Dulcie Leimbach

LYNNE
RIENNER
PUBLISHERS

BOULDER
LONDON

Published in the United States of America in 2016 by
Lynne Rienner Publishers, Inc.
1800 30th Street, Boulder, Colorado 80301
www.rienner.com

and in the United Kingdom by
Lynne Rienner Publishers, Inc.
3 Henrietta Street, Covent Garden, London WC2E 8LU

Library of Congress Cataloging-in-Publication Data
Names: Wurst, James.
Title: The UN Association of the USA : a little known history of advocacy
and action / by James Wurst.
Description: Boulder, Colorado : Lynne Rienner Publishers, Inc., 2016. |
    Includes bibliographical references and index.
Identifiers: LCCN 2016016379 (print) | LCCN 2016022243 (ebook) |
    ISBN 9781626375475 (hardcover : alk. paper) |
    ISBN 9781626375482 (pbk. : alk. paper) | ISBN 9781626375499 (ebook)
Subjects: LCSH: United Nations Association of the United States of
    America—History. | United Nations—United States—History. | United
    States—Foreign relations—1945–1989.
Classification: LCC JZ4997.5.U6 W87 2016 (print) | LCC JZ4997.5.U6 (ebook) |
    DDC 341.2306/073—dc23
LC record available at https://lccn.loc.gov/2016016379

British Cataloguing in Publication Data
A Cataloguing in Publication record for this book
is available from the British Library.

Printed and bound in the United States of America

5 4 3 2 1

To the late John C. Whitehead
and the thousands of other Americans whose endeavors have
increased understanding of and support for the United Nations
over more than seventy years

and

To my wife, Rosa

Contents

Foreword

Andrea Bartoli

With great pleasure, I present this important work. There is much to be learned from the history of the United Nations Association of the United States of America (UNA-USA), which has been vital to US support for the United Nations since its founding.

Why do we write about the past, and why do we need a history of UNA-USA? The way we create a meaningful future is by building on the ideals that emerged from our past successes. In understanding how this innovative vision of the UN, which set the stage for globalization, could become a reality under seemingly impossible conditions, one can imagine ways in which impossible global challenges of today can be overcome.

The value of the contributions made by UNA-USA is very relevant, especially to those who remember well the state-centered international system and the relative newness of nongovernmental organizations (NGOs), which seem ever-present in the international system today. UNA-USA was ahead of its time in advocating for the importance of multilateralism in a way that many NGOs would like to replicate today. The association was a locus of experimentation and creativity that allowed for explorations that would have been difficult (if not impossible) for state actors. In a bilateral international system that could not navigate global commonalities and differences, UNA-USA offered a more effective future.

Intriguingly, UNA-USA protagonists did not shy away from the enormous challenges ahead, but instead sought a network of competent and committed scholars, practitioners, and advocates who could imagine, encourage, and support change. The need for such collaboration continues to this day. Issues ranging from poverty to partnerships, from peacekeeping to protection, demonstrate that there is nothing that can be done by UN member states in isolation. The generative ability of the independent sector, of which UNA-USA has been a model and a champion, is an essential component of our evolving international system.

At the beginning of my term as dean of the School of Diplomacy and International Relations in 2013, I was asked to continue the school's institutional support of Ed Elmendorf and James Wurst in their effort to write the history of UNA-USA. What an auspicious beginning. Reflecting on that history was an invitation to rediscover the very roots of the School of Diplomacy and set the right tone for that school's new era. The first school of international affairs founded after the Cold War, Seton Hall's School of Diplomacy and International Relations was conceived through an exclusive relationship with UNA-USA that is still vibrant and fruitful. The timing could not have been more propitious: the merger with the United Nations Foundation, the seventieth anniversary of the United Nations, the new UN Global Goals for Sustainable Development, and a new period of growth for Seton Hall University.

Centers of higher education such as the School of Diplomacy and International Relations are going to play an increasingly significant role in understanding, framing, communicating, and addressing contemporary challenges. They will continue to function—as UNA-USA did—as catalysts for options that would have been impossible to explore without the space in between, the gray area of opportunity not controlled by overreaching states.

An element of this process, and one of the emerging dimensions of this history, is the role of the people, of the ordinary citizens, who, without official mandate, explore new models of international governance and collective action. The UN system has openly embraced this role of the people in the new millennium. After Secretary-General Kofi Annan's "Millennium Report" in 2000, his reference to the people of the world has become an essential thread. Around the world, so many seek the level of representation and political relevance that UNA-USA has fostered and witnessed. There are now many more United Nations associations worldwide, and an important global conversation about their relevance and impact can begin with this volume.

I am grateful to my School of Diplomacy colleagues, who made this collaboration possible and who kept alive, for many years, the unique connection between the school and the UN system. In particular, I would like to recognize Professor Courtney Smith, whose UN Intensive Summer Study Program has for nearly twenty years brought people from around the world to New York to learn about the UN through an engaged and productive pedagogy; and Professor Martin Edwards, who accepted the challenge of directing our Center for UN and Global Governance Studies and has grown it rapidly into a relevant player in the UN system. In addition, I want to recognize the many students, colleagues, and friends who have been contribut-

ing to the fruitful collaboration of UNA-USA and the School of Diplo
This nearly twenty years has been a productive beginning, and this history
makes that collaboration stronger and more compelling moving forward.

As chair of the advisory committee for this book, I also thank its dis-
tinguished members for their invaluable contributions to the publication—
namely, Steven Dimoff, Bill Draper, Fred Eckhard, Toby Gati, Jeff Laurenti,
William McDonough, Karen Mulhauser, Jim Olson, Tom Pickering,
Jonathan Roberts, Steve Schlesinger, Gillian Sorensen, William vanden
Heuvel, Christopher Whatley, and the late John C. Whitehead.

—Andrea Bartoli
Dean of the School of Diplomacy and International Relations,
Seton Hall University

Foreword

A. Edward Elmendorf

Early in 2010, the UNA-USA Board of Directors cochair, Ambassador Tom Pickering, asked me to lead UNA-USA through the final design, negotiation, and approval of its planned alliance with the UN Foundation. As a former US diplomat at the United Nations, a former UN official, and a previous UNA-USA volunteer leader, I was pleased to assume this new role. As I took up these responsibilities, I became increasingly aware of the organization's long, rich history and of the risks that a failure to preserve the written record, interview as many of the key players as possible, and document UNA-USA's many-faceted activities would imply the loss of an important thread in contemporary US history. Indeed, this is a story of linking private citizens with their government and with the United Nations, under the auspices of the United Nations Association of the USA and its predecessor, the American Association for the UN (AAUN)—hence this history and the associated assumption of the UNA-USA archives by Seton Hall University.

As I delved into the records and talked with vital stakeholders in UNA-USA and beyond, I began to see more clearly the critical importance of citizen input into foreign policy decisions, be they large or small. I also saw the significance, for US involvement in the UN, of over seventy years of independent, committed voices, all supporting an active, internationalist US engagement rooted in international law, the UN Charter, and the architecture of multilateral organizations created under US leadership at the end of World War II. AAUN and UNA-USA have also increased the public visibility of the United Nations with the executive and legislative branches of our government in Washington, DC. Conferences and meetings, multiple policy studies enriched by UNA-USA member input, collaborations with UN associations in other countries, and public events and private meetings organized by the many UNA-USA chapters around the country have all contributed.

Civil society is important to the United Nations and to US engagement in the UN. While UN observers and UN actors themselves tend to focus on the high policy drama taking place at the intergovernmental level, there is critically important long-term work being done by the hundreds of UN commissions and committees and thousands of personnel around the world. Among the thousands of nongovernmental organizations active at the United Nations, UNA-USA has held a unique position as an independent source of policy input and support with only one value at the root of its actions: the purposes, principles, and procedures outlined in the UN Charter. To do this, UNA-USA occasionally has had to criticize US policies and UN actions and sometimes engaged in fierce internal debate. At the same time, UNA-USA has evolved in response to the changing global scene and its impact on the United Nations; it has suffered and benefited from mood swings in the United Nations and in the US public.

As this book demonstrates, UNA-USA has mobilized widespread interest and involvement in the UN and in US policies affecting the UN, including among public figures such as Eleanor Roosevelt and Elliot Richardson; business leaders such as John Whitehead and Arthur Ross; and NGO personnel, teachers, students, and schoolchildren across the country. It has helped to open the United Nations to the US public, starting with UN tour guides provided by AAUN in the early years, and it has helped Americans to understand and visit the occasionally opaque organization.

Like other membership organizations, UNA-USA has suffered from changes in how US citizens have participated in civil society organizations over the past seventy years, as well as from the present reality that communication takes place most frequently in the e-world rather than in person. As the UN has become less visible to the broad US public, and as dramatic tensions and civil conflict in other countries have come to occupy more of public attention, the advocacy and public education activities of an independent civil society organization such as UNA-USA have become even more important to the United States in its role as a responsible and collaborative, but no longer single dominant, global player.

UNA-USA leaders throughout the country have been trailblazers in promoting and supporting a peaceful world through the many programs and activities of the United Nations, ranging from traditional peacekeeping to efforts in the realms of economic policy, social development, humanitarian affairs, and human rights. The element of surprise in the history of AAUN and UNA-USA lies in how little has been known before the writing of this book about so much of its work: the contacts by AAUN executive director Clark Eichelberger with President Franklin D. Roosevelt during World War

II to lobby for an active, effective United Nations even before it was created; the extensive volunteer work of Eleanor Roosevelt at AAUN; the interactions between the civil rights movement of the 1960s and AAUN; the work of UNA-USA in helping to define post–Cold War roles for the UN in peacekeeping and development; and the mobilization of Americans in defense of the UN against ill-informed criticism and assaults calling for US disengagement.

I want to express deep personal appreciation to James Wurst, the author of this study; to Dulcie Leimbach, the editor of the book; and to Andrea Bartoli, dean of Seton Hall University's School of Diplomacy and International Relations, which has provided institutional and fiduciary oversight for the UNA-USA history project. I also thank the leaders and supporters of UNA-USA from across the country in the years immediately before its alliance with the UN Foundation, whose belief in the importance of the project and confidence in the skills and commitment of the study team led them to provide financial support: Christopher Brody, William and Judith Cottle, Edison Dick, William Draper III, Ambassador James Leonard, William McDonough, Ambassador Thomas R. Pickering, Jonathan Roberts, Janet Ross, Gillian Sorensen, David Squire, Judith Thayer, Katrina vanden Heuvel, Ambassador William vanden Heuvel, Josh Weston, and the late John C. Whitehead. Financial assistance also came from the Carnegie Corporation of New York, the Community Foundation for the National Capital Region, and the Dick Family Foundation. Special appreciation is given to Janet Ross for her extraordinarily generous support and to Tom Pickering for introducing the history project to potential financial supporters.

—A. Edward Elmendorf
Former president and chief executive of UNA and
study director for the UNA-USA History Project

Preface

This book covers more than seventy years of the history of an extraordinary civil society organization. From the League of Nations Association to the American Association for the United Nations (AAUN) to the United Nations Association of the USA (UNA-USA), the overarching vision has been the belief that the world works best when people cooperate, not when they fight. Members of UNA-USA have always maintained faith that the world coming together as the United Nations was the greatest goal of our civilization.

The book starts in one of the most miserable years of the twentieth century—1938—when the worst war in human history was beginning to spread and when dedicated internationalists on both sides of the Atlantic sought not only an end to Nazism but also the establishment of a cooperative world order. The United Nations was born from these years, shaped in no small measure by the same Americans who headed the AAUN. While the postwar unity unraveled, AAUN took the lead in the campaign to keep the United Nations central to the political and public life of the United States. In this work, the association had a great champion—Eleanor Roosevelt.

As domestic and international situations changed, UNA-USA changed as well, branching into new fields, such as the unofficial diplomacy of its Parallel Studies Program and the creation of a body of visionary writings that helped shape the internationalist debate for decades. The end of the Cold War opened new opportunities for the UN, and UNA-USA was quick to promote a stronger UN role in peacekeeping, human rights, international law, the environment, and development.

One of UNA-USA's enduring strengths has been its network of chapters and citizens from around the United States. The pages that follow afford an in-depth look at the role these chapters have played on the local, national, and international stages. The book also examines the lives of some of the social, political, and business leaders who dedicated so much of their talent to UNA-USA.

The book has been a collaborative effort in the finest sense of the word. The first people to thank are the members of the core team that conceived the project: Ed Elmendorf, Dulcie Leimbach, and Tino Calabia. Jeff Laurenti, Angie Drakulich, and Doug Garr made invaluable contributions in researching and critiquing various drafts of the manuscript. In addition, I thank all the people named in these pages who shared their memories, insights, and in some cases personal archives. Their contributions are more than could fit in a single volume, so the UNA-USA History Project will continue with a website hosted by Seton Hall (http://blogs.shu.edu/UNA-USA) that will include an oral history, other research, and reports and photos from the UNA archives.

On the subject of archives, I offer a tremendous thank you to two extraordinary libraries. I spent weeks in these wonderful institutions, reliving the history of these important years. The Manuscripts and Archives Division of the New York Public Library (Astor, Lenox, and Tilden Foundations) houses the Clark Eichelberger archives, and the staff there helped me navigate 200-plus boxes of papers. The Seton Hall University library houses the UNA-USA archives, and the university archivist, Alan Delozier, and his team were knowledgeable and enthusiastic supporters of the project.

The School of Diplomacy and International Relations at Seton Hall University, under the leadership of Dean Andrea Bartoli, served as the institutional home for this project. More than that, the school's high ethical and academic standards enriched the project. I thank Professor Bartoli and the school's faculty, including Martin S. Edwards, Elizabeth V. Halpin, Catherine Ruby, and Courtney B. Smith.

In other phases of my career, I worked with interns from the Seton Hall School of Diplomacy, and they were consistently energetic and creative. That tradition of excellence continues with the interns who contributed to this book: Omar Ahmad, Bridget B. Brady, Jared A. Daly, Brian Dolan, Fabio Faschi, John J. Pollack, and Mariah G. Ross (as well as Haoran Sun of American University). Thank you.

And, of course, I thank my wife, Rosa, who put up with my turning our dining room into a research library for far too long.

I'm saving my final thanks for Estelle Linzer and Margaret Olson. They worked for decades in various positions for AAUN and UNA-USA, keeping the offices running, reaching out to the membership and general public, and organizing the files. After months at the New York Public Library, it became clear to me that while the archives were in Eichelberger's name, the work of preserving all these documents was due to the diligence of these two women. Without their dedication and foresight, this book would have been impossible, and, as a result, the rich history of one of this country's most important citizen movements would have been lost.

—*James Wurst*

1

A Citizens' Movement for Founding the United Nations, 1938–1943

Two days after the attack on Pearl Harbor in 1941, President Franklin D. Roosevelt delivered a radio address, saying, "There is no such thing as security for any nation—or any individual—in a world ruled by the principles of gangsterism. There is no such thing as impregnable defense against powerful aggressors who sneak up in the dark and strike without warning. . . . We are going to win the war and we are going to win the peace that follows. And in the dark hours of this day— and through dark days that may be yet to come—we will know that the vast majority of the members of the human race are on our side."

The next day, FDR's personal secretary received a letter from Clark Eichelberger, the director of the League of Nations Association, offering its services and those of related groups to help the president construct "the organization of the world for peace and justice."[1]

This was not a spontaneous idea born from shock of the attack. For more than twenty years, Eichelberger, the LNA, as it was known, and others had carried the banner for a "world organization" as declared by the League of Nations. And though the league itself was slipping into irrelevance through its inability to marshal effective global responses to the aggressions of the emerging Axis powers in the early 1930s and the Allied powers' military reactions, the association that supported it still promoted the league's ideals, calling for revisions of its covenant to make the world body both more effective and more acceptable to the United States. By the time World War II reached its bloodiest peak in the early 1940s, a consensus was finally reached among the Allies that a new organization for international security—not simply a victors' peace— was necessary long before the shooting stopped, so that when peace came, the world would have a new strong foundation on which to build.

The LNA itself was an early grassroots base in the United States with an internationalist outlook. It was founded in 1923 through the

1

merger of the American Association for International Cooperation and the League of Nations Non-Partisan Committee, after the Paris Peace Treaty, which had set the terms of victory following World War I and which had included the creation of the League of Nations. Despite ultimate US congressional and popular rejection of the league, it continued to campaign for international US engagement abroad. Even as the LNA struggled to garner support over the decades, it nevertheless became the founding organization of the American Association for the United Nations (AAUN) in 1945 and later of the United Nations Association of the United States of America (UNA-USA) in 1964.

Eichelberger's life paralleled the political history of the century. Born in 1896 in Illinois, he served as a US Army corporal in World War I, "loading boxcars," as he said, in France. (His brother, Robert, had a military career of greater longevity, having been a West Point graduate and a four-star general in the Pacific theater during World War II.[2]) In the early 1920s, Clark Eichelberger traveled to Geneva to study the League of Nations. His connection to the league began in 1927, when he became the director of its Chicago office. In 1933, he became the executive director, and in 1938, he was in Geneva for what was to be the last League Assembly, just as Britain and France fatally forced the cessation of the Sudetenland region of Czechoslovakia to Germany in the name of peace. Eichelberger was a member of the US State Department committee that wrote the first draft of the UN Charter and a consultant to the 1945 San Francisco Conference. After 1933, depending on the year, he was either the director or the executive director of LNA, AAUN, UNA, or related coalitions until his retirement in 1964. He then continued to serve in advisory capacities for UNA and the Commission to Study the Organization of Peace (CSOP), the research arm of the LNA, until his death in 1980.

The other important figure in global peace advocate circles during those decades was James T. Shotwell. Born in Canada in 1874 to US Quaker parents, Shotwell's academic and political careers included milestones in international affairs. He was a US delegate to the 1919 Paris Peace Conference and the author of the charter of the International Labour Organization (ILO). Shotwell was named president of the LNA in 1935. Four years later, he and Eichelberger founded CSOP. In his role on a State Department subcommittee, Shotwell was largely responsible for the working paper that formed the basis of the UN Charter (see below). Eichelberger and Shotwell complemented each other's skills. Eichelberger was the detail-oriented organizer, and Shotwell, the intellectual, developing the next great idea.

Clark Eichelberger
(Photo courtesy of the Clark M.
Eichelberger papers,
Manuscripts and Archives
Division, The New York Public
Library. Astor, Lenox, and Tilden
Foundations.)

It was Eichelberger who mobilized the grassroots base, and it was Shotwell who created the frameworks for international organizations, including the ILO and the UN. It was Eichelberger who lobbied presidents and congressional leaders; it was Shotwell who designed the building blocks of a new international security structure for the United States.

The single overarching obsession of these and other internationalists—starting with Franklin D. Roosevelt, himself—was to ensure that the multiple failures of the League of Nations would not be repeated. Globally, this meant creating an organization that had real authority and that was not created as a victors' peace. In the United States, this meant engaging as broad a spectrum as possible of political (especially congressional) and popular opinion. Fewer than twenty years had passed between the Paris Peace Conference of 1919 and Adolf Hitler's annexation of the Sudetenland in 1938; for most political and military leaders in the late 1930s, the Great War was living memory. Harry Truman, Dwight Eisenhower, and Eichelberger were soldiers in that war; FDR was a junior cabinet official at the time; Herbert Hoover was a relief worker in Belgium; FDR's future secretary of state, Cordell Hull, and his first vice president, John Nance Garner, were members of the House of Representatives.

In her memoirs, *This I Remember,* Eleanor Roosevelt recalled the first UN General Assembly meeting in London in 1946, which brought up ghosts of previous failures. "So many of the Europeans were older men who had made the effort with the League of Nations and were a little doubtful about a second international effort to keep the world at peace," she wrote. "The loss of a generation makes itself felt acutely twenty to twenty-five years later, when many men who would have been leaders are just not there to lead."[3]

Among the internationalists, there was no debate that the failure of 1919 had led directly to the next world war, and it certainly was not a question of hindsight. In 1919, President Woodrow Wilson said, "I can predict with absolute certainty that within a generation there will be another world war." Paul Kennedy, in *The Parliament of Man,* reproduced a chilling political cartoon from 1919, titled "Peace and the Cannon Fodder," from the London *Daily Herald.* It depicts the Great War victors strolling out of the Paris conference, while cowering behind a column is a small naked boy, labeled "1940 class."[4]

A Horrible Summer, 1938

Eichelberger traveled to Europe in the summer of 1938, first to attend the International Federation of League of Nations Societies in Copenhagen, followed by a trip to Prague in July for meetings with government officials, and then on to the annual Assembly of the League of Nations in September in Geneva. Before leaving the United States, he met with FDR on June 9 at the White House and broached his favorite policy proposal: an international conference to revise the League of Nations' Covenant to make it more authoritative and more acceptable to the United States. Eichelberger quoted Roosevelt as saying, "That's the thing. That's good; I believe it's about time for something to be done along that line."[5]

Europe was consumed by the crisis in Czechoslovakia. Hitler was demanding the annexation of the German-speaking portion of the country, called the Sudetenland. He had annexed Austria in March and was claiming to represent the "oppressed" ethnic Germans of western Czechoslovakia. The nineteenth session of the League of Nations Assembly met in Geneva beginning on September 12. Eichelberger described it as "an unreal Assembly," in which the official agenda was taken up with routine matters and with only one mention of Czechoslovakia, while "outside the Assembly Hall very little was spoken of except the increasing threat of Germany to Czechoslovakia and the efforts of the British and French governments to force Czechoslovakia to a hideous surrender."[6] Eichelberger's disdain for the political maneuvering was vehement. He clearly saw the sacrifice of Czechoslovakia as a betrayal of an ally behaving legally and undercutting the remaining authority of the league.

Edward R. Murrow, the CBS News chief correspondent in London, asked Eichelberger for radio reports from the assembly. In his radio broadcast commentary on September 11, Eichelberger, despite his anger, sounded an optimistic note. "We must not permit any catastrophe to destroy our faith," he said. "No adversity should stop us for a moment from fulfilling the task of our generation, which is the outlawry of war and the establishment of the institutions of peaceful international society."

On September 21, British prime minister Neville Chamberlain met with Hitler at his retreat at Berchtesgaden in the Bavarian Alps, where Chamberlain accepted Hitler's claim to the Sudetenland. Eichelberger, in a September 26 radio address on CBS, was blunt, complaining that Britain and France "have maneuvered Prague into the position of a defeated power being presented with ultimatums from friends and enemies alike. There is universal resentment . . . that a law-abiding democratic state such as Czechoslovakia should be placed in this position."[7]

At the Munich summit with Germany and Italy on one side and Britain and France on the other, an agreement was signed (with no Czech officials present), ceding the Sudetenland to Germany on September 30. This was the infamous "peace is at hand" summit. A historic irony is that the League of Nations Assembly also ended on the same day. Eichelberger later wrote that while he was at a dinner with league leaders that evening, "[I] could hardly contain myself as I listened to the hypocritical tributes" as to how Munich was the road to peace. "I believed it was the beginning of the Second World War," Eichelberger wrote. The assembly never met again.

Back in the United States, the LNA and other coalitions were organizing demonstrations and prayer meetings in support of Czechoslovakia. On September 25, thirty mass meetings were held around the country. At the Chicago rally, 65,000 people attended. An overflow crowd of 23,000 filled the meeting in Madison Square Garden in New York City. In a message to that rally, Eichelberger said, "The refusal of the United States to join the League of Nations twenty years ago and the abandonment of its principles by other great powers are finally bearing fruit."[8]

Despite Munich and the neutering of the league, the LNA continued to advocate for its role in international affairs, so its work was not officially over, despite the assembly's collapse. However, after the league's successive failures to defend Ethiopia against Italian aggression, as well as Austria and Czechoslovakia against Germany, the LNA abandoned hope that it could play a part in political or security issues; it focused instead on strengthening its work in economic, social, and humanitarian affairs. This was not grasping at straws. Indeed, this work had already been relatively productive, particularly with the ILO, which was functioning as intended with US support. After its creation in 1919 from the ashes of the Great War, the ILO pursued fair, universal labor practices based on social justice. (Later, the ILO became the first specialized agency of the UN in 1946.) Moreover, the United States had actively supported the league's efforts in this regard while staying out of the league itself. The LNA had not given up on international solutions to political issues, though; it had just given up on the league as the vehicle for those solutions.

The Rise of Internationalism

Internationalism was not the dominant school of thought throughout the United States in the 1920s and 1930s. The LNA soldiered on long after the bulk of US governmental and popular opinion gave up on it and returned to their traditional isolationism. Eichelberger, Shotwell, and company used their skills, nevertheless, to convince Americans that they needed to look outward; yet, the public debate on such foreign policy was won through the more powerful voices of William Randolph Hearst, the publisher; Father Charles Coughlin, the Detroit-based radio demagogue; and isolationist members of Congress. At the time, those members included the preponderance of the Republican Party and a large share of the Democratic Party.

By 1938, with the next war looming in Europe, Eichelberger and other LNA officials knew that FDR's heart remained with them, but the Neutrality Acts, which prevented the United States from favoring one belligerent over another in wartime, and political realities strongly favored US cautious impartiality. Eichelberger met with FDR eight times from 1936 to 1944, seeking to gauge his feelings on creating an international organization and briefing him on LNA's work.[9] Although FDR was an advocate of international engagement, he could not always promote that position publicly. As president, however, he filled his State Department with Wilsonians: Secretary of State Cordell Hull, Undersecretary of State Sumner Welles, and Ambassador Joseph Davies, among others.[10] In 1939, Roosevelt had instructed the State Department to start drafting the outlines for a world organization. FDR was content to feed ideas to Eichelberger, knowing that Eichelberger agreed with him and that the president would not have to take responsibility for these trial balloons.[11]

On September 1, 1939, Germany invaded Poland. Two days later, Britain and France declared war on Germany, and World War II began in force. Although the United States was still officially neutral, official and public opinion generally favored the European democracies over the German dictatorship. But that sympathy did not include abandoning neutrality.

Two internationalist groups were established after the declaration of war in Europe: the Committee to Defend America by Aiding the Allies (CDAAA), founded in May 1940, and Fight for Freedom (FFF), founded in April 1941. The main difference between the two was that the CDAAA focused on maximizing aid to European allies (in policy terms, this meant repealing the Neutrality Acts), while the more militant FFF group wanted a declaration of war. Both opposed the isolationist America First Committee, and both refused to work with Communists. Eichelberger, Shotwell, and other LNA figures helped to create the CDAAA, as they shared offices. The Fight for Freedom entity was chaired by Ulric Bell, a former editor of the *Courier-Journal* in Louisville, Kentucky, who later ran Americans United for World Organization after Fight for Freedom folded. In 1943, he was named by Robert E. Sherwood to run the Los Angeles branch of the Office of War Information, acting as a liaison to the motion picture industry.

Both the CDAAA and the FFF adopted the strategy of putting on a nonpartisan and populist face. Drawing on the strategy of the LNA, both groups worked to build chapters across the country and enlist distinguished public figures. Demographically, this meant focusing on getting midwestern Republicans to counter the Democratic/East Coast–heavy boards and committees. From that perspective, the Committee to Defend America hit the trifecta with William Allen White, the publisher of the *Emporia Gazette* in Kansas, a Pulitzer Prize winner, a nationally known author (including the articles "What's the Matter with Kansas?" and "Mary White," about his daughter), and a dedicated Republican. But White was a "Teddy Roosevelt Republican," meaning he supported the Bull Moose Party and the League of Nations and opposed isolationism and the Republican Party's conservative wing. The Fight for Freedom's honorary chairmen were Henry W. Hobson, the Episcopal Church's bishop for southern Ohio, and Senator Carter Glass, Democrat of Virginia.

Both Hobson and Glass succeeded in establishing chapters around the country, but the CDAAA did a better job. By the time of the Pearl Harbor attack in 1941, the committee had more than 800 chapters, whereas the

Fight for Freedom had 372. In an article analyzing the two groups, Andrew Johnstone, a lecturer at the University of Leicester in Britain, wrote that the purpose of the chapters was to demonstrate popular support and to counter the criticism of representing only the "elite Eastern Establishment."[12] He argued that the FFF had superior outreach to labor and African Americans (African American leaders in the group included A. Philip Randolph and Adam Clayton Powell). Both groups, through Eichelberger and Bell, had the ear of the White House, but Eichelberger could boast a closer personal relationship with FDR. In addition, FDR's steps to aid the British, in particular the Lend-Lease Program, were more aligned with CDAAA thinking. "Despite its non-partisan nature and Republican Chairman, the CDAAA was clearly sympathetic to the foreign policy aims of the Roosevelt Administration. In fact, it often went out of its way to act as a propaganda agency for those policies," Johnstone wrote.[13]

Popularly known as the White Committee, the CDAAA was unveiled to the public on May 20, 1940. In his statement to the press, White said, "The time has come when the United States should throw its economic and moral weight on the side of the nations of western Europe. . . . It would be folly to hold this nation chained to a neutrality policy determined in the light of last year's facts. The new situation requires a new attitude." The group sought to attract support from leading public figures and chapters nationwide. Well-known endorsers included James B. Conant, the president of Harvard; Governor Herbert Lehman of New York; the boxer Gene Tunney; playwright Robert Sherwood; historian Henry Steele Commager; theologian Reinhold Niebuhr; and General John Pershing. "The genius of the Committee," Eichelberger wrote, "was to get information and suggestions for action out to the country and in turn channel expressions of opinion to Washington."[14]

The strategy of the committee in the period between the annexation of Czechoslovakia in 1938 and the attack on Pearl Harbor in 1941 can be found in the *Washington Office Information Letter*. Published by CDAAA, starting in early 1941, it was a weekly mimeographed publication promoting the CDAAA's agenda and examining practical matters such as industrial production. Written over the year alternately by Livingston Hartley, Donald C. Blaisdell, Frank S. Goodwin, Roger S. Greene, and E. Fred Cullen, the newsletter made the case of supporting Britain, Russia, and China in every way short of military force. In a July 24, 1941, article, titled "Hitler's Objectives in Russia," the committee argued that Hitler not only aimed for control of Russia's wheat and oil but also "intends to use a defeated Russia as an instrument in his drive to dominate the world," in which he would "gain invaluable strategic positions for use against the British Empire." The fall of Russia and the absolute isolation of Britain would lead to a "Germanized Europe."

After the attack on Pearl Harbor, the December 19 issue (#49) stated, "America's entry into the war lays finally the specter of an appeasement peace. . . . Our country is now the central power house of the Allies, and our country is fighting for total victory." The last newsletter in the Eichelberger archives, dated December 24, 1941 (#50), dealt with Winston Churchill's arrival in Washington, DC, which the committee saw as the beginning of a formal alliance between the two countries. (It was: the Declaration by the United Nations by Roosevelt and Churchill was announced the next week.) The issue also analyzed the Pacific front and politics in Germany and provided a "Retrospect" on whether war could have been avoided. The short answer to that question was no—any appeasement of Japan and Germany "could have brought us peace, only temporarily. . . . The inevitable showdown with them both either would have come before now, or else would loom directly ahead. And that showdown would then have been a two-ocean war for survival, without any effective allies—a battle of America."[15]

Germany's invasion of the Soviet Union in June 1941 shook up political alliances. Ever since the 1939 Molotov-Ribbentrop Nonaggression Pact (by which each pledged to remain neutral should either nation be attacked by a third party), American Communists had supported isolationism. After the invasion, however, they became interventionists and left the isolationist, pro-German America First Committee; but neither CDAAA nor FFF accepted them as members.

Another change at this time was that the committee shortened its name, dropping "by Aiding the Allies," so that it was simply the Committee to Defend America (CDA). The July 4, 1941, issue of the *Washington Office Information Letter* was the last to use the full title. In the next issue, July 11, the committee was now Committee to Defend America, with a subhead: "By Aiding the Allies—By Defeating the Axis Powers—By Developing Means for Permanent Peace." No explanation for the name change was given.[16]

A *New York Herald Tribune* article on July 4, 1941, noted the change and quoted a CDA Executive Committee statement saying that the long title "was always too cumbersome" and that it was "limited as a complete definition of the committee's aims."[17] The timing suggests that the committee did not want its name to imply an alliance with the Soviet Union, though that was not explicitly stated.

FDR and Churchill met on August 14, 1941, aboard the HMS *Prince of Wales*, where they agreed on a set of principles for international cooperation. Dubbed the Atlantic Charter, the nonbinding agreement was a declaration "of certain common principles in the national policies of their respective countries on which they based their hopes for a better future for the world." Once the charter was released, the internationalists seized it as a rallying agenda for a global organization.

Eichelberger flew to Britain in September 1941 to seek a better sense of British political thinking after the signing of the charter. His agenda included meetings with US and British officials and governments-in-exile based in London, including the Czech foreign minister, Jan Masaryk, and the Free French leader, Charles de Gaulle. But Eichelberger's main interest was meeting with the British Research Sub-Committee on International Organization, the politically kindred spirit to the Commission to Study the Organization of Peace, the LNA's think tank. Eichelberger discovered from his talks with the British group that, other than the need for a postwar organization and a commitment to the disarmament and economic recovery of Germany, the two organizations had little in common. "One might say that the British were too close to the war to engage in postwar planning, whereas the Americans were too far removed from it to have a sense of reality about it," he wrote.[18]

Eichelberger was also invited to a small private lunch at 10 Downing Street with Winston Churchill. After the meal, drinks, and a monologue by the prime minister, Eichelberger—true to form—asked Churchill one question: What would take the place of the League of Nations in the postwar world? Churchill was noncommittal, saying he was too old to think beyond the war itself; it was up to FDR to create such an entity.[19] In a CBS radio broadcast soon after, on September 21 from London, Eichelberger said, "It would be a disaster if the war were so prolonged that at its close the victorious nations would be too tired to build or guarantee an adequate peace." Foreshadowing the speech FDR would make on December 8 after Pearl Harbor, Eichelberger added, "Winning the war should be a job of a few years; winning the peace will require the best efforts of our generation."[20]

The December 7, 1941, Japanese attack on Pearl Harbor ended the isolationist/internationalist debate entirely. The Committee to Defend America, the Fight for Freedom, and America First all ceased to exist by early 1942. The LNA, CSOP, CDA, and other affiliated groups created a grand coalition called Citizens for Victory. "As a result, in addition to the vast effort to mobilize the American public against the fascist threat, further significance of such networks lay in their potential for years to come," Johnstone wrote.[21]

Winning the Peace

On December 8, 1941, Congress declared war on Japan, and on December 11, Germany and Italy declared war on the United States, and the United States reciprocated. World War II was now virtually global. The LNA, like the vast majority of Americans, mobilized for battle. Citizens for Victory, the LNA, and all the various permutations of acronyms, agendas, and personalities from the past two decades or so crystallized themselves through a two-prong goal: win the war and win the peace.

Churchill visited Washington on December 22. By January 1, 1942, he and FDR announced a sweeping alliance, called the Declaration by United Nations. The declaration, which was ultimately signed by twenty-six governments, reaffirmed "a common program of purposes and principles" set out in the Atlantic Charter, with each state pledging to "employ its full resources" in "the struggle for victory over Hitlerism." (Its original name was merely Declaration, but after it was signed, the phrase "by United Nations" was added.[22]) The LNA's goal of developing a world organization before the end of the war, dedicated to securing peace through international cooperation, played out in tandem with the official policy of the US government.

FDR continued to communicate with Eichelberger and the LNA, encouraging them to say what he could not yet declare openly. "I have read with interest of your plan to inform our people of the United Nations' aspect of the struggle," he wrote in an April 30, 1942, letter to Eichelberger. "Nothing could be more important than that the people of the United States and of the world should fully realize the magnitude of the united effort required in this fight."[23]

Earlier, in February 1942, the CSOP published its long-planned report titled "The United Nations and the Organization of Peace," which continued to refine the vision of both the CSOP and the LNA for the UN world body. This vision was based on the principles of the Atlantic Charter and the Declaration by United Nations.

As long ago as 1939, Secretary of State Hull had assigned State Department officials to begin a discreet study of postwar peace and reconstruction through his advisory committee on problems of foreign relations. Hull stayed with this work throughout the war but had to face the imperatives of the war itself, as well as other agencies wanting "a piece of the United Nations action" and the potential wrath of isolationists.[24] In September 1941, Hull and Welles, undersecretary of state, finally got approval from FDR for the State Department to become the exclusive home for postwar planning. The new Advisory Committee on Postwar Foreign Policy met for the first time on February 12, 1942 — two months after Pearl Harbor and five weeks after the publication of the Declaration by United Nations.

The postwar committee was chaired by Hull, with Welles as vice chair. But Welles was also the chair of the subcommittee on political problems, which put a world organization in his portfolio. (The other subcommittees were security, territorial problems, economics, political, and legal, as well as one on a possible European federation.) Welles and Leo Pasvolsky, Hull's personal assistant and an economist, recruited outside experts (including Eichelberger and Shotwell) to begin creating a world body. This was the only time in his career that Eichelberger received a salary from the US government. At this point, the committee was still secret; so when Eichelberger toured the country visiting LNA chapters, he never revealed that their collective goal was now under serious consideration in the White House.

By March 1943, the subcommittee had a rough draft ready, presenting a major world organization. Although the paper was the product of the political subcommittee (the Welles Committee), there was some disagreement, no surprise, as to who deserved the most credit: in his book, *Act of Creation: The Founding of the United Nations*, historian Stephen C. Schlesinger said it was Pasvolsky; but Eichelberger credited Shotwell. Regardless, the fundamentals of what would become the UN Charter were apparent: a General Assembly, a Security Council, an International Court of Justice, an Economic and Social Council, and a Trusteeship Council. The exact membership and voting rights of the Security Council were still unsettled, but FDR's one nonnegotiable point — that the four major powers (the United States, Britain, Russia, and China) would have special policing powers and responsibilities — was in place.[25] The president signed off on the plan, and on June 15, 1943, he mentioned for the first time, publicly, that the government was working on a blueprint for an international organization.[26]

The first draft of the UN Charter was complete.

The First UN Association

Despite the basic common interest in "winning the war/winning the peace," there was still a plethora of internationalist organizations during the war years — many of them housed at LNA headquarters at 8 West 40th Street in New York City and with Eichelberger and/or Shotwell in leadership positions. As noted earlier, Citizens for Victory (also located

at 8 West 40th Street) served as the major umbrella organization starting in 1942. Hugh Moore, the founder and president of the Dixie Cup
Company, was the executive director, and Eichelberger was vice chair.
(Moore was on the executive committee of LNA and was a founding
member of CDAAA. He founded the Hugh Moore Fund for International Peace in 1944 and remained involved in foreign policy and civic
groups for the rest of his life.) The Free World Association was founded
in 1941, also with Moore as the executive director. Yet there were
attempts "to unite the internationalist movement under one banner,"
Johnstone wrote, first with the Non-Partisan Council to Win the Peace
in 1943 and then Americans United for World Organization in 1944.
Although the goal was coordination, Johnstone stated that "both merely
added to public confusion and caused as much division within the
movement as unity."[27] The Non-Partisan Council was based in Chicago;
the other groups were housed at 8 West 40th Street, though, by 1942,
the Free World Association had moved into its own building—Free
World House on Bleecker Street in New York.[28]

The first organization to be called the United Nations Association
came into being in July 1943. As tax-exempt, nonprofit organizations,
the LNA and the CSOP were legally barred from advocating for or
against specific bills before Congress or from conducting campaigns
targeting specific candidates. The UNA, however, was created as a tax-
able organization to launch such campaigns.

The UNA's incorporation said that it had been established "for the
declared purpose of carrying on an educational campaign throughout the
country in support of the principles of the Atlantic Charter and of the formation and participation therein by the United States of an international
organization for the maintenance of security and justice throughout the
world."[29] Shotwell, besides being the director of the Carnegie Endowment for International Peace and chair of the CSOP, was also chair of the
UNA board. Eichelberger was the executive director.

Eichelberger and Shotwell set out nationwide to garner support for
House and Senate resolutions endorsing a world organization, praising
members of Congress who backed the bills, and working against those
who opposed them. Two congressional resolutions made up the heart of
the campaign. Representative J. William Fulbright (D-Arkansas) offered
a resolution in 1941 that simply said Congress favored "the creation of
appropriate international machinery with power adequate to establish and
to maintain a just and lasting peace, among the nations of the world." The
bipartisan Ball-Burton-Hatch-Hill Senate resolution of 1943 (proposed by
Joseph H. Ball, R-Minnesota; Harold H. Burton, R-Ohio; Carl A. Hatch,

D–New Mexico; and Lister Hill, D-Alabama) was more detailed, calling on the United States to "take the initiative in calling meetings of representatives of the United Nations" to plan for postwar peace, including relief and assistance for countries liberated from the Axis powers, procedures "for the peaceful settlement of disputes and disagreements between nations," and the establishment of "a United Nations military force" to suppress "any future attempt at military aggression by any nation."

A UNA pamphlet sent to supporters cited the "urgency of writing the peace while the war still is being waged. . . . We support actual organization of the United Nations as quickly as possible; [there are] positive indications by the United States Congress and the Executive that the United States will join a world organization" that has police powers, has authority for the peaceful settlement of disputes, will cooperate to improve "the standard of living of all peoples," and will establish democratic governments where UN aid is used in reconstruction.[30] In other words, the goals of the UNA and LNA lined up identically, under the same leadership and same street address; the difference was the legal necessity of segregating the partisan and nonpartisan sides.

In meeting minutes from May 19, 1944, Eichelberger reported that in the summer of 1943, UNA had arranged tours for representatives and senators to twenty-nine states to speak on "the Ball-Burton-Hatch-Hill resolution specifically, and on international organization generally." The touring congressional members included Senators Harry Truman (D-Missouri) and Albert Gore (D-Tennessee), the father of the future vice president.[31]

The Fulbright resolution was adopted on September 21, 1943. The Ball-Burton-Hatch-Hill resolution was opposed by the Senate majority leader, Tom Connally (D-Texas), so it never advanced from committee. Instead, Connally offered his own resolution that covered the same territory more generally. But before that vote was taken, the Moscow Declaration by the United States, Britain, and Russia was issued on November 1. In addition to committing themselves to seeing the war through to the end as a united group, the declaration said the powers "recognize the necessity of establishing at the earliest practicable date a general international organization." Connally incorporated that language into his resolution, which was adopted on November 6. The White House now had Congress on record endorsing a world organization.[32]

In 1944, the UNA, "having achieved its stated purpose with the tours, was later folded into a coalition of organizations working toward American acceptance of membership in a future world organization," Estelle Linzer, the manager of UNA, wrote.[33] The hard part—establishing the need for a world organization—appears to have been approved, with much of the credit going to Eichelberger and Shotwell and the rest of the LNA. Yet the real work in formulating that body was just beginning.

Notes

1. Andrew Johnstone, *Dilemmas of Internationalism: The American Association for the United Nations and US Foreign Policy, 1941–1948* (Surry and Burlington, VT: Ashgate, 2009), 15.
2. Alfred E. Clark, "Clark Eichelberger, 83; Directed American Association for U.N.," *New York Times,* January 27, 1980.
3. Eleanor Roosevelt, *This I Remember* (New York: Harper & Brothers, 1949), 60.
4. Paul Kennedy, *The Parliament of Man: The Past, Present, and Future of the United Nations* (New York: Random House, 2006), 17.
5. Clark M. Eichelberger, *Organizing for Peace: A Personal History of the Founding of the United Nations* (New York: Harper & Row, 1977), 70.
6. Ibid., 76.
7. Ibid., 79.
8. Ibid., 80.
9. Ibid., 224–248.
10. Stephen C. Schlesinger, *Act of Creation: The Founding of the United Nations* (Cambridge, MA: Westview, 2003), 29.
11. Johnstone, *Dilemmas of Internationalism*, 33.
12. Andrew Johnstone, "To Mobilize a Nation: Citizens' Organizations and Intervention on the Eve of World War II," in *The US Public and American Foreign Policy* (Routledge Studies in US Foreign Policy), ed. Andrew Johnstone and Helen Laville (London: Taylor & Francis Publishing, 2010), 26–40.
13. Ibid., 35.
14. Eichelberger, *Organizing for Peace*, 121–126.
15. The Clark M. Eichelberger Papers, Manuscripts and Archives Division, New York Public Library. Astor, Lenox, and Tilden Foundations. (NYPL Archives), box 50.
16. Ibid.
17. Ibid., box 45.
18. Eichelberger, *Organizing for Peace*, 172–177.
19. Ibid., 180–181.
20. Ibid., 184–185.
21. Johnstone, "To Mobilize a Nation," 38.
22. Tony Millett, "The UN's Real History: A Response to Dan Plesch," Open Democracy, November 22, 2005, https://www.opendemocracy.net/globalization -UN/UN_3053.jsp.
23. NYPL Archives, box 56.
24. Schlesinger, *Act of Creation*, 36.
25. Ibid., 40.
26. Ibid., 47.
27. Johnstone, *Dilemmas of Internationalism*, 87.
28. NYPL Archives, box 54.

29. Ibid., box 56.

30. Ibid.

31. Ibid.

32. Eichelberger, *Organizing for Peace,* 220–221.

33. Estelle Linzer, "The Way We Were: An Informal History of the American Association for the United Nations from 1945 Through 1964 When It Merged with the United States Committee for the United Nations to Become the United Nations Association of the United States of America" (unpublished manuscript, 1995, pages unnumbered).

2

"We the Peoples," 1944–1946

Dumbarton Oaks, Washington, DC

By now, the world organization was very much a US invention. The members of the State Department's Political Committee and its subcommittees were all American; not even the British were involved. The Atlantic Charter was bilateral. Although twenty-six countries had signed the charter, people in Washington, DC, and London had written the Declaration by United Nations. In spring 1944, Cordell Hull began talks with the British and Soviet ambassadors to discuss the procedures for the conference that would create this potential world body.

Personal and policy tensions had been building between Hull and Sumner Welles throughout the work of the Political Committee. Those tensions finally resulted in Welles's resignation in September 1943. Edward Stettinius Jr., the former chair of US Steel and former administrator of the Lend-Lease Program, replaced him as undersecretary of state. Stettinius quickly became secretary of state in December 1944, when Hull resigned because of ill health. The Dumbarton Oaks Conference, which convened in the months preceding Hull's resignation, became his last major initiative in the White House.[1]

The sprawling Dumbarton Oaks estate in Georgetown, with its Renaissance revival mansion at its heart, was the home of Mildred and Robert Woods Bliss, art collectors and patrons. The Blisses had granted the estate and their collections of books and artwork to Harvard University in 1940. The White House wanted the conference to stay as close as possible to Washington, and Harvard agreed to lend the estate to the US government for the conference.

Friction immediately ensued among the four major powers. Russia refused to sit down with the Nationalist government of China because the latter had not declared war on Japan, an action Moscow insisted was a precondition for attendance at the talks. Therefore, it was agreed that two rounds of talks at Dumbarton Oaks would be held: the United States,

17

Britain, and Russia would meet from August 21 through September 28, 1944; and the United States, Britain, and China would meet from September 28 through October 7. Despite this split, the countries worked productively. Two elements worked in favor of a smooth-running conference. In the first, the United States had laid a solid framework, both with the Welles Committee draft and with Hull's consultations. In the second, the other three countries were not particularly engaged. The British submitted one paper, but otherwise none of the countries "seemed to take the preparatory work very seriously," Stephen Schlesinger wrote in *Act of Creation*. Since there was "nothing of serious consequence, the Welles Committee draft became the basic frame of reference for building a plan of world organization."[2] So, when the Dumbarton Oaks proposals were issued by the four powers on October 7, they looked much like what Welles, Leo Pasvolsky, and James Shotwell had brought into the conference.

With the basic structure settled—General Assembly, Security Council, Economic and Social Council, Trusteeship Council, and the International Court of Justice—the discussions "mainly centered on how to distribute powers among the various branches."[3] Of these issues, the extent of the Security Council veto was by far the most contentious. Russia insisted on an absolute veto for the permanent members, which would have meant the power to block even consideration of an issue. Pasvolsky proposed a compromise: the veto could be used only for substantive or enforcement issues but not for simple procedural issues. Russia held firm to its position and was eventually joined by Britain.[4] On September 21, Franklin Roosevelt met with his delegation and told them to conclude the conference, leaving the remaining issues for him to settle at the next summit.[5]

Meanwhile, with the United Nations taking shape in governmental and public circles, the LNA and CSOP made the Dumbarton Oaks proposals the rallying theme of their campaign, even before the proposals were announced. On September 28, the CSOP invited more than fifty organizations to an October 6 meeting in New York to "help plan a tremendous coordinated campaign of popular education on the purport of the Dumbarton Oaks agreements. . . . We should devise a general plan, map our strategy, and determine what each of us can best contribute to our common effort." Forty groups attended the meeting in the Wilson Library of the CSOP offices in New York to devise coordinated educational campaigns without creating a new formal organization.[6]

Once the proposals were made public, a group of internationalists, including LNA and CSOP officials, wrote to Secretary of State Stettinius, welcoming the proposals, but they also noted concern "about certain areas of incompletion." They listed six: (1) granting the General Assembly and the Economic and Social Council "responsibility for the promotion of human rights and essential freedoms"; (2) "adequate provision" to administer the "colonial territories taken away from Italy and Japan" and the creation of a Trusteeship Council for the well-being of "non-self governing peoples"; (3) the creation of the Permanent Court of International Justice; (4) consideration of the need for "the regulation of armaments in the postwar period"; (5) provision in the use of the Security Council rules that a great power "should have no vote in consideration of dispute to which it is a party"; and (6) the "express provision . . . for an international agency whose function it will be to develop the climate in which world organization can live and grow." If the sixth concern can be viewed as the seeds for the United Nations Educational, Scientific, and Cultural Organization (UNESCO), then serious, sometimes pivotal, efforts were made to incorporate five of the six recommendations into the charter. But attempts to limit the strength of the great powers in the Security Council routinely failed and continue to do so today.

For most of World War II, the term *United Nations* referred to the allies fighting the war and not to any international organization. Thinking that the phrase would become the name of the world organization, LNA tried to register it so that only the LNA could use it in a future organization. LNA changed its name, for starters, to the American Association for the United Nations (AAUN) in February 1945. That it began using the term *United Nations* before the formation of the UN demonstrated the association's single-mindedness. As early as 1942, Eichelberger asked FDR what would be the name of the world organization. He wanted to know if it would be the phrase the president and Winston Churchill had been using for the allies—United Nations. The president was noncommittal.

Dan Plesch, a British academic, has written that Roosevelt first used the phrase to a naked Churchill, on the morning of December 29, 1941. Winston was emerging from his morning bath in a guest room in the White House when he heard the wheelchair-bound US president calling him—just weeks after Pearl Harbor and after Adolf Hitler's declaration of war against the United States—to say that Roosevelt had hit upon the name "United Nations" to define the countries allied against the Axis powers. The State Department had come up with the more tedious and infinitely less catchy "Associated Powers," which Roosevelt discarded.[7]

Back in 1944, Eichelberger wanted to lay claim to the name to pre-empt other nongovernment groups from grabbing it. In 1944, in a message from FDR to Eichelberger, transmitted by Belle Roosevelt (the wife of Kermit Roosevelt, a son of Teddy Roosevelt), Roosevelt said, "Inform Clark that the name of the Association should be changed to include the words 'United Nations.'" FDR was sure his and Churchill's formulation would be accepted.[8]

San Francisco: "We the Peoples"

The story of how the UN was realized is well known. On April 12, 1945, FDR, while on vacation in Hot Springs, Georgia, after his grueling trip to the Yalta Conference with Churchill and Joseph Stalin to end the war and allot territories, was sitting for a portrait by Elizabeth Shoumatoff. He slumped over, saying, "I have a terrific headache." That afternoon—thirteen days before the San Francisco Conference to begin to organize the UN, eighteen days before the suicide of Hitler, and twenty days before the fall of Berlin—the man who had been president longer than anyone else in US history died. It was now up to Harry Truman to finish the war and win the peace.

Eichelberger argued, and the record backs him up, that the San Francisco Conference was FDR's overarching priority in his last days. Even though he was exhausted from the trip to Yalta, FDR planned to attend the conference. In his final interview, he told journalist Anne O'Hare McCormick that he was looking forward to the meeting. "He was looking to the inauguration of the San Francisco Conference as the crowning act of his career," she wrote. "This was his project." He told Robert Sherwood, the playwright who was FDR's speechwriter at the time, "I'm going to be there at the start and at the finish, too." On April 6, he asked Archibald MacLeish, the writer and poet, to begin drafting his speech for the opening of the conference. Roosevelt was even considering resigning as president to become the first UN Secretary-General.[9]

Eichelberger tried in vain to hold a meeting with Truman before the conference, but failing to lobby Truman in person was not imperative, since advocating for an international organization to Truman would have been preaching to the choir. Truman's support did not begin with his presidency. He had made the case for an international organization in the Senate and took part in the 1943 tour to support the pro-UN congressional resolutions. Just weeks before becoming president, he had delivered a speech calling for greater cooperation among nations. "The only rational alternative to existing international anarchy lies in some reasonable form of international organization among so-called sovereign states," he said.[10] Famously well read, Truman carried with him a clipping from the Alfred Lord Tennyson poem "Locksley Hall":

> Till the war-drum throbb'd no longer, and the battle-flags were furl'd
> In the Parliament of man, the Federation of the world.
> There the common sense of most shall hold a fretful realm in awe,
> And the kindly earth shall slumber, lapt in universal law.

Whenever asked about his backing of an international organization at the conference, Truman "was happy to reach into his wallet and read that passage from 'Locksley Hall,'" historian Paul Kennedy wrote.[11]

FDR was buried at Hyde Park, New York, his family's estate, on Sunday morning, April 15. By the afternoon of April 16, Truman was addressing a joint session of Congress. Announcing that within his first hour as president he had ordered the San Francisco Conference to proceed, he said, "The task of creating a sound international organization is complicated and difficult. Yet, without such an organization, the rights of men on earth cannot be protected."[12]

All year, supporters of the UN had been making plans for Dumbarton Oaks Week from April 16 to April 22. The goal was to rally support for the UN as world leaders headed to San Francisco. Despite the death of FDR only days before, organizers, with Truman's blessing, went ahead with the plans. The day after FDR's death, Eichelberger sent a telegram to the AAUN membership, recalling the president's commitment and noting that "his greatest ambition" was to see that out of victory "there would grow a world organization to guarantee permanent security. . . . The only tribute we can pay worthy of him is to see to it that the world organization is created with American membership just as quickly as possible." Dumbarton Oaks Week "would go forward just as planned."[13]

The United Nations Conference on International Organization, the formal name for the San Francisco Conference, was called to order on April 25. The US delegation arriving in the city was the one that FDR had named, with Secretary of State Stettinius as the chair. The bulk of the delegation were members of Congress from both parties, including Senators Tom Connally (D-Texas) and Arthur Vandenberg (R-Michigan). Only two members were not government officials: Harold Stassen, a former governor of Minnesota, and Virginia Gildersleeve, the dean of Barnard College in New York, the only female delegate, and an early supporter of the League of Nations. Truman, however, consumed with the steep learning curve he faced as the new president, did not stick to FDR's plan to attend the conference personally, though he addressed the conference by radio.

Despite the popular image of the UN as an inclusive "Parliament of Man," the conference was limited to countries that had declared war against Germany and Japan—that is, the twenty-six original signatories to the January 1942 Declaration by United Nations, plus those that had declared war on Germany and Japan by March 1945. Foreshadowing the Cold War, Poland was not seated, because the Western powers favored one delegation from the country, while Russia supported another. In total, fifty countries became negotiators in San Francisco.

The State Department and some of the civil society groups who were at Dumbarton Oaks were responsible for an important innovation: the creation of the role of consultants, who represented civil society organizations. These people were not part of the official governmental delegation, yet they worked with the delegates in developing strategies and proposals. The State Department invited forty-two national groups to send one consultant and two alternates to the conference. Eichelberger represented AAUN; the Carnegie Endowment for International Peace was represented by Shotwell and by Malcolm W. Davis, the Carnegie director. Margaret Olson, who became a longtime staff member of AAUN, was an AAUN alternate. The full roster of consultants was an impressive cross-section of US political, social, and economic life, including the American Legion, the Brotherhood of Railroad Trainmen, the Federal Council of the Churches of Christ in America, the National Association for the Advancement of Colored People (W. E. B. Du Bois was the consultant), the National Council of Farmer Cooperatives, National Council of Jewish Women, National Lawyers Guild, Southern Baptist Convention, World Government Association, and the YMCA. They all served the dual purpose of tapping into a wealth of experience and knowledge and opening a conduit between the government and the broader public—a classic setup of civil society, or grassroots, at work. This arrangement enabled Eichelberger, Shotwell, Du Bois, and the others to help shape the UN Charter and public opinion. The consultants further organized themselves into a nine-member core committee, including Eichelberger and Shotwell.

Stettinius called the creation of the consultants "an experiment." Dorothy Robins-Mowry, who started working for the LNA on education in 1942 and later focused on the organization's Model UN program, wrote in *Experiment in Democracy* that the government knew it was "perhaps opening a Pandora's box. The consultant process was an experiment in democracy in action on the diplomatic level."[14]

Estelle Linzer, the AAUN manager, wrote, "The consultants were, for the most part, concerned with 'humanizing the Charter,' in the words of Foreign Policy Association leader Vera Micheles Dean [a Russian American political scientist]," by pressing for human rights provisions and strengthening the economic and social components of the charter. The consultants also played another surprisingly crucial role. Alerted by Gildersleeve that "many details were being left out of the proposed Charter in order to shorten it," the AAUN intensified its lobbying, especially on education, human rights, and trusteeship.[15]

As they did at Dumbarton Oaks, the consultants came with proposals designed to found the strongest international body possible. In early February 1945, the AAUN board laid out its priorities for San Francisco:

1. To make the Charter and the activities of the United Nations known and understood by the people of the United States.
2. To advocate and support those policies by our Government which will make United States membership effective in the United Nations.
3. To study the means by which the United Nations can be strengthened to meet the needs of an ever-changing world.
4. To cooperate with UN associations in other countries in building a strong public opinion in support of the United Nations.[16]

Linzer wrote that these same principles served as the AAUN's Resolution of Welcome when Trygve Lie, a Norwegian, became the UN's first Secretary-General in 1946.

Robins-Mowry said in an interview for this book, at age ninety-four, that so many groups participated at the San Francisco Conference that "the experience tied them together and gave them a sense of strength, which I don't think they had before." She continued to explain that the AAUN seemed to recognize "that they could really play a role in American foreign policy." In her book *Experiment in Democracy,* Robins-Mowry explained how the consultants organized into a working group dubbed ABLE, drawn from the types of organizations involved: agriculture, business, labor, and education.[17] Initially, ABLE worked to ensure education issues were addressed in the charter, but it later expanded its scope to deal with all the issues on the consultants' priority list.

The consultants lobbied hard to get those priorities into the draft charter. These priorities could be distilled to four points: the infrastructure to promote economic and social benefits, including education; UN trusteeship of colonies and the strategic bases captured in the war; the inclusion of a vibrant human rights component; and a formal status for nongovernmental organizations (NGOs) in the UN system. At the same time, they were also mobilizing their supporters. During May, Eichelberger sent a series of telegrams to Linzer in New York, loaded with optimistic reports on the negotiations and recommending how chapters could be mobilized to promote work in San Francisco.[18]

A May 2, 1945, letter to Stettinius from the consultants urged amendments to give "new purpose" to the draft. All the amendments were written to strengthen the draft's human rights element, including the establishment of a commission and the text that the "assurance to every human being of the fundamental rights of life, liberty, and the pursuit of happiness is essential not only to domestic but also international peace."[19]

Merging the consultants' commitment to ensuring human rights and trusteeship was integral to the charter, and Du Bois argued in a May 1 letter that any International Bill of Rights had to specify colonialized people. "If it were clearly understood, this would be a great and fateful step," the civil rights leader wrote. "The omission of specific reference to these people is almost advertisement of their tacit exclusion as not citizens of free states, and that their welfare and freedom would be considered only at the will of the countries owning them and not at the demand of enlightened world public opinion."[20] A CSOP memo of May 5 concluded that "inclusion in the Charter of most of what we have recommended on human rights" has been achieved.[21]

Another area of success was lobbying for the inclusion of a formal role for NGOs in the UN Charter. Building on the success of ABLE, a working group chaired by Shotwell sent a letter to Stettinius on May 15, laying out a comprehensive list of proposals, including the idea that NGOs should have a formal status within the Economic and Social Council (ECOSOC). The official US delegation accepted this idea, which resulted in Article 71 of the charter.[22] Thus, at the birth of the United Nations, the consultants, under AAUN leadership, succeeded both by example and by their effectiveness in enshrining the fundamental role of "the peoples" in the order created by the UN.

Local, national, and global media reported on the conference. In addition, AAUN and other consultants distributed regular reports from the event. In a reversal of the secrecy surrounding Dumbarton Oaks, the conference itself published a daily newsletter called *The United Nations Conference on International Organizations Journal*. (The style of that journal implies it was the model for the UN's *Daily Journal*, still printed today.) The *San Francisco Chronicle* covered the conference daily, reporting on everything from high-profile speeches to subcommittee deliberations, treating it as both a local and an international story. One page from *The New York Times* (May 18, 1945) preserved in the

Eichelberger archives offers a useful snapshot: two articles datelined San Francisco have the headlines "Unity Is Revealed on Economic Plan" and "Widen Definition of Human Rights." That page also carried a column called "A Serviceman's View," in which a recently decommissioned Navy lieutenant described the "fundamental distrust between Britain and the United States on the one hand, and Russia on the other"; yet he was hopeful that with "firmness and confidence, we may yet win years of peace for which so much has been sacrificed."

That lieutenant's name? John F. Kennedy.[23]

The conference ended on June 26 with the unanimous adoption of the UN Charter. (The statutes of the International Court of Justice were also ratified that day, replacing the Permanent Court of International Justice, a League of Nations creation that had ended in 1939. From 1921 to 1939, the permanent court had issued thirty-two decisions and twenty-seven advisory opinions.[24])

In her book about the founding of the UN, *Experiment in Democracy,* Robins-Mowry wrote:

> By the time the Charter was in the final stages of completion, many of the original consultants had [left San Francisco and] returned to their offices to begin the final drive for ratification. Many of the techniques and practices that the organizations had learned and used during the months of the Dumbarton Oaks educational campaign were refurbished to do battle for the United Nations.[25]

Bearing in mind that the League of Nations had been debated in the Senate for nine months, the consultants planned a conference, called "What Happened at San Francisco," for June 23 at the Commodore Hotel in New York. Seven hundred organizations were invited to attend "to initiate the push toward accepting the Charter."[26] In addition, there was a strategy session on July 16. "In actuality, Senate approval of the Charter came so rapidly that the issue was determined almost before a proper nationwide educational and pressure program could get underway," Robins-Mowry wrote. "Sentiment in favor of the Charter was so strong that no serious opposition materialized either within the Senate or from the public."[27]

The US Senate ratified the charter on July 28 by a vote of 89 to 2, after one week of debate. The years of preparation, informing, researching, worrying, and lobbying Congress and the public had unequivocally paid off. "The ease, rapidity and overwhelmingly large vote of approval by the United States Senate undoubtedly stemmed from the careful planning, preparation, and activity of the governmental administration and the non-governmental organizations in the years and months preceding submission of the Charter to the Senate," Robins-Mowry wrote.[28] The United Nations was off to a better start than the League of Nations had been.

To enter into force, the charter had to be ratified by the five great powers (France was now officially in the club) and a majority of the other states. That benchmark was reached on October 24, 1945, now recognized as UN Day.

Eichelberger finally met Truman on August 27, after the president's trip to the Potsdam Conference, at which the victors worked out postwar issues in Europe. In a letter to Welles on September 26, Eichelberger summarized the meeting by listing three issues he had raised with Truman: states had to be ready to discuss the atomic bomb, as the secret of the bomb "will not be a secret very long"; a "watering down" of the trusteeship agreements on Pacific bases, because the Navy "has prevented the formulation of a forthright program on this point"; and rapid withdrawal of troops from Europe and Asia. "I sympathize with the desire of the men to come home," he wrote, "but pulling out may lead to tragedy." In concluding the letter, Eichelberger wrote: "I had a talk with President Truman several weeks ago. I believe he agrees with these policies."[29]

Popular Support

Mobilizing public support for the UN before it existed was a priority of the LNA and the AAUN and a specialty of Eichelberger's. Ever since the Atlantic Charter and Dumbarton Oaks, the association had redoubled its efforts not only to keep the public informed but also to actively engage it, fearing slackening of intensity would lessen interest. Americans in 1943 were as internationalist as Americans had been isolationist in 1936. The war was the fight for civilization itself, and the UN was considered the hope for the future. It also helped that the UN was essentially a US idea.

A telegram from Truman to Eichelberger on July 30, 1945, called the ratification of the charter "not so much an end as a beginning"; he also stated that it was up to the US people "to see to it that the Charter work insofar as it lies within their power to make it work. Only if they understand what the Charter is and what it can mean to the peace of the world will the document become a living human reality." He ended, "Organizations and individuals working toward the fullest possible understanding of the Charter of the United Nations deserve the gratitude and support of all of us."[30]

Public backing was broad. Historically, the LNA, Committee to Defend America, Fight for Freedom, and the other internationalist organizations had viewed public engagement as vital. The emphasis on local chapters and mobilization was written into the internationalists' DNA, with an unprecedented enlistment occurring across professional, religious, economic, racial, and geographic lines. Industrialists such as the Rockefellers, Thomas Watson of IBM, and Murray Bullis, the chair of General Mills, were early supporters. The country's leading labor organizations—the American Federation of Labor (AFL), the Congress of Industrial Organizations (CIO), and the Farm Union—were ensconced in the internationalist camp. The US Chamber of Commerce, the AFL, and the American Farm Bureau Federation published a document called "A Declaration on Postwar Problems" in March 1944. Names of Hollywood stars like Orson Welles, James Cagney, and Bette Davis turn up on letterheads and letters of endorsement. Douglas Fairbanks Jr. and Eichelberger regularly exchanged letters, with the latter updating Fairbanks on such issues as atomic energy and Palestine. (During the war, Fairbanks had been a commissioned naval commander, so his direct involvement with the LNA was curtailed.)

Toward the end of the war, AAUN hosted the Servicemen's Wives for the United Nations, an ad hoc group promoting the creation of the UN to avoid future wars. Belle Wyatt "Clochette" Palfrey—wife of John G. Palfrey Jr., a granddaughter of Theodore Roosevelt, and daughter of Belle Roosevelt—was the national chair. The national advisory committee included the Honorable Emily Taft Douglas, the Honorable Helen Gahagan Douglas, Belle Roosevelt (wife of Kermit Roosevelt), and Esther Stassen (Mrs. Harold E. Stassen).

In a March 1945 telegram, Eleanor Roosevelt wrote that she was "delighted to hear of the Committee which is being formed by the Servicemen's Wives to work for peace. My very best wishes to all of you." A public letter by Eichelberger in August of that year reported that the group had chapters in twenty-two states. "These young women, waiting for their husbands to return, find the Servicemen's Wives Committees an outlet for their desire to do something actively so that their husbands and the next generation will not have to participate in a Third World War," he wrote. The organization prepared a radio series called "Listen: Mrs. America." They also published a comic book, "prepared by the staff of *True Comics* Magazine," called *A Third World War Can Be Prevented NOW!* Undated but clearly published after the San Francisco Conference, its message stated, "That these dead shall not have died in vain, we must support the United Nations Organization to prevent recurring world wars!"[31]

Other pro-UN organizations attracted a who's who of celebrities and literary giants. The masthead of the Writers' War Board in 1945 listed the detective fiction author Rex Stout as chair, backed by such supporters as Paul Gallico, Oscar Hammerstein II, William L. Shirer, Pearl S. Buck, Edna Ferber, Langston Hughes, George S. Kaufman, Edna St. Vincent Millay, Edward R. Murrow, Clifford Odets, Eugene O'Neill, John Steinbeck, and Thornton Wilder.

In September 1945, Murrow wrote a public letter supporting the AAUN:

> For the last nine years I have viewed the United States and its policies from abroad, and I am persuaded that now more than ever before American policy will be decisive in determining whether the suffering, sacrifice, and achievement of the last six years will have produced anything more than a temporary respite from death and destruction. We are confronted with a choice between a new world and none at all.

Murrow continued: "[AAUN] is not going to prevent another war, but it is doing something to illuminate the alternatives that confront us."[32]

The Eichelberger archives also preserved examples of ordinary citizens promoting the UN, expressing support for it with songs, radio plays, comic books, and pamphlets. A doctor in Idaho even sent Eichelberger his sketch for the UN flag that had four bars representing the Four Freedoms and a six-pointed star in the center that the doctor described as "the Creator's star or double triangle symboliz[ing] unity of spirit and matter," but that would be more recognizable as a Star of David.[33]

As the San Francisco Conference approached and with it the real possibility of a meaningful world organization, a new political movement emerged. World Federalists argued that the pending body would be insufficient, and what was needed was a world government in which states relinquished significant sovereignty. With the fulfillment of his life's work within view, Eichelberger vigorously criticized the idea as unrealistic and a threat to the UN before it could even be established. After the charter was ratified, the World Federalists immediately pressed for junking the charter for a world government constitution. Predictably, Eichelberger actively campaigned against that idea. In a September 16, 1945, letter to Sumner Welles, Eichelberger wrote,

> I am as alarmed as you are over the desire of some so-called Liberals to scrap the Charter and begin with a constitution for world government. . . . The world government people will undoubtedly make a dramatic appeal to a certain minority. But I think the majority of the people will respond to a practical program of immediate steps.

The World Federalist Movement had its defining event in Dublin, New Hampshire, a haven for Bostonians' summer homes. The October 1945 conference called for a world federal government to replace the UN. The AAUN's response on October 27 noted that the Senate had just approved the UN overwhelmingly and that Dublin "offers no alternative which could provide immediate machinery. . . . With the reaction that has set in since San Francisco, it is obvious that nothing stronger than the Charter could be agreed upon in the near future."[34]

Tremendous Optimism: A Year of Firsts

Summer 1945 saw the definitive end of the war with Japan's surrender. But it also brought the dawn of an ominous new power—the atomic bomb. The bombing of Hiroshima and Nagasaki, among other acts, created a new potential for war on an obliterating scale. The AAUN immediately called for the UN to control atomic energy for peaceful purposes, while banning it militarily. Atomic energy joined the list of AAUN priorities, along with trusteeship, human rights, refugee relief and food aid, and economic and social initiatives—all urgent items that needed to be on the new UN agenda.

The first observation of UN Week, from October 24 to 28, included a campaign that drew 105,000 American signers from forty-eight states in a message of fraternity and support for the UN. In New York, Belle Roosevelt served as the New York City chairwoman, and Mayor William O'Dwyer was honorary chairman. Nelson Rockefeller hosted the UN Week dinner at the Waldorf-Astoria; among the speakers were Secretary-General Trygve Lie and the first General Assembly president, Paul-Henri Spaak of Belgium.

The first General Assembly (GA) was called to order in London on January 10, 1946. The number of members had increased from fifty to fifty-one, with the addition of Poland (Stalin got his preferred government seated). The US delegation was headed by Stettinius and included ranking members of Congress from both chambers and both houses. The first delegation also included Eleanor Roosevelt, who was assigned to the Third Committee, where she took the lead on human rights issues and drafting the Declaration of Human Rights. The GA's first resolution was adopted on January 24, calling for the establishment of a commission to deal with the problems raised by the discovery of atomic energy.

The first meeting of the Security Council took place on January 17. In addition to procedural issues, the first matters before the council dealt with Iran, Spain, and the admission of the first new members beyond the original fifty-one: Afghanistan, Iceland, and Sweden. On Spain, the council decided that the Fascist dictatorship of Francisco Franco should not be allowed into the UN. The Iranian issue was more difficult, since it involved a dispute between two member states, with the second state being the Soviet Union. Moscow still had troops in Iran past the deadline for the removal of all foreign troops, as agreed in 1942. Even though Russia withdrew its troops in 1947, the item remained on the council's agenda for two decades.

Between the London session and the reconvened New York session of the first GA later that year, the AAUN executive committee issued a statement on March 15 outlining three points that it contended were needed to guide US foreign policy as the UN took shape: (1) "All efforts for the achievement of security should be undertaken through the United Nations. Such problems as Iran, Manchuria, and Spain should be handled through the Security Council"; (2) "Every effort should be made to reach an understanding with Russia and to reduce the psychological tension which places Russia in an antagonistic position towards Britain and the United States"; and (3) "The United States should indicate clearly now that it will support the Charter against any aggression anywhere."[35]

By then, interest in the UN extended far beyond the traditional internationalist circles. For example, the US Chamber of Commerce adopted a resolution on the UN on May 2, saying,

> Because of our devotion to the cause of peace and our great power we have an obligation to assert our strength in the face of wrong. The United States of America should expend every possible effort to bring the United Nations organization through this testing period, to the end that it, with whatever refinements and evolutionary perfections may be necessary, shall become in fact as it now is in hope, the final safeguard of mankind against the ravages of brutal strife.[36]

In August, the World Federation of UNAs (WFUNA) held its inaugural conference in Luxembourg, with twenty-two UN national associations attending. Eichelberger was present. WFUNA was established to assist the national groups in supporting the UN and the principles of the charter. The group elected the Czech foreign minister, Jan Masaryk, as its president.

The second session of the first GA started on September 12 in New York. Senators Connally and Vandenberg, the ranking Democratic and Republican members of the Senate Foreign Relations Committee, were part of the delegation, though both men questioned whether having two elected officials on the delegation was a conflict of interest, given that they had the most to do regarding any UN issue to come before the Senate.[37] Disarmament, control of atomic energy, trusteeship, new members, the decision on the permanent headquarters, the official seal of the UN, international law (including the crime of genocide), and the transfer to the UN of the remaining League of Nations assets (such as property, funds, and files) topped the agenda. Summarizing the session in a newsletter he sent to AAUN chapters, Eichelberger wrote unstintingly of his enthusiasm. He wrote that the assembly concluded on December 15, "in a wave of sincere appreciation on the part of the delegates for what had been done. The world today is on a higher plane because of the decisions of the Assembly."[38]

Remembering those first days, Robins-Mowry said she and her colleagues "were all so interwoven. . . . We all knew each other, those at the US Mission and AAUN. . . . It was almost like a big family. In 1945, 1946, those early days were very exciting. And we were part of building this whole operation." In the interview for this book, she said further, "The sense of excitement we had about building a new thing. A new thing—the United Nations—which was going to bring the US really into the world and get us over the terrible hump of having rejected the League of Nations. . . . There was a tremendous sense of optimism."

A Permanent Home

When the UN held its first General Assembly, the organization was still nomadic. Interest in Geneva as the capital had faded, largely because of the city's association with the ghost of the League of Nations, which had been based there. Eichelberger, among others, objected to Geneva on the grounds that Swiss neutrality would have meant the UN could not authorize military action from Swiss soil. He argued this meant the Security Council could not meet in Geneva.[39] The emerging consensus was that the permanent headquarters should be in the United States; Truman had officially made the offer to the UN, but there was no decision on the exact location. San Francisco seemed a natural choice, but European governments and Russia preferred the East Coast, as it was much closer to their capitals.

In a May 24, 1946, statement, the UN Permanent Site Committee complained about the "passive attitude" of the US government in the decisionmaking. "A tragedy may result if the United Nations officials and their peoples get the feeling that the organization is not welcome in this country," it said. "While being close to a metropolitan area so that cultural advantages were to be available, . . . the headquarters itself was to be a sufficient distance away so that it might develop an independent character."

The AAUN supported this "original option" and favored the US "eastern seaboard," leaning toward Greenwich, Connecticut; however, it noted the local opposition, which deemed the potential traffic jams forbidding. At the same time, the AAUN felt "the City of New York is too large to permit the proper development of the United Nations headquarters within its metropolitan area. It would be easier for the headquarters to develop in almost any other metropolitan area." With only four months left before the GA resumed its session in New York, the statement said that if the issue were not settled, "the offer of the City of San Francisco and the hospitality of the people there seem most attractive."

San Francisco reminded governments that the world body would be welcomed. Mayor Roger D. Lapham, in an August 20, 1946, speech, said that he supported the idea not only for "provincial motives" but also because "an analysis of the situation would at least give grounds for the conclusion" in favor of his city. He touted the city's "friendly atmosphere as well as its physical advantages" and "a more give-and-take and tolerant attitude perhaps more than in any other section of these United States." He concluded, "What better atmosphere could there be in which to nurture and develop the young United Nations Organization?"[40]

Motivated as always by the fear that drift would slacken the US public's interest in the UN, in early 1946 AAUN pressed the US government to make a decision on the UN's permanent home. An October 14 statement by several organizations, including the AAUN, League of Women Voters, and the Federal Council of Churches of Christ in America, criticized the Truman administration: "It is time that we Americans fulfilled the responsibilities which we assumed when the United Nations was officially invited to this country."[41]

The two most talked-about locations remained in suburbia: near Greenwich-Stamford in Connecticut and in Westchester County, New York, just north of New York City. Both regions opposed the suggestions. Competition to locate the UN within other towns or cities manifested in the unlikeliest of places, such as in Claremore, Oklahoma, or in the Black Hills of South Dakota, wrote Charlene Mires in *Capital of the World: The Race to Host the United Nations*. Philadelphia vied for the prize, too, citing its historical roots in liberty and freedom movements.[42]

Mayor O'Dwyer of New York had been lobbying that the UN be built on the ash pit in Flushing Meadows, Queens (the "valley of the ashes" described in *The Great Gatsby* and the future home of the 1964–1965 World's Fair).[43] At the UN Week dinner at the Waldorf-Astoria, the program featured an unsubtle, two-page spread pitching the Flushing Meadows site (which O'Dwyer called a "park"), complete with a schematic for the UN campus.[44] The search committee did not favor Flushing, but Robert Moses, the master builder of New York City during those years, told the UN it must be Flushing or nothing.

The AAUN, which was based in New York, nevertheless dismissed the idea of the headquarters in the city, noting that the original study committee envisioned a site up to forty-one square miles (for comparison, Manhattan island is thirty-four square miles). It dismissed the "college campus" idea—specifically, Flushing Meadows.

The second session of the first GA met in September 1946 at three temporary sites in the New York metropolitan area: the majority of the offices were located in the village of Lake Success on Long Island, in a former gyroscope factory; the Security Council met at Hunter College's Bronx campus, in the school's gym; and the General Assembly, in Queens. The AAUN made a decision on the permanent headquarters a priority for the session. It sent a telegram to Secretary of State James Byrnes, reminding him of Truman's promise.

With the UN, the Truman administration, and the City of New York deadlocked, interested parties, including Eichelberger, asked Nelson Rockefeller to intervene with substantial results. In December 1946, John D. Rockefeller Jr., Nelson's father, announced that he was giving the UN $8.5 million to buy a parcel of land on the very unfashionable East Side of Manhattan at 42nd Street, in a former slaughterhouse site of seventeen acres, which was owned by William Zeckendorf, the real estate mogul. The deal was signed and construction began in 1948. The cornerstone was laid on UN Day 1949.

Notes

1. Stephen C. Schlesinger, *Act of Creation: The Founding of the United Nations* (Cambridge, MA: Westview, 2003), 55.

2. Ibid., 47.

3. Ibid., 49.

4. Ibid., 50.

5. Ibid., 51.

6. Clark M. Eichelberger, *Organizing for Peace: A Personal History of the Founding of the United Nations* (New York: Harper & Row, 1977), 250–252.

7. United Nations Association, "The West Triangle World" (newsletter, April 2013), http://www.una-westtriangle.org/newsletterMay13.htm.

8. Eichelberger, *Organizing for Peace*, 276–277.

9. Schlesinger, *Act of Creation*, 71–72.

10. Ibid., 7.

11. Paul Kennedy, *The Parliament of Man: The Past, Present, and Future of the United Nations* (New York: Random House, 2006), xi–xii.

12. Schlesinger, *Act of Creation*, 15.

13. The Clark M. Eichelberger Papers, Manuscripts and Archives Division, New York Public Library. Astor, Lenox, and Tilden Foundations (NYPL Archives), box 58.

14. Dorothy B. Robins-Mowry, *Experiment in Democracy: The Story of US Citizen Organizations in Forging the Charter of the United Nations* (New York: Parkside Press, 1971), 104.

15. Ibid., 130.

16. Estelle Linzer, "The Way We Were: An Informal History of the American Association for the United Nations from 1945 Through 1964 When It Merged with the United States Committee for the United Nations to Become the United Nations Association of the United States of America" (unpublished manuscript, 1995, pages unnumbered).

17. Robins-Mowry, *Experiment in Democracy*, 118–119.

18. NYPL Archives, box 59.

19. Ibid., box 60.

20. Ibid.

21. Ibid., box 59.

22. Robins-Mowry, *Experiment in Democracy*, 122–124. Also "Letter Submitted to Secretary Stettinius by Consultants, Known as ABLE, May 15, 1945," reprinted in Robins-Mowry, *Experiment in Democracy,* 216–218.

23. NYPL Archives, box 61.

24. *Permanent Court of International Justice (PCIJ) Overview, League of Nations Archives,* Geneva and the Center for the Study of Global Change, Bloomington, Indiana, http://www.indiana.edu/~league/pcijoverview.htm.

25. Robins-Mowry, *Experiment in Democracy*, 141.

26. Ibid., 142.

27. Ibid., 146, 148.

28. Ibid., 149.

29. NYPL Archives, box 61.

30. Ibid.

31. Ibid., box 60.

32. Ibid., box 59.

33. Ibid., box 58.

34. Ibid.

35. Ibid., box 63.

36. Ibid., box 62.

37. Eichelberger, *Organizing for Peace*, 287–288.

38. NYPL Archives, box 62.

39. Eichelberger, *Organizing for Peace*, 284.

40. NYPL Archives, box 63.

41. Ibid.

42. Lucia Mouat, "Why the UN Was Built in New York and Not in South Dakota," PassBlue.com, July 18, 2013, http://passblue.com/2013/07/18/why-the-un-was-built-in-new-york-and-not-in-south-dakota/.

43. Lisa L. Colangelo, "1964 World's Fair: When the World Came to Queens," *New York Daily News*, http://creative.nydailynews.com/worldsfair.

44. NYPL Archives, box 62.

3

The American Association for
the United Nations, 1947–1964

The euphoria and consensus that accompanied the unequivocal defeat of the Axis powers and the creation of the United Nations did not last long. No one was calling it a Cold War yet, but the chill had set in. Without the unifying menace of Hitler, US politics reverted to a polarized mode, and the mutual distrust between the United States and the Soviet Union resurfaced. This was an immediate validation of the internationalists' position that the creation of the postwar world body had to be agreed on before the end of the war. The first few years of the UN's existence were proof that the UN Charter could never have been written in 1946.

Yet, the basic machinery of the UN was running as planned. At the beginning of 1947, the UN had its first Secretary-General and its first General Assembly behind it, though it had no permanent home. The real-world applications of the letter and spirit of the charter were playing out in postwar reconstruction, military remnants of the war, the beginning of decolonization, and the first tremors of the Cold War.

Dorothy Robins-Mowry, who started working for the League of Nations Association and continued with the AAUN, recalled in an interview for this book that after the horrors of World War II, every problem seemed capable of being surmounted: "Even after the Cold War broke out, the optimism continued. The Cold War was [seen as just another] problem."

Like any new organization with a large but fluid mandate, the UN had to continue to invent itself as time passed. Haunted by the inert role adopted by the league's first secretary-general, Eric Drummond, and the impact that approach had on the league's failure, Trygve Lie, the first UN Secretary-General and a Norwegian, struggled to balance passivity with an assertiveness that would not offend governments, wrote journalist Stanley Meisler in *United Nations: The First Fifty Years*. Lie used

Two AAUN staff members, Betty Sheffer, left, and Mary Pensyl, at the display of newspaper clippings about United Nations Week; September 1947 or 1948. The theme of the week was "There's a yoU in the United Nations." (Photo courtesy of Clark M. Eichelberger papers, Manuscripts and Archives Division, The New York Public Library. Astor, Lenox, and Tilden Foundations.)

Article 99 of the UN Charter, which gives the Secretary-General the authority to "bring to the attention of the Security Council any matter which in his opinion may threaten the maintenance of international peace and security," thus opening the door to a more flexible view of the Secretary-General's role.[1] The AAUN supported Lie in this interpretation.

In Eichelberger's histories of the UN, a recurring theme was the liberal versus strict constructionist view of the charter. Eichelberger and AAUN were, naturally, advocates of the liberal interpretation. Eichelberger saw the Soviet Union as the leader of the strict constructionists, whereas the United States usually sided with liberals. Eichelberger was pleased by the expansive views that Lie (and later, Dag Hammarskjöld and U Thant) took of their mandate. Eichelberger wrote,

> The expanding role [of the Secretary-General] has been one of the most important developments in the history of the organization. It has resulted from courage and wisdom on the part of three successive Secretaries-General, and because of the existence of certain vacuums which the General Assembly (GA) and the Security Council have asked the Secretary-General to fill.[2]

One way that Lie made liberal use of the charter's description of his role included attending Security Council meetings and recommending courses of action for the council. This approach turned out to be a theme in UNA's work through its policy studies programs and its posture in advocacy work.

Eichelberger argued for a liberal interpretation of the charter to maximize its authority, especially welcoming the increasing role of the GA when the Security Council was deadlocked. The General Assembly replacing the council as the "principle peacemaking organ . . . is unquestionably the most significant constitutional development which has taken place in the United Nations."[3] AAUN was supportive of the Uniting for Peace mechanism, a procedure by which the General Assembly can take up an issue of international security if the Security Council fails to act.[4] "The most spectacular example of a liberal interpretation of the Charter occurred with the adoption of the Uniting for Peace resolution," Eichelberger wrote. When council disagreements among the veto powers regarding a threat to peace lead to inaction, the GA can take up the matter "and recommend collective measures, including, in the case of a breach of the peace or act of aggression, the use of armed force."

The first years of the UN also saw that what happened outside it was more consequential than what happened inside it. Lie had not been Secretary-General for two weeks, in 1946, when Stalin released his Five-Year Plan on February 9, calling for rearmament because "no peaceful international order is possible" between Communist and capitalist countries. On February 22, George Kennan, the American diplomat and adviser, wrote his famous "long telegram" contending that Moscow viewed the rest of the world as evil and that therefore US policy should be one of "strong resistance." This was the genesis of the policy of containment to which he is credited. Then on March 5, Winston Churchill delivered his Iron Curtain speech, prompting Stalin to call the former prime minister "a firebrand of war," adding, "And Mr. Churchill is not alone here." Soon, the basic postures of the Cold War were put in place.[5]

Eichelberger took a philosophical approach to this threat to international cooperation. The causes of conflict "go back to antiquity," he wrote. "This is one of the reasons that, in some instances, the United Nations has been able to stop fighting and secure an armistice, but has not been able to translate the armistice into peaceful and permanent settlements."[6] Furthermore, he emphasized the importance of "moral unity."

"It is doubtful that the world would have survived this long," he wrote. "The disruptive potentialities of the changes in the immediate post-war period were so great and their capacity for destruction so terrible that without the unifying moral force of the United Nations the world might have destroyed itself."[7]

Stalin's arm's-length attitude toward the UN was largely linked to arithmetic: there were more pro-US members of the General Assembly than pro-Russian; therefore, Russia would always lose a one-state-one-vote showdown. The Security Council—in particular, the veto power of the big five—was Moscow's insurance, which Stalin used regularly. In February 1946, the Soviet Union was the first to use the Security Council veto. In the first ten years, Russia used the veto nearly fifty times, more than the other four veto-wielding states combined; the United States did not use its veto until 1970, against a resolution concerning Southern Rhodesia (now Zimbabwe).[8]

Throughout the 1950s, the Soviet Union grew increasingly hostile to the UN and its Secretaries-General. Although initially supportive of Lie and Hammarskjöld, Soviet attitudes ended up seeing them (especially Hammarskjöld, a Swede) as servants of the West. In 1960, the Soviet Union proposed a troika to replace the individual Secretary-General—a three-person presidium representing the East, West, and "neutrals." The proposal stemmed from Hammarskjöld's angering the Soviet Union, partly by his efforts to resolve the Congo-Katanga secessionist crisis. Arguing that Hammarskjöld was taking on too many political issues and grabbing too much authority, Moscow refused to pay its Congo peacekeeping assessments for a time and urged for the troika, rather than a solo brand of leadership, at the UN helm.

Eichelberger called this "an attack by the Soviet Union upon the office of the Secretary-General and on Dag Hammarskjöld personally." He added, "The small states overwhelmingly rejected the troika plan as fallacious. To them the Secretary-General played a particularly sympathetic role. . . . The small states were quick to see that a three-headed Secretary-General would rob them of this independent friend."[9] To sidestep the issue when Hammarskjöld died, U Thant was elected acting Secretary-General and was later elected for a full term as Secretary-General without further mention of a troika, especially because the Soviets found little support outside their Eastern European allies.

The charter held open the possibility of a review conference ten years after ratification. The General Assembly put the item on its agenda as that anniversary drew near, but the idea was greeted with ambivalence by AAUN. In *UN: The First Ten Years*, Eichelberger wrote, "The wisdom of holding a conference should not be confused with the desire to improve the Charter," implying that such a review might result in a weaker, rather than stronger, United Nations. Although he maintained his thesis, "supported by public opinion polls, that the people overwhelmingly want a stronger United Nations to preserve the peace,"[10] he worried that a review conference could strengthen the UN or could "check the evolution of the United Nations toward increasing authority."[11] The GA continued to put the review on its annual agenda and to then defer it. The conference was not held then, nor has it been held more recently.

Looking back at the UN's first decade, Eichelberger cited four key developments in the international system: "the break-up of the five-power system, the advent of the atomic age, the rapid liquidation of the colonial system, and the revolt against misery by the underprivileged half of mankind." He added that it was "a sufficient tribute" to the UN that "it has survived these changes."[12] Yet five years later, in 1960, Eichelberger said at an AAUN conference that the UN was facing "a different kind of crisis, because it's not dramatic, it's the problem of an interest slipping away from the United Nations." He added, "It has yet to be proven that to fragmentize the world's concerns and weaken the moral concern of the United Nations for peace problems will in any way lead to their solution in a more rapid way."[13]

International Crises

The international community faced a rapid series of security crises with vastly different origins requiring nimbleness on the part of the UN to devise responses. The creation of Israel in 1948 and the subsequent clashes between Israel and the Arab states, the Korean War, the Suez crisis, the Cuban missile crisis, and the Congo civil war all tested the UN's ability to reinvent itself with each challenge to peace and security. The constant in AAUN policy amid these crises was that it favored initiatives that strengthened the UN's authority.

China

In 1937, the Nationalists of Chiang Kai-shek and the Communists under Mao Zedong called a truce in their civil war to fight the common enemy of Imperial Japan. During the war, Chiang was the acknowledged leader of China, so his representatives participated in the negotiations over the UN and signed the UN Charter. With Japan defeated, the two opponents in China resumed their own fight. When Mao took control in 1949, Chiang fled the mainland and set up his Nationalist government in Taiwan (called Formosa). He also retained the Chinese seat in the UN, leaving the Beijing government unrepresented. This geopolitical contest lasted for more than twenty years.

The question of Chinese representation placed the AAUN in a bind, because it pitted two of its guiding principles—the universality of the UN and anticommunism—in conflict. On the one hand, the AAUN did not want to legitimize a Communist government, but on the other, AAUN's commitment to universality made it impossible to ignore that the Beijing government controlled the majority of territory and people of China. Throughout the 1950s, the association's annual statement of policy reflected this indecision. For example, the 1956 statement on China said,

> We can no longer hide our heads in the sand and refuse to recognize the problem of Communist China. Certainly it is impossible to accept the delegates of a nation so long as it is in a state of war with the United Nations. But eventually peoples must be represented in the United Nations by the governments in effective control, whether they are democratic or not.[14]

Korea

Korea was divided between the north and south at the end of World War II. The demarcation line was supposed to be temporary, but it turned into one of the first Cold War stalemates. The north invaded the south on June 25, 1950. At the request of the United States, the Security Council met to deal with the attack. Since the Soviet Union was boycotting the council at the time, it could not exercise a veto to protect its ally. The council condemned North Korea, but the advance continued, with North Korean troops capturing Seoul on June 28, 1950. On July 7, the council passed a resolution creating a unified UN command in Korea under US leadership. By September, a counteroffensive, led by US General Douglas MacArthur, had regained much of the lost territory. Both Secretary-General Lie and President Harry Truman saw the invasion as a test of the UN. "Korea was the first true test of the UN," Meisler wrote, "and he [Lie] intended to show its mettle. The Security Council had a clear duty to defend South Korea, and he was prepared to demand that it fulfill its duty."[15] Truman simply said, "We can't let the UN down."[16]

The Soviet Union ended its boycott of the council just in time to take its turn in the rotating presidency seat on August 1. Naturally, there were no more council resolutions on Korea. The United States then used the novel Uniting for Peace strategy, which allowed the General Assembly to deal with security matters as long as the issues were not on the Security Council agenda and two-thirds of the GA members agreed. Thus, the GA became the focus of the UN's Korea diplomacy. The assembly approved a resolution recommending (not demanding, as the assembly has no enforcement authority) "appropriate steps be taken to ensure conditions for stability throughout Korea."

The AAUN saw the response to Korea as precisely what the UN was intended to accomplish. A July 1950 statement expressed the AAUN's "admiration and support for the way in which the United Nations, its members and particularly the Government of the United States have functioned in the Korean crisis. Collective security is functioning."[17] Eichelberger wrote, "The Uniting for Peace resolution provides one of the most spectacular illustrations of a liberal interpretation of the Charter. The framers of the Charter did not contemplate the General Assembly assuming powers at the expense of the Security Council."[18]

As the US-led UN force pushed against the North Koreans, the United States, and MacArthur, in particular, entertained the idea of pushing beyond the demarcation line at the thirty-eighth parallel to invade North Korea and reunite the country. But Truman was ready to negotiate a peace based on the status quo at the demarcation line. When MacArthur wanted to push north of the thirty-eighth parallel, the AAUN sided with Truman. An AAUN April 19, 1951, statement said that Truman had no choice but to relieve MacArthur "when the General's public statements were clearly at variance with the government's policies as expressed by the President." Neither the US government nor the UN had authorized such a policy. Unification must come through mediation, the statement added.[19]

Following the same reasoning, an April 1954 statement on Indochina (Vietnam, Laos, and Cambodia) supported the US position that the issue was "not just an internal sovereign affair, but is a threat to the peace" and the US "is ready to assume a heavy responsibility to repel the threat to freedom and peace." However, the association called on all parties to seek a solution through UN mediation. "Like the problem of Korea before it, the problem of Indo-China must be met through the moral and material strength of United Nations action."

While anticommunism was fundamental to the AAUN outlook, the association's pro-UN impulses always trumped its anticommunism ones. Eichelberger wrote to Secretary of State George Marshall on July 11, 1947, referring to a series of Senate resolutions aimed at revising the UN Charter. Noting that one set "is designed to force Russia out of the United Nations," he wrote, "Nothing could be more harmful." Likewise, the AAUN opposed a proposal that would commit the United States to withdrawing from the UN if Beijing were handed the Chinese seat. A July 13, 1954, statement by AAUN President Charles Mayo backed Dwight Eisenhower and John Foster Dulles in rejecting the idea (the statement does not say who proposed it). "Would it be for us to throw away our moral influence and leadership in the world community and allow the communist dictatorships to fall heir to the leadership which now belongs to this country and the whole free world?" Mayo wrote. "Nothing could be more advantageous to the totalitarian cause or weakening to our friends."[20]

The Middle East

During World War I, Britain and France made a secret arrangement, the Sykes-Picot Agreement, to divide the Arab lands taken from the Ottoman Empire into certain spheres of influence. France ended up with a League of Nations mandate for what is now Lebanon and Syria, while Britain assumed league mandates for Iraq, Transjordan, and Palestine, opening the last territory to Jewish immigration to establish a national home for the Jewish people. After World War II and the Holocaust, the calls for a Jewish homeland became impossible for the international community to ignore. London passed the issue to the UN. A special committee of the General Assembly in the summer of 1947 proposed that Palestine "within its present borders . . . shall be constituted into an independent Arab state, an independent Jewish state, and the [international] city of Jerusalem." In a shake-up of traditional alliances, the United States and the Soviet Union supported the creation of a Jewish state through partition, with Britain suspicious of US motivations.

The AAUN endorsed the UN drive to create the Jewish state. The association's Palestine Committee issued a position paper in October 1947, condemning "the bitter extremists on both sides." It did not mention the special committee or its proposal, but it did say the United States must state its position and "must make it very clear that once a decision has been agreed [by the General Assembly], it will assist through the United Nations in whatever way is necessary to carry out the solution agreed upon."[21]

On November 29, 1947, the General Assembly adopted Resolution 181 endorsing the partition plan, deciding that the Jewish state and the Arab state would be established in May 1948. The Arab states objected to the plan. On May 14, 1948, Israel declared itself an independent nation. On the same day, the United States recognized the new state, while Arab forces (from neighboring countries and within Palestine) moved to take control of land held by the armed forces of the emerging Jewish state. While repelling the attackers, Israeli units also pressed Arab inhabitants out of many places that the units secured for the new state. UN mediation began first under Count Folke Bernadotte of Sweden and then under Ralph Bunche, an African American diplomat originally from Detroit, after the Stern Gang, an extremist Zionist group, assassinated Bernadotte. The talks resulted in the deployment of unarmed military observers and two cease-fires. But the UN, more than sixty years later, is still unable to broker a stable peace.

On May 17, three days after Israel's independence, the AAUN issued a statement welcoming the establishment of Israel and applauding the rapid recognition of Israel by the United States, while calling for further steps to fully implement the partition plan. The statement, issued by AAUN President William Emerson and Eichelberger, called on the Security Council to "prevent or stop declared Arab warfare upon Israel"; it also called on the United States to "now propose that all possible steps be taken through [ECOSOC] for the promotion of economic union . . . and for all of the broad policies of joint economic cooperation outlined in the resolution of November 29" and to promote the "establishment of the special international regime for Jerusalem . . . a statute for which has already been carefully worked out by the Trusteeship Council."[22] Subsequent annual statements of policy stopped calling for an economic union and international control over Jerusalem.

Suez

The 1956 clash over the Suez Canal was the first great confrontation between colonial powers of the north and the emerging powers of the south to land on the UN agenda. It was a unique challenge to the UN's ability to improvise. On July 23, 1956, Egyptian president Gamal Abdel Nasser seized the Suez Canal. Britain, which had held the canal since World War I, and France, the second-largest shareholder in the Suez Canal Company after Britain, called the seizure illegal. President Eisenhower did not side with the two European allies and urged them instead to take their case to the United Nations. After three months of private negotiations involving Britain, France, and the United States (but boycotted by Egypt), the two European powers agreed to take their case to the Security Council. But while publicly agreeing to a council meeting, Britain and France were secretly planning an invasion to take back the canal.[23]

Security Council meetings began on October 5, 1956. Hammarskjöld also organized private meetings in his offices that resulted in "six principles," including respect for free transit through the canal and for Egypt's sovereignty and the settlement of disputes by arbitration. Those principles became the basis for a council resolution that was adopted unanimously on October 13. However, France, Britain, and Israel devised a plan in Paris the next week to take back the canal: Israel would invade Egypt and take the waterway; Britain and France would then issue ultimatums to Egypt and Israel to stop fighting, withdraw their troops ten miles from the canal (meaning Israel would be allowed to stay in Egypt), and allow an Anglo-French force to secure the waterway. The first step on October 31 worked as planned—Israel reached the canal in one day. As expected, Nasser rejected the ultimatum, and Britain and France began bombing Egypt, with troops arriving the next week.

Eisenhower was furious. The United States had not been consulted, and the president called the invasion an "error."[24] The United States immediately took the issue to the Security Council. After Britain and France vetoed a draft resolution calling for the withdrawal of all foreign forces, Yugoslavia invoked the Uniting for Peace precedent and called for an emergency session of the General Assembly to address the issue. On November 7, the GA called on Hammarskjöld to create a UN Emergency Force (UNEF), which he did within forty-eight hours,[25] making it the first UN peacekeeping mission. The first "blue helmets"—all Danes—arrived on November 15 (the actual helmets were US Army surplus quickly painted UN blue). Nasser agreed to the force, providing that UNEF supervised only the *withdrawal* of foreign forces and that the canal would be solely in Egyptian hands. By early 1957, all foreign troops were out of Egypt, and UNEF remained in the country for nine years. Meisler wrote that the crisis "enhanced the reputation of Dag Hammarskjöld, who worked incessantly to carve out a peaceful exit for the thrashed colonial powers and to create the first UN peacekeeping force."[26]

Despite the AAUN's strong championship of decolonization and self-determination for newly independent states, the association was sympathetic to Britain and France in this matter. In *UN: The First Twenty Years*, Eichelberger called the seizure of the canal a "great provocation" but passed no judgment on the invasion.[27] AAUN was strongly in favor, however, of UN involvement in the crisis. An AAUN statement on September 25, 1957, said the association was pleased the issue "has finally reached the United Nations." It called the reactions by Britain and France "understandable" but insisted the solution must come from the UN, not from the military actions of the two countries. "Such a solution would not mark a triumph either of the Western Powers over Egypt or of anti-colonialism over the Western powers." A statement on October 4 made four recommendations for Security Council action: all parties must avoid the threat of war; the UN should request an advisory opinion from the International Court of Justice (ICJ) "on the right of the Egyptian Government to nationalize the Company for operating the Suez Canal"; pending an ICJ opinion, the Security Council should establish "a supervisory commission to assure to all nations, including Israel, fair and efficient observance of the guarantees of free and equal use" of the canal; the Security Council should seek "a positive long range solution," including the establishment of "an international waterways commission to study and recommend" to governments arrangements for "free and equal navigation for all nations in all pertinent canals and waterways."[28]

The last recommendation was based on a CSOP plan on international waterways from 1951. An October 11 letter to *The New York Times* said the United States should "keep the Suez question before the United Nations until a settlement is achieved" and urged Secretary of State Dulles and other foreign ministers to attend the Security Council. The letter was signed by Eleanor Roosevelt, chair of the Board of Governors; President Charles Mayo; Oscar de Lima, chair of the board of directors; and Eichelberger.[29]

Congo

The Congo civil war was not only a bloody, painful affair but also a watershed event for the UN. It required the largest, most complex peacekeeping operation at the time, and it was the first instance of the UN taking sides in a shooting war. The wounds inflicted on Africa and the UN by Congo remain unhealed today. (Now called the Democratic Republic of Congo (DRC), it was called Zaire from 1971 to 1997, before it reverted to its earlier name, or DRC.)

The Congolese revolution gained popularity between 1958 and 1960. Belgium, its colonial power, granted the country independence on June 30, 1960. However, "few colonies came to independence as unprepared as the Congo," Meisler wrote. "Belgian colonialism had been harsh and exploitative. . . . Unlike the British or French, the Belgians provided no period of self-rule to prepare their colony for independence."[30] As a result, the country's burst into independence led to its immediate collapse, with mutinies and murders of Europeans and Congolese. At that juncture Katanga, a Congolese province rich in minerals and under the leadership of Moise Tshombe, backed by the Belgians, declared its independence from the rest of Congo (then called the Republic of Congo).

On July 10, 1960, Belgium sent a military force to restore order, over the objection of the new leaders of the country, Prime Minister Patrice Lumumba and President Joseph Kaša-Vubu, who requested US assistance. (Lumumba was the first elected leader of the nation since its independence.) President Eisenhower said no and urged Congo to bring its case to the UN. On July 14, Hammarskjöld requested and received authority from the Security Council to send a peacekeeping force to Congo. Within a year, Opération des Nations Unies au Congo (ONUC) reached close to 20,000 troops from thirty countries and stayed for four years.

Walter Lippmann, the American journalist, wrote, "This UN enterprise is the most advanced and the most sophisticated experiment in international cooperation ever attempted."[31] Since there was no peace to keep, the force inevitably took sides in the fighting, alternately enraging and satisfying the supporters of the Lumumba government. The force succeeded in restoring some order—notably, ending the Katanga secession in 1961; but the uneasy peace did not last long after the mission left in 1964. Hammarskjöld died in a plane crash on September 17, 1961, while en route to negotiate a truce in Katanga. (A UN peacekeeping force was sent in 1993 and has remained there since.)

The AAUN backed Hammarskjöld's ambitious peacekeeping operation. In its 1962 Statement of Policy (dated November 17), the Third Biennial Convention also backed acting Secretary-General U Thant's plan of reconciliation. Blaming Tshombe's "recalcitrance" and European powers' "inability or reluctance" to help U Thant, the association urged the US government "to continue to support and if possible improve this Plan and to help the Secretary-General to carry it out." Saying the plan "should be applied immediately," the statement said the plan would "strengthen the hands of the moderate Congolese government against extremists" and would "enable the United Nations [to] gradually reduce the expenses of its military establishment and concentrate on the economic and social recovery."[32]

Cuba

The Cuban missile crisis of 1962 was the biggest public display of nuclear brinksmanship the world has ever witnessed. Playing out over thirteen days, Washington and Moscow pushed each other closer to the edge after the United States discovered that Russia was placing missiles—many of them nuclear armed—in Cuba. While the high-stakes moves and countermoves were taking place behind closed doors in Moscow and Washington, the Security Council was the scene of one of history's most memorable displays of public diplomacy.

On October 23, the day after John Kennedy announced the blockade of Cuba, the council met in an emergency session, where US Ambassador Adlai Stevenson II and Soviet Ambassador Valerian Zorin traded charges and tabled resolutions condemning each other. On the third day, Stevenson shifted from addressing the council and spoke directly to Zorin: "Do you, Ambassador Zorin, deny that the USSR has placed and is placing medium and intermediate range missiles and sites in Cuba? Yes or no—don't wait for the translation—yes or no?" When Zorin refused to answer, Stevenson continued: "I am prepared to wait for my answer until hell freezes over, if that's your decision. And I am also prepared to present the evidence in this room." With that, the US staff brought into the room U2 spy plane photos of the Soviet missile sites in Cuba. Harlan Cleveland, the US assistant secretary of state for international organizations, later said, "The drama of that . . . worked, as far as anything can work in politics, perfectly, and was very persuasive to everyone."[33]

There are many analyses that argue that the UN—and the Security Council, in particular—was a sideshow, that Stevenson's challenge at the council was great theater but irrelevant politics. According to Meisler, "It is popularly regarded as Adlai Stevenson's finest hour at the United Nations—though the historic record makes it clear that neither he nor the UN played major roles in ending the crisis."[34] Not surprisingly, Eichelberger credited the UN for helping avoid catastrophe. "The Cuban crisis in 1962 demonstrated that the United Nations had both the authority and the skill to interpose itself between two superpowers who were on a collision course," he wrote. "One could say that if there had been no United Nations the two giants might have confronted each other with disaster. It has been said many times that the United Nations has made the difference between the uneasy peace in which the world now lives and catastrophe."[35]

"Conditions of Stability and Well-Being"

As detailed in Chapter 2, the LNA/AAUN not only promoted the creation of the UN but also offered specific ideas on what issues should be on the UN's agenda: human rights, decolonization and trusteeship, disarmament, and economic and social improvements. This targeted, expanded agenda continued into the first sessions of the General Assembly and Security Council. As always, the guiding principle was that the initiative should strengthen the UN's authority. Because the Security Council was either deadlocked on most of these issues or these issues were not on its agenda, the UN and its supporters—including AAUN—focused their attention on the GA, ECOSOC, the Secretary-General, and the specialized agencies. The association applauded Lie's and Hammarskjöld's initiatives to expand the authority of their office; lobbied to increase the number and mandate of specialized agencies; and continually advocated for greater GA involvement in all issues, including security.

Citing Article 55 of the charter, Eichelberger wrote that this article was proof that the founders wanted "a well-rounded organization" that would promote peaceful settlements of disputes and promote human rights and economic development, meaning its "long-range task [is] the promotion of a better life for the peoples of the earth." The article illustrates "the fact that the United Nations is more than a league of states—that it has very considerable authority as an entity."[36] Article 55 states:

> With a view to the creation of conditions of stability and well-being which are necessary for peaceful and friendly relations among nations based on respect for the principle of equal rights and self-determination of peoples, the United Nations shall promote:
>   Higher standards of living, full employment, and conditions of economic and social progress and development;
>   Solutions of international economic, social, health, and related problems; and international cultural and educational cooperation; and
>   Universal respect for, and observance of, human rights and fundamental freedoms for all without distinction as to race, sex, language, or religion.

Not only did this open-ended mandate provide a basis for a robust and inclusive role for the UN in economic and social issues, but also, by linking "stability and well-being" with "peaceful and friendly relations among nations," it fit perfectly with the AAUN's view of rights and freedom as being closely tied to peace and security.

A higher purpose also became part of the association's thinking. Eichelberger quoted the director-general of the UN Technical Assistance Administration, Hugh Keenleyside, calling such assistance "kindliness" and "the spirit behind the various tech assistance programs." This idea to "help people help themselves," wrote Keenleyside, "goes back to antiquity" and finds modern manifestations in the work of the Rockefeller Foundation, which "has provided examples of organized philanthropic technical assistance." Such development assistance and advice is "considered one of the most important and constructive of United Nations activities," Keenleyside wrote. Eichelberger endorsed this concept, writing, "No United Nations program provides a better illustration of the organization's expansion based upon a liberal application of the Charter."[37]

Human Rights

Human rights were regularly invoked as the nexus of providing technical assistance to governments to advance the UN's role. They were also arguably the issues that consumed the AAUN the most. Even before Dumbarton Oaks and San Francisco, the LNA/AAUN considered it essential that human rights be enshrined in the charter to ensure a just, lasting peace. Ensuring that human rights were embedded in the charter — not only as a concept, but also as integral to the functioning of the UN as a source for peaceful settlement of disputes and economic development — was a notion expressed clearly by Eichelberger: "The Charter of the United Nations places human rights and the dignity and worth of the human person as one of its first objectives."[38] (The issue of human rights is dealt with more in Chapter 14.)

Decolonization*

In the AAUN worldview, one of the greatest human rights was the elimination of colonialism. Human rights, economic and social freedoms, and security could never be achieved without decolonization. "When a sentiment for freedom sweeps an area, it cannot be held back. Freedom cannot be rationed," Eichelberger wrote.[39] The issue is an important component of the charter: Chapter XI of the charter outlines principles for decolonization; Article 73 states that the UN member states were to aid trusteeship territories, "to develop self-government, to take due account of the political aspirations of the people, and to assist them in the progressive development of their free political institutions, according to the particular circumstances of each territory and its peoples and their varying stages of advancement"; and Chapter XII established the international trusteeship system, which was "for the administration and supervision of such territories as may be placed thereunder by subsequent individual agreements. These territories are hereinafter referred to as trust territories."

An entire council of the UN was dedicated to trusteeship, a body parallel to the Security Council, the General Assembly, and the Economic and Social Council. The Trusteeship Council's mandate was to consider reports given to it by the administering authority; the members were to accept and examine petitions along with the administering authority; and they could then plan periodic visits to various trust territories, provided the council received approval from the administering authority.

---

* Mariah G. Ross contributed research to this section.

As Eichelberger wrote, "The eventual doom of the colonial system was foreshadowed in a number of liberal provisions of the Charter."[40] He noted that the colonial powers promised independence as a reward for support during World War II. At San Francisco, "the powers, aware of this situation, wrote into the Charter obligations to advance self-government and independence which they might not have agreed to in some of their reactionary moods following the war."[41]

Progress in decolonization was rapid and was reflected in the AAUN's policy statements. In 1952, the association noted that "the most dramatic political and economic developments of the post-war years lie in the extraordinary movements of colonial peoples for national independence, and in the equally determined and continuing demands for relief from poverty, feudalism and racial subjection." It also noted that one-quarter of the world's population had won its independence since the UN was founded. Ten years later, the statement of policy by the Third Biennial Convention declared, "Today, less than two percent of the entire world is still in colonial status. Almost forty-four percent of the membership of the United Nations is made up of members which were not independent states when the second world war began." Drawing strikingly on the language of the US Supreme Court on school desegregation, the AAUN called for the remaining colonies to "receive their independence with all deliberate speed—fast enough to stimulate and maintain hope in the people of these territories, but deliberate enough to avoid a repetition of the Congo disaster."[42]

A related AAUN campaign urged the United States to turn over lands captured from the Japanese in World War II to UN trusteeship. The September 21, 1945, program of the AAUN Executive Committee urged that all strategic bases held by the United States should not be annexed but rather should be maintained by the United States "as a trustee for the world organization, thus protecting itself, but at the same time developing the world organization and maintaining police stations for world security." This was not US policy, however, and thus AAUN's impatience with the US government grew. On July 17, 1946, the CSOP wrote to Secretary of State James Byrnes, saying, "It is our belief that the refusal so far of nations to work out a coordinated United Nations policy for strategic bases is possible second only to the lack of international control of the atomic bomb in promoting insecurity." Byrnes replied on July 26, saying the United States will continue to be engaged in trusteeship issues, "with a view to establishing in them [the trusteeship agreements] the purposes and principles regarding trusteeship which were laid down in the United Nations Charter." As to strategic bases, Byrnes wrote that the outcome "will be consistent with the purposes and principles" of the charter.[43]

The AAUN persisted. "The question of strategic bases is one of the most important and yet one of the least discussed in the problems of collective security and disarmament," Eichelberger wrote. "They should no longer be factors contributing to the world's insecurity."[44] The bases were never turned into UN trusteeships; however, over the decades, they were either decommissioned or returned to the original country.

Disarmament

The UN Charter envisioned disarmament based on the regulation of armaments, multilateral reductions in arms and armed forces, and "the least diversion" of resources to arms from development (Article 26).[45] Embracing this concept, LNA/AAUN pressed for disarmament through mutual agreement rather than through coercion. This was a special concern for James Shotwell and CSOP, the latter of which made disarmament a focus of much of its research in the 1930s and early 1940s, promoting the case for the orderly regulation of disarmament that found its way into the charter. Shotwell was the lead author of Carnegie Endowment's 1946 proposal for the control of nuclear material and for a draft convention on international inspections.[46]

A letter from AAUN officials and others to Secretary of State Stettinius (undated but most likely written soon after the Dumbarton Oaks Conference) said, "In harmony with the Atlantic Charter, the Moscow Declaration and the Declaration of the United Nations, all of which have reaffirmed the need for the regulation of armaments in the postwar period, we earnestly commend to you the necessity of giving adequate consideration to universal reduction of armaments within the basic framework of the international organization."

Later policy statements elaborated on this principle. The 1953 statement of policy, for example, said, "In the interest of common survival all nations must quicken their efforts within the United Nations if they are to free the world of the burdens and fears of armaments and the scourge of war." With the atomic bombings of Hiroshima and Nagasaki in August 1945, disarmament took on a new, more immediate meaning. On August 9, the day the bomb was dropped on Nagasaki, Eichelberger telegrammed President Truman, urging him to take "decisive action through the United Nations to prevent . . . universal destruction." He wrote, "It was your destiny to announce to the world a scientific achievement so overwhelming that mankind enters the atomic age." Eichelberger suggested both a national committee to "study how the

United States can best utilize this discovery for our own well being and that of the world" and the "necessity of rigid world inspection." Eichelberger suggested that two committees be set up to deal with the issue: one, under the authority of the Security Council, dedicated to "the working out of the controls necessary to maintain universal peace and prevent universal destruction"; and another, under the Economic and Social Council, that would explore how atomic technology could be put to beneficial industrial and social uses.[47]

On August 12, three days after the destruction of Nagasaki, Shotwell wrote an article for the *New York Herald Tribune,* saying, "There is no more pressing need in all the world than that of the immediate control and direction of this new force." Warning of what would, in fact, happen in a few years, he wrote, "The history of science leaves no doubt that the fundamental principles of this great discovery, like all those of the past, cannot long be kept secret either of any one group of scientists or of any one nation. Therefore arrangements for international as well as national control must be worked out quickly."

Furthermore, Shotwell anticipated the long-range nuclear missile arms race in which the United States and the Soviet Union would soon engage:

> Strategic frontiers are a thing of the past. This had already become true with the invention of the rocket bomb [Nazi Germany's V2 rocket] traveling through the stratosphere to anywhere on earth. That invention is now reinforced a thousand-fold, for it must be remembered that both rocket and atomic bombs are only in their infancy.

Rejecting the idea that the bomb "has rendered useless all the plans" for the UN Charter, Shotwell argued the opposite: "The charter was drafted upon a principle which makes possible an adequate directorate for the use of the atomic bomb both to police the world for peace and to insure its proper use in peacetime pursuits." He concluded by elaborating on Eichelberger's two-committee proposal.[48]

In *UN: The First Ten Years*, Eichelberger wrote that John Foster Dulles had told him that if the negotiators at San Francisco had known that the bomb lay on the horizon, "they would have made the Charter a stronger document with authority for the control of weapons of mass destruction."[49]

While comprehensive disarmament, including banning land mines and controlling the use of small arms, has been dealt with on the UN agenda, nuclear disarmament remains stuck in limbo, a fixture on the agenda from the start. "Comprehensive plans for global disarmament were proposed soon after the UN began to function, but were quickly abandoned in favor of a more targeted approach."[50] The first GA resolution on January 24, 1946, established the Atomic Energy Commission with the mandate to "make specific proposals for the elimination of atomic weapons and other weapons of mass destruction and help ensure that atomic energy would be used only for peaceful purposes." While the United States maintained its monopoly, it was willing to consider controls. Most notable was the Baruch Plan of June 1946. Bernard Baruch, the US representative to the UN Atomic Energy Commission, proposed creating an International Atomic Development Authority "to promote and regulate the peaceful uses of atomic energy and establish an international system of on-site inspections and sanctions."

Opposed to any plan that would lock in the US monopoly on the knowledge to build the bomb, the Soviet Union rejected the plan and made a counterproposal later that year dubbed the Gromyko Plan, after Soviet Foreign Minister Andrei Gromyko. This plan called for the elimination of all nuclear weapons, followed by a verification regime.[51] The website Atomic Archive summarized the stalemate: "The United States position, then, was that international agreement must precede any American reductions, while the Soviets maintained that the bomb must be banned before meaningful negotiations could take place."[52]

Shotwell and his colleagues at the Carnegie Endowment developed their own draft treaty for the control of nuclear technology. The treaty would create an Atomic Development Authority, an international body that "would have absolute control of all 'dangerous' activities in the atomic energy field and would closely supervise through licensing and inspection all 'non-dangerous' activities."[53]

According to Harold Josephson, the author of *James T. Shotwell and the Rise of Internationalism in America,* the Shotwell/Carnegie plan was considered a compromise between the two positions, though Shotwell himself did not see it that way. Rather than appear to be working counter to the US government, Shotwell withdrew the Carnegie proposal. "The Endowment's draft convention proved neither technically feasible nor politically adequate," Josephson concluded.[54]

Nevertheless, AAUN persisted. Every AAUN annual convention and policy statement advocated general and nuclear disarmament, in fulfillment of both the charter and the first resolution of the General Assembly.

AAUN was not alone in this campaign. Various coalitions of scientists, including some who had worked on the Manhattan Project, argued for international control. The National Committee on Atomic Information included among its scientific consultants Albert Einstein, J. Robert Oppenheimer, and the Nobelists Leo Szilard and Harold C. Urey. The Committee on Atomic Energy was set up in 1946 explicitly to support the ultimately successful McMahon Bill, which transferred control of atomic weapons and technology from military to civilian control. Celebrity endorsers of this group included the actors James Cagney, Bette Davis, and Paul Robeson; the composer Aaron Copland; and the writers Langston Hughes, Lillian Hellman, and Howard Koch.[55]

The UN continued to work on a framework for disarmament through several permutations of a multilateral negotiating body that is known today as the Conference on Disarmament, based in Geneva. Nuclear disarmament continued to be a primary focus of AAUN/UNA. When UNA began its Multilateral Studies program in 1968, its chapters chose the Nuclear Nonproliferation Treaty (NPT) as its first study (see Chapter 9).

By the early 1960s, the AAUN was advocating the expansion of UN authority to new areas: Antarctica, the seabed, and outer space (conventions covering these environments were indeed established). Within a few years, the idea of UN authority over the moon was taken seriously as the race to it and other celestial ambitions began in earnest between the United States and the Soviet Union.

Notes

1. Stanley Meisler, *United Nations: The First Fifty Years* (New York: The Atlantic Monthly Press, 1995), 31.

2. Clark Eichelberger, *UN: The First Twenty Years* (New York: Harper & Row, 1965), 42.

3. Clark Eichelberger, *UN: The First Ten Years* (New York: Harper & Brothers, 1955), 15.

4. Eichelberger, *UN: The First Twenty Years*, 16–17.

5. Meisler, *United Nations*, 24–26.

6. Eichelberger, *UN: The First Twenty Years*, 49.

7. Eichelberger, *UN: The First Ten Years*, 5.

8. United Nations, "Security Council: Quick Links," Dag Hammarskjöld Library Research Guides, http://research.un.org/en/docs/sc/quick/veto.

9. Eichelberger, *UN: The First Twenty Years*, 44–45.

10. Gallup polls from 1953 to 1955 showed that between 55 percent and 80 percent of the US public approved of the UN's work. Comprehensive polling data are available on the UNA-USA History Project website: http://blogs.shu.edu/UNA-USA/.

11. Eichelberger, *UN: The First Ten Years*, 87–88.

12. Ibid., 1.

13. The Clark M. Eichelberger Papers, Manuscripts and Archives Division, New York Public Library. Astor, Lenox, and Tilden Foundations (NYPL Archives), box 116.

14. Ibid., box 122.
15. Meisler, *United Nations*, 57.
16. Ibid., 59.
17. NYPL Archives, box 122.
18. Clark Eichelberger, *UN: The First Fifteen Years* (New York: Harper & Brothers, 1960), 100.
19. NYPL Archives, box 122.
20. Ibid.
21. Ibid., box 65.
22. Ibid., box 120.
23. Meisler, *United Nations*, 105–107.
24. Ibid., 106.
25. Eichelberger, *UN: The First Twenty Years*, 29.
26. Meisler, *United Nations*, 95.
27. Eichelberger, *UN: The First Twenty Years*, 29.
28. NYPL Archives, box 122.
29. Ibid.
30. Meisler, *United Nations*, 116–117.
31. Quoted in Brian Urquhart, *Ralph Bunche: An American Life* (New York: Norton, 1993), 319.
32. Seton Hall University (SHU Archives), The Msgr. William Noé Field Archives and Special Collections Center, South Orange, NJ, box 908.
33. Meisler, *United Nations*, 146–147.
34. Ibid., 141.
35. Eichelberger, *UN: The First Twenty Years*, 46–47.
36. Ibid., 105–106.
37. Eichelberger, *UN: The First Ten Years*, 54.
38. Ibid., 70.
39. Eichelberger, *UN: The First Fifteen Years*, 71.
40. Eichelberger, *UN: The First Ten Years*, 3.
41. Ibid., 64–65.
42. NYPL Archives, box 117.
43. Ibid., box 64.
44. Eichelberger, *UN: The First Ten Years*, 30.
45. Mariah G. Ross contributed research to this section.
46. Harold Josephson, *James T. Shotwell and the Rise of Internationalism in America* (Teaneck, NJ: Fairleigh Dickinson University Press, 1975), 274.
47. NYPL Archives, box 59.
48. Ibid.
49. Eichelberger, *UN: The First Ten Years*, 3.
50. Edmund Piasecki and Toby Trister Gati, *The United Nations and Disarmament* (New York: UNA-USA, 1993), 1.
51. Ibid., 2–3.
52. "The Manhattan Project: Making the Atomic Bomb," AtomicArchive.com, http://www.atomicarchive.com/History/mp/p6s5.shtml.
53. Josephson, *James T. Shotwell*, 268.
54. Ibid., 280.
55. NYPL Archives, box 62.

4

AAUN Internationalism and Domestic Political Disputes, 1947–1964

Marginalized for most of the years between the world wars, the LNA/AAUN found its brand of internationalism prevailing throughout the war. At war's end, isolationism regained some favor but still lost to internationalism both in Washington and among the general public. By that time, however, many definitions of internationalism had emerged. The AAUN was the dominant civil society organization promoting internationalism in general and at the UN in particular. Starting in 1947, the AAUN arranged annual conferences that attracted up to 110 organizations and were designed to keep AAUN's foreign policy approaches in the forefront.

Because the US public still viewed the UN as a guarantor of peace, it retained public support. A Gallup poll taken in September 1947 found that when asked, "Are you in favor of the United Nations Organization?" 85 percent said yes; 6 percent, no; and 9 percent, no opinion. A majority (51 percent) was dissatisfied with "the progress made to date by the U.N. Organization," though one main reason for that dissatisfaction was "the [UN's] lack of power and authority to carry out decisions." The UN was also creating its own celebrity culture by default. The same poll found that Soviet Ambassador Andrei Gromyko was the best known of the "big four" ambassadors. Three times as many Americans could name Gromyko than they could name the US ambassador (Warren Austin); less than 1 percent knew the name of the French ambassador (Alexandre Parodi).

The roster of celebrities supporting the UN continued after the war. In addition to Douglas Fairbanks Jr. and Myrna Loy was a newer contingent of artists—notably, actor Danny Kaye's involvement with the UN Children's Fund (UNICEF). In an interview with Edward R. Murrow, the composer Oscar Hammerstein II (*South Pacific, Oklahoma, The King and I*) included a defense of the UN among questions about his creative process and home furnishings. An anarchist could never be elected mayor or dog-catcher, he said: "Nevertheless we seem to subscribe to anarchy in international affairs; we resist government. Many of us resist even the United Nations which is a mild form of law and order. And many think it is weak and should be abolished. I think it is weak and should be made much stronger. I think it is our only hope for peace."[1]

The return of politics as usual in the United States required maneuvering by the AAUN to maintain its bipartisan character. This was always a difficult task because the key officials, including Eichelberger and Shotwell, were Democrats, and the AAUN's most effective advocate was arguably the most famous unelected Democrat in the United States: Eleanor Roosevelt. Going back to the time of the Committee to Defend America by Aiding the Allies (the White Commission) in the lead-up to US entry into the war, the organization always worked for a bipartisan nature. Because the majority of Republicans supported the creation of the UN, the AAUN had a deep bench of prominent Republicans upon whom it could count as friends, including Dwight Eisenhower, Senator Arthur Vandenberg of Michigan, Ambassador Henry Cabot Lodge Jr., and Nelson Rockefeller. Even John Foster Dulles—who, as Eisenhower's secretary of state, was a leading Cold Warrior—spoke of the UN in glowing terms and was often featured at AAUN events. Regardless of who was president, the AAUN's annual conferences began with the reading of a letter from the White House, with Vice President Richard Nixon addressing an AAUN conference in 1956.

AAUN also appears to have escaped the attention of the anticommunists in Congress. The activities of the House Un-American Activities Committee and the McCarthy witch-hunts in the Senate were set up to undermine the New Deal as much as they were constructed to root out Communists. Although the LNA/AAUN had a long history of opposing communism, being internationalists was often enough to gain congressional attention. Even the Alger Hiss case did not seem to touch AAUN. Hiss was deeply involved in creating the UN and was a colleague of Shotwell at the Carnegie Endowment, but he had no direct role in the AAUN. Likewise, Alger's brother Donald worked with Carnegie and published papers supporting the UN; Donald was investigated and cleared. This appears to be as close as the AAUN got to the investigations.

Occasionally in her syndicated "My Day" column, Eleanor Roosevelt would criticize Red Scare tactics as an affront to civil liberties or as plain silliness, such as when the Illinois American Legion voted to withdraw support for the Girl Scouts because of pro-UN material in their publications. "I wonder why it seems to the Legion a bad thing to indoctrinate members of the Girl Scouts with an interest in the U.N.," she wrote. "No one in the U.N. is talking about world government or handing out propaganda on the subject, and that is one of the first things the Illinois American Legion had better learn. The U.N. is made up of sovereign states."[2] Although she defended people who came under investigation—for example, the Alabama lawyer Clifford Judkins Durr, who represented many civil rights defendants, including Rosa Parks— none of those she defended had AAUN links.

AAUN combined its commitment to human rights at home and abroad with its desire to have the UN Charter enshrined in the US founding documents in a landmark racial discrimination case. In its October 1947 term, two cases on the US Supreme Court docket (*McGhee v. Sipes* and *Shelley v. Kraemer*) challenged the constitution- ality of "restrictive covenants," or laws under which African Americans were not permitted to own homes in certain neighborhoods. The AAUN filed an amicus brief in support of the African American homeowners, making the self-evident argument that such discrimination was a viola- tion of the Fourteenth Amendment of the US Constitution. But AAUN (joined by the Carnegie Endowment, the American Jewish Committee, and several law professors from Yale and Columbia Universities) went further, claiming the states were violating the UN Charter as well. In a December 4, 1947, statement, William Emerson, the AAUN president, explained why the AAUN had filed the brief:

> It [AAUN] believes that restrictive housing covenants and similar manifestations of racial and religious discrimination are both viola- tions of the Fourteenth Amendment of the United States Constitution and the obligations of the United States subscribed to under the Charter of the United Nations to promote human rights and fundamen- tal freedoms without distinction as to race, language, sex or religion.

Judging by press reports and AAUN's own statements at the time, this appears to be the first time the UN Charter was invoked as the law of the land before the Supreme Court. A *New York Times* article on December 5, 1947, described the AAUN as "taking the position that racial restrictions on the use of land violates the terms of the United Nations Charter," which, because it was ratified by the US Senate, should "become superior to municipal or state law."[3] The Supreme Court ruled the following year that such covenants were unconstitutional.

The other side of the issue — that is, isolationists who wanted to restrict US compliance with international law — was best represented by Senator John W. Bricker (R-Ohio), who championed a proposed amendment to the US Constitution that would have restricted presidential authority to conclude international agreements. At the time, *Foreign Policy* magazine, in its October 1953 issue, said the proposed amendment "would provide the legal basis for radically altering the present division of powers between the legislative and executive branches of the Federal Government in respect to the formulation and conduct of this country's foreign policy, and for necessary participation by State Governments in the execution of such policy in certain areas."[4] Another reason, less often stated, was the fear that international agreements would interfere with state and national segregation laws.

Although the Truman and Eisenhower administrations opposed the initiative, Bricker continued to introduce many versions of it between 1951 and 1954, as well as later in the decade. The most successful amendment, in 1954, failed to reach the two-thirds threshold necessary to send it to the states for ratification by a single vote. Supporters of the Bricker amendment cited as executive overreach some key international agreements of the previous decade, including the North Atlantic Charter (the founding document of NATO) and the UN Charter. Yet, Bricker had voted for the NATO treaty and the Marshall Plan.

Paul G. Hoffman, chair of the Studebaker Corporation and president of the Pasadena AAUN chapter, wrote a pamphlet for AAUN in 1953 criticizing the Bricker initiative. (The role of Hoffman, who later became the first administrator of the UN Development Programme, is explored further in Chapter 15.) Hoffman wrote: "A group of frightened lawyers are going up and down the country trying to terrify our people" by arguing to change the constitution "so as to incapacitate ourselves to deal as a nation with matters which have been a subject of treaties since the first days of the nation." The Bricker amendment would also "grant Congress 'the power to regulate' all executive and other international agreements [which would] impair if not destroy the independence of the Executive Branch."[5]

While trying to kill the amendment in the Senate, the Eisenhower administration also tried to placate Bricker and his supporters. For example, in 1953, the US government announced that it would not submit to the Senate for ratification any human rights treaties or covenants that might be negotiated at the UN, including the Convention on the Prevention and Punishment of the Crime of Genocide (Genocide Convention), nor would it participate in the General Assembly committees drafting these conventions. Eichelberger wrote that this preemptive rejection of the covenants damaged the US position:

> While these [covenants] were still being drafted, the United States Government announced at a meeting of the subcommittee of the Senate Judiciary Committee considering the Bricker Resolution that it would not submit the human rights covenants when completed to the Senate, taking the position that there were better ways than the treaty method to advance human rights. By this act the United States reduced its capacity to influence the documents in the drafting stage.[6]

In April 1955, Eichelberger also wrote to Eleanor Roosevelt, who was about to testify before the Senate regarding yet another Bricker amendment, about his own recent testimony. (For more information on her role regarding that amendment, see Chapter 5.)

As for major international treaties, the United States did not ratify the Genocide Convention until 1988, and it only ratified the International Covenant on Civil and Political Rights in 1992. It has not ratified the International Covenant on Economic, Social and Cultural Rights or the Convention on the Rights of the Child, the Convention on the Rights of Persons with Disabilities, or the Convention on the Elimination of All Forms of Discrimination Against Women.

Estelle Linzer, longtime AAUN manager, speaking at a 1994 event held by the Eleanor Roosevelt Center at Val-Kill, in Hyde Park, NY. First Lady Hillary Clinton is seated center in the first row. (Photo courtesy of Bill Urbin/National Parks Service.)

Giving Birth to the United Nations Association of the United States of America

For more than a decade in the life of the UN, two broad-based civil society organizations had "United Nations" in their titles—the AAUN and the US Committee for the United Nations. The AAUN had organized the official events for the first UN Days in 1946 and 1947. Behind the scenes, however, criticisms of AAUN's "outspoken policy stands" seem to have led to the State Department's refusal to name AAUN as the lead organization for the US observance of UN Day in 1948. Instead, the State Department created a "quasi-governmental" body.[7] (See Box 4.1.) The US Committee for the UN became the official US organizer of UN Day, with the president of the committee appointed by the US president.

It appears that the public never fully grasped that these were two different organizations. The Eichelberger archives contain letters from people asking why there were two groups—for example, people complained that they were still asked for money when they had already contributed, without realizing the appeals were coming from separate entities.[8] Throughout the 1950s, Eleanor Roosevelt, as the chair of the AAUN Board of Governors, sought to merge the two organizations, but US Committee chairmen rebuffed her. Reporting to the AAUN Executive Committee on December 21, 1955, she said she had met with the US Committee national chair, James S. McDonnell (of McDonnell Aircraft Corporation, who later became a UNA-USA leader and donated about $1 million through his estate to the organization's endowment). According to Roosevelt, McDonnell "had come to the conclusion that there was no way in which the AAUN and the US Committee could work together."[9]

Roosevelt wrote to John D. Rockefeller III, conveying her disappointment after hearing of McDonnell's conclusion. She was "upset to find that Mr. McDonnell" had concluded that, because of the difference in the two organizations' objectives—"in other words because we educate on all points of view and sometimes take positions"—he did not think it possible to merge. "Mr. McDonnell thinks competition is good in business and that it might be possible in this work. I do not agree with him." On November 7, 1955, McDonnell proposed (perhaps to mollify AAUN) that it might merge with the Women United for the United Nations to hold a yearlong joint finance campaign, but that proposal was not pursued.

Structurally, the distinction between the two organizations was obvious: the US Committee was a product of the State Department; AAUN was an autonomous civil society organization. After that, however, the

Box 4.1 Estelle Linzer: The Way We Were

Estelle Linzer was one of the longest-serving and most important people in the history of UNA-USA, serving as a staff member and later as a volunteer leader from the 1940s until her death in the late 1990s. She began at the AAUN as a close colleague of Clark Eichelberger; after 1951, she accompanied Eleanor Roosevelt on some of the former first lady's travels across the nation on behalf of AAUN.

After the AAUN and the US Committee for the UN merged in 1964, Linzer left her staff position during the management of Porter McKeever. Thereafter, she worked as a volunteer leader for UNA in many capacities: as vice chair of the UNA; officer of the Southern New York State Division and of the UNA of New York; member of UNA-USA delegations to the World Federation of UNA; and the UN representative (and thus a member of the Council of Organizations) of the Johnson Foundation in Racine, Wisconsin. In the last role, Linzer helped organize policy sessions on the UN at Wingspread, the Johnson conference center.

At the UN, she was a respected and senior member of the NGO community. Even when Linzer was a volunteer, she championed UNA staff members, especially those in middle management or support positions. During the early 1990s, she chaired a staff relations committee.

Throughout her life, Linzer wrote and lectured on the UN work of Eleanor Roosevelt. Linzer's anecdotes about "Mrs. R." were warm, witty, and riveting. Linzer was especially interested in human rights, as was Roosevelt. In addition, Linzer served as a board member and leader of the Eleanor Roosevelt Center at Val-Kill, Roosevelt's cottage in Hyde Park, New York. Linzer also worked to preserve the AAUN's history, organizing and donating its records to the New York City Public Library. Her typescript chronicle of the AAUN, "The Way We Were," reflects a concerted effort to assemble and record the organization's chronology, activities, and leadership and serves as a vital research tool on the AAUN's history.

—Jim Olson

differences were muddled. The distinction of purpose was so obscure that it had to be explained even to AAUN members. Addressing the first AAUN biennial in November 1958, Stanley Rumbough Jr., chair of the US Committee at the time, said the only differences between the two organizations were "in terms of function, because we have had no differences whatever with the AAUN." He said the US Committee strived to "arouse" the interest of its 120–130 member organizations (one of which was the AAUN) and other national groups (representing civic, business, labor, agriculture, war veterans, religion, education, youth, women, trade, and service associations); to work with the committee's Advertising Council on public awareness; to disseminate literature; and, above all, to promote UN Day. When the US president issues the annual UN Day proclamation, Rumbough said, "We take this proclamation, and we send it to every governor in every state and territory. We ask him to appoint a state chairman for UN Day and we ask him to issue a proclamation."[10]

In 1958, a memo written to Roosevelt from Rumbough, who was by then becoming more attuned to the merger, reiterated that there was "no conflict in the purpose, structure or the activities of the two organizations." He went on to say that, in fact,

> the work of each organization serves to supplement the work of the other. The AAUN is a voluntary national organization of State and local chapters with dues-paying individual members. They have a total of 45,000 members, 40 State associations and over 400 local adult and college chapters throughout the country. The purpose of the AAUN is to develop a well-informed public opinion in support of the United Nations. From time to time, the AAUN issues policy statements on problems before the United Nations.

Rumbough continued:

> The US Committee, on the other hand, is a semiofficial organization whose chairman is appointed by the President of the United States. It is made up exclusively of national organizations, including the AAUN. The purpose . . . is to disseminate facts about the United Nations and to promote the observance of UN Day in the United States. The Committee does not take stands on UN or US policy.[11]

Although AAUN leadership favored a merger, the chapters worried that it would rob the association of its ability to promote policy. Acknowledging this when the AAUN/US Committee merger finally came to fruition in 1964, Eichelberger said, "The historical tradition of the Association [will be] preserved. . . . Our right to speak freely, to speak our mind, to make policy statements" will remain the same. "Your work in the community must be undisturbed by the merger."[12] (See Box 4.2.)

Other more practical matters were involved regarding the merger. At the AAUN Board of Directors meeting in May 1964, where the vote to merge was passed, Oscar de Lima (who, at the time, was the chair of both the AAUN Merger Committee and the AAUN Executive Committee) pointed out that the US Committee was not given a budget by the government, so it had to raise its own money. "This of course, began to

Box 4.2 Peggy Carlin: "Chins Up!"

Peggy Sanford Carlin served in senior positions at UNA-USA from about the late 1960s through her retirement in 1989. Born in Vienna, Austria, Carlin and her family fled Nazi oppression and migrated to New York City via London. Before joining the UNA-USA staff, Carlin had been an actress and a host for Voice of America, where she had her own German-language talk show called *Peggy Sanford Plaudert* (loosely translated, "Chatting with Peggy"). Her radio scripts are deposited with the University of Texas, Austin (http://www.lib.utexas.edu/taro/utcah/00165/cah-00165.html).

At UNA, Carlin was responsible for the Council of Organizations, which numbered 100-plus civic organizations, service clubs, religious groups, labor unions, and advocacy groups as its members. Carlin and her assistant, Carol Christian, coordinated the work of the Conference of UN Representatives in New York (the representatives of American NGOs in the Council of Organizations) and the Conference of Washington Representatives for the UN (a DC-based staff of Council of Organizations members). Each group met monthly, offering briefings that emphasized the US role in issues on the UN agenda. Carlin's work with two organizational members of the council was especially noteworthy. She and Christian arranged annual events at UN headquarters for Lions Clubs International and the National Education Association. These events drew hundreds of members nationwide and provided another channel for building grassroots support for the UN.

Carlin worked with the UNA-USA development staff (especially Robert Ratner in the 1970s and Stan Raisen in the 1980s) to coordinate two major UNA-USA fund-raising events—the fall ambassadors' ball and the spring dinner, both held in New York City. These events drew top UN Secretariat officials and ambassadors, as well as US business leaders, providing a large source of revenue and visibility for UNA-USA. Ratner, Raisen, and their staffs raised the money, and Carlin made sure the events were elegant and fun and that protocol was observed. She took great care with the seating arrangements so guests could mingle with UN officials and diplomats.

For many people in the UN community, Carlin was the face (or a major face) of UNA-USA. Her apartment, in New York City, visited a few years ago, was adorned with old photos of her dancing with or greeting Secretaries-General, ambassadors (such as George H. W. Bush), and other celebrities (like Paul Newman, who was a member of the US delegation to the First UN Special Session on Disarmament in 1978).

Lastly, Carlin organized UNA's national conventions during the 1970s and 1980s. Held at a prominent New York hotel, the conventions combined business and substantive sessions with a visit to UN headquarters. Chapter leaders, representatives of the members of the Council of Organizations, and members of UNA's board of governors and National Council came together at these events, held four times each decade.

Carlin's responsibilities expanded so much at UNA that when she retired as a senior vice president, she supervised not only the Council of Organizations, the ball and dinner, and the convention, but also membership, relations with chapters, and Model UN and youth programs. After her retirement, she remained active in the UNA of New York City and helped stage the 1995 UNA-USA National Convention in San Francisco as part of the UN's fiftieth anniversary observance.

At UNA, Carlin, who is now in her mid-nineties, was always sophisticated, funny, a great supervisor (her admonition to discouraged staff members was "Chins up!"), and an excellent communicator with a strong sense of style and protocol.

—*Jim Olson*

cross lines with the AAUN," he said. Local chapters "found themselves in conflict with petitions and appeals from the United States Committee," and as the committee grew, "the lines crossing with the AAUN have been more difficult and more frequent."[13]

At the same meeting, Norman Cousins, editor of *The Saturday Review* and AAUN board member, called the situation "unnatural, illogical, irrelevant and indefensible, and this is the existence of two organizations, both of which are concerned with developing the fullest possible public support for the United Nations but the mutual existence of which does not make for the achievement of a mutual objective." He added,

There is no reason in the world why we should run after history with a mop. There is every reason in the world why there should be in existence a powerful organization with many, many times our present membership, an organization which not only indicates active support to the UN but, indeed, an organization which can give leadership to Congress and indeed to the world.[14]

Under Presidents Kennedy and Johnson, the State Department—and thus the US Committee—was more open than in previous years to a merger. In addition, because the US Committee had to raise funds, the two groups with similar agendas were seeking money from the same pool of donors, making it clear that finances were an overriding concern of both organizations. Indeed, fund-raising for each group suffered. The merger also became more realistic when Robert S. Benjamin became chair of the US Committee. (Presidents Kennedy and Johnson appointed him to the post from 1961 to 1964, respectively—the only time a chairman served more than one year.) Benjamin, an entertainment lawyer and a cochair of United Artists, had a long history of supporting the UN and having personal relationships with key AAUN figures, including Eleanor Roosevelt. Recalling the negotiations leading up to the merger, Benjamin said the philosophy of the national organizations did not bother him or Roosevelt, "but the people in the grassroots wanted the AAUN to be a position-taking organization, people who advocated causes specifically, rather than just the cause—the vitality of the United Nations as an institution."[15]

Proponents of the merger from both sides ultimately convinced their memberships of the value of coming together. The AAUN Board of Directors' vote on May 8, 1964, was unanimous in favor, as was the vote of the board of the US Committee earlier that day.[16] In 1965, the two became the United Nations Association of the United States of America, resulting in what Benjamin described as "a vibrant organization [that] has all the businesses and community supporting it, has got the grassroots support Mrs. Roosevelt generated, and has a national organization for the country."[17] (See Box 4.3.)

Box 4.3 UN Tours and the Central Fountain

In the early days of the UN, AAUN established two of the most enduring and visible components of the UN compound: the guided tours and the Central Fountain in front of the Secretariat Building.

At first, AAUN was cool to the idea of UN headquarters being located in the city, preferring a nonurban environment where the UN would not be restricted in its physical growth. But once the East River site was settled, the association was enthusiastic. It recognized the potential of making the UN accessible to the public, which also turned out to be profitable. As early as 1947, the AAUN's annual report said, "The location of the site of the United Nations in the United States confronts the Association with a magnified task which it performed in a minor way in Geneva, that is the setting-up of proper staff to act as guides to the many thousands of people who will visit the headquarters." At that point, the headquarters were still under construction.

AAUN organized the first tours using female volunteers from the organization. The first tour, in October 1952, cost one dollar for most visitors, though students and veterans paid only fifty cents. In a report on the guides, journalist Cindy Adams described them as an "international corps of brains and beauty" who explained the "workings of the United Nations to over a million visitors a year" and consisted of a "passel of guides (all ladies, from Pakistan, Denmark, Brazil, Israel, Canada, Taiwan, Russia and points East)." (For more details, see Chapter 17.) In 1955, the association turned over the guided tour service to the UN.

The AAUN was also responsible for the Central Fountain, which was commissioned by the AAUN and the Governors' Wives Committee. In 1950, Ruth Price, the director of the Northwest Office of AAUN, came up with the idea for a gift to the UN from American schoolchildren. After consulting with UN officials, including Ralph Bunche, the proposal switched from a carillon to an artwork. Eventually, $50,000 was raised, and the fountain was dedicated on June 26, 1952.[18] (The Jacob and Hilda Blaustein Foundation, as a memorial to Dag Hammarskjöld, commissioned the sculpture that now stands in the center of the foundation after his death in 1961. The statue—*Single Form*, by Barbara Hepworth—was installed in 1964. Jacob Blaustein had been a US delegate to the United Nations.)

—*James Wurst*

Notes

1. Edward R. Murrow, *Person to Person*, May 13, 1955.

2. Eleanor Roosevelt, "My Day," August 11, 1954.

3. The Clark M. Eichelberger Papers, Manuscripts and Archives Division, New York Public Library. Astor, Lenox, and Tilden Foundations (NYPL Archives), box 64.

4. The *Foreign Policy* magazine quoted in this book is a different publication from the current magazine bearing that name, which was founded in 1970.

5. NYPL Archives, box 115.

6. Clark Eichelberger, *UN: The First Ten Years* (New York: Harper & Brothers, 1955), 72.

7. Estelle Linzer. "The Way We Were: An Informal History of the American Association for the United Naitons from 1945 Through 1964." Unpublished manuscript, 1995.

8. NYPL Archives, box 125.

9. Ibid., box 122.

10. Ibid., box 115.

11. Ibid., box 133.

12. Ibid., box 118.

13. Ibid.

14. Ibid.

15. Robert Benjamin, "Franklin D. Roosevelt Oral History Program: Interview with Robert Benjamin," by Dr. Thomas Soapes, Franklin D. Roosevelt Library, Hyde Park, NY, 1977.

16. NYPL Archives, box 118.

17. Benjamin interview.

18. Seton Hall University (SHU Archives), The Msgr. William Noé Field Archives and Special Collections Center, South Orange, NJ, box 908.

5

Eleanor Roosevelt Stumps for the AAUN and the United Nations, 1953–1962

Dulcie Leimbach

Eleanor Roosevelt may have been the wife of one of the most popular presidents in the history of the United States, but she pursued her own ambitions in the political arena long before her husband, Franklin D. Roosevelt, was first voted into the governorship in New York and later into the White House.

Roosevelt's role as first lady has been extensively chronicled, including an autobiography and columns she wrote for magazines and newspapers over decades. She operated from an insatiable need to please, attracting a devoted audience of admirers wherever she traveled. One of her great gifts was her ability to relate to all kinds of people with a joyful ease.

But what is little known about Roosevelt was her volunteer work, from 1953 to her death in 1962, with the American Association of the United Nations, the predecessor organization of the UNA-USA. While acting as an unofficial AAUN ambassador, Roosevelt helped not only to promote the UN itself, a beloved cause of hers, but also to shape the AAUN into a larger national network of chapters and divisions and enhance its influence in the United States and overseas. A review of the papers and letters related specifically to Eleanor Roosevelt from the Clark Eichelberger archives at the New York Public Library reveals how Roosevelt's role at AAUN solidified her image as an activist and promoter of democratic and international causes.

Roosevelt's twelve years at the White House, during the Great Depression and World War II, grounded her in the nitty-gritty world of politics, even though she never ran for public office. As an envoy for her husband, she developed her deft way with crowds and individuals.

Her marriage in 1905 to FDR, a cousin five times removed, began in the typical fashion of a young woman bred in lofty circles in New York; she learned the art of standing by her man while he started and nurtured his political career. With five children born in ten years, Eleanor kept herself almost maniacally busy throughout the first two decades of her marriage, which also entailed the brutal discovery of FDR's affair with his secretary, Lucy Mercer.

FDR's infidelity became an emotional turning point for Eleanor Roosevelt, whose restless soul found solace by immersing herself in soft politics and charity—altruism that her famous uncle, Teddy Roosevelt, had instilled in her during her childhood visits to his family's estate, Sagamore Hill, in Oyster Bay Cove, New York. Roosevelt dived into volunteer work, beginning with the American Red Cross in 1917, which was a perfect outlet for her, as she enjoyed comforting people, particularly outsiders.

By the time the Roosevelt clan arrived at the White House in 1933, Eleanor had joined such civic organizations as the national League of Women Voters and the Women's Trade Union League. In 1935, she began a nationally syndicated newspaper column, "My Day," mixing the personal with the political in her plain style. The column lasted for decades and was carried by at least 200 papers. Roosevelt also delved into writing her first autobiography, *This Is My Story*. Throughout FDR's three terms, as well as during the first leg of his unprecedented fourth term, which ended abruptly in spring 1945, Roosevelt jumped at every chance to see more of the world and pitch in to what she considered causes that helped the masses.

When FDR died in April 1945 and the Roosevelts had to suddenly vacate Pennsylvania Avenue, President Harry Truman appointed Eleanor to the US delegation to the United Nations soon after the world body had emerged as a reality from the San Francisco Conference. Truman understood the political gain of having FDR's widow on his team.

The UN work became a natural continuance of life at the White House for Eleanor. Her tasks as a delegate involved more traveling and meeting foreign dignitaries, negotiating, and diplomacy. It also became arguably one of the most important achievements in her public life. Yet, as the only US woman delegate at the UN at the time, sixty-two-year-old Roosevelt, who had never acquired a college education, believed she had to prove herself twice over, despite her years as first lady of the United States. "How could I be a delegate to help organize the United Nations when I have no background or experience in international meetings?" she wrote in her autobiography, *On My Own*.[1]

Senator William Fulbright and others involved in US foreign affairs reinforced her nagging sense of self-doubt. Fulbright was concerned that her presence on the bipartisan delegation would signal a lack of seriousness about the UN, according to *A World Made New,* a book by Mary Ann Glendon on how the Universal Declaration of Human Rights came into being. But Truman prevailed, and Roosevelt's nomination in the Senate was sealed, grumblings notwithstanding.[2]

Her triumph as a delegate came accidentally, however. She was assigned a "safe" committee in the General Assembly—on social, humanitarian, and cultural affairs—where she and others surmised she could do little harm. Yet the role qualified her to chair the original, separate committee charged with creating the UN Commission on Human Rights, part of the newly formed Economic and Social Council. There, Roosevelt honed her diplomatic skills, hammering out over several years, with dozens of other delegates from all over the world, the Universal Declaration of Human Rights, adopted by the General Assembly in 1948.

First as chair of the committee and then of the Human Rights Commission, Glendon wrote, Roosevelt was credited with fostering a "cross-cultural understanding" among the delegates working with her on drafting the declaration. She even held teas and dinners at her Washington Square home in New York, so that everyone could get to know one another.

According to Estelle Linzer, the longtime manager of AAUN who wrote of Roosevelt's years on the commission, Roosevelt "labored long and hard to weld together the differing viewpoints of men who represent nations."[3] Even harder was Roosevelt's task as chairwoman, when she had "to listen hour upon hour." In a letter to her daughter Anna, Roosevelt described how

> during the entire London session of the [General] Assembly I walked on eggs. I knew that as the only woman on the delegation I was not very welcome. Moreover, if I failed to be a useful member, it would not be considered merely that I as an individual had failed but that all women had failed, and there would be little chance for others to serve in the near future.

When the historic vote on the declaration took place in the General Assembly, Eleanor read her speech wearing, as if for good luck, a fleur-de-lis brooch that was a replica of the three-feathered Roosevelt crest her husband had given her on their wedding day forty-three years earlier.

The vote, held in the Palais de Chaillot in Paris, started before midnight on December 9 and ended early on December 10, culminating in a standing ovation for Roosevelt. Yet she was reportedly more pensive than exultant in her response to the vote, Glendon contended, perhaps out of exhaustion. "It was after midnight when I left the Palais de Chaillot," Roosevelt wrote.[4] "I was tired. I wondered whether a mere state-

ment of rights, without legal obligation, would inspire governments to
see that these rights were observed."

Eleanor resigned from the delegation in 1952 (though, in 1961, she
rejoined the US mission to the UN as an adviser to the US ambassador,
Adlai Stevenson), when Dwight Eisenhower was elected president. She
was aware that a Republican appointee would replace her.

Her departure benefited the AAUN, as she knocked on the organization's door in New York in 1952. Approaching Clark Eichelberger, the
executive director, she declared that she was ready to volunteer. Eichelberger almost fell off his chair, he recounted, having no trouble accepting Roosevelt's offer.[5]

By late December 1952, a memo from Linzer to AAUN staff members said, in part, that "Mrs. Franklin Roosevelt will begin coming into
the AAUN office as a volunteer on January fifth. She will be here two
days a week, and through the kindness of Eleanor Gardner and Ruth
Berridge, will occupy their office. Mrs. Roosevelt will occupy herself
with chapter liaison activities."

She actually arrived on January 10 in the offices, a townhouse at 45
E. 65th Street, next door to the home, it turned out, that her mother-in-
law had bought for Eleanor and FDR soon after they were married. Hers
was a small, sparsely furnished office, but she said it would "do." The
staff members, once broken of their awe, became used to her habits:
being prompt for meetings and appointments; preferring face-to-face
talks rather than talking on the phone; going into her colleagues' offices
rather than summoning them into hers; and gently dismissing overlong
visitors by pushing back her chair, standing, and extending her hand for
a farewell shake.

Roosevelt, who was addressed as Mrs. Roosevelt, was soon jetting
or taking the train across the United States with Eichelberger. In tow
was a secretary—Patricia Baillargeon (see Box 5.1) or Linzer, who by
then was associate director. Together, she and Eichelberger worked to
educate the public about the UN and to expand the AAUN. Already, the
UN was a difficult-to-grasp entity for many Americans, who savored
their sovereignty but craved peace after two world wars.

"Perhaps this . . . is a good time to remind you that staff members
are due in at 9 o'clock in the morning," Linzer continued in her memo
to the office. "And could you please stow the coffee containers?"

It is hard to imagine Roosevelt taking umbrage at the sight of coffee containers. She delved into the AAUN, where she shared an office
with Baillargeon, who was from Seattle and a recent graduate of Mills
College. Roosevelt decided that growing local chapters and increasing

Box 5.1 Patricia Baillargeon: Serving "Mrs. Roosevelt"

Within four years of graduating from Mills College in Oakland, California, Patricia Baillargeon landed a job that any graduate in history and government would consider plumb: working for Eleanor Roosevelt.

At twenty-three years old, Baillargeon was a Seattle delegate and a volunteer at the annual conference in Washington, DC, that the AAUN put on for NGOs. The time was March 1953, and she had been promised a job with the Voice of America, but the McCarthy hearings were being conducted, and hiring for some jobs with the government had been frozen.

A month later, Baillargeon began working with Mrs. Roosevelt, who was sixty-eight then, in a position to last six weeks, to "help the person who was helping Mrs. Roosevelt," she said in a phone interview from Seattle in July 2014. Soon, the AAUN offered her a full-time position as Mrs. Roosevelt's secretary, which involved traveling across the United States to promote the UN and the AAUN. Baillargeon worked with Roosevelt from nearly the day Baillargeon arrived at the AAUN in 1953 not long before Roosevelt's death in 1962.

Baillargeon recalled her first impression of the office she shared with Roosevelt: it was "the same size as everyone else's." The AAUN was located on East 65th Street in a townhouse but soon moved into the Carnegie Building, at 345 E. 46th Street, directly across from the UN on First Avenue.

Roosevelt and Eichelberger would meet in his office—at the end of the hall, off-center from the traffic—and discuss strategies for spreading the word about the UN around the United States. A big part of what they needed to do, they agreed, was to go out and speak to people across the country.

"They carved up the map and said, 'Let's go to this section of the country next,'" Baillargeon said, adding that they might visit a couple of states at a time but always went to a different city each day. The format was similar for every trip. Roosevelt, Eichelberger, and Baillargeon would arrive at their destination early in the morning or late the night before, going by plane or by train. They would have a breakfast meeting with the groups that had organized the visits. They went to cities with AAUN chapters or were invited by local NGOs, but the visits came through the work of the chapter. A joint press conference with Eichelberger and Roosevelt would be held in the morning, as they "didn't waste any part of the day."

Late in the morning, after the press conference, where the "working press loved Mrs. Roosevelt," they would move on to a luncheon, which was usually open to local nonprofit groups. Occasionally, Eichelberger would speak separately to an all-male luncheon. In the afternoon, both Eichelberger and Roosevelt held more appointments. She would then return to her hotel or to other places she stayed—as a guest at a chapter member's home, say—and dictate her daily "My Day" newspaper column to Baillargeon. Sometimes, she'd take a short nap. (When Roosevelt was not traveling, her personal secretary, Maureen Corr, handled the dictation at Roosevelt's home in New York.)

In the evenings, at the largest hall in every city, Eichelberger gave a short speech, followed by Roosevelt, who gave longer speeches to a packed crowd. Baillargeon said she never saw Roosevelt use notes, speaking generally on the same topic on each trip, but framing it in a local way to engage the audience. As Baillargeon said, "When she spoke, everybody was silent and focused." Roosevelt had a "wonderful sense of the humor of daily life" that imbued her speeches and took everything in stride because, as Baillargeon said, "these were the last years of a difficult life" for her.

"She knew there was a huge amount to do" in improving the world, Baillargeon added, and in enlarging AAUN's membership. As part of her visits, Roosevelt also incorporated stops at colleges and universities, having become involved in this work through the Collegiate Council for the UN, which operated in a different office from the AAUN and had chapters of its own.

When Roosevelt was at the AAUN in New York, she kept close ties to the UN, managing a "huge string of appointments," Baillargeon said. Roosevelt would occasionally dip out for lunch at the UN Delegates Dining Lounge but mostly ate at her desk.

For people she could not fit into her schedule at the office, she met at her home on the Upper East Side, including visitors from overseas. "She gave it [the mission of AAUN] enormous momentum; she worked harder than anyone else; her drive and her goals were unwavering," Baillargeon explained. "She gave AAUN a great reaffirmation, helping to galvanize its presence across the US."

In addition to her "My Day" column, which she wrote for decades, Roosevelt also wrote a question and answer column for the *Ladies' Home Journal*, in which she provided the answers herself, with Baillargeon typing them up and Roosevelt editing them. Although she didn't hesitate to answer the big and small questions people posed to her about geopolitical crises, it was her impulse to want to solve a problem no matter how complicated. Most important, she spoke out.

—*D. L.*

membership would be her top priorities. "Mrs. Roosevelt was always on time for her appointments no matter how trivial they may have seemed to others to be," Linzer wrote. "She was impatient with the telephone, preferring to see the person with whom she was communicating."

During Roosevelt's nearly ten years at the AAUN, she worked closely with Eichelberger in building up the association in the 1950s and into the early 1960s, doubling the number of chapters to nearly fifty (though such numbers are impossible to verify and vary widely, depending on the source). She made recommendations about changing AAUN's structure and enhancing its stature. In fact, she came to AAUN with a work plan, outlined in an early communication to chapter and state leaders, calling for a regional chair for each region and a "Plan of Work."

"If this plan can be followed, I think we would gradually bring to the people of the United States a fundamental knowledge on all UN activities up-to-date," she wrote. "This seems to me the important thing to achieve if we are going to fight the attacks on the UN." She closed: "Our Association is the only organization that can do this in an organized and orderly fashion."

Her legendary energy did not flag during her time with the AAUN, recalled grandson John Roosevelt Boettiger in an e-mail to this writer: "Traveling with her during her AAUN years could leave us young folk ready to turn in with the sunset; she was just getting her 2nd wind."

As noted, the AAUN's precise chapter membership numbers have been consistently hard to confirm. By 1958, Stanley M. Rumbough, chair of the US Committee for the UN, wrote a memo to Roosevelt about a possible merger of the two organizations. According to Rumbough, AAUN had "45,000 members, 40 State associations and over 400 local adult and college chapters throughout the country."

A survey done for the Manhattan chapter in 1957, however, reveals its demographics, possibly emblematic of other AAUN city chapters: 78 percent of the members were women, about 95 percent were older than 43 years, about 49 percent were married, and 51 percent were not married. Astonishingly, 72 percent had not attended a meeting in the preceding year. (For more information on AAUN membership, see Chapter 13.)

Roosevelt deemed her "work sessions" with AAUN chapters the best way to recruit more members. As such, she followed a steady routine of hopscotching around the United States. She found an ideal niche for her passions; although she did her work as a volunteer, the archives include references of her transferring money from her charity to AAUN projects or to pay for her traveling expenses. On May 20, 1955, for example, she made a $1,000 "transfer" from her charity fund at New York Trust to pay for a booklet that a "Mrs. Jean Picker" was writing with Eleanor, called "The United Nations: What You Should Know About It." The collaboration with Picker, a journalist and eventual American delegate to the UN, evolved into a warm friendship. Two months later, in July 1955, Eleanor wrote to Eichelberger that she "transferred to you today the sum of $4,000.00 from the New York

Trust Co. This will cover my expenses as well as, I hope, leave a small contribution for the Association."

Roosevelt knew how to convey the role of the UN and the AAUN to a wide audience. She was certain of what members and potential members needed to hear for them to fully engage with the organization's message—that the world could be improved through the UN and that the AAUN in New York and its national grassroots base provided the support for that goal. The archives include hundreds of letters to and from AAUN supporters—from corporate chiefs like Thomas J. Hargrave of Eastman Kodak, Robert Benjamin of United Artists, and Thomas Watson of IBM, to union bigwigs (George Meany and Walter Reuther), to the unlikeliest politicians (Governor Orval Faubus in Arkansas, who defied the Supreme Court decision to desegregate the state's public schools), to private citizens writing to her on their engraved stationery. Through her correspondence, Eleanor Roosevelt reinforced the value of the UN and AAUN.

Over the years, she also counted on many friends in the right places to help support the AAUN through speaking engagements or other favors. In addition to her labor pals, she called on Dr. Charles Mayo, of the clinic fame; Henry Cabot Lodge Jr., US ambassador to the UN; Edward R. Murrow; Nelson Rockefeller and John D. Rockefeller; George Whitney of JP Morgan; Palmer Hoyt of the *Denver Post*; Edith Wilson, widow of President Woodrow Wilson; and Arnold Constable, of the Constable & Company department store chain, among others. For example, she persuaded Dr. Mayo, who was the national president of the organization from 1953 to 1957, to speak at a UN rally at the Shrine Auditorium in Los Angeles in 1954. But a telegram to Henry Cabot Lodge Jr., asking him to speak at the same rally, was turned down. Similarly, Dag Hammarskjöld, the UN Secretary-General, refused to speak, based on his principle of not showing favoritism toward nongovernmental organizations.

She also did not blanch at asking for money to keep AAUN solvent; it was money, she emphasized, that went toward its programs, such as education, or to help defray costs of special events. A typical letter soliciting donations reinforced how AAUN helped to plan and promote UN commemorations, such as the annual UN Week. Writing in 1956 to the philanthropist George F. Baker Jr., for example, she invited him to participate in that year's program, which "is used for special efforts to educate and orient adults and youth alike in the functions of the United Nations." Similar solicitations were sent to other foundations, executives, and financiers, including John Cowles of the *Star and Tribune* in

Minneapolis; J. Russell Parsons at Chubb and Son; Dore Schary of MGM Studios; Mr. and Mrs. William Vanderbilt III; and Marshall Field III of the *Chicago Sun-Times*.

Contributions could be minuscule but symbolic. A gift of $25 from Igor Sikorsky of Sikorsky Aircraft in Bridgeport, Connecticut, on April 9, 1954, contained this aperçu from him: "My relatively modest personal means are heavily taxed by numerous requests for personal help which I am constantly receiving, many from numerous former compatriots who fled the terrors of communism and the revolution and who find themselves spread virtually all over the world. In view of this, I am able to forward you only a token donation, together with best wishes for continued success."

Though donations may have never deluged AAUN, Roosevelt's presence inspired a wide scope of sources to send checks, including the J. Seward Johnson Sr. Charitable Trust and the H. J. Heinz Company Foundation. A large sum came from Marshall Field III, who sent $300,000 to AAUN on October 10, 1955. In May 1962, a donation of $25 from Ilse Oppenheimer, six months before Eleanor Roosevelt died, was sent to contribute to "the vitally important work of the AAUN."

Paradoxically, Nikita Khrushchev's controversial behavior at the UN incited many Roosevelt fans and cronies to write checks to the AAUN. Edna Ferber contributed in 1961, saying, "I'm sure that the combined contributions of all the writers in the United States could not compensate for Khrushchev's financial withdrawal from the United Nations."

But not everyone felt eager to donate to the AAUN, despite Roosevelt's prestige. In 1955, *The New York Times* said no to a request from Roosevelt. Amory H. Bradford, the paper's secretary, explained: "I regret that I have to report to you that we have reached a negative decision. . . . Our decision in this, as in many similar cases, has to be that we should not make a financial contribution in an area where we can, we believe, make our most effective contribution in the pages of The Times itself."

Roosevelt also managed internal AAUN tiffs, such as addressing tensions running through chapters in Southern California in the 1950s. She tackled tough assignments, such as responding to ambivalent, if not hostile, attitudes toward the UN by some members of the US Congress—mainly, Senator John Bricker's (R-Ohio) attack on the integrity of the UN, which collectively became several proposed constitutional amendments, all bearing his name. Throughout the 1950s, Bricker sought to limit US ratification of international treaties and participation in international organizations. (See Chapter 4 for more information.)

In a letter from Clark Eichelberger to Roosevelt, dated April 21, 1955, he related his own recent experience on speaking to the US Senate regarding the continual proposal of Bricker amendments:

> The Senators yesterday were all friendly. In the morning Senator Alexander Smith [R–New Jersey], taking issue with Senator Bricker, said his experience at the United Nations was the Assembly could resolve, but that there was no coercion of the United States. He asked Mr. Gross if it were not true that conventions of the United Nations Specialized Agencies had to be ratified by the United States Senate.

He went on:

> Senator [Alexander] Wiley [R-Wisconsin] questioned me. Again, all friendly questions to elicit favorable answers. He asked me where the world would be if it were not for the United Nations, and I said probably in a third world war or in a state of disintegration. He asked me what were the major achievements of the United Nations to date, etc. The purposes of the people who spoke yesterday from the negative side led by Senator Bricker were to plead for a restricted United Nations. They would turn the clock back and make the United Nations a league of states. Several speakers emphasized (and this seems to be the new party line) that the Charter is not a "constitution" but rather a treaty and therefore is not subject to liberal interpretation and growth as would be a constitution.

It appeared from this letter that Roosevelt was going to speak to Congress, too, as Eichelberger wrote to her:

> I do not think you would want to put yourself in a position of answering Senator Bricker's specific points as such, although you might want to be prepared to answer his suggestions for Charter amendments. They are all silly; particularly the one that would strike "We, the Peoples" from the United Nations Charter for fear that this means a United Nations citizenship.

In this context, he wrote that Roosevelt "would have a good occasion to conduct a seminar on human rights." (It is unclear whether Roosevelt actually testified.)

Mostly, Roosevelt participated actively in AAUN plans for commemorative programs to raise public knowledge of the UN. The AAUN was often a large presence, if not the main one, behind these programs, hiring public relations people for the UN's tenth anniversary, for example, and suggesting other modes of promotion, some of which the UN accepted and others that seemed to fall by the wayside. This promotional role became an avid focus of AAUN's work in the 1950s. The UN relied on the AAUN for its advice and administrative help, as the world body hardly excelled at getting its name out properly, stymied by bureaucracy, an international staff, and a sense of modesty that it wanted to maintain.

The plan at the AAUN was to both promote the UN and to recruit members into its own ranks by using George Randall, a publicist based in Los Angeles who was a local chapter member and former public relations director for the Richfield Oil Corporation. Randall, however, quickly revealed himself as unreliable, according to the Eichelberger archives,[6] bartering for favors through the Roosevelt name. He went so far as to send out an announcement, unbeknown to the family, of a new advertising and public relations company, called Randall & Roosevelt, being formed by him and Elliott Roosevelt, one of Eleanor's four sons. "Accounts to be handled include AAUN, New York," the announcement read. Soon Randall was ousted (officially, he resigned) when Eleanor Roosevelt got word of his shenanigans. In a classic Roosevelt lashing out—she could cut people off with a fast swipe of the pen, signing her name at the end of blunt letters—she wrote to him in a draft letter, then scratched it out: "Almost from the beginning we found you very difficult to work with. In the first place you wanted the Association to forego [sic] its entire program and do nothing but to carry out your suggestions for the stunts for Decennial Day."

Eleanor Roosevelt, AAUN chair of the Board of Governors, speaking at the AAUN Washington conference luncheon, Feb. 28, 1955. (Photo courtesy of the Clark M. Eichelberger papers, Manuscripts and Archives Division, The New York Public Library. Astor, Lenox, and Tilden Foundations.)

In the same draft, she accused Randall of having a "persecution complex" and had "one more point": you were not "dismissed as you imply . . . you have seen fit to resign." The letters to Randall go back and forth over months, revealing Roosevelt's ability to pinpoint a problem with specificity. Decennial Day went on without Randall.

The other work that kept Roosevelt frantically busy was responding to invitations from AAUN members and others interested in the UN. Baillargeon, Roosevelt's personal secretary, said in an interview for this book that a large pile of requests for visits always sat on Roosevelt's desk. Roosevelt answered the correspondence herself in a personable, but always professional, manner. She also never overlooked people close by—for example, thanking the AAUN staff for remembering, every year, her birthday on October 11. As one card in 1955 attests, she signed it in her formal fashion, "Very cordially yours, Eleanor Roosevelt."

Her letters and cards expressed a tireless tone. In Arkansas in January 1955, she thanked Governor Orval Faubus for meeting her in Little Rock when she came through town: "I was delighted with the response to the United Nations meetings which was evident that day, and I am extremely anxious that the support of the United Nations in your area will continue to grow. I hope that the American Association for the United Nations in Arkansas continues to enjoy your support of its program."

Roosevelt was inclined to accept most of the invitations and speaking engagements across the United States, which invariably involved socializing; she often spent the night as a guest in someone's home when she came to town. Baillargeon described in detail the itineraries of Roosevelt and Eichelberger on their trips, as the two or three of them (sometimes with Linzer joining them as a fourth) dropped into small and big American cities with military precision. Roosevelt also traveled to capitals of Europe and Asia for other engagements as a former first lady and as a US delegate to the UN.

For nearly a decade, she kept a dizzying schedule, including stops and overnights to such places as Portland, Oregon; Wilkes-Barre, Pennsylvania; Akron, Ohio; Lincoln and Omaha, Nebraska; Madison, Wisconsin; Los Angeles; Miami; Atlanta; Baltimore; Helena, Montana; New Orleans; Chicago; Anderson, Indiana; Detroit; Reno; Durham, New Hampshire; East Lansing and Kalamazoo, Michigan; Syracuse; Austin; Santa Barbara, California; Huron, South Dakota; Pittsburgh; and Brooklyn, New York.

She stayed on topic—that is, the UN—with the same focus she displayed as a girl refining her personal goals—the more difficult, the better. When she experienced misgivings about the UN, she discussed them, expressing over and over that war was not a choice that any nation or individual should encourage, let alone force.

Linzer described Roosevelt as never asking for or expecting special attention.

> Planes, trains and cars were equal to her if they got her there. All except that four-seater private plane belonging to the President of a large company in Michigan. When Mrs. Roosevelt and I were escorted on to it, she looked at me with a small smile playing about her lips and said: "I've never liked these things since I flew in one over the Rockies with my son." But gamely we flew from Detroit to Kalamazoo in the bright sunshine, in that four-seater plane. And Mrs. Roosevelt made one of the best speeches on the United Nations she had ever made, that evening. We had to fly back to Detroit on the same four-seater that night, too!

On a separate trip to Miami, Roosevelt was to appear on TV and to meet with the board of the AAUN chapter. As the plane landed, she noticed all the TV cameras nearby and a red carpet rolled out to the plane's entrance. Linzer wrote, "She turned to me and said: 'Estelle, there must be a celebrity on this plane. Look at all the fuss they're making!'"

Roosevelt's visits to AAUN chapters were usually fruitful. From the San Diego chapter, which she visited in 1954, a letter thanking her for her April 3 stop "not only enticed new membership (already about 25 percent) but converted a number of 'antis.' The inspiration you brought will long be with us and help us do a better job."

Her excitement at attracting large interest in AAUN could be palpable, as if she were counting votes. (She often tracked her numbers of new members.) In a telegram she sent to Eichelberger in February 1953 from Fayetteville, Arkansas, she wrote that in Los Angeles, "they have interested 5 major oil companies and the Bank of America who are asking their publicity directors to become members of the AAUN." Although who "they" refers to is unclear, it is most likely an AAUN chapter in Southern California. The telegram continues: "They want to start a tremendous membership drive and they feel it will be successful if we can have Dr. Mayo or Ambassador Lodge, Senator Cooper or Margaret Chase Smith there. They will make it the biggest meeting ever held and they hope to get 6 thousand members that night. You can reach me at Hotel Di Lido in Miami."

Her bipartisan approach to reaching out rarely failed. It was as if she lay awake at night—either at her home on the Upper East Side, say, or at her cottage in Val-Kill in Hyde Park, New York—compulsively calculating whether her campaigning had covered every base. Sometimes, her letters asking for support revealed an obsessive quality. She leaned on George Meany on February 6, 1953, confiding that she was "extremely anxious that the labor groups become more familiar with the work of the United Nations and I would be very glad if our chapters [of AAUN] made contact with your representatives in different areas and if you would be kind enough to send word on the way down the line that they may cooperate with us." Her objective, she added, was

> to get more truthful information about the United Nations into the hands of the people and to get what help we can from the people's organizations. For instance, it seems to me that in almost every state some labor people might like to become experts on the International Labor Organization, to be listed with our chapters as possible speakers to other groups and to hold themselves, occasional meetings in their own organizations where matters of interest to them pertaining to world affairs and the United Nations could be discussed.

Meany's response, still as president of the AFL, in a letter dated February 25, 1953, said he agreed that it was important for the US people to

> become more and more familiar with the work which the United Nations is doing. I also agree with you that it would be well, in order to assist in this additional work, to bring about a liaison of some type between the local chapters of the American Association for the United Nations and various local affiliates of the American Federation of Labor.

Yet, she did not admire everyone in high circles. Writing to H. L. Hunt Jr., the oil magnate in Dallas, on March 9, 1953, Roosevelt declined to do a six-minute recording on his "Facts Forum" conservative radio program, regarding what she considered might be a biased discussion against UNESCO and the US backing of it. She explained her decision:

> I do not feel that [this] would be adequate presentation. Also, I have carefully been over much of your material. I consider that it is slanted material. While you present the side for the United Nations fairly, you invariably present the opposite side in such a manner as to make it carry greater weight with uninformed persons. So that I do not feel inclined to accept your invitation.

Indeed, her relationships with labor leaders were far more aligned with the Democrat-leaning membership makeup of AAUN. To William Dunn of the Communications Workers of America, she wrote on March

12, 1954, that the Congress of Industrial Organizations (CIO) would help "us promote memberships in our forthcoming membership drive." She emphasized that the AAUN "must become a mass membership organization" and that it was seeking both individual and organizational memberships. "I hope that your unions will promote both kinds," she continued, noting that individual memberships ranged from $3 to $5 to $10 or more and included a monthly publication from the AAUN, "which will help him keep up to date on the activities of the United Nations and our Government's role in it." The publication also contained a newsletter that she wrote herself. "I believe that this publication will serve two purposes," she said. "It will keep the member informed; it will help him become a part of informed public opinion."

The AAUN encouraged all types of organizations to join its ranks. A group with a membership of up to a hundred people cost $25, with the scale increasing at an additional $25 for each hundred additional members or fraction thereof. The benefits for organizational memberships were program kits of "material and suggestions to help inform the group about the UN." Roosevelt noted, "Of course we cannot supply material to individuals in such a group." She strategized in one letter: the AAUN was announcing the opening of its membership drive in San Francisco, and, she wondered, "If I could announce then a number of organizations had enrolled some thousands of members through their organization memberships, it would have an important psychological effect."

The AAUN staff members were so respectful of her privacy and feelings that when her dog died, they kept the news from her while she traveled in Asia. A note to Eichelberger from a staff member shows how painful this death might be for Roosevelt, noting,

> Estelle [Linzer] just telephoned that Mrs. Roosevelt's Scotty Tamas [a grandson of Fala, the family's Scotty during their life in the White House] died. I thought it would be best if she is not told until she is back at the hotel as she will be very upset. If [the word "if" underlined three times] we can get her back without speaking to reporters as Estelle says the press know already.

Roosevelt attracted immediate attention wherever she set foot, even when she hid her face under a broad-rimmed hat or cloaked herself under a heavy wool coat dangling with her trademark raccoon-fur stole. In January 1955, she described to the *New York World-Telegram* the pleasures of her AAUN stumping, saying, "It is stimulating to be out in the country where one gets a feeling of how the general public is thinking." One woman, she noted in the interview, "had been told that the

American Association for the United Nations was subversive and the only thing you could do was ask people to study the groups a little more. In this way they would soon find out that neither the UN nor the AAUN were in any way subversive."

Anti-UN agitation was not uncommon, even though the majority of Americans supported the world body in its abstract form. Its universalism unnerved the critics: Could it dictate American laws? Seize property? Bar the government from doing what it wanted? Roosevelt had plenty to do to counter the skepticism. One such instance was brewing in the AAUN chapter in Beverly Hills, California, which wrote to Roosevelt, bemoaning the drift in Southern California in the anti-UN direction. The slogan of the opposition, the letter writer said, was "Out of the UN in '55!," an alarming prospect, no doubt, for the AAUN chapter. The letter writer added that the chapters in the region were also "adrift" from the national base and acting on their own, with poor finances.

Such discontent from AAUN chapters was expected in a grassroots organization that had its headquarters in New York, far from many members and seemingly aloof to the interests of small towns or cities. Collecting funds and disbursing them from local chapters to regional bases and on to New York became a constant friction throughout the AAUN's existence.

Eichelberger conferred regularly with Roosevelt, an acknowledgment of her star power and experience. He relied on her to connect with members, whereas he might have been too much of an egghead to make that social, if not political, leap. Throughout the 1950s, the AAUN repeatedly evaluated its mission, as it did in future decades. As Americans displayed more disenchantment with the UN for various reasons, Eichelberger and the AAUN tried to address these problems.

In one internal paper, Eichelberger listed the UNA's three-point plan: to make the UN Charter and the activities known and understood by Americans; to advocate and support those policies "by our Government which will make United States membership effective in the United Nations"; and "to study the means by which the United Nations can be strengthened to meet the needs of an ever-changing world." That ever-evolving world proved to be the biggest challenge for the UN and, indirectly, for the AAUN, as sentiments declined from favorably to less so toward the world body. Eichelberger's occasional hurrahs became necessary measures for AAUN's evolution and prosperity. Although the AAUN took stances on controversial matters on many occasions, sometimes its politics or policy proposals, or even its promotional campaigns, could seem inappropriate in the more straitlaced UN.

Even as optimism for the UN stayed intact throughout the 1950s, Americans' romance for it waned considerably during the anticommunist fervor that hit the United States throughout the decade; it continued, albeit to a lesser extent, into the early 1960s and the 1970s, as the Cold War froze out many backers. All the shifts in public opinion had begun to chip away at the UN during Roosevelt's time with the AAUN.

The decrease in popularity toward the UN did not diminish Roosevelt's fervor as she kept up her work promoting the AAUN. In 1961, for example, she was still meeting with top UN officials, including Dr. Ralph Bunche, the American diplomat who worked in the UN Secretariat at the time, to "discuss the problems of the United States and the United States Delegation to the United Nations in the next session"— presumably, in the General Assembly.

Meanwhile, the AAUN raised money at every chance. Its annual gala in the 1950s became a tradition that has lasted ever since, in one form or another. In the 1950s, it consisted of a luncheon or dinner at the Waldorf-Astoria (where it held galas until 2008). In 1956, Mary Lasker of the Albert and Mary Lasker Foundation presented a check of $10,000 to Roosevelt at the party as chair of the AAUN Board of Governors. Lasker said that the money was to be used to "develop the college chapters of the AAUN."

Roosevelt was involved in organizing the galas; perhaps the largest one at the time revolved around her seventieth birthday. The celebration dinner was held at the Grand Ballroom of the Roosevelt Hotel, with reservations at $15 a person. Tributes were solicited, as were contributions to the Eleanor Roosevelt 70th Birthday Fund, to finance her work with the AAUN.

Roosevelt was also a member of the AAUN's board, a position she used to lure important people into the AAUN orbit. In 1956, she approached Palmer Hoyt of the *Denver Post* to become president of the board, though without success. She had even invited him to her home at 211 E. 62nd Street, for a "very informal" dinner to discuss the possibility. Nelson Rockefeller also cited his busy schedule to turn down the offer that year. The name of Joseph Pulitzer Jr. of the St. Louis publishing family, came up, though reservations about him put the nix on him quickly. In a letter to a Mrs. George Gellhorn, of St. Louis in 1956, Roosevelt wrote, "This is a very confidential letter. . . . In the event that [Nelson Rockefeller] cannot" accept the presidency, "the Association would like to approach Mr. Joseph Pulitzer." But one board member, she wrote, believed that Pulitzer "at times drinks too much. Now I have absolutely no way of knowing anything about this, but I wonder if on a

Eleanor Roosevelt (left) with Frances Humphrey Howard in Huron, South Dakota, in 1954. Howard, the sister of future US vice president Hubert Humphrey, was the first executive secretary and publicity director of the United Nations Association of South Dakota. She also served as Roosevelt's special assistant in the Office of Civilian Defense during World War II. (Photo courtesy of the family of Frances Humphrey Howard.)

personal and very confidential basis you would tell me whether there is any truth in this. We would like to invite him but not if this is something that effects [sic] his character."

The organization was also looking perennially for like-minded groups to help build its base. Talk began in 1955 of merging the AAUN with the US Committee for the UN, the semiofficial government group led by a personal appointee of the US president. It was made up of national organizations, including the AAUN, to "disseminate facts about the United Nations and to promote the observance of UN Day in the United States." The committee, however, did not take stands on US or UN policy, unlike the AAUN, which is why the merger did not happen for nine years (see Chapter 4).

Roosevelt kept up her syndicated column, "My Day," which ran in such papers as the *New York Post* and the *Baltimore Sun*. The columns were mercifully short, like a blog post today, often concentrating on politics and AAUN chapter news. From Brussels on September 10, 1958, she wrote that delegations in the capital arriving for the meetings of the World Federation of United Nations Associations "were invited the other night to visit the German pavilion at the World's Fair." Every-

one, she noted, "enjoyed sitting around in the cool evening air and looking at the lighted buildings."

On September 22, 1958, in a column from Moscow, she talked
about the AAUN and its Russian counterpart on the subject of money:

> The other afternoon our delegation from the American Association for
> the United Nations met with the Soviet Association for the UN, and it
> was a lively two-hour session. . . . We were questioned at length about
> publications and the source of our income. The Soviets seemed much
> interested in our budget, how our money is spent, and where it comes
> from in the first place. At a later session we shall have the opportunity
> to put the same questions of organization to them. Not a single contro-
> versial question was raised at this first meeting.

Roosevelt was chair of the AAUN Board of Directors for many
terms (she was also chair of the Board of Governors at one point).
Later, when she chaired the AAUN committee on chapters, her responsibilities ranged from looking after the national field staff to handling
the regional field directors. In a 1962 field report to the board, she said,
"[The] over-all field picture is a growing, expanding one, with constantly untapped local interest and leadership coming to the fore
through national and regional field directors' trips to open up new territories. However, loss may be reported in a few areas: chapters are no
longer active in Eugene, Oregon; Vancouver, Washington; Missoula,
Montana, South Nassau [Long Island], N.Y."

She summarized the persistent problems of the AAUN:

> One could be the absence of strong leadership; another might be the lack
> of enough leadership so that one person's defection to other geographi-
> cal areas means chapter drop-out. It is our experience that when a chap-
> ter fails, it is best to let the area "cool off" for a while and begin anew
> with entirely fresh personnel and this is the pattern which we follow.

In that period of the early 1960s, she added,

> The need for some type of action by individuals and groups has
> become compelling and the AAUN is reflecting this need through the
> steady growth of chapters in various parts of the country. No longer do
> people just want to discuss; now they want to "do something about it."
> Talking and acting on issues before us in the United Nations has
> become a major activity in this country. . . . It would seem that a major
> job for AAUN chapters today and in the future would be to extend the
> hand of help by focusing the attention of these individuals toward the
> constructive work of the United Nations.

AAUN chapters, moreover, are "becoming more and more the center for UN activity programs and action in their areas; the national office of the Association must encourage this at all times."

As of December 30, 1960, membership remained steady—reportedly, at 42,493—operating with an annual budget of $340,000. "So if divided by 42,000 members," Eichelberger wrote to Roosevelt, the "cost of each is about $8, but that does not include the service of providing AAUN News and postage." He noted the hard time collecting membership dues on time, adding, like an irritated accountant, that the "national office is not a superstate that can penalize chapters for not sending their membership amounts." The draft budget for 1962 put expenses for the combined operations of AAUN, CSOP, and Collegiate Council for the UN (CCUN) and speaker services at $450,000 and possible income at $430,000.

Roosevelt's health faltered by the early 1960s; she couldn't have been more prophetic when she said in December 1960, "These crowded hours have been interesting and stimulating. They have, I hope, been useful. They have, at least, been lived to the hilt." The hilt arrived on November 7, 1962, when she died of bone-marrow tuberculosis in her home on the Upper East Side at age seventy-eight.

Linzer, in a memo two days later to the AAUN accounting office, detailed the obituary announcements the office sent to the *New York Times*: "One notice from the Officers and Board of Directors and one from the staff in tribute and memory for Mrs. Roosevelt were placed in the New York TIMES November 8, 9 and 10. Authorization for this came from Mr. Eichelberger, Wednesday evening, November 7th, when Mrs. Roosevelt died."

Adlai Stevenson, a close friend and US ambassador to the UN, wrote a long eulogy for a memorial service held at Hyde Park: "Darkness had no place in the life of Eleanor Roosevelt; and it has even less place in her remembrance. For hers was a radiance that warmed the cold, beckoned to the lost, and kindled hope where none had ever flamed."

When she died, a score of eulogies was delivered to the UN General Assembly from every corner of the globe—the first and only time a private citizen was so honored. Stevenson said, "I recalled that she gave her faith not only to those who shared the privilege of knowing her and of working by her side, but to countless men, women and children in every part of the world who loved her even as she loved them."

"There were no doubts," he said, in her life.

Notes

1. Mary Ann Glendon, *A World Made New: Eleanor Roosevelt and the Universal Declaration of Human Rights* (New York: Random House, 2001), 21–22; originally published by Eleanor Roosevelt, *On My Own* (New York: Harper, 1958), 39.

2. Glendon, *A World Made New*, 21–22.

3. The Clark M. Eichelberger Papers, Manuscripts and Archives Division, New York Public Library. Astor, Lenox, and Tilden Foundations (NYPL Archives), box 133.

4. Glendon, *A World Made New,* 170.

5. NYPL Archives, box 132.

6. Ibid., box 133.

6

Citizen Advocacy:
The UNA-USA and the
US Government Since the 1970s

The personal relationships between the AAUN and US government officials—up to and including President Roosevelt—throughout the 1930s and 1940s were never replicated after FDR's death. Eichelberger and others had cordial relationships with presidents, State Department officials, and on Capitol Hill during the post-FDR years, but nothing approached the closeness of wartime. What AAUN/UNA succeeded in doing throughout the decades of Democratic and Republican administrations and congressional terms was forging dedicated relationships with luminaries who were committed to helping the association. From Sumner Welles and Henry Wallace in the 1940s and 1950s to Elliot Richardson and John C. Whitehead in the 1980s and 1990s and up to Thomas Pickering and William Luers in the twenty-first century, the association counted on goodwill from many knowledgeable practitioners of Washington politics.

Beyond the personal and professional relationships, the main vehicle for reaching out to the Washington (and New York) establishment was a series of high-profile conferences. The AAUN used these settings to draw together civil society and political leaders to advance the UN agenda. The first conference, held on December 14, 1945, was titled "Looking to the United Nations Assembly." This lead-up to the first General Assembly featured Eichelberger; John Foster Dulles, speaking on the General Assembly; Thomas Watson of IBM, speaking on "Economic and Social Progress"; the future Nobel Peace Prize winner Ralph Bunche, speaking on trusteeship; and James T. Shotwell, on disarmament.[1]

During the 1950s and 1960s, the AAUN also sent bipartisan questionnaires to congressional candidates to get their views on UN-related issues. For the November 1952 elections, the association created a proposal for a UN plank in each party's platform that said that the UN Charter obligations "should be the heart of our foreign policy" and that

Americans should "dedicate ourselves to strengthening the United Nations through use, evolution, and modification where necessary." Specific proposals included creating UN armed forces, increasing the power of the General Assembly, developing a "strong" UN human rights program, and creating technical assistance for economic development; these themes have resonated for decades in UN debates and continue to be argued today. In one UNA demand, for a "strong human rights program," notable progress has been made, such as creation of the post of UN High Commissioner for Human Rights and an increasingly active and more effective Human Rights Council after the United States decided to join the body, which replaced the much-criticized Human Rights Commission.

Eichelberger addressed the Democratic National Committee's platform committee for the 1960 presidential convention, urging the party to adopt a distinctly non–Cold War policy of cooperation. The United States should help new states develop and should work on "winning the allegiance and support of the new states," he said. "Their allegiance cannot be won if we ask them to choose sides in a world of power politics." Speaking long after the Soviet Sputnik and before the pledge of President Kennedy to place a man on the moon in the 1960s, Eichelberger argued for "cooperative control" over new scientific discoveries: "We believe that the possibility of landing on celestial bodies presents a great world moral problem and we urge the United Nations law be extended to the frontier of outer space." The United States should also pursue general and complete disarmament, make greater use of the International Court of Justice and summit meetings to avoid deadlock, and "move toward a more relaxed state." While the United States should continue bilateral economic agreements, Eichelberger said, "It is to the advantage of the United States to make it possible for the United Nations to meet the challenge. If we give the most through the United Nations, the nations will know it." On human rights, he said the US "refusal to ratify the Genocide Convention and other human rights conventions and to participate in the completion of the human rights covenants has served to delay the advancement of human rights through the United Nations."[2]

By 1950, the AAUN had settled into a pattern of presenting an annual conference in Washington, designed to inform the power establishment on key UN issues, to highlight the work of civil society, and to offer advice on how the US government could strengthen the UN's work. The Conference of National Organizations called by the AAUN drew the support of 85–120 national organizations, including civil and human rights groups, trade unions, women's rights organizations, and faith-based organizations, following the precedent set by the coalition that promoted the creation of the United Nations.

Vice President Richard Nixon, Senator Hubert Humphrey, Dean Rusk (then the president of the Rockefeller Foundation and later US secretary of state), and Harold Stassen were among the Washington figures to address these conferences. (The policy positions taken at these first conferences are discussed further in Chapter 3.)

The eleventh conference, held in March 1961, was unusual, as previous conferences had had more scholarly themes, such as "Great Issues Before the United Nations," "Year of Appraisal and Dedication," and "Conference on United States Responsibility for World Leadership." The theme in 1961, however, was "The United Nations in Crisis." Yet there was little indication which crisis it was referring to: Suez hung in the past, and the full horror of the Congo and of the Cuban missile crises were to come. President Kennedy's message to the conference spoke of the "crisis in the world":

> The United Nations offers our most hopeful channel for finding reasonable and just solutions to them. Never has there been a greater need for the people of this country, and indeed for those of all members of the United Nations, to understand these critical issues. The United Nations must succeed because the alternative is the abandonment of the principle of a world governed by law to a world dominated by force.[3]

By contrast, the themes of the panels were based on the relatively optimistic quotes from Kennedy's inaugural address: "To Strengthen the Shield of the New and the Weak" and "To Preserve the United Nations, to Defend the United Nations, and to Strengthen the United Nations." It was also to be Eleanor Roosevelt's last address to an AAUN meeting, as she had just been named to the US delegation to the UN General Assembly. Working under Ambassador Adlai Stevenson, this was to be her second and final government appointment before her death in 1962.

The 1962 conference again took a JFK speech as its organizing theme, but this time it was more visionary: "UN Decade of Development."[4] Drawn from his September 25, 1961, General Assembly address, the conference program said that the AAUN's 1970 annual conference "will total the score to see what progress has been made" after a decade and then "a grand conference will determine how successful the world has been in achieving the goals" of the decade. These themes reverberated in the UN and UNA-USA into the twenty-first century, with discussions on a new international development agenda, known as the Millennium Development Goals (which was succeeded by the Sustainable Development Goals in 2015).

UNA established a full-time office in Washington in 1972, with Roger Cochetti as director. Its primary responsibilities were to liaise with the State Department, educate Congress about the UN, and keep UNA membership apprised of UN-related issues on the congressional agenda. The office's *Washington Weekly Report,* which debuted in 1973, became the main vehicle for reaching the Washington and New York policy communities and the national membership, focusing on such issues as countries' annual dues, peacekeeping, international law, and the efforts to constrain UN actions.

Although the *Weekly Report,* which lasted until 1998, when it was replaced by the online *Washington Report* until 2010, may have covered the key substantive issues of the day, UN finances always took a prominent position. Throughout the 1970s and 1980s, "Assessed Contributions" and "Voluntary Contributions" inevitably led the topics in each issue. Other issues of concern included the Genocide Convention, peacekeeping, refugee assistance, the Law of the Sea treaty, the Zionism resolution and the push for its repeal, and the Middle East. After the end of the Cold War and the shift from Ronald Reagan to George H. W. Bush to Bill Clinton, financial issues gave way to Iraq; peacekeeping missions in Africa and Cambodia; repeal of the Zionism resolution; social issues, especially relating to women's health (the UN Population Fund, or UNFPA, and the "Mexico City" policy, concerning contraception and abortion); and the megaconferences of the 1990s (the UN Conference on Environment and Development and the Beijing Fourth World Conference on Women, addressed by First Lady Hillary Clinton). Yet financial issues were not settled.[5]

Steven A. Dimoff worked in the Washington office from 1979 until the merger with the UN Foundation in 2010, making him one of the longest-serving UNA officials. After graduating with a master's degree in international affairs from the Johns Hopkins School of Advanced International Studies in 1977, Dimoff started his career working on the staffs of several members of Congress, including Charles J. Carney, a Democratic representative from Ohio, Dimoff's home state. Before coming to Washington, Dimoff had been exposed to the UNA in high school and was aware of some of the issues unfolding in the UN. While Dimoff was on Carney's staff, the UN General Assembly passed the momentous resolution equating Zionism with racism, turning the UN position into what a large number of supporters considered an anti-Israel stance. "There was this constant bickering back and forth about whether the United States should stop all funding to the UN or withdraw from the UN as a result of the General Assembly vote on Zionism and racism," Dimoff said in an interview for this book. "A little bit of work that I did was on the Zionism/racism [resolution] and trying to convince the congressman not to go off the deep end on this."

Answering an advertisement for a job opening, Dimoff was hired by the UNA in 1979 as the assistant director for Congressional Relations and Research. The Zionism resolution followed him from Capitol Hill to the UNA. Although the UNA vigorously opposed the resolution, the association was a victim of the anti-UN fever generated by the resolution; so Dimoff spent his time trying to convince congressional members not to view the UN through this one lens (see Chapter 7). "There were a lot of changes in the [UNA] staff within a short period," he recalled. By 1983, he was director of the office. Sometimes, the staff consisted of just two people. Over the years, Dimoff earned other positions: executive director, vice president of the Washington office, and vice president of policy and advocacy.

To Fund or Not to Fund the UN

Despite all the UN-related issues before Congress, Dimoff found that his main responsibility was keeping track of congressional actions affecting US funding of the UN. Even when the US position was in ascendency at the UN in the 1950s, there were often congressional initiatives to cut off UN financing over some controversy. It was not until the 1970s, however, that this strategy became embedded in the national debate. "Almost from the moment I joined," Dimoff said, "I was surprised at the constant arguing over the US financial commitment to the UN." This strategy was not limited to the United States. During its time in relative isolation, the Soviet Union also threatened to withhold funding from the UN, especially during the Korean War and matters involving China. The Soviet Union did withhold funds, leading to the cancellation of the 1964 General Assembly. In the US budget debate, withholding funds from the UN threatened serious problems for the UN budget, even though the money allotted for foreign policy matters was minuscule. The constant tug over financing the UN reflected political scorekeeping between the two parties in Congress and the White House.

As a result, these issues took up "a good chunk" of staff time, at a time when the office consisted of three to four people. "We worked closely with the State Department and other NGOs back in those days," Dimoff said. "The *Washington Weekly Report* was really written to keep everyone apprised. In those days, it was . . . talking on the phone, one person after another." He added that "if we had had the Internet," the job would have been easier. Instead, "it was a great coordination by telephone."

In making the case for the United States to pay up, UNA first started the argument by simply reminding officials that the assessed contributions were a legal responsibility under the UN Charter; if the government was unhappy with the allocation, the UN's Committee on Contributions was the venue for reassessing contributions. Second, Dimoff said they stressed "the importance of the work of the UN to the goals of US foreign policy. . . . There was always an issue, usually more than one, that really spoke to the kind of role the UN could play in helping the US advance its own foreign policy objectives." This argument echoed Eichelberger's vision: "We believe that the United Nations is the very foundation of American foreign policy, and that there are many ways in which it can be used."

According to Dimoff, "the issue of the financial support for the organization was one that intruded upon just about everything all the time. Sometimes, the Congress was balking at paying the dues. Sometimes it was the administration didn't want to put in the effort." US contributions to the UN operating budget were part of the State Department's budget; "it was on the lowest rung of interest of everyone [in State] because they also had to worry about salaries and pensions of State Department employees, embassy construction, and bilateral relationships with other countries."

According to Article 19 of the UN Charter, a member state loses its voting rights in the General Assembly if the country falls two years behind in its assessed contribution (the Security Council's vote is not affected). "We almost lost our vote in the General Assembly at one point," Dimoff said. "The United States would always pay just enough to avoid it. So, there was never any real consequence, and Congress never saw any consequence." But for the UNA, the payments were "a bread-and-butter issue; all members of the association in leadership felt it was very important that the United States meet the obligations—and that it meet them in full, on time, and without conditions. . . . If there's one issue, one position that UNA took over those years, and I'm sure still continues to take, it is that."

The election of Ronald Reagan introduced a new dimension into the equation. Reagan's director of the Office of Management and Budget (OMB), David Stockman, proposed delaying UN payments one year "in order to make some budget savings," which meant that even if the United States paid in full, it would always be one year behind. According to Dimoff, "To this day, that still exists. The multiple attempts to overturn it failed."

The next front in the budget war was launched by Senator Nancy Kassebaum (R-Kansas). In 1983, she proposed an amendment to the State Department's authorization that would unilaterally reduce the US contribution to the UN and specialized agencies, including UNESCO, the Food and Agriculture Organization (FAO), and the World Health Organization (WHO). Later joined, with provisions, by Representative Gerald Solomon (R–New York), the Kassebaum-Solomon amendment was attached to the annual appropriations bill from 1984 to 1989. The amendment also stipulated that future payments would be contingent on the UN's acceptance of contribution-weighted voting on budgetary matters, which could not be legally instituted without amending the UN Charter. "One of UNA's really important accomplishments," Dimoff said, was its ability to work with Kassebaum in trying to modify the restrictions.

> We never got there, but there was enough progress made in New York that we were able to go back to Senator Kassebaum over and over again, and we were able to have progressive modification of the Kassebaum-Solomon amendment. . . . Eventually—it took about six years—it got to the point where the United States was back on track [to] paying most of what it owed, but we were still dealing with the issue of how to pay back what we had owed from the past.

Paying the assessed contributions for peacekeeping was a particular annoyance for other member states. As a permanent member of the Security Council, no peacekeeping mission can be approved without the support of the United States, and Washington vigorously backed some of the missions in the 1990s. Yet Washington still balked at paying its assessed share. During that decade, "when peacekeeping was in the ascendency," UNA tried to shift the peacekeeping budget from State to the Defense Department (DoD), Dimoff said. The policy was that "peacekeeping was no longer what it had been traditionally thought to be—kind of a thin blue line between warring parties"; it had become more traditional military operations. According to Dimoff,

> Can you really do it [peacekeeping] in the context of the State Department? The State Department could work with DoD in terms of coordinating policy with regard to UN peacekeeping, but in terms of the kinds of efforts needed, wouldn't it make more sense to have peacekeeping in the Department of Defense? Quite honestly, the DoD had far more funding to be able to provide for this kind of thing, and DoD was becoming increasingly involved anyway.

Although both departments were willing to consider the idea, "the main opposition came from Capitol Hill, because . . . the main issue was changing committee jurisdiction. When you're a congressman who has control over a UN peacekeeping budget that's over a billion dollars a year, you're not going to be giving it up . . . all that easily to someone else," said Dimoff. (The chairs of the Foreign Relations Committee during this period were two Republicans, Charles Percy and Richard Lugar, from 1981 to 1987; Claiborne Pell, Democrat, from 1987 to 1995; Jesse Helms, Republican, from 1995 to 2001; Joseph Biden, Democrat, from 2001 to 2003; and then back to Lugar in 2003.)

According to Dimoff, UNA "conducted a series of programs for congressional staff on a variety of . . . timely subjects about the UN, because there really was not much of a body of knowledge about the UN on Capitol Hill" due to "a large turnover" in Congress. UNA was "trying to . . . establish a base of knowledge that could give you some institutional memory within the Congress, but we spent a lot of time trying to point out what previous Congresses had done on any number of issues related to the US and the UN."

Dimoff said that UNA had a unique asset in making its case on behalf of the UN: Elliot Richardson. For nearly a decade, Richardson, as chair of UNA-USA, would make appointments with members of congress to discuss the importance of the issues before the United Nations. "Of course, everyone was willing to sit down with Elliot Richardson," Dimoff recalled. His name "in Washington was legendary, he was just the type of guy that everybody wanted to see, and he could make very convincing arguments to people at a geopolitical level, that people understood and appreciated."

Richardson holds a special place in US political history for all the positions he held. Dubbed "the former everything,"[6] he held more cabinet-level posts than anyone else in US history. He was also the ambassador to Britain under President Ford and chief negotiator to the UN Convention on the Law of the Sea for President Carter. Most famously— the first line in nearly every obituary of him when he died on December 31, 1999—was his role in defying President Richard Nixon during the Watergate scandal. On Saturday, October 20, 1973, as Nixon's attorney general, Richardson resigned rather than carry out the president's order to fire the special prosecutor investigating Watergate. Richardson's second-in-command also refused. It was not until Nixon reached the third-ranking Justice Department official, Robert Bork, that prosecutor Archibald Cox was fired. What became known as the Saturday Night Massacre was "widely lauded as a special moment of integrity and rectitude that secured him [Richardson] a place in the nation's history."[7]

UNA-USA president Edward
C. Luck, standing, with Elliot
Richardson, UNA-USA Board
of Directors chairman, 1988.
(Photo courtesy of the Arthur
Ross Archives.)

Richardson used his prestige to promote UNA, serving as chairman of the board from 1980 to 1988 and then as cochair (along with Cyrus Vance) of UNA's National Council until his death. Richardson was also ready to serve UNA in small ways, such as speaking to a graduate fellows seminar organized by the UNA chapter in Washington, DC. "It was really a pleasure and honor to work with him through those years on those issues. He took a personal responsibility as chairman of UNA to see that these issues were addressed," Dimoff said.

Richardson was born in Boston in 1920. His first government service was during the Eisenhower administration. He was named US attorney for Massachusetts in 1961 and entered electoral politics in 1964, first as lieutenant governor and then as attorney general of Massachusetts. President Nixon brought him to Washington in 1969 as secretary of health, education, and welfare; he later became secretary of defense and, in 1974, attorney general. After Nixon's resignation, he held three posts under President Gerald Ford. After leaving public office in 1980, he divided his time between a law practice and civil organizations, including UNA.

Ultraconservative Opposition

The cumulative effect of budget tricks, other priorities, and tying a legal obligation to unilateral conditions weighed down the UNA throughout the 1980s. And then there was Jesse Helms.

For more than two decades, regardless of which party held the White House or Congress, US policy toward the UN was often shaped by the anti-UN views of the ultraconservative Senator Helms of North Carolina. When the Republicans ran the Senate, he was either chairman or in the leadership of the Foreign Relations Committee. When the Republicans were out of power, he used his senatorial privileges to try to enforce his will. Holding up UN dues and blocking presidential appointees were his key tactics.

President Reagan named John C. Whitehead, a future chairman of the UNA board, as deputy secretary of state in 1985. Whitehead's official responsibilities focused on Eastern Europe. One of his first assignments, however, was negotiating with Helms. Helms was using his privilege to hold up thirty-eight State Department nominees, including Whitehead. "Helms didn't believe in our ambassadors. He thought our ambassadors were all Communists and that they had been unfaithful to the United States by making compromises with our enemies," Whitehead recalled in an interview for this book. (Whitehead died in February 2015.) "Claiborne Pell was chairman, but Jesse Helms was always the veto on the Foreign Relations Committee and held up—as he had the right to do and as any senator could hold something up—for 'further investigation.'" Whitehead, a former chair of Goldman Sachs, brokered a deal with Helms that ended the logjam and gave Reagan the appointees he wanted.

In his autobiography, *A Life in Leadership,* Whitehead wrote, "Jesse's obstructionism was taken as a fact of life. No one made the effort to understand what he was trying to achieve. As it happened, he enjoyed all the attention that came with causing such a logjam. But more deeply, he wanted respect. And I showed him respect by asking what he wanted."[8] Whitehead was less diplomatic decades later. In his interview for this history, he called Helms "our enemy." He said, "I spent four years as deputy secretary of state and was involved with all the UN activities and dealt with people like Jesse Helms, who were enemies of the United Nations and didn't like diplomats at all." Simply wanting to be in the Foreign Service "made them suspect." He added, "I can't say that I overcame his hatred, but I dealt with it the best I could—not always successfully."

The most-used weapon in Helms's arsenal was the purse. Like Kassebaum, he promoted financial amendments meant to accomplish a political purpose—that is, to weaken the United Nations. In 1979, Helms proposed an amendment to the International Development Cooperation Act that would have made contributions to international technical agencies voluntary. Opponents argued "that the real issue was that the Helms amendment prohibited all UN assessed contributions from the US and that this would injure programs which are directly beneficial to the US."[9] Although the amendment was included in the final bill, it was later repealed, largely through the efforts of Representative Michael Barnes (D-Maryland).

Whitehead also had to deal with hard-liners in the White House, including Chief of Staff Donald Regan and Attorney General Ed Meese, who were also not interested in paying the UN dues. But Whitehead found an unexpected ally—Nancy Reagan, the first lady. Thinking that the president was "more sympathetic to the plight of the UN" than were his advisers, Whitehead met with Mrs. Reagan and told her that the US failure to pay the dues was pushing the UN into bankruptcy. In his autobiography, Whitehead said the first lady was shocked that the situation was so serious and said she would look into it. "Shortly afterward," Whitehead wrote, he was invited to a small luncheon in the White House with Reagan, UN Secretary-General Javier Pérez de Cuéllar, and a few staff members (but not Mrs. Reagan). After the Secretary-General spoke, Reagan "said he hadn't realized the seriousness of the UN's financial problems and, now that he knew, he wanted Pérez de Cuéllar to know that the United States fully supported his program." The next budget had the UN dues intact.[10]

Budget proposals during the Reagan administration incorporated the Kassebaum/Helms conditions, and UN funding suffered accordingly. But by Reagan's last budget (fiscal year 1989), the administration recommended "near full funding" of the UN and specialized agencies, reflecting the wishes of the incoming Bush administration: $205.5 million of the $216.0 million owed for the regular budget and the full $269.0 million for eleven specialized agencies. "In its final budget presentation, the Reagan administration had argued that recent United Nations successes in mediation of regional conflicts and continued implementation of administrative and budgetary reform compelled the United States to 'resume its responsibility to pay its past and present obligations.'"[11]

With the end of the Cold War and the election of George H. W. Bush as president of the United States, the problem eased. Bush, a former ambassador to the UN, was more supportive of the world body. Although he appointed a Helms ally, John Bolton, as undersecretary of state for international organizations, Bush also relied more on the UN, especially after Iraq's annexation of Kuwait. In addition, Whitehead, then a private citizen, accepted the post of chairman of UNA in 1989, allowing him to be freer to make the UN's case in Washington.

During the Clinton administration, the Republicans regained control of the Senate in 1994, giving the Foreign Relations Committee to Helms. So, Helms returned to his strategy of constraining the UN through the budget. In 1997, after the election of Kofi Annan as UN Secretary-General, Helms and Biden, the ranking members of the Foreign Affairs Committee, struck a deal to pay US arrears on the condition that certain reforms were instituted.[12]

"It was really an extremely difficult situation because the Helms-Biden agreement as finally passed had something like thirty-eight conditions, but originally it had about seventy. So, it was just micromanaging the UN to death," Dimoff said. While "the State Department obviously played a key role on how that was handled," Dimoff added,

> It really demonstrated to our board that all hands were required to be on deck. That meant the board would form an Advocacy Committee to review, to help, to collaborate. That was great because you had dedicated board members who really felt this was important. Up until that time, quite honestly, it was pretty much the president and the chairman of the association who decided, and they generally had been very supportive, but the buy-in of the board was really . . . a new important development.

(See Chapter 13 for more information.)

The 1999 Helms-Biden Act (the proper name was the United Nations Reform Act of 1999) linked payments of arrears ($926 million) to reforms, including reducing the US share of the regular budget to 22 percent from 25 percent and its share of the peacekeeping budget to 25 percent from 30 percent. In December 1999, under President Bill Clinton, the United States made the first arrears payment of $100 million. The final payments were made under George W. Bush shortly after the 9/11 terrorist attacks.

Day on the Hill

A major innovation of the Washington office was the Day on the Hill. Started by Whitehead and Dimoff in 1993, the project became an important vehicle for channeling UNA members' concerns to the power brokers in the capital. As Dimoff said,

> It became clear that grassroots' involvement was the only way to get traction on many of these issues. . . . If Congressmen and women did not hear from their constituents, they were that much less likely to listen to what you were saying. So, we were asking our chapters—which

had always been active in their communities—to now invite members
of Congress to their meetings, to ask them to meet with them on a regular basis. We were also asking those folks to come to Washington to
meet with members of Congress.

The program ran every other June. (The first one was actually held in
March, but Dimoff recalled it snowed too much to make traveling easy.)

"UNA folks were highly motivated, I was always appreciative of
their willingness to do these kinds of things," Dimoff explained. "We
would prepare the briefing papers for them. We would try to give them
everything they needed so it would not be a terribly challenging situation for members of Congress and their staffs. . . . Our folks generally
were more thoughtful types; . . . they acquitted themselves well."

Katy Hansen, the UNA Iowa division leader, said in an interview
for this book that Day on the Hill proved to be successful for advocacy
and fulfilling for participants. More recently, UNA-USA instituted
Well-Worn Advocacy awards, recognizing the symbolic wear and tear
on shoes in advocacy visits. This was awarded to chapters for creating
long-term relationships with members of Congress and their staffs. The
East Bay and Sarasota-Manistee chapters have been honored with the
award.

Day on the Hill was linked to the UNA Chapter and Division meeting, with the final day of the conference dedicated to the program. Participants usually met with seventy-five representatives and senators.
"The way we did it was to schedule appointments for folks with their
elected representative," Dimoff said. "When this first started, it was
such a curiosity for members of Congress that they would meet with the
members because they were so surprised anyone would come from such
a distance to talk about this."

Records of UNA in the UNA archives at Seton Hall detail how the
program worked. Each UNA member had a sheet of talking points and
questions to discuss with the congressional member, as well as a space
for recording the replies. Although specific topics for discussion were
agreed on beforehand, "they could also talk about what their chapter
was doing," Dimoff said. "You know, 'We're raising money to help
eliminate mine fields around the world.' So, to my mind, it was a win-
win. Win for national, win for chapters, because they were able to
showcase a little bit of the activity of their chapters to their elected representative. Some members of Congress became members of chapters."

Dimoff gave an example of how personal the political could be in
this program. Bill Miller, who worked in the Kentucky legislature and
was a member of the Kentucky UNA chapter, worked with another

member of the chapter "who happened to have been the high school teacher of a member [of Congress] who was critical of the UN." Dimoff continued:

> You find these things out completely by surprise. They would come out in the conversation and those kinds of little facts that you would learn, then later on you could call on folks individually. "Hey, could you pay a visit or could you make a phone call to the senator's office? There's a vote tomorrow on this." I always found they were quite willing to do it. Nobody said I don't have time.

Dimoff, who was also a member of the Washington, DC, chapter (UNA's largest), said it was really advocacy work. "It was the beginning of a far more active UNA in terms of its membership, and it couldn't have come at a more critical moment with these funding issues, but also with UNESCO."

These two elements—the knowledgeable Washington staff and the informed members—were complemented by support from influential Washington figures related to UNA. Whitehead and Richardson "were just key to whatever success UNA-USA had in this area," Dimoff said. "Without them, we would've been do-gooders, but with them we were do-gooders with gravitas and with authority." Whitehead "came down for that snowy first meeting." They "had the kind of entrée that enabled them to meet with really key members of Congress."

But UNA's high-visibility leadership was viewed as a "kind of an elitist organization, part of the foreign policy establishment, right in there with the Council on Foreign Relations and the Trilateral Commission. So it didn't have a lot of credibility with a good number of people—Democrats and Republicans, by the way," Dimoff said.

Other groups interested in international cooperation, such as Citizens for Global Solutions, had developed similar programs. "It was kind of a coming of age for a lot of organizations, because when we first did it, there weren't that many. . . . By the time we were seven or so years into it, everybody was up there. The day we were up there, it would also be the American Diabetes Association Day; there were so many different groups going around."

The Washington office also originated the UNA Congressional Leadership Award, which was given to Senator Claiborne Pell (D–Rhode Island), who had been a junior foreign service officer at the San Francisco Conference founding the UN. It was also awarded to Representative Jim Leach (R-Iowa), Senator Richard Lugar (R-Indiana), and Senator Chuck Hagel (R-Nebraska and a future defense secretary under President Barack Obama).

Advocacy with elected representatives was not limited to Congress. Some chapters also engaged in such activities at the state and local levels. Priya Desai, for example, led the UNA–Oklahoma City chapter's Jeane Kirkpatrick Society advocacy team, named for the first woman to serve as US ambassador to the UN. Desai's team learned of actions proposed in the Oklahoma legislature against the UN's Agenda 21, a voluntary program adopted by the Rio Conference on Environment and Development during the administration of George H. W. Bush. She mobilized chapter members to contact legislators of the Republican-controlled House and Senate; eventually, the bill was killed in a Senate committee.

In 2005, the UNA San Francisco chapter cosponsored a five-day observance of UN World Environment Day—the first time a US city gained global recognition for exceptional environmental practices. The mayor then, Gavin Newsom, launched a citywide Green Cities Expo, featuring best practices in sustainability from over fifty cities throughout the United States.

In Seattle, when the city government celebrates Human Rights Day, the chapter joins by presenting its annual Human Rights Award, now named after Eleanor Roosevelt. Similarly, in Washington, the UNA chapter has cooperated with the DC Civil Rights Commission to honor leaders on Human Rights Day. The UNA chapter in Westchester County, New York, has partnered with the county board of legislators in saluting outstanding local women who work with the UN, including in 2014 the minority leader of the House Appropriations Committee, Nita Lowey. (More information on UNA chapter work is provided in Chapter 13.)

Over the years, UNA-USA became increasingly visible in Washington. Dimoff said that UNA-USA leaders in New York decided the organization should heighten its presence even more in the capital; it did so through holding events at such fashionable venues as the Kennedy Center. The United Nations Concert and Dinner became an important diplomatic and social event, featuring performers like Ella Fitzgerald and drawing in cabinet secretaries, well-placed congressional members, and Secretary-General Kofi Annan. The events, which ran from 1976 to 1985, regularly raised $500,000 to $600,000 (about $2.5 to $3.0 million in 2014 dollars).

The Advocacy Committee

Although advocacy had been vital to the association's work for decades, a formal UNA Advocacy Committee was not established until December 2000. Starting as a subcommittee of the International Policy Committee (which, in turn, answered to the UNA Board of Directors), it examined key issues and made annual recommendations for priority issues to the Council of Chapters and Divisions, the Council of Organizations, and the National Council in order to develop a comprehensive strategy for the next year. These recommendations became the core of UNA's legislative strategy for the US Congress.

The board of directors authorized the subcommittee in September 2000; the first meeting took place on December 7, 2000, at the UNA Washington office. The first chair of the subcommittee was Edison Dick, a member of the National Board and of the International Policy Committee. In an interview for this book, Dick said "a principal purpose" of the subcommittee "was to collect all such policies for inclusion in the yearly advocacy agenda that was intended as a guide for UNA-USA to inform and influence the UN as well as Congress." The committee solicited the views of the International Policy Committee and local chapters to formulate the agenda, he said. The first and "toughest of all the challenges" was trying to convince Congress to pay its dues and arrears to the UN and to pay for peacekeeping operations. Beyond that, other important issues, according to Dick, were providing advocacy support for the International Criminal Court (of which the United States is not a member), as well as for human rights treaties (the Conventions on the Elimination of All Forms of Discrimination Against Women, the Rights of the Child, and the Prevention and Punishment of the Crime of Genocide), the Convention on the Law of the Sea, the Framework Convention on Climate Change (the Kyoto Protocol), and arms control and nuclear test ban agreements.

Dimoff said, "These issues were becoming . . . quite controversial. There was a whole slew of them. So, the Policy Committee and the Advocacy Committee worked in tandem, very closely. In fact, at one point, the Advocacy Committee was actually a subcommittee of the Policy Committee, but it was felt that they should be freestanding Committees of the Board."

Dimoff explained that the Advocacy Committee helped address a dichotomy that had hampered UNA's work. "There was this tendency in New York to focus on the UN Secretariat building and the diplomatic core, which is important, but the main kind of engine for the development of US foreign policy in relationship to the UN" was shaped in Washington, he said. "Particularly after 1995, a lot of the board members felt we just need to all be involved in this more than we have been. We need to give it more visibility than we had. We have to participate more actively." He added, "Up until that time, quite honestly, it was pretty much the president and the chairman of the association who decided, and they generally had been very supportive, but the buy-in of the board was really, again, a new important development" because now "everyone was moving in the same direction" and the chapters (through their board representatives) felt that "everyone could now participate."

One issue that prevented UNA from establishing such a committee earlier was the persistent challenge of any NGO: how far could an NGO go in trying to influence government policy without risking its nonpartisan, nonprofit legal status? Dimoff said this was a concern that board members raised often. He said he assured everyone,

> We were not going to be running up against our percentage of our UNA budget—I think [it] was 20 percent [dedicated to advocacy]. In any case [we were] always very sensitive to the way we presented ourselves as an organization. We were, at heart, a public education organization. We valued discussion, debate; we weren't trying to pull anything over anyone's eyes. I think that the Advocacy Committee gave our work greater focus.

UNA-USA headquarters also encouraged chapters to set up advocacy committees locally, but the idea met with only moderate success, according to Dick.

The UNESCO Controversy

At one time or another, nearly every UN agency drew the ire of someone in Washington: President Ford took the United States out of the International Labour Organization; during Reagan's first term, he withdrew the United States from the UN Industrial Development Organization (UNIDO); the UN Population Fund (UNFPA) regularly got caught—and still does—in the domestic debate over contraception and abortion; and the International Atomic Energy Agency (IAEA) was criticized for not catching violations of the Nuclear Nonproliferation Treaty (NPT). But it was the United Nations Educational, Scientific, and Cultural Organization (UNESCO) that attracted the most sustained fire over the years. When the UN was created, the AAUN considered the UN Charter's commitment to economic and social issues vital to the world body fulfilling its mission for a more peaceful world. UNESCO, with the slogan "Building peace in the minds of men and women," was to be the vehicle for those goals, and it played a large role in the writing of the Universal Declaration of Human Rights. Its mandate was ambitious, but eventually real and perceived issues of mismanagement and politicization defined the relationship of the agency, which is based in Paris, with the US government.

This controversy "really kind of raised the stakes, as it were, because UNESCO was one of the premier international organizations in the UN system," Dimoff said. "Education, culture, science were areas of cooperation where you could work on substantive issues."

Calling UNESCO pro-Communist, anti-Israel, and hostile to free speech and capitalism, as well as citing financial mismanagement, President Reagan pulled the United States out of UNESCO in 1984. But, according to Dimoff, "UNESCO was extremely important because there were several important members of Congress who felt very strongly about it and felt that UNA should be leading an effort [to change the minds of members of Congress]. Congressman Jim Leach of Iowa really pushed that."

A *Washington Weekly Report* from March 16, 1984, quoted Leach, a Republican, testifying before a House committee that the "problems attendant with human foible should be rooted out, yet the US should not allow concern for one director's management style to mask ideological pouting at home." While acknowledging financial problems and policy differences, Leach called leaving UNESCO "an unjustified response to an exaggerated problem." He said that US participation in the agency had moderated its behavior in the past—notably, protecting Israel's right to participate and in restraining its budget.[13]

Dimoff said, "There were numerous kinds of projects we undertook over the years, including trying to develop a plan for the US return to UNESCO." Jeffrey Laurenti, the director of multilateral studies at UNA, was the lead person on the global policy project in 1988. A US/international task force, chaired by Leach, produced a US-focused report on US interests in UNESCO. The task force had two goals, Laurenti said in an interview for this book: one was to build international support for reforms reinvigorating the organization and "the other was to define the terms and process for US re-entry."

After the report was written, chapters lobbied the national office to take up the cause. But that support never came. Laurenti said, "Chapter leaders pleaded with national to speak out, North Carolina's Jack Fobes [a former deputy director-general of UNESCO] presented resolutions at conventions and National Council meetings, but UNESCO had become politically toxic in Washington, and the national headquarters apparently only issued an anodyne statement calling for cooler heads to prevail."

The task force did not make any progress during the first Bush administration, but they did have more luck after Bill Clinton was elected president in 1992. Working through Assistant Secretary of State Douglas Bennet, the team met with Tim Wirth, the undersecretary for global affairs (and future UN Foundation president). "While State was behind it, we worked very closely with" Bennet, Wirth, and Deputy Secretary of State Strobe Talbott. "They put the UNESCO money for dues in the budget they presented at the end of 1994 to OMB."

On another front, Laurenti said, "it had been a big uphill slog" with people on the National Security Council (NSC) staff, who said, "'Why the blank are we talking about going back into the UNESCO? We don't need to do that.' These were hard security types. So all this is a diversion for them." The plan stalled in the NSC for seven months, Laurenti recalled, and by then the Republicans gained the Senate majority in the 1994 elections, giving the chairmanship of the Foreign Relations Committee to Helms. "The 1994 election sealed its doom," Laurenti said of the UNESCO program. The State Department "preemptively" removed UNESCO funding from its budget proposal.

The United States did not rejoin UNESCO until 2003. Speaking at the UNESCO General Conference, Laura Bush, then first lady, said, "We raise our flag to join the flags of 189 UNESCO member states in seeking the very best of our human hopes for liberty, dignity, and peace." That year, Mrs. Bush was designated UNESCO Honorary Ambassador for the UN Literacy Decade (2003–2012) by the agency's director-general.[14]

In 2013, however, more trouble ensued with the United States and UNESCO, when the former lost its voting rights on UNESCO's board because it had stopped paying its annual dues in 2011, after the agency had accepted Palestine as a member. That action triggered a US law that forbids the United States to contribute funds to any UN agency that allows Palestine to join.

The Emergency Coalition for US Financial Support of the UN

The issues of budget arrears and UN reform peaked in 1996. The United States was $1.1 billion in arrears for the assessed budget and the peacekeeping budget—it was even behind in paying for peacekeeping missions that it had approved. The Emergency Coalition for US Financial Support of the United Nations was started "to find a solution to the arrears problem," Dimoff said, and UNA was quick to join it. According to Dimoff, "The primary focus [was] going on the Hill, going to the State Department, trying to drum up some energy on the part of the State Department to address these issues."

The coalition was the brainchild of David E. Birenbaum, the US ambassador to the UN for management and reform under President Clinton from 1994 to 1996. For those two years, "I was on the front line, explaining to others what we are doing or not doing," Birenbaum said in an interview for this book. Consequently, "I saw it was enormously frustrating, and [I saw] how much damage [the arrears] did to us." Since most of the arrears were for peacekeeping, he said, "There was no justification whatsoever."

He conceived the idea for a coalition when he was still an ambassador; he raised it with Richard H. Stanley, the president of the Stanley Foundation, because, as a government official, Birenbaum could not introduce such an initiative himself. Stanley, based in Iowa, organized a few meetings; when Birenbaum left government, "I just reached out to people."

The coalition became a grand collection of organizations and individuals in which UNA was a player. Not since the 1945 San Francisco Conference had such a high-level coalition of political, social, business, and labor leaders organized themselves around a UN issue. The coalition also boasted a bipartisan Leadership Council (a board of advisers) and a nonpartisan group of some of the most recognizable public figures of the day, including former President Jimmy Carter; Senators (and former Senators) Mark Hatfield, George Mitchell, Claiborne Pell, Charles Percy, and Paul Simon; leading Washington figures who had held key posts in both Democratic and Republican administrations, such as Frank C. Carlucci, Lawrence Eagleburger, Rita E. Hauser, Margaret Heckler, Max M. Kampelman, Sargent Shriver, Abraham Sofaer, and Andrew Young; industrial philanthropists like David Rockefeller and George Soros; labor leaders like Lane Kirkland and John Sweeney; and figures closely associated with UNA, such as the stalwarts Elliot Richardson and John Whitehead.

A July 25, 1997, letter to Helms urging him "to support full funding of the outstanding and current US legal obligations to the United Nations" was signed by every former secretary of state of both parties. Henry Kissinger's was the first signature. "The continued failure of the US to honor its legal obligations threatens the financial viability of the United Nations," the letter said. "While continued reform is necessary, the United Nations advances important US interests and deserves the support of the President and the Congress as well as the American people." (The signees were Kissinger, Alexander Haig Jr., George Shultz, Cyrus Vance, James Baker III, Lawrence Eagleburger, and Warren Christopher.)[15]

Birenbaum was chairman of the group; a former UNA president, James Leonard, was the president; Charles William Maynes, the editor of *Foreign Policy*, was the treasurer; Richard H. Stanley of the Stanley Foundation was secretary; and Victoria K. Holt, a senior associate at the Henry L. Stimson Center and future deputy assistant secretary of state, Bureau of International Affairs, was initially executive director.

The coalition had a single objective, did not have members à la UNA, and was meant to dissolve once its mission was completed. Although it was a nonprofit group, contributions were not tax deductible, thus allowing the coalition to lobby Congress on specific legislation. Whitehead, who was at the time UNA board chair, was "completely supportive," Birenbaum said. The coalition generated hundreds of newspaper advertisements and letters to the editor and articles.

The formation of the coalition coincided with Ted Turner's $1 billion gift for UN causes and the subsequent creation of the UN Foundation as a conduit for the contribution, since the UN could not accept the gift directly. Perceiving that the coalition and the evolving mandate of the UNF did not conflict, "we supported each other," Birenbaum said. Tim Wirth, as a former senator, met with fellow senators on the issue. Birenbaum added that the UN Foundation provided the coalition with some money.

The strategy was to focus on the annual appropriations bill rather than on a specific policy-oriented bill. At the same time, however, Secretary of State Madeleine Albright was negotiating with Helms over the arrears issue. Those talks, Birenbaum said, led to what became the Helms-Biden bill. The bill was not a reaction to the coalition; rather the bill "emerged because the politics of the situation were such that we had to get the buy-in of a major conservative, and Helms was willing to play that role." Helms-Biden "helped create a climate where [Congress] was more receptive to paying," Birenbaum said.

Richard Holbrooke, the US ambassador to the UN at the time, also took a leading role in the initiative's success. "I don't want to be naive about this, but Richard Holbrooke had a great deal to do with it," Birenbaum said. "He was a force of nature and lobbied very enthusiastically and effectively in support of it." The deal "was not easy," Birenbaum said, because if the US contribution went down, others would have to go up. "It was a huge effort to shave off peanuts," he said, and "totally meaningless" to the overall US budget.

Birenbaum speculated that they would have succeeded even without Holbrooke because of the terrorist attacks of September 2001. "Once 9/11 happened, there was no question that we were going to pay our dues." President George W. Bush announced that the United States would make a $100 million payment. Dimoff said, "That payment was like pulling teeth," but it cleared the bulk of the debt. The coalition dissolved in March 2002, transferring its few assets to the UNA Washington office.

Although this specific coalition succeeded in its clearly defined goals, the broader campaign to maintain US government support for the UN has been a continuing mission. Even when the UN was enormously popular with the US public in the 1950s, isolationists worked to undermine it (see Chapter 4). As this chapter illustrated, by the early 1970s fundamental changes had occurred in international politics that tested UNA's ability to rally support for the UN.

Notes

1. The Clark M. Eichelberger Papers, Manuscripts and Archives Division, New York Public Library. Astor, Lenox, and Tilden Foundations (NYPL Archives), box 114.

2. Ibid., box 116.

3. Ibid., box 117.

4. Ibid.

5. Seton Hall University (SHU Archives), The Msgr. William Noé Field Archives and Special Collections Center, South Orange, NJ, box 16.

6. Neil A. Lewis, "Elliot Richardson Dies at 79; Stood Up to Nixon and Resigned in 'Saturday Night Massacre,'" *New York Times*, January 1, 2000.

7. Ibid.

8. John C. Whitehead, *A Life in Leadership: From D-Day to Ground Zero* (New York: A New America Book, Basic Books, 2005), 147.

9. *Washington Weekly Report*, April 6, 1979.

10. Whitehead, *A Life in Leadership*, 200–202.

11. *Washington Weekly Report*, April 6, 1979.

12. Vita Bite, "United Nations System Funding: Congressional Issues," *Congressional Research Service,* http://fpc.state.gov/documents/organization /55841.pdf.

13. *Washington Weekly Report*, March 16, 1984.

14. UNESCO press release 2003-67, September 29, 2003, http://portal.unesco .org/en/ev.php-URL_ID=15744&URL_DO=DO_PRINTPAGE&URL_SECTION =201.html.

15. SHU Archives, box 16.

7

The Decline of
Popular Support for the UN:
UNA-USA in the 1970s

By the early 1970s, the UN had made great strides in fulfilling one of the charter's fundamental mandates—decolonization. When the charter was signed in 1945, fifty member states existed. Countries that are key global southern powers today, including Algeria, Indonesia, Jordan, Libya, Malaysia, Nigeria, Pakistan, Democratic Republic of Congo (formerly Zaire), and Zimbabwe (formerly Rhodesia), were not present at the UN's founding in San Francisco because they were not independent nations. By 1970, the number of UN member states had increased to 142, primarily through decolonization. The inevitable result was that as the UN became more universal, US dominance of the world body's agenda weakened, despite its role as top financial contributor. The 1970s, therefore, saw numerous UN decisions that the United States viewed as hostile, resulting in US public support dropping, with a subsequent decrease in support for UNA-USA. During this period, the General Assembly took on three issues that alienated the United States: voting to give the Chinese seat to the Beijing government, promoting a New International Economic Order (NIEO), and the Zionism-as-racism resolution. The most far-reaching of these for the United Nations was the 1971 vote on China.

China, under the Nanjing-based Republic of China, led by the wartime leader Chiang Kai-shek, was an original signatory of the UN Charter in 1945. Mao Zedong's revolution established the People's Republic of China (PRC) in October 1949, taking control of mainland China and forcing the Republic of China government to flee to Taiwan, then called Formosa. Despite having lost the war, the Taiwan-based government retained the Chinese seat (including the Security Council seat and its veto power) at the UN. Attempts had been made over many years to deal with the matter, including proposing a two-seat solution or total expulsion of the Taiwan entity, but they all failed. There was no question, however, that mainland China needed to have a major say at the UN, given the sheer size of its population, but its Communist government put off many Western countries. The UNA was similarly divided between principle and logic. As discussed in Chapter 3, throughout the 1950s and 1960s, the AAUN/UNA took a one-hand/other-hand position.

By 1971, enough votes in the General Assembly shifted the balance; on October 25, 1971, the General Assembly voted 76 to 35, with 17 abstentions, to seat Beijing, while expelling the Republic of China in Taipei. Although the United States attempted to have both governments admitted, Washington could not garner enough support for this plan. Resolution 2758 declared that "the restoration of the lawful rights" of the People's Republic of China was "essential" and recognized the country as "the only legitimate representatives of China to the United Nations." Members of Congress reacted angrily, cutting financial contributions to the UN. The Nixon administration was more muted, with its attention focused on the significant visit of the president to Beijing scheduled for early 1972.

The New International Economic Order

Another initiative in the 1970s that caused both the US government and the US business community to sour on the UN was the New International Economic Order, an initiative originating among the recently independent states seeking to create new controls over the global economic system. The NIEO had no legal standing nor was it an organized body, but it was an organizing principle for promoting the agenda of the Group of 77 developing states, or G77. The UNA did not enter the debate over the NIEO.

The NIEO originated in decolonization and the subsequent consolidation of developing countries into a coalition. The United Nations Conference on Trade and Development (UNCTAD) offered a bureaucratic organizing body at the UN. UNCTAD was another result of the "two movements for political independence and an end to economic dependency," wrote Robert F. Meagher, a professor of international law at the Fletcher School of Law and Diplomacy at Tufts University. He added, "These movements came together in 1964 when [UNCTAD] became a permanent subsidiary of the General Assembly."[1]

The NIEO was "more a political program than an economic one," Stephen D. Krasner wrote in *The US, the UN, and the Management of Global Change*, a UNA book published in 1983. The economic plan was not especially radical, Krasner wrote, but it was "accompanied by attacks on the basic assumptions of the existing order and by demands for effective control over international decision-making machinery." It was the "political component" that made the NIEO distinctive.[2] The role of state control of the economy appealed to the Soviet Union as much as it appalled laissez-faire capitalists in the West. It thus became another indictment against the UN, despite the general agreement on most of the provisions of the Charter of Economic Rights and the Duties of States.

(Another initiative—the New World Information and Communication Order—was also opposed by the US government, but it was an issue on the UNA's agenda.)

A 1980 memo by the director of communications of the US mission to the UN, Jill A. Schuker, to the ambassador at the time, Donald McHenry, underlined the general acceptance, and lack of hostility, within the US government. "We recognized the goal, long advanced by the developing countries, of achieving a New International Economic Order, in keeping with the new political and economic realities of the post colonial period." She quoted Ambassador Andrew Young in 1977 as saying that the United States "indeed supported the evolving process of a new system of international cooperation for economic progress," thus helping to "avoid sterile, confrontational debate." Schuker wrote that "bombast" helped divide the United States from the newly independent developing countries. "Our lack of sensitivity led to a perception that the United States . . . had little or no interest in or awareness of the developing world's priority political and economic concerns."[3]

McHenry and Schuker were officials under President Carter. Shortly after his election, President Reagan unequivocally rejected NIEO at the Cancún Summit on International Development Issues in 1981 in Mexico.

Zionism as Racism

The vote on China and the debate over the NIEO were soon overshadowed by another move at the UN that created lasting ill will among US officials and the public and profoundly affected the standing of the UNA. On November 10, 1975, the General Assembly passed a resolution equating Zionism with racism, on a vote of 72 to 35, with 32 abstentions. The proper name of Resolution 3379 was "Elimination of All Forms of Racial Discrimination." It endorsed the 1975 Declaration of Mexico on the Equality of Women and Their Contribution to Development and Peace, which called for "the elimination of colonialism and neo-colonialism, foreign occupation, Zionism, apartheid, and racial discrimination in all its forms" and therefore "determines that Zionism is a form of racism and racial discrimination."

The US delegation to the Mexico City conference was doubly enraged. The delegates, led by Bella Abzug, the American Congress member, not only complained about the idea but also said it had no place in a conference about women.[4]

After Mexico City, the issue moved to the General Assembly. The United States signaled its opposition to the idea as the draft resolution was wending through the Social and Humanitarian Committee of the General Assembly. Leonard Garment, who represented the United States in the committee as a diplomat, warned that the text endorsed anti-Semitism and called it "an obscene act." On UN Day, October 24, 1975, President Gerald Ford issued a statement, saying, "Such action undermines the principles upon which the United Nations is based." In an interview for this book, James Leonard, who had become UNA president as the controversy grew, considered the draft still "incipient" at the time, as it was just percolating through the preliminary procedures in the UN. Consequently, Leonard tried to find out how to forestall the problem.

The UNA also publicly rallied against the resolution between Mexico City and that autumn's General Assembly annual debate. Edward Luck, who was then a researcher at UNA and would become its president in 1984, said in an interview for this book that this was the first time the association took a public position on a UN resolution. As a junior staff member, Luck said he was not involved in the planning but that "UNA-USA had never taken a position, apparently, as an organization on an issue before the UN, and that's why they created policy panels, so the policy panels would take positions and UNA wouldn't. But people were saying, 'You've got to take a position on this, this is fundamental.'"

After the vote was taken in the General Assembly, Daniel Patrick Moynihan, a Democrat who had been appointed US ambassador to the UN by President Ford, a Republican, delivered a blistering speech from the podium in the General Assembly Hall. The United States "does not acknowledge, it will not abide by, it will never acquiesce in this infamous act," he said. "There will be time enough to contemplate the harm this act will have done the United Nations. Historians will do that for us. It is sufficient to note for the moment only one foreboding fact: a great evil has been loosed upon the world." The speech made him a national hero, though there was continuing controversy over his role in the whole affair.

Although a majority of reports praised Moynihan for eloquence and righteous rage, others said he could have handled it more diplomatically and that he was looking for a fight. In *United Nations: The First Fifty Years,* Stanley Meisler quoted several diplomats and scholars who said the resolution could have been buried if Moynihan had taken a less confrontational approach. The British ambassador at the time, Ivor Richard, said in a speech to the UNA, "I spend a lot of time preventing rows at the UN—not looking for them. Whatever else the place is, it is not the OK Corral, and I am hardly Wyatt Earp." It took no imagination to guess who Richard thought was Wyatt Earp. Rita E. Hauser, a Republican who had been a US delegate to the UN Human Rights Commission, said the resolution "could easily have been buried in the Third Committee" if Moynihan had not been so aggressive. "By doing that he compelled the issue to the table, which to me is folly when you don't have the votes."[5]

Leonard said he was told by "midlevel people" at the US mission that "they thought it [the controversy] could have been avoided. But Moynihan had seen this as an opportunity. Now, for an admirer of Moynihan, this all seems very slanderous," said Leonard, who emphasized that he did not know whether what he was told was just rumor. In an interview for the Association for Diplomatic Studies and Training, Leonard said,

> There was an awful lot of criticism of Moynihan's handling of that in the Mission by the people who were watching it up close and there were even those who felt that in a way he had provoked it in order to provide himself a platform for then making himself very popular with the Jewish groups and the American people generally, who were outraged by the famous resolution. I just honestly have no way of knowing whether that was true.[6]

Moynihan was elected to the US Senate from New York the following year.

The resolution enraged Capitol Hill. The day after the GA vote, the Senate unanimously passed a resolution "sharply condemning" the resolution. Even supporters of the UN blasted it; some even said they were ready to wash their hands of the world body. Senator Abraham Ribicoff (D-Connecticut) said, "I have long supported the United Nations and the important role that this nation must play in it if that body is to survive. Today, I am no longer able to rise in defense of the United Nations. I am no longer optimistic about the future of that one-time community of nations that has now fallen so far." Senator Joseph Biden (D-Delaware at the time) called the resolution "stupid," adding "the UN is weakened by its passage." Senator Charles Mathias (R-Maryland), said, "To those of us who have supported efforts to make the United Nations a more viable organization, the vote must be taken as a signal to rethink the basic assumptions on which such support was based."[7]

Despite the rhetoric from the White House and Congress, there were no serious attempts to withdraw US membership in the UN. That could not be said, however, about threats to cut financial contributions to the world body, which were bound to have major repercussions. In his study of US financing of the UN, Meagher named the China and Zionism decisions, plus resolutions on the NIEO, as crucial turning points for the punitive financial actions taken by Congress. "In these cases criticisms emanated from both houses of Congress and demands were made to either cut US contributions or in some cases to withdraw from the UN. The executive branch, through the State Department, joined in the criticism of the actions but did not endorse either a cut in contributions or withdrawal."[8]

Leonard, who had been an ambassador, knew the bill to cut funding was working its way through Congress, so he consulted with the US mission to the UN on how to derail it. He said that the question for UNA-USA quickly became, what was it going to do about the accusation against Israel? In an analysis of the impact of the Zionism-as-racism resolution, Luck, in his interview for this book, said, "UNA-USA for the first time in its history took a political stand by opposing the proposed resolution and by appealing to each of the then 141 other national missions to reject it." Besides writing to the missions, Luck said Leonard also wrote to all the UNA chapters and members, soliciting their views and support.

In a 1987 paper prepared for the International Legal Conference on Anti-Semitism, Anti-Zionism, and the United Nations, Luck wrote, "The long-term impact of the Zionism-Racism Resolution was not so much to swell the ranks of those 'hostile' to the UN . . . , as to erode the ranks and to sap the enthusiasm of the 'faithful.'" He wrote that the resolution gave "conservative critics of the world organization an opportunity to seize the political initiative. And they did, with extraordinary results." Conservatives "found an attractive way to appeal for sympathy and support from American Jews and from many others who prior to this had hardly given them the time of day."[9]

UNA-USA had a special problem on its hands regarding the resolution. US Jews had been strong political and financial backers of the organization since its founding. As Leonard noted in the interview, "A large part of our financial support came from generous Jewish leaders, including Bob Benjamin, who was chairman of the board, a Democrat, and a liberal" and "a loyal supporter." Other supporters included Arthur Krim, an entertainment lawyer, chair of Orion Pictures and United Artists, and a "very big donor to the Democratic Party and to Israel," and Phil Klutznick, a real estate businessman in Chicago who was "the hugest donor," an adviser to three presidents, and a member of the UNA-USA board.

"The resolution hit the New York Jewish community very hard," Leonard said. "And many became quite outspoken. Managing all of that was really the principal task." Despite actively campaigning against the resolution, UNA-USA membership became a victim of the passage of the resolution. "In the sixteen months following the introduction of this issue in the General Assembly, UNA-USA lost 18 percent of its members (from just over 29,000 to around 24,000). The drop was even more spectacular in some areas," Luck wrote.[10]

Felice Gaer held several positions in UNA (but not during this period), as well as in human rights groups, including as the director for the Jacob Blaustein Institute for the Advancement of Human Rights. She stated that UNA "did an amazing amount of what I would call programming with high-level UN diplomats all through that period." She added, "I know the positions they took. I know Ed Luck did some very important things at the time."

For Toby Trister Gati and other policy experts at UNA-USA, the controversy made their work in drafting policy positions more complex. A UN-centric response to every issue—a stance Gati said was widely favored by the chapters—was unrealistic given events like the Zionism resolution. "You couldn't say that the UN was being a neutral force when some of the resolutions were clearly anti-Israel, anti-US, anti-West," she said in an interview for the book. What was needed "was much more a nuanced approach."

Luck wrote of a "qualitative shift in the basic perceptions of the UN held by many Americans," saying that "in passing the Zionism-Racism Resolution . . . the UN was not only once again failing to do something right, it was consciously doing something that the vast majority of Americans believed to be morally wrong."[11] On the other hand, Luck wrote, "Over the long-run, however, the resolution did have a salutary effect in compelling those who believed most in the UN to confront some of the difficult political problems standing between the existing UN and its high ideals. Paradoxically, it in essence politicized a number of observers who had felt that the UN itself should somehow be above politics."

Luck's analysis, written four years before the resolution was repealed in 1991, looked to the future with hope:

> The UN of 1985–86 is not the UN of 1975. Efforts are still made by some Member States to resurrect the Zionism-Racism language in various UN documents, and these need to be resisted firmly and vigilantly. But the critical change over the past decade has been that these efforts are regularly rebuffed by a combination of Western and moderate Third World countries.

By 1986–1987, there was "serious discussion about asking the General Assembly to reverse its early action and to deny the linkage between Zionism and Racism." Luck listed reasons that included the decreasing clout of the Organization of the Petroleum-Exporting Countries (OPEC); the African Arab coalition "becoming frayed"; the "widespread disillusionment with Socialist economic models"; and the disillusionment "with Soviet aggression in Afghanistan encouraging more moderate political trends in the Third World, with positive spin-offs for the Israeli and American positions in the UN."

Luck's optimism was well founded. The resolution was repealed in December 1991 on a 111-to-25 vote, with 13 abstentions and 17 other countries, including Egypt and Kuwait, not participating. The one-line resolution simply had the GA decide "to revoke the determination contained in its resolution 3379 of 10 November 1975."

In its article on the vote, *The New York Times* reported, "The vote reflected the shifting political currents of recent years, the Persian Gulf war in particular, which split the Arab and Islamic worlds, and the changes in the former Soviet bloc, fostered by the collapse of Communism."[12] Another change that Luck noted was that "compared to the major exodus of members in the late 1970s and early 1980s, UNA-USA has enjoyed a modest, but steady, expansion of membership."

Notes

1. Robert F. Meagher, "United States Financing of the United Nations," in *The US, the UN, and the Management of Global Change* (A UNA-USA Publication), ed. Toby Trister Gati (New York and London: New York University Press, 1983), 110.

2. Stephen D. Krasner, "The United Nations and Political Conflict between the North and the South," in *The US, the UN, and the Management of Global Change* (A UNA-USA Publication), ed. Toby Trister Gati (New York and London: New York University Press, 1983), 214–215.

3. William vanden Heuvel, private archives.

4. Stanley Meisler, *United Nations: The First Fifty Years* (New York: The Atlantic Monthly Press, 1995), 204.

5. Ibid., 216–217.

6. James Leonard, "The Association for Diplomatic Studies and Training Foreign Affairs Oral History Project: Interview with James Leonard," by Warren Unna, March 10, 1993, http://www.adst.org/OH%20TOCs/Leonard,%20James%20.toc.pdf.

7. Edward C. Luck, "The Impact of the Zionism-Racism Resolution on the Standing of the United Nations in the United States," in *Israel Yearbook on Human Rights*, published under the auspices of the Faculty of Law, Tel Aviv University (Dordrecht/Boston/London: Martinus Nijhoff Publishers, 1987), 104–105.

8. Meagher, "United States Financing," 102.

9. Luck, "The Impact of the Zionism-Racism Resolution," 107.

10. Ibid., 106.

11. Ibid.

12. Paul Lewis, "UN Repeals Its '75 Resolution Equating Zionism with Racism," *The New York Times*, December 17, 1991.

8

The UNA-USA Parallel Studies Program and Track II Talks, 1968–1992

Whether or not top Soviet leaders recognized the United Nations as an important arena to influence world opinion, they deigned to engage with it directly on only two memorable occasions, providing vivid, lasting images of the height and then the end of the Cold War. First, there was the iconic image of Nikita Khrushchev, the Soviet leader, pounding his delegate desk in the General Assembly in 1960 — it is still not clear whether he did the pounding with his shoe, as it was not captured on film or in a photograph but remains legendary. Then, standing in the same hall in 1988, Mikhail Gorbachev, the Soviet Communist Party chief, told the world that the Soviet Union would unilaterally cut its troop strength by half a million and pull back its forces from Eastern Europe, signaling that Moscow was abandoning its policy of keeping Warsaw Pact countries in its orbit by force. Less than one year later, the Berlin Wall fell; on December 31, 1991, the Soviet Union ceased to exist.

During these decades, private, unofficial efforts and visits were made to cool tensions and find common ground between the United States and the Soviet Union. UNA-USA's contribution to these efforts was an important, behind-the-scenes Parallel Studies Program that defined the international outreach of UNA for at least three decades. It had a huge influence on the political direction of Soviet politics, as former UNA president Edward C. Luck explained in an interview for this book.

In the late 1960s, the Policy Studies Committee of the UNA board decided that the most urgent foreign policy issue was the tension between East and West. A Policy Studies Program brought together US experts to discuss important security issues in the US-Soviet relationship; later, a Parallel Studies Program brought together US and Soviet experts to discuss a range of issues. The first policy study program was undertaken with partners in the USSR; subsequent programs involved Japan and the

People's Republic of China. The initiative with the Soviet Union started during a relatively calm period in US-Soviet relations in the late 1960s, when the two superpowers were cooperating on several arms-control ventures, including the Nuclear Nonproliferation Treaty (NPT), the Anti-Ballistic Missile (ABM) Treaty, and the first agreement limiting the stock of strategic ballistic missiles—the SALT I Treaty. Under President Nixon, arms control was high on the priority list of both Washington and Moscow as a means of reducing tensions between the two capitals.

UNA began its policy studies program in the mid-1960s under UNA vice president Elmore Jackson, whom Porter McKeever, then UNA's president, had recruited from the State Department in 1966. Jackson hired a team that included David Lenefsky. In an interview for this book, Lenefsky, who ran the program, called Jackson "an extraordinary, sophisticated human being. He was a quiet guy, religious. He had an extraordinarily sophisticated mind, and he was self-effacing—one of the few people who never had a career in government as high as he should have." Lenefsky added, "In terms of diplomacy, he was a genius; people trusted him." He said McKeever and Jackson were "beloved," so the combination of the two "allowed you to attract an extraordinary group of people under the policy study program."

Jackson, a Quaker who worked for the American Friends Service Committee from 1936 to 1961, was central to one of history's great "what might have beens." In 1955, as the Quaker representative to the UN, "he was asked by an envoy of Gamal Abdel Nasser, then the Egyptian Prime Minister, to set up a meeting between Egyptian and Israeli officials," according to the *New York Times* obituary of Jackson. Jackson "made three trips to Egypt and Israel, where David Ben-Gurion, then the Defense Minister, also welcomed his efforts. Mr. Jackson had the backing of the United States, the State Department said. The mission failed when fighting between Israelis and Arabs broke out in the Gaza Strip."[1]

Lenefsky said the first policy report dealt with the question of Chinese membership in the UN, and the second was on conflict resolution. "UNA in those years never came down one way or another on China," he said. "On one hand, UN should be universal; on the other hand, China is a bad actor." In the report, UNA's conclusions favored the universality argument.

By the late 1960s, informal consultations with the Russian Academy of Sciences led to the creation of the Parallel Studies Program. Lenefsky said the idea originated with the academy; the UNA-USSR, "which was obviously a function of the Soviet government"; and the

World Federation of UN Associations (WFUNA). According to Lenef-sky, "the Soviet UNA asked our UNA to come to Moscow" to discuss the possibility of setting up a program.

At this point, the Parallel and Policy Studies programs were not yet "separate and distinct," said Lenefsky, who was the project director of both programs. The first joint projects focused on nuclear nonprolifera-tion and cooperation on environmental issues. The chair of the nuclear project was Robert V. Roosa, the chair of the environmental project was Robert O. Anderson, board chairman of Atlantic Richfield.

According to James Leonard, who was an arms-control negotiator for the United States at the time and later became president of UNA-USA (1973–1977), the United States pursued "a small treaty because [Henry] Kissinger wanted to show it was possible to talk with the Rus-sians." That "small treaty" was the Seabed Arms Control Treaty, an agreement, signed by the United States, Britain, the Soviet Union, and eighty-four other countries, that banned placement of nuclear weapons or other weapons of mass destruction on the ocean floor beyond a twelve-mile coastal zone. The Biological Weapons Convention followed in 1972. International realities and the interests and skills of UNA offi-cials coincided, resulting in arms control topping the agenda of the Par-allel Studies Programs.

This convergence worked well for Leonard, as he had an extensive background in arms control, had served in Moscow as a foreign service officer, and had Russian-language skills (see Chapter 12). Two other UNA experts who steered the Parallel Studies Program through those years were Toby Trister Gati and Ed Luck.

One of Lenefsky's last acts before leaving UNA in 1972 was to hire Gati, who had just earned her master's degree in international affairs from Columbia University. While still at Columbia, Gati had asked a former US ambassador to the UN, Charles Yost, who was teaching at the university, for career advice, and he directed her to UNA. She was hired as a researcher and became the Parallel Studies project director in 1974. Luck, her classmate, was hired in 1974, first as a researcher and eventually as a project director. As project directors, "We wrote articles together and worked extremely well together," Gati said in an interview for this book. She and Luck would divide up an article, each of them writing different parts that would then come seamlessly together. In addition, "We had to do fund-raising, because every one of these proj-ects had to be self-supporting. It was more than that. Our programs became a net contributor to the UNA budget." In 1984, Gati was named senior vice president for political, security, and multilateral issues.

A UNA report from 1980 lists four priorities for the Parallel Studies Program with the Soviet Union: political relations, strategic arms control, European security, and involvement in the Third World. Later reports showed an expanded, fine-tuned agenda, including an international development strategy, weapons in outer space, the strengthening of UN abilities, settlement of regional conflicts, and the possibility of a UN naval peacekeeping force for the Persian Gulf in 1987. Before a major conference on the NPT in 1985, UNA-USA and UNA-USSR, both part of the WFUNA global membership network, issued joint statements on strengthening the nonproliferation regime and exploring ways to use the UN's untapped potential in the arena of international peace and security. (An earlier statement in March 1975 had called for strengthening the nuclear nonproliferation regime by expanding the number of state parties to the treaty—neither China nor France was a party at that point—and improving safeguards to ensure that nuclear technology could be used exclusively for peaceful purposes. It also linked nonproliferation—and international security, in general—to making the US-Soviet "process of détente irreversible."[2])

Arms control was also high on the bilateral agenda of the USSR and the United States, as it was a key matter for both countries. Gati said that because of the Cold War, there were subjects that the United States and the USSR could not agree on, but "we and the Russians—the Soviets at that time—had a common interest in the nonproliferation regimes. So we could talk about that. That's how it started." The US participants knew well that while "we weren't going to change the world, nonproliferation policies were always evolving," Gati added. "There were new challenges, and new countries were thinking of going nuclear. There was discussion of strengthening the international regime" with an international system of inspections or other preventive means to avoid nuclear disaster.

Gati recalled a meeting in Moscow where Russians pulled the US experts aside and mentioned that some Soviet leaders were considering using nuclear weapons to change the direction of the rivers in Siberia. The idea was that the force from a few small nuclear weapons explosions could create shock waves that could reverse the direction of the waters from north to south, so that more water would flow to support industry and agriculture in a part of Siberia where there were more people and a better climate. Gati said the Russian scientists were appalled by the idea; they were concerned about not only the environmental chaos that could ensue but also the precedent of using nuclear weapons for anything. "So they asked UNA to put together some scientific papers for them, which we did, on what the likely negative impacts of such explosions would be," Gati said. "The Russian scientists said that our Western analysis would have much more weight with the Soviet leadership than theirs would. And it turned out to be the case—we sent them some papers on this issue and the idea quietly disappeared, to everyone's relief."

Besides influencing Soviet thinking on these issues, "we brought ideas back to the State Department and the White House," Gati said. Like many US embassies around the world, those in the Eastern bloc were isolated; the US embassy in Moscow, for example, "didn't have many of the contacts we had." In fact, "the embassy rarely saw people from the politburo, but we often did." As a result, "there was not that much information on the Soviet Union at that time and what it was thinking," she said. So, after returning home from meetings in the Soviet Union, UNA-USA members would find themselves cited in *The New York Times* about the policy implications of what they had learned in their discussions abroad. For example, as noted later in this chapter, in December 1991, Gati and Richard N. Gardner, a former deputy assistant secretary of state and former US ambassador to Italy and Spain, published an op-ed in *The New York Times* on allocating to Russia the Soviet seat in the Security Council.

These were insights that UNA could relay to the UN itself. "We had a unique understanding of those issues. We had very close relationships with every Secretary-General. We could go in and talk about any subject . . . on our agenda," Gati said. "We had our reports on UN reform, or on nonproliferation, or on economics—whatever issue, we had entrée into the highest level of the UN to discuss. I remember holding sessions on different topics and inviting ambassadors from all over based on work that UNA-USA had done."

Indeed, the Parallel Studies Program had several built-in advantages when it began working with the Soviet Union. For one, UNA-USA could work with a natural counterpart—UNA-USSR. Gati said that the latter group was in a position to bring "in people with a little more flexibility than maybe government would have had." It was clear that this organization did not have "any true dissidents in the group"; rather, it had participants with "different views on the ways to defend Russian/Soviet interests in the international system." UNA-USA and UNA-USSR also held many sessions together on the UN's peace and security functions, on how its economic activities should be structured, and on reform of the UN.

Another advantage was the number of high-profile people involved in the program. These former officials drew on their government experience, and if they went back into government service (which many did), they could draw on their UNA experiences. The first chair of the Parallel Studies Program, Walter J. Stoessel Jr., was a former deputy secretary of state and ambassador to the Soviet Union. William Scranton, a former governor of Pennsylvania and former UN ambassador, who also chaired the East Asia program of UNA-USA, followed him. The UNA-USA core group included former secretary of state Cyrus Vance; Professor Marshall Shulman of Columbia University; Vance's special adviser on Soviet affairs, Elliot Richardson; President Carter's Treasury secretary, W. Michael Blumenthal; Francis Bator of Harvard's Kennedy School; MIT professor Lincoln Bloomfield Sr.; former undersecretary of state for management, Ivan Selin; and former undersecretary of the Treasury, Robert Roosa (who also chaired UNA's economic policy program with the USSR).

Business leaders, including James McDonnell, a co-founder of McDonnell Douglas, and investment banker Arthur Ross also lent their financial support to the work. Brent Scowcroft, who was national security adviser to Presidents Ford and George H. W. Bush and a military assistant to President Nixon, chaired sessions once he left government. "If you want to have an impact, it's very nice to have a Brent Scowcroft on your side," Gati noted.

The Parallel Studies Program provided a financial cushion for UNA. In the mid-1970s, there were new money strains in the association, largely because funds for UNA had been drying up over donor disgust with the Zionism-as-racism resolution (see Chapter 7). But as Luck pointed out, "most of the big foundations were good supporters of our work." That list included the John D. and Catherine T. MacArthur Foundation, the Rockefeller Brothers Fund, W. Alton Jones, the Carnegie Corporation, the Ford Foundation, and the Ploughshares Fund.

The key figure on the Soviet side was an academician, Georgy Arbatov, the founding director of the Russian Academy of Science's Institute for US and Canadian Studies, who, Gati said, was "very close to several Politburo members and who invited very good people" to participate. It was the Institute for US and Canadian Studies—the "gatekeeper," Gati called it—that sponsored UNA-USSR members when they visited the United States. According to Leonard, once Gorbachev came to power,

> Arbatov . . . was a Central Committee member [and] the expert on America. That made him something a bit special. I think that he was in constant contact with Gorbachev and with other people, probably staff members of the Central Committee, who were encouraging him to feed in the kinds of things that he was getting from the UNA group about the importance of Russia in America, in Washington, in our public opinions.

Luck, in his interview, gave an example of how ideas worked their way into Soviet thinking. After Gorbachev announced his new policies of glasnost and perestroika in 1985, Vladimir Petrovsky, a participant in the dialogue who later became deputy foreign minister and UN under-secretary-general, approached Luck and asked him what he thought of the policies. "I said: 'Well, it's quite a break with the past and a lot of promising elements. It's really quite something.' And he said, 'Did it look familiar?' I said, 'Some of the ideas sounded a little bit familiar.'" Petrovsky told him they drew some of the ideas from a background paper Luck had written. "I don't even remember the paper," Luck said.

UNA-USA's impact on disarmament was felt strongly at the UN. As Leonard noted,

> What I think UNA did was to give encouragement to the great majority of UN members who always felt that the US was dragging its feet on disarmament. We in a sense gave a validation of continuing US interest. We were in close contact; I mean, Vance, even before being secretary of state, had been a deputy secretary for defense. I think they saw that the UNA membership wanted more disarmament than they were getting.

Gati wrote in the 1985 annual report: "These efforts reflect UNA-USA's long-term commitment to constructive engagement and quiet

A meeting of the UNA Parallel Studies Arms Control Group in Moscow in December 1987 with Georgy Arbatov, left, secretary of UNA-USSR and director of the Institute on US and Canadian Studies of the USSR Academy of Sciences; and US Senator John Tower (R-Texas), chairman of the UNA-USA Group on Arms Control. (Photo courtesy of Toby Trister Gati.)

dialogue, rather than highly charged public exchanges. The ongoing nature of the contacts provides a sense of purpose and continuity that opens up opportunities for the exploration of new ideas during periods of international calm and gives a critically needed sense of perspective when the international climate is stormy."[3]

By 1980, the US-Soviet relationship had flipped and begun a downward spiral, starting with the Soviet invasion of Afghanistan in 1979. Ronald Reagan, a fierce critic of détente, devoted his first term to intensifying the confrontation with what he called the "evil empire," overseeing the largest buildup of nuclear weapons in history and promoting new weapons systems (most notably the Strategic Defense Initiative, also known as Star Wars). Meanwhile, the Soviet Union went from one aging old-school leader to another, remained bogged down in Afghanistan, deployed nuclear weapons ever closer to Western Europe, and suffered from economic stagnation. In the United States and Europe, grassroots movements, repelled by a world of 50,000 nuclear weapons and the notion of a "winnable" nuclear war, pressured both superpowers.

After President Reagan's reelection in 1984 and the ascension of Gorbachev as the Soviet party leader in 1985, the two countries began to pull back from their nuclear brinkmanship. In 1985, the two leaders met in Geneva and issued an official joint statement proclaiming, "A nuclear war cannot be won and should never be fought." Then, at the extraordinary summit at Reykjavik, Iceland, in October 1986, the two leaders came close to actually agreeing to negotiate to zero nuclear weapons, to the horror of conservative advisers on both sides and stymied only by Reagan's insistence on pursuing Star Wars.

Yet, history moved quickly. The two countries signed the Intermediate-Range Nuclear Forces Treaty in 1987, eliminating an entire class of weapons that had raised tensions across Europe. Gorbachev's 1988 UN speech, in which he renounced the use of force to hold its Eastern European allies in line, ended the Brezhnev Doctrine and laid the groundwork for the dissolution of the Eastern bloc. In early 1989, the last Soviet troops pulled out of Afghanistan.

It was not only policy but also personalities that were influenced by the open dialogue of the Parallel Studies Programs. The meetings between UNA-USA and UNA-USSR in the 1970s and early 1980s helped persuade a new generation of people to consider novel ways of thinking and later became part of what Gati described as "Soviet political life." In this way, US participants came to know many Russians who had risen to power, especially under Boris Yeltsin, the first elected Russian president. Soviet junior officials who participated in the Parallel Studies Program and rose through the ranks included Sergey Lavrov (who became Russian ambassador to the UN and later foreign minister); Alexey Yablokov (environmental adviser to both Gorbachev and Yeltsin and a coauthor of a study of the Chernobyl disaster); Vladimir Lukin (Russian ambassador to the United States and Russian human rights ombudsman); Yevgeny Primakov (Russian foreign minister and then prime minister); Andrey Kozyrev (foreign minister under Yeltsin); Roald Sagdeev (a senior science adviser to Gorbachev); and Andrea Kolosovsky (Russian ambassador to the UN in Geneva). Others involved in the Parallel Studies Program included Roza Otunbayeva, who later became president of Kyrgyzstan. Arbatov and Sagdeev had been members of Gorbachev's delegation to the Geneva summit in 1985 as well.

Post-Soviet Programs

With the end of the Soviet Union, the Parallel Studies Program continued, but it shifted focus to what a post-USSR world would look like. In an op-ed for *The New York Times* in December 1991, just weeks before the Soviet Union dissolved, Gardner and Gati, writing on behalf of UNA-USA, argued for allocating to Russia the Soviet seats in the Security Council, with the other Soviet republics joining as new member states. As self-evident as this may sound, it was not the only option being discussed. Some delegates, opinion makers, and policy experts did not want to give Russia that much power and argued for the Commonwealth of Independent States (CIS) to take over the Soviet seat (perhaps with rotating leadership), even though the charter applies to states, not coalitions or confederations.

Just as the Parallel Studies Program's expertise helped improve mutual relations during the Cold War, that same knowledge helped the US government come to grips with the new order. Because of the program's contacts, UNA officials could fill in gaps in Washington's understanding of the changes going on in Yeltsin's Russia. UNA experts worked to get the US government to change its attention and approach to the emerging country. The administration of George H. W. Bush was "invested in Gorbachev," Gati said. "They weren't paying attention to Yeltsin." In June 1992, Gati arranged a meeting between Yeltsin and then presidential candidate Bill Clinton, "because nobody else knew the people around Yeltsin, and I knew them all and was able to do that," she said. "I know that the White House didn't want that meeting to happen and wasn't going to assist in arranging it."

In 1992, Gati wrote a memo proposing a UNA program called International Organizations and the Role of the Newly Independent States to "focus on the role of the new Commonwealth states in the international system or regional and global institutions and on the contribution international organizations can make to a peaceful transformation in the region." Several projects were launched after the breakup of the Soviet Union, including one concentrating on the CIS, one on Eastern and Central Europe, and another on the "Russian-American Dialogue on UN Peace Enforcement."

Gati left UNA in 1993 to work in the Clinton administration. She served as special assistant to the president and senior director for Russia, Ukraine, and the Eurasian States at the National Security Council and then as assistant secretary of state for intelligence and research until 1997. While working at the State Department, one of her initiatives was a publication called "Peacekeeping Perspectives." As she explained,

> When I went to the State Department, there was so much the UN was doing and people didn't know about it. The new publication was designed to keep all the regional bureaus updated on what the UN was doing in their region. Most of them never paid attention until there was a problem, and then they said, "Oh, the UN was there?" And the publication became very, very important. I used my UNA background when I got to the State Department and often called upon people that I had known when we needed information or analysis. That was a very important input for US policy.

After leaving government, Gati became a senior international adviser for Akin Gump Strauss Hauer & Feld, a Washington law firm with an emphasis on Russia and Eurasia, various politically sensitive regions of the world, and the workings of international political and economic institutions.

Japan and China

The success of the Parallel Studies Program with the USSR inspired two more programs—one with Japan and the other with China. The Japan project, which started in 1973, was notably different from the Soviet initiative, as UNA was dealing with a US ally rather than an adversary. Officially called the Parallel Studies Program with the Asia Pacific Association of Japan (APAJ), it highlighted common political and security issues, including the rise of China, as well as more specific matters on strategic relationships in the region, such as the implications for East Asia of global and regional arms control, regional flashpoints, and the course of Sino-American and Sino-Japanese relations. A 1975 report outlined the goals of the UNA Parallel Studies and APAJ Program as an effort to "seek improved methods of maintaining peace and stability in Asia and to identify ways in which the UN and other international organizations might contribute to Japanese and American security needs in today's changing global environment."[4]

When UNA began its Japan program, Richard Snyder, who had been a State Department specialist in Japanese and Russian affairs, chaired the UNA-USA sessions with Sadako Ogata, a future UN high commissioner for refugees, for UNA-Japan. (UNA-Japan was brought into the process by APAJ.) Two conferences were held in 1973—one in Tokyo and another in Washington. Cyrus Vance, then chair of UNA's Policy Studies Committee, chaired the US delegation. The program's first report, "Framework for an Alliance: Options for US-Japanese Security Relations," was published in August 1975. Focusing primarily on security, the report concluded that the Mutual Cooperation and Security Treaty "should be maintained in its present form" and that the two governments "should negotiate a minimum stable structure of US bases and facilities in Japan." Later studies dealt with economic issues (especially in light of the 1970s energy crisis) and Japan's expanding role in multilateral institutions.[5]

Once the Gorbachev era in the Soviet Union began, the dialogue in the Japan program adapted to explore how Soviet "new thinking" might impact the region. A 1989 paper entitled "Gorbachev's Asian Policy: Refashioning American and Japanese Policy Towards the Soviet Union" was the result of a series of panels chaired by McGeorge Bundy, President Kennedy's national security adviser, and Yoshio Okawara, Japan's ambassador to the United States. The paper took a cautious approach to Gorbachev's policy pronouncements on the Asia Pacific region. Warning that perestroika might still fail, the panel concluded that the "uncertainty may argue against an overly enthusiastic response to Gorbachev's initiative in Asia, but it is no excuse for inaction."[6] The paper was followed by a series of expert panels chaired by Joseph Nye, Harvard University political scientist, and Ogata on how to enhance the UN and regional security organizations.

Engagement on Chinese issues started in 1979 as a UNA policy program without direct Chinese involvement. One of the more substantive reports on China issued by UNA was a 1979 study called "Beyond Normalization," written by the UNA/USA National Policy Panel to Study US-China Relations. The report's recommendations reflect the tense relationship between the two powers at the time on issues that included Taiwan, Korea, US arms sales to the region, business opportunities, and the development of greater scientific and cultural exchanges. The panel recommended "an equilibrium strategy" that would recognize both Chinese and Soviet security concerns and would "resist Chinese pressure to adopt a strategy based on a united front against the Soviet Union."[7]

By 1984, as China became more politically and economically engaged, UNA began a parallel program with Chinese partners. William A. Hewitt, chairman of Deere & Company, and Brent Scowcroft led the China Parallel Policy Program, which lasted ten years. According to Luck, the idea for the program came from the Chinese. He was approached by a military attaché from the Chinese mission to the UN in 1979, who said, "You have this very interesting project with the Soviet Union. Why don't you start a similar project with China?" UNA-USA saw this as an opportunity to develop better understanding of the policies and intentions of each side. Many on the Chinese side of the discussions came from the Beijing Institute for International Strategic Studies (the think tank of the People's Liberation Army, now called the China Institute for International Strategic Studies) or the Shanghai Institutes for International Studies. Two generals—Xu Xin and Xu Yimin—represented the Beijing Institute.

The China program was a classic example of the value of UNA's ability to draw on a bipartisan roster of participants. Scowcroft was well known to the Chinese, Luck said, because he had helped lay the groundwork for President Nixon's visit to China. He accompanied Secretary of State Henry Kissinger on the visit that preceded Nixon's. "In fact," Luck said, "present at one of our meetings over in China was the vice minister of Foreign Affairs, who had been one of the two people who greeted Brent when he first got off the plane in setting up the Kissinger meetings. . . . It was a very warm, emotional sort of thing. Brent really valued being part of that program."

Gati said the Chinese partners "seemed not to have given much thought to certain subjects of global engagement, such as their possible role in peacekeeping" or other ways to participate in UN activities. "On many subjects, they really didn't want to—or couldn't yet—respond. They were not the kind of people who will give you their opinion until they really had thought it out." Consequently, "you're not going to have a Eureka! moment, where the Chinese announce something. But I think they gradually became more amenable to some of the UN reform ideas, maybe also on proliferation. They wanted to talk not about bilateral arms control, as we did with the [Soviets], but about multilateral arms control and what their role might be in such discussions."

As the programs matured, quadrilateral programs involving the United States, USSR, China, and Japan were held in 1990 in San Francisco, in 1991 in Vladivostok, and in 1992 in Beijing. That program was chaired by Frank Carlucci, a former secretary of defense. Gati called the quadrilateral programs "a unique opening," since the Russians and Chinese had never met in this format and the four had never met before to discuss Asian security. They agreed to do so because they trusted that UNA-USA "would not blindside them." Luck pointed out that for those few years, "we had three programs going, and it was a very dynamic combination."

Gati said, "What we had been doing for twenty years all of a sudden made this huge leap" from bilateral discussions to the global stage. "The programs built up expertise and trust, and each side benefited from the discussion as they built up a track record of breaking new ground. In addition, participants went to hold senior positions in their security establishments." Despite the demonstrable contributions the programs made to international relations, however, questions were raised within UNA as to how these dialogues advanced UNA's core mission to promote a stronger United Nations. These questions continued as UNA became involved in more multilateral projects, as detailed in the next chapters.

Notes

1. "Elmore Jackson, 78, Quaker Mideast Envoy," *The New York Times*, January 19, 1989.

2. Seton Hall University, The Msgr. William Noé Field Archives and Special Collections Center, South Orange, NJ, box 21.

3. Ibid., box 2012.0039.

4. *Framework for an Alliance: Options for US-Japanese Security Relations*, a Report by Task Forces of the United Nations Association of the USA and the Asia Pacific Association of Japan, August 1975.

5. Ibid.

6. Ibid.

7. Ibid.

9

Post–Cold War Openings: The UNA-USA Multilateral Studies, 1984–2000

As the Parallel Studies Program proceeded in its calibrated, influential manner, UNA was also publicly engaged in matters of international security by researching and publishing an increasing number of studies and reports that delved into such topics as nuclear disarmament, hunger, the environment, and enhancing UNA's policy role. This last subject included recommendations on election monitoring, which the UN adopted by adding such work to its own political and peacekeeping tools. These reports enhanced UNA's regular array of publications for members and the general public on foreign affairs and the UN itself, detailed in Chapter 17.

The Multilateral Project (and its successor, the Global Policy Project) drew on UNA's two greatest strengths: its unparalleled access to both the UN Secretariat and missions of the member states, which trusted UNA as a player in US foreign-policy debates; and its nationwide membership, which could take the debate on international issues to local communities around the country. An international policy issue, identified by UNA program staff in consultation with the UNA chapter network, would be researched and presented in a briefing book. The briefing would set out policy quandaries and alternative ideas to deal with the issues, ranging in approach from "realist" and unilateralist to internationalist and multilateraist. UNA chapters would then organize study groups and public forums in their communities to debate the issues and would write reports addressing the policy questions posed by the briefing book. The project's director would assemble a national advisory group of recognized policy experts and political personalities who would advise on ways to sharpen the recommendations from the chapter-led discussion groups. The final report would strive for policy sophistication, while also reflecting the preponderance of views of the nationwide participants. As an example, in 1984, the briefing book titled

On the Front Lines: The United Nations' Role in Preventing and Containing Conflict was distributed to UNA chapters. The book and the UNA chapters' comments were incorporated into the final report, *Keeping the Peace in Troubled Times: Recommendations for Multilateral Action,* published in 1985.

The final report would then be presented at public events in both New York and Washington, with private meetings at high levels both at the United Nations and in the US government, often with members of Congress controlling relevant committees. The leaders of local study groups would be asked to follow up with their own contacts to their members of Congress on specific recommendations where Congress could make a difference. On issues ranging from peacekeeping to the environment to reforming the UN, the series of reports demonstrated an ability to make recommendations that were both ahead of the curve and achievable.

These multilateral study projects had historic precedents in the work of the Commission to Study the Organization of Peace (CSOP). As detailed in Chapter 1, CSOP was founded in 1938 to provide the academic and political grounding for the arguments that the League of Nations Association made in favor of an international organization—a "think tank," in current parlance. Clark Eichelberger and James T. Shotwell were the driving force behind the creation of the commission.

Shotwell joined the faculty of Columbia University in 1905. He was a member of the committee appointed by President Wilson to work out the principles of the peace agreement after World War I. Shotwell was a US delegate to the 1919 Paris Peace Conference, the author of the charter of the International Labour Organization, and a contributor to *Encyclopedia Britannica*. In 1917, he became the director of research at the Carnegie Endowment for International Peace, where he held a variety of posts over the next three decades, including president in 1947. Shotwell was the president of the League of Nations Association from 1935 to 1939; he resigned after he and Eichelberger founded CSOP. Shotwell became CSOP's first president and served until 1947. When the State Department set up its advisory committee on postwar planning in 1941, Shotwell was named to the political subcommittee, which was largely responsible for the working paper that formed the basis of the UN Charter. After the war, he left CSOP but remained involved at Carnegie, focusing mostly on his writing. In 1962, Shotwell and his wife, Margaret, retired to their country home in Woodstock, New York, a house they had built in 1910. Margaret, his wife of sixty-four years, died in July 1965. Shotwell died six days later.

Harold Josephson, a biographer of Shotwell, wrote, "Although Shotwell participated in the debate over America's wartime policy, he focused most of his attention on the nature of the peace which had to follow. As early as the summer of 1939, he and Eichelberger made plans to organize a Commission of Enquiry" to study an international organization. That commission became CSOP.[1]

In the commission's first publication in 1939, Shotwell, who had become the chair of CSOP, wrote,

> The supreme problem of our time is how, without entering upon a fruitless war of ideas, we can organize peace upon a basis of freedom and justice. It is a problem which cannot be solved by wishful thinking or by merely repeating, as in a creed, formulas of democracy. It calls for the critical reexamination of the lessons of history and a clear-sighted view of the real interests and the actual possibilities of our cooperation with other nations in building the world of tomorrow.

That document outlined the series of studies CSOP intended to produce to support the government's war aims and the structure of the postwar peace.[2]

The commission members came largely from academia—Barnard, New York University, Princeton, University of North Carolina, University of California, Columbia, the New School for Social Research, Smith College, University of Michigan, the Fletcher School of Law and Diplomacy at Tufts, and Oberlin College—but also included the Rotary, the League of Women Voters, the International Chamber of Commerce, the American Federation of Labor, the Rockefeller Foundation, bankers, economists, and church leaders. Some early members became government and academic luminaries, such as Secretary of State John Foster Dulles; his brother and future CIA director, Allen Dulles; Virginia Gildersleeve of Barnard; Ursula Hubbard of the Carnegie Endowment; and William Allen White. Eichelberger was the director.

CSOP's first report was published the next year, on November 12, 1940—Armistice Day. Simply called *Preliminary Report,* it said CSOP's goal was to ensure that the United States "shall not again fail to play its part in any opportunity which may be offered to organize a durable peace." The next reports came in rapid succession, all meant to make the political and technical arguments in favor of an international organization. The second report (February 1942), *The Transition Period,* coming two months after the Pearl Harbor attack, stressed the urgency of making plans for postwar reconstruction before the war ended. The third report (February 1943), *The United Nations and the*

Organization of Peace, called on the Allies to begin, as soon as possible, to plan for a peace settlement. The fourth report (November 1943), *Fundamentals of the International Organization,* provided "a precise blueprint for a new world organization," including "an assembly open to all nations, an executive council composed of a limited number of nations, . . . and a secretariat to study international problems and provide information and secretarial services."[3]

While the reports provided the core of CSOP's work, the commission also produced less academic and more timely material, including radio broadcasts on CBS in 1940 called *Which Way to Lasting Peace?* and broadcasts on NBC in 1943 called *For This We Fight.* This material consisted of statements analyzing the news of the day, such as the Atlantic Charter and the creation of a Youth Education Committee.[4]

After the war and the establishment of the UN, the reports stopped being massive compilations on multiple issues and, instead, focused on one theme. For example, the fifth report (June 1947) was titled, *Security and Disarmament Under the United Nations,* and the eighth (June 1953) concentrated on regional arrangements. The fourteenth report (January 1962) was called *The UN Secretary-General: His Role in World Politics.* The twenty-fifth report, issued in 1975, was titled *Protecting Human Rights.* The twenty-ninth, and final, report in 1980 was called *Regional Promotion and Protection of Human Rights in Africa.*[5] A thirtieth report was planned but never written. Because of dwindling finances, the executive committee voted to dissolve CSOP in May 1981. All remaining assets were transferred to the Clark Eichelberger Memorial Fund. In its final days, CSOP operated out of Estelle Linzer's apartment.[6]

Echoes of CSOP's goal of presenting realistic, comprehensive programs can be found fifty years later in the philosophy for the UNA Multilateral Project reports. For example, Shotwell wrote in 1939 that CSOP's vision was to "clarify and enlighten public opinion, to explain to the world in which we were living and to propose the way for building the structure of peace."[7] In the 1988 study *Pulling Together: A Program for America in the United Nations,* Elliot Richardson, the chair of the UNA, wrote, "It was essential that the issues raised by the panel should enter the mainstream of public debate in the United States."

1980s

The Multilateral Project began in 1984 as a way to stimulate policymakers and the public to consider multilateralism as a way to manage international affairs peacefully. The project's agenda was driven with significant input by UNA chapters. The first executive director of the Multilateral Project was Fred Eckhard (who eventually became Secretary-General Kofi Annan's spokesperson); the directors were Edward and Ann Florini (Ann went on to work at the Carnegie Endowment for International Peace, among other institutions). The advisory board was chaired by Matthew Nimetz, a lawyer and future special envoy for both the US government and the UN. Leading figures included Richard Gardner (a professor of international law at Columbia and a future ambassador), Jessica Tuchman Mathews (a vice president of the World Resources Institute and future president of the Carnegie Endowment), Charles William Maynes (editor of *Foreign Policy* magazine), and William vanden Heuvel (future ambassador and chair of the UNA Board of Governors).

The Florinis began the project by engaging UNA membership and organizing consultations, said Jeffrey Laurenti, who became the executive director in 1987. "They were asked to try to bring in as wide a range of people in their communities as possible," Laurenti added in an interview for the book. "So that the chapters that did it well and would reach into the political class would reach out to other organizations that might have some interest in the subject." The next step was for the national office to work with policy experts. "We would assemble a fair number of people who might not have had any real relation with the UN at all but knew of that particular subject area and could give a sharper edge to ideas that had gotten support from chapters."

The first Multilateral Project studies dealt with nuclear weapons—an issue that engaged the chapters and the UN for the entire existence of the world body. *Nuclear Proliferation: A Citizen's Guide to Policy Choices,* by Ann Florini, detailed for participating local study groups the numerous nuclear proliferation issues facing the world at the time, including India's nuclear bomb; the Israeli destruction of the nuclear reactor at Osirak, Iraq, under construction; and the spread of weapons-grade nuclear materials and the skills needed to use them. The final report of the study, *Nuclear Proliferation: Toward Global Restraint,* was issued the next year and proposed policy options on the subject ahead of the 1985 Review Conference for the Nonproliferation Treaty. The report's recommendations included strengthening the UN's International Atomic Energy Agency's watchdog abilities, resuming talks for a comprehensive nuclear test ban treaty, creating nuclear-weapons-free zones, and developing a full US nonproliferation policy covering weapons-grade nuclear materials and export controls.

International peace and security was the theme for the second study. The 1984 *On the Front Lines: The United Nations' Role in Preventing and Containing Conflict,* by Ann Florini and Nina Tannenwald, a UNA consultant who became a political science professor at Brown University, was the briefing book for the nationwide community-level debate organized by UNA chapters. Their submissions were distilled in the final report, *Keeping the Peace in Troubled Times: Recommendations for Multilateral Action,* published in 1985. Written when UN peacekeeping was largely confined to policing cease-fires, *On the Front Lines* suggested greater engagement by UN bodies overall: the Security Council should do more follow-through on the implementation of its resolutions; the General Assembly should streamline its agenda to deal with a few items "on which debate would be most useful and about which informal pre-Assembly consultations might produce compromise resolutions or consensus"; and the Secretary-General's "capacity to preempt and manage international violence" should be enhanced. Building on the concepts found in *On the Front Lines, Keeping the Peace* included recommendations for strengthening peacekeeping, regional organizations, and the rule of law. A memo from Florini after a meeting with Secretary-General Javier Pérez de Cuéllar said that he was "enthusiastic" about the report, and he had "made it clear that he intends to implement those recommendations that he can."

The third study was *The Next Giant Leap in Space: An Agenda for International Cooperation* in 1986, a topic that also engaged the UN for at least a decade, given the race to space by the United States and the Soviet Union. UNA recommended that the superpowers renew their bilateral agreements on space and make greater use of multilateral forums—including the UN Committee on the Peaceful Uses of Outer Space—to develop "international space law," to limit space-based weaponry, and, in a particularly forward-looking proposal, to use space technology "to adopt an extensive program of research into global [climate] change." That was followed by *A Time to Plant: International Cooperation to End Hunger* (1987), which explored ways to reduce malnutrition and hunger.

A break with the single-issue studies came in 1988, with the publication of the briefing book *A Stronger Hand: Shaping an American Agenda for a More Effective United Nations,* written by Laurenti. He wrote it not only with an eye to the change in US administrations (George H. W. Bush became president in 1989), but also at the cusp of the changes ushered in with the end of the Cold War. The world— especially the major powers—was looking at the UN in a new light, considering ways it could work on global issues that would have been unthinkable during the Cold War paralysis, which had left most international problems off the agenda except for some African hot spots and the Middle East. *A Stronger Hand* looked at eight issues that UNA viewed as potential openings for greater UN involvement: arms control beyond the superpower monopoly, Afghanistan, the World Court, human rights, drug abuse, health, environment, and labor. Drawing on the landmark 1987 report of an international task force that UNA had assembled on UN management and decisionmaking, the briefing book also discussed proposals to revise the system-wide authority and structure of the UN's Economic and Social Council.

"This was a particularly complicated project," Laurenti said. The logic was "let's look at the whole gambit of UN issues that would have a major constituency." Therefore, according to Laurenti, "it was much thinner in terms of how it looked in each issue area than the typical GPP [Global Policy Project] would be because you are trying to do a broad waterfront with large consultations." UNA-USA saw opportunities at this time for the UN because 1988 was a presidential election year with no incumbent running; thus, "you could inform a new administration without criticizing an old one," Laurenti said. "You could view [George H. W.] Bush as a continuation of the same, but he turned out very much not to be," Laurenti said, referring to the transition from the Reagan era to the Bush era. He added that the recommendations in *Pulling Together* that were the most perceptive were those on Afghanistan, which included recommendations of UN monitoring of frontiers and supporting government reconstruction.

Another issue that came out of the membership consultations was the idea of UN election monitoring. "We would have maybe a dozen chapters saying, 'Yes, we think there should be a UN Elections unit.' So that was requisite blessing, or the imprimatur, to allow us to include in the report," Laurenti said. "Of course, it was a staff judgment, What of all the many recommendations in the report are the ones that might have the strongest legs? And that clearly was one of them." The report that was developed from *A Stronger Hand* was called *Pulling Together: A Program for America in the United Nations*, published in 1988.

The recommendation for a UN elections body was viewed, Laurenti said, "as ahead of its time, at the end of 1988 when it was made, but the sudden collapse of the Communist regimes in Eastern Europe in the fall of 1989 suddenly made it topical." He said that he and Ed Luck presented *Pulling Together* to Tom Pickering when he was the US permanent representative to the UN—"that was a multifaceted project, and he [Pickering] went through the items that he thought would be saleable within the administration and those that would be harder to sell. And this is when he said he thought that election monitoring could be sold. Indeed, the elder Bush presented a proposal for a UN elections commissioner's unit. This would become the UN elections office."

In the preface to *Pulling Together,* Elliot Richardson, the UNA chair, wrote that the report "comes at a critical time, when a new realism in both the Third World and the Soviet Union have created new opportunities for international cooperation at the UN—but also when America's own relations with the UN are in disarray." In addition to election monitoring and Afghanistan, the report contained recommendations for controlling weapons of mass destruction, addressing AIDS, and improving UN decisionmaking and management.[8]

Richardson chaired the executive council of the Multilateral Project, and Nimetz chaired the advisory group for these five studies. The James S. McDonnell Foundation and the Armand Hammer Foundation provided the bulk of the funding for the first briefing books; McDonnell and the Ford Foundation funded *Pulling Together.* After *Pulling Together,* the Multilateral Project was renamed the Global Policy Project because, Laurenti said, "Nobody liked the word 'multilateral,' least of all in chapterland."

Another significant contribution by UNA during this period was a project separate from the Global Policy Project. UNA's United Nations Management and Decision-Making Project (1985–1987) was designed to study means to strengthen "the effectiveness of the United Nations and its immediate affiliated organs by offering constructive criticism regarding the management, governance and role of the world organization." A series of panel meetings and a preliminary report culminated in *A Successor Vision: The United Nations of Tomorrow*, a book edited by Peter J. Fromuth, the project's staff director and former staff member of Senator Ted Stevens (R-Alaska). The book concluded that the UN's role was "determined by two factors, each pulling in opposite directions"—namely, that the challenges facing governments are international, while "the authority for dealing with these problems remain[s] vested in nation states." The project examines ways in which the UN could be reformed to deal with this basic contradiction. Richardson chaired the project, which was funded by the Ford Foundation.

Transitioning to a New World Order

The early 1990s saw a proliferation of UNA studies meant to influence the post–Cold War debate over the UN's role. The decade's early years were defined by the demise of the Cold War—however arbitrarily that date was defined—and the launching of the 1991 Gulf War, when Iraq invaded Kuwait. Part of UNA's contribution to this debate was a series of "occasional papers," written by specialists on topics high on the UN agenda—in particular, the Middle East, peacekeeping, and the environment.

The Gulf War was the first major test of the UN after the Cold War thaw. The Security Council, freed from that division, acted swiftly after Iraq's invasion of Kuwait in August 2, 1990. The council's first resolution (Resolution 660) on the matter was passed the same day, condemning the invasion and calling on Iraq to withdraw unconditionally. Four days later, Resolution 661 imposed trade and financial sanctions on Iraq. In all, a record number of twelve resolutions, all dealing with the crisis in such a short period, were adopted by the time the United States and its allies began their aerial bombardment of Iraq on January 16, 1991, followed by the land invasion of Kuwait on February 25. On April 3, the Security Council adopted Resolution 687, setting unprecedentedly detailed terms for an unconditional cease-fire; Iraq accepted that resolution on April 6, officially ending the hostilities. While rapid and effective response helped shorten the war, the council's uncharacteristic swiftness was also based on unique issues—in particular, Saddam Hussein's flouting of international law in this invasion, starting the earlier Iran-Iraq War, and his use of chemical weapons in that conflict.

UNA's first occasional paper was "The United Nations in the Gulf Crisis and Options for US Policy" (October 1990), written by David J. Scheffer and financed by the Ploughshares Fund. Scheffer, an American international lawyer, was a senior associate at the Carnegie Endowment for International Peace at the time; he later served as the US ambassador to the negotiations for the founding of the International Criminal Court and then as a senior vice president of UNA (see Chapter 14). The paper analyzed Security Council reactions and potential further actions, framed in the context of the UN Charter, particularly regarding collective self-defense, including the potential for military action. The paper also foreshadowed the weapons inspections regime and the establishment of the ICC. Excerpts from the report were read into the *Congressional Record* by Senator Terry Sanford (D–North Carolina).

UNA followed up on Scheffer's paper in February 1991 with "Roles for the United Nations After the Gulf War." Written while the war was going on, the paper said, "Just as the United Nations played a crucial role in consolidating international resolve against Iraqi aggression, so will the UN be deeply involved in international efforts after the war." The paper (no author or editor was credited) recommended that "the US should take the lead once again to engage the UN in developing a strong international response to these postwar challenges." It outlined fields where the UN could take new responsibilities in the Middle East, such as a new peace-keeping operation in parts of Iraq and Kuwait; deploying a UN-flagged naval force in the Persian Gulf; monitoring sanctions, refugee and humanitarian assistance, and arms control (expansion of UN abilities to monitor weapons of mass destruction and missiles in the Middle East); coordinating financial compensation by Iraq; prosecuting alleged Iraqi violations of the laws of war; and convening a peace conference. The paper noted, "The long-standing but controversial proposal for a Middle East peace conference to resolve the conflicts between Israelis, Palestinians and Arabs may assume more urgency following the Gulf War."

The paper also suggested a permanent UN enforcement capability, whereby states would agree to provide "on call" forces for Security Council–sanctioned action—what became known as standby forces or rapid-reaction forces—arguing that if such an arrangement had existed, "the Security Council might have been in a position in early August 1990 to deploy troops rapidly to Kuwait to forestall a complete takeover of that country."[9]

After the Gulf War, UNA-USA took a long view toward proposing ways to ensure a stable peace in the region with a December 1992 Occasional Paper, "Curbing the Middle East Arms Race: Policy Options for the United States and the United Nations," compiled by Edmund T. Piasecki, a staff member. It drew on the facts of "increasing pressures" to supply sophisticated conventional weapons to the region, coupled with "the increased interest in the UN's potential for facilitating and implementing regional arms limitation agreements that has been evidenced since the Gulf War." While primary responsibility lies with the states of the region, the paper argued that the UN "can play a crucial secondary role" in implementing any agreements through strong verification mechanisms and "personnel to enforce the compromises." Ploughshares Fund also financed the report.

The 1992 Global Policy Project sought to apply the lessons from the Gulf War to the need for peacekeeping and enforcement to the broader international community. A briefing book, *Partners for Peace,* and a final report, *The Common Defense* (both funded by the Ford Foundation), were written around the concept that "suddenly, it seemed possible to realize the vision of collective security," as John Whitehead, the chair of UNA, wrote in *The Common Defense*. Peacekeeping, which was expanding the number of missions and their mandates, was a focus of the study, but the interlocking issues of peace enforcing, peace building, initiatives to integrate international law, economic development, and arms control and disarmament were all woven into a comprehensive vision. "The UN framework for collective security founded on law once again becomes a viable one," Laurenti wrote. The chair of the advisory committee for this report was James Woolsey Jr., who would soon be appointed the director of the CIA.

The January 31, 1992, Security Council summit was another remarkable event signaling an interest in promoting security through the UN. Designed to be an obvious sign that the council was putting the Cold War behind it and working toward consensus on international issues, the summit requested UN Secretary-General Boutros Boutros-Ghali to produce a report on strengthening preventive diplomacy, peacekeeping, and peacemaking—a mandate that became *An Agenda for Peace*. In response to the summit and Boutros-Ghali's public call for comments, UNA published "Directions and Dilemmas in Collective Security" (January 1992) by Laurenti, and "A UN Revitalized" (May 1992), compiled by Russell M. Dallen Jr., a senior fellow in Policy Studies at UNA-USA; both publications focused on the summit.

"Never before has so much been expected of the UN, nor its potential seemed so great," Dallen wrote. Laurenti argued that as states "find

A meeting held at UNA-USA's Arthur Ross Conference Center in 1992. From left: Jeffrey Laurenti, UNA executive director of multilateral studies; Richard Thornburgh, UN undersecretary-general for management; Toby Trister Gati, UNA executive vice president; and UNA president Edward C. Luck.
(Photo courtesy of Toby Trister Gati.)

a growing convergence of security interests, it will become possible to transfer a widening range of security functions to the international level." The UNA-USA papers presented an ambitious agenda of their own, dealing with a range of issues that included giving regional powers "semi-permanent" seats (meaning a multiple-year term) on the Security Council, providing substantive responsibilities to the Military Staff Committee (a group of the big five of the Security Council that was created by the charter but rarely used), explicitly linking (where possible) peacekeeping operations to negotiations to resolve the dispute, establishing a "fully capitalized standby peacekeeping reserve fund," establishing a rapid-deployment force, clarifying the Secretary-General's role in preventing and managing conflicts, supporting regional efforts at conflict resolution, strengthening treaties against weapons proliferation, and creating an International Criminal Court.[10]

Environment and Development: UNA Occasional Papers

Two of the nine occasional papers, plus a multilateral study conducted by UNA and the Sierra Club, dealt with environmental matters. Ahead of the UN Conference on Environment and Development (UNCED), which was held in Rio de Janeiro in June 1992, the studies called for greater attention to environmental problems and how international cooperation through new institutional structures could address those problems. The conference, known as the Earth Summit, produced an action plan called Agenda 21, which called for voluntary actions from the local level to the global level to contend with environmental matters and promote sustainable development. (Agenda 21 has since morphed into a right-wing talking point in the United States—that is, the UN is trying to rob the United States of its sovereignty over its use of its land, water, and air.) One recommendation in Agenda 21 was to create a Commission for Sustainable Development (CSD) that could "enhance international cooperation and rationalize the intergovernmental decision-making capacity for the integration of environmental and development issues."[11]

Two UNA occasional papers—one before and one after the Rio meeting—promoted the notion of linking the causes of environmental protection to sustainable development and of creating legal frameworks to promote international solutions. "Making UNCED Work: Building the Legal and Institutional Framework for Sustainable Development at the Earth Summit and Beyond" (March 1992) was written by Catherine Tinker, a senior policy analyst at UNA-USA who later participated in the Dialogue Among Civilizations (see Chapter 10). The paper asserted that enhancing international cooperation could be achieved by better use of existing laws (the International Law Commission and treaties that included the 1985 Vienna Convention for the Protection of the Ozone Layer) and making institutional changes to standing UN bodies and agencies, such as ECOSOC and the UN Environment Programme.

"Institutionalizing the Earth Summit: The United Nations Commission on Sustainable Development" (October 1992) was written by Kathryn G. Sessions, a policy analyst in UNA's Washington office. "One striking feature of the UNCED process was its ability to spur an evolution in understanding of environmental and development issues," wrote Sessions, who represented UNA at the summit. Although negotiators and experts came to Rio focused on their specific concerns, "as the negotiations proceeded, . . . there developed a new appreciation not only of the urgency of the problems in each area but also of their interdependence," she wrote. If the summit meeting did represent such a turning point, she noted, then "there is room for optimism about the future of the CSD." The UN General Assembly created the Commission on Sustainable Development in December 1992.

The Multilateral Project in 1990 started with the briefing book, *One Earth, Many Nations: The International System and Problems of the Global Environment*, by Jeffrey Laurenti and Francesca Lyman, a Seattle journalist specializing in environmental issues. This was the first collaboration between UNA-USA and the Sierra Club. With a foreword by Senator Al Gore (D–Tennessee) and Senator John H. Chafee (R–Rhode Island), the book explored issues entering the UN and public lexicon that are now daily concerns, such as global warming, overfishing, and sustainable development. The final publication, released later that year, was called *Uniting Nations for the Earth: An Environmental Agenda for the World Community*. The project was funded by the McDonnell Foundation and the Florence and John Schumann Foundation. Introduced on the twentieth anniversary of Earth Day and ahead of the 1992 Earth Summit in Rio, the report was meant to stimulate debate among the US public on "what should be the direction of global environmental policy." The paper, written under Laurenti's direction, recommended immediate negotiations on a "global warming pact" in time for the 1992 conference and commitments to cut emissions contributing to global warming and ozone depletion. It also called on the United States to strengthen the federal Clean Air Act and to ratify the Law of the Sea Convention. While the United States has yet to follow through on either of these recommendations, the analyses in these reports remain part of the international debate over climate change.

Later Global Policy Studies

UNA-USA was determined that the United Nations also be viewed and judged by the US people and policymakers for its work beyond political and military security. The Global Policy Project presented numerous other subjects for public debate and policy formulation in the 1990s, many of which—notably in the human rights and environmental fields—were pioneering works that remain relevant today.

• *The Global Connection: New International Approaches for Controlling Narcotic Drugs* was a report of the Global Policy Project (1991), chaired by Richard S. Williamson, an assistant secretary of state under Reagan (see Box 9.1), with Laurenti as project director.

• "A Consensus for Change: Transforming the United Nations' Role in Global Economics" was written in 1994 by Shareen Hertel, a consultant who later became a professor of political science at the University of Connecticut. It was funded by the Ford Foundation and the John D. and Catherine T. MacArthur Foundation. The paper, said Boutros-Ghali in *An Agenda for Peace* (issued in 1992), "articulated a bold vision of security," in that "staving off military conflict" required not only military means but also "promoting the political, social and economic conditions necessary to sustain peace."

• *Inalienable Rights, Fundamental Freedoms: A UN Agenda for Advancing Human Rights in the World Community* was published in 1996 by a national advisory committee led by former Oregon legislator Les AuCoin. John Whitehead, the chair of UNA, wrote that the report "makes a major contribution in locating international human rights policy in a context of America's own remarkable social history of democratic enlargement." The paper made many recommendations for strengthening existing human rights instruments and for enacting new ones, including the much-anticipated International Criminal Court. According to Laurenti, the most novel recommendation—"the one that would reverberate for a dozen years in the national and international debate"—was the call for a UN Democracy Caucus, which became part of the rationale for the Community of Democracies that Madeleine Albright and Mort Halperin created late in the decade. The briefing book *Promises to Keep: Securing Human Rights in a Changing World,* written in 1992 by Hertel, explored how the evolving definitions and understandings of human rights could take a more comprehensive approach in UN work.

• The 1997 *Crisis and Reform in United Nations Financing* was a reaction to the Republican Congress's methodical refusal to release funds for UN dues. The report made the case for the United States' paying its assessed contributions without conditions, and called on the GA and the US Congress "to compromise on the peacekeeping formula." It followed on from the 1996 briefing book called *National Taxpayers, International Organizations*. The advisory committee cochairs were

---

Box 9.1 Richard Williamson

Richard Williamson was a native of Chicago and a leader of the Illinois Republican Party. He served in the administrations of Ronald Reagan, George H. W. Bush, and George W. Bush. Under the elder Bush, Williamson was the assistant secretary of state for international organization affairs. He served as ambassador to the United Nations Commission on Human Rights and as the special envoy to Sudan under the younger Bush, working to end the genocide in Darfur. Williamson also served as a senior policy adviser for the presidential campaigns of John McCain and Mitt Romney. One of his last endeavors was coauthoring a report with former secretary of state Madeleine Albright, a Democrat, on the prevention of genocide. The report was published in July 2013. He died in December of that year.

When he was not in government, he devoted time to UNA as a member of the board and as a participant in such projects as the dialogues with Russia, China, and Iran and the Transitional Justice Global Initiative. Steve Dimoff said one of Williamson's most important contributions to UNA was his chairing (along with Charles Maynes, another former assistant secretary of state for international organization affairs) a multilateral policy project on US financing of the UN. The 1995 report was called *National Taxpayers, International Organizations: Sharing the Burden of Financing the United Nations*. Dimoff said it was "important to show to Washington that someone cared about these issues."

In an interview for this book, Suzanne DiMaggio, who was the vice president of Policy Programs at UNA-USA from 1998 to 2007 and is now a director at New America Enterprise, called Williamson "a very unique person . . . one of these rare Republicans that had an internationalist perspective and was a big supporter of UN." Such a person "was hard to find then and certainly hard to find now." He had good contacts with congressional Republicans and "played a very constructive role in getting our work to the [Republican] leadership," she said. Dimoff agreed that Williamson played a special role in reaching out to fellow Republicans, saying, "He was taken seriously." Williamson, Dimoff added, "was one of the few people who actually sought positions at the UN; he was very comfortable with that."

—*J. W.*

William Maynes (a Democrat) and Richard Williamson (a Republican), and Laurenti wrote the reports.

• *Options and Opportunities: Arms Control and Disarmament for the 21st Century* was a briefing book by Laurenti and Jonathan Dean, a former US ambassador to arms-control negotiations and president of the UNA Washington chapter from 1997 to 2001. Published in 1997, it explored how the international community could further promote post–Cold War reductions in nuclear, chemical, biological, and conventional arms. This study did not result in a final report, Laurenti said, because UNA was "unable to secure a nationally recognizable figure to chair a national advisory committee, despite eight months of sending invitations from John Whitehead to one potential chair after another." Laurenti said this was an indication that it was becoming increasingly difficult to recruit national Republican political figures for UN-related projects.

• *Workers' Rights in the Global Economy* was a briefing book by Elizabeth McKeon, written in 1999. It examined workers' rights amid increasing globalization, job loss, and deindustrialization. Topics also included the role of unions, when it is appropriate for governments to intervene in markets, restrictions on management, the role and relevance of the International Labor Organization, NGOs' highlighting abuse of workers, international enforcement of laws against forced labor, child labor, and the North American Free Trade Agreement and other trade agreements.

According to Laurenti, the Global Policy Project lost its core energy by the late 1990s: "There came to be a sense of overload, or exhaustion for a lot of chapters." Participation, he added, began dropping in the late 1990s, which may have been "a function of just chapters themselves being worn out." The last two briefing books—*Options and Opportunities: Arms Control and Disarmament for the 21st Century* and *Workers' Rights in the Global Economy*—were written, but neither resulted in a final report. Moreover, foundations were losing interest in the format, and funding for the study projects dried up. "Bill Luers arrived as president of UNA, he looked at the realities of falling participation and funding, and he drew the obvious conclusions," Laurenti said.

More Groundbreaking UNA Reports

UNA documents from this period touched on other topics high on the international agenda:

• *Strengthening UN Fiscal Oversight Machinery: The Debate on an Inspector-General*, written by Laurenti in 1994, was prompted by a report from the UN Board of Auditors in 1992 that focused on the US proposal for creating an Office of Inspector-General at the UN to strengthen accountability and oversight. "There are reasons for skepticism that an inspector-general is a panacea for management and financial control issues," Laurenti wrote. While stressing the importance of independence for the post, "The Congress has come to identify withholding US contributions to United Nations activities as its strongest leverage in speeding action through the slow, consensus-based political process in New York." In the interview for this book, Laurenti said this was "an issue on which UNA had an outsized impact, in effect mediating between Washington's demands and UN sensibilities and resulting in a significant institutional reform that has UNA fingerprints all over it." The result was the UN's Office of Internal Oversight Services.

• *Nonproliferation and the UN Security Council: Prevention, Compliance and Enforcement* emanated from an October 1995 event sponsored by UNA-USA and chaired by McGeorge Bundy, a scholar-in-residence at the Carnegie Corporation of New York and former special assistant for national security under Presidents Kennedy and Johnson. The threat of the proliferation of weapons of mass destruction "has emerged as one of the most urgent threats" to peace and security, wrote Ed Luck, UNA's president emeritus at the time. He added, "At the apex of the nonproliferation regime stands the UN Security Council, the only body with both the authority and responsibility to take the political, economic and military measures necessary to preserve international peace and security." The conference, made up primarily of international specialists and government representatives, dealt with conflicting aims of encouraging a more engaged council and of antagonism against a more activist council.

• *Towards Tomorrow's United Nations: A Sino-American Study on UN Reform*, from August 1996, was a joint effort by the Shanghai Institute for International Studies and UNA-USA. The project's goal was to explore fields of UN reform on which the two groups could agree, on the basis that "no serious reform of the United Nations would be possible without some degree of agreement, if not cooperation, between the US and China." Calling the initiative "a starting point for an ongoing dialogue," it explored such issues as reforming and strengthening ECOSOC; enacting Agenda 21 and promoting the work of the Commission on Sustainable Development; clarifying the "operational guidelines" for UN peacekeeping missions; defining the next steps in nuclear disarmament; requiring "the commitment and leadership of the five permanent members of the Security Council" (though participants disagreed as to what those next steps should be); and reforming the Security Council and Secretariat. For UNA, the panel was chaired by Ronald Spiers, the former UN undersecretary-general for political affairs; it included Luck and John Bolton (then a private citizen).

• *Partners Apart: A Review of the Relationship Between the US-Based Major Groups and the United Nations in the Area of Sustainable Development* was written by Kathryn G. Sessions of UNA-USA in April 1997. Noting "a sense of disconnect between US communities and the United Nations," the report promoted strengthening relations between the Commission on Sustainable Development and civil society by recommending that the CSD place more emphasis on the expertise of civil society and that greater distribution be made of the CSD's findings to the general public.

• *Combating Terrorism: Does the UN Matter . . . and How?* was a 2002 policy report, featuring the wreckage of the World Trade Center on the cover. It tracked how the international community had already developed a body of treaty law to suppress specified terrorist acts, regardless of political motive, even as a comprehensive definition remained stymied. It also showed how new Security Council mandates on all member states to track terrorist funding and operatives were transforming international security. Written by Laurenti, the report said that although terrorism had been on the UN agenda for years, the UN's capacity to act would be limited until the Security Council gave the UN a more proactive mandate in addressing the threat.

Collective Security

For the first four decades of the UN, peacekeeping consisted essentially of truce monitors and buffer forces between two combatants, usually over disputed territory (such as Kashmir, Cyprus, the Middle East). But that changed in the 1990s as a liberated Security Council, free of Cold War shackles, approved many new missions with expansive mandates aimed at resolving conflicts—not merely freezing them. This period also saw an expansion of traditional peacekeeping, especially in countries where Cold War proxy wars (or apartheid South Africa's meddling) ended, and the UN was called on to rebuild war-weary countries. Such missions were undertaken, with wildly varying degrees of success, in Angola, Cambodia, East Timor, El Salvador, Liberia, Mozambique, Namibia, Rwanda, Sierra Leone, and the former Yugoslavia.

Starting with its analysis of the Gulf War, UNA sought to influence the debate in favor of stronger, more rapidly deployable peacekeeping and peace-enforcement missions that had clear mandates, adhered to the rule of law, and were properly financed. "Peace building" also entered the lexicon by way of Secretary-General Boutros-Ghali's *An Agenda for Peace*. This ambitious concept promoted an enlarged role for the UN, backed by the Security Council, in staying behind after a conflict ended to help consolidate peace through economic and social reconstruction, including disarming combatants, establishing reconciliation councils, monitoring elections, repatriating refugees, and rebuilding government institutions. While successes occurred in peace building, the unmitigated horrors of the failure to prevent the Rwandan genocide of 1994 and the slaughter of about eight thousand Bosnian men and boys in Srebrenica in 1995 reflected major powers' resistance to shouldering the political and financial costs of UN intervention and UN officials' grave lapses in judgment; they also prompted serious soul searching by the UN.

A cornerstone to UNA's contributions in the field of peace enforcement was the International Task Force on the Enforcement of UN Security Council Resolutions. Begun in 1995, it consisted of a series of dialogues and research papers. Lord Carrington, the former British foreign secretary and secretary-general of NATO, served as chair. Other members of the panel were Gro Harlem Brundtland, the former prime minister of Norway; Sergey Lavrov, Russia's ambassador to the UN and now the foreign minister; Cyril Ramaphosa, the former secretary-general of the African National Congress; Moeen Qureshi, the former prime minister of Pakistan; and Brent Scowcroft, the former US national security adviser. It was unique for UNA to create such a broadly international panel. "Recognizing both the weaknesses of existing international enforcement machinery and the reluctance of many UN member states to grapple seriously" with enforcing council resolutions, UNA convened the task force "to consider fresh approaches to this longstanding dilemma."[12] The task force was financed by the Carnegie Corporation of New York and the John D. and Catherine T. MacArthur Foundation.

The task force released seven reports, all looking at dimensions of collective security, including applying the NATO model to Security Council missions and using sanctions. The work culminated in a final report, *Words to Deeds: Strengthening the UN's Enforcement Capabilities,* in December 1997. The report called on states to strengthen the UN's capacity for early warning and preventive diplomacy; to respect the "primacy" of the council "to mandate enforcement actions"; to improve the UN's mechanisms for organizing and implementing enforcement actions; and to avoid the use of force, though when there is no choice, force should be deployed "through multilateral rather than unilateral means."[13] Laurenti said the report's recommendations on the use of sanctions by the Security Council were likely the most significant contribution. "The report's recommendations against merely symbolic sanctions, its cautions against total embargoes, and its call for more serious monitoring through the Security Council's sanctions committees of states' implementation of UN sanctions regimes became a feature of sanctions mandated by the council in the years following," he added.

Boutros-Ghali's successor, Kofi Annan, appointed a panel on UN Peace Operations to assess the UN's shortcomings and to make recommendations that could ensure that the crimes committed in Rwanda and the massacre at Srebrenica would not be repeated. Chaired by Lakhdar Brahimi, a former foreign minister of Algeria who had become a UN negotiator in various conflict situations, the study became known as the Brahimi Report. Presented to the Security Council on November 13, 2000, it called for significant structural changes in the UN system and for renewed political commitment by member states. Like so many other UN initiatives, the report's ambitious vision was met with middling success, prompting a new panel to study peacekeeping's agenda (in 2015), especially as it grows in complexity in combating, for example, transnational crime and terrorism.

UNA entered this phase of the peace and security debate with a policy report called *The Preparedness Gap: Making Peace Operations Work in the 21st Century,* published in 2001. Produced under the guidance of Laurenti as the executive director of Policy Studies, it looked at how the UN could improve its peacekeeping and peace-building capacities and how the United States could aid in this campaign. The recommendations for the UN included the inception of a rapid deployment force, a "reserve police capacity," a standby "civil administrator corps," a unity of command, and "a clear assignment of responsibilities." UNA also called on Washington to encourage military and police personnel to train for UN missions, provide up-to-date materiel, and promptly pay the money owed to the UN for peacekeeping and regular budget contributions.

UNA conducted a joint venture with Harvard University called the Project on Justice in Times of Transition at Harvard University (since renamed Beyond Conflict). Its 2003 report, *A Policy Report on the Partnership Program on Peace-Building and Rule of Law,* had two goals: "heightening awareness in the policy community on the importance of establishing the rule of law to the success of international peace and stability operations" and "generating fresh recommendations" on how the UN and other multilateral institutions "can improve their capacity to support the establishment of the rule of law in post-conflict societies." Working with the UN Secretariat, the project conducted regional workshops in Singapore, Botswana, Istanbul, and New York. "Rule of law matters in post-conflict peace-building because it is the key link that connects each factor in a nation's successful restoration," Kimberly Dasher, a UNA policy associate, wrote in the introduction. Although it is difficult to sustain order in a country emerging from conflict, she wrote, "the failure to start building such institutions may relegate a society to continued turmoil."[14]

During these decades, UNA-USA built on the tradition of CSOP and made substantive contributions to the debate over collective security both during and after the Cold War. The pairing of grassroots activism and policy experts created a unique contribution to the debate.

Notes

1. Harold Josephson, *James T. Shotwell and the Rise of Internationalism in America* (Teaneck, NJ: Fairleigh Dickinson University Press, 1975), 237.

2. The Clark M. Eichelberger Papers, Manuscripts and Archives Division, New York Public Library. Astor, Lenox, and Tilden Foundations (NYPL Archives), box 151.

3. Josephson, *James T. Shotwell*, 242–244.

4. NYPL Archives, box 151.

5. Ibid., boxes 186–188.

6. Ibid., box 191.

7. Josephson, *James T. Shotwell*, 238.

8. Jeffrey Laurenti, *Pulling Together: A Program for America in the United Nations* (New York: UNA-USA, 1988); Seton Hall University (SHU Archives), The Msgr. William Noé Field Archives and Special Collections Center, South Orange, NJ, box 12.

9. "Roles for the United Nations After the Gulf War," a UNA-USA paper, 1991. SHU Archives, box 12.

10. Russell M. Dallen Jr., ed., *A UN Revitalized: A Compilation of UNA-USA Recommendations on Strengthening the Role of the United Nations in Peacemaking, Peacekeeping, and Conflict Prevention* (New York: UNA-USA), May 1992. SHU Archives, box 21.

11. "United Nations Conference on Environment and Development: Agenda 21," Chapter 38. June 1992.

12. "International Task Force on the Enforcement of UN Security Council Resolutions" (New York: UNA-USA), 1997.

13. *Words to Deeds: Strengthening the UN's Enforcement Capabilities,* final report, December 1997. SHU Archives, box 15.

14. *A Policy Report on the Partnership Program on Peace-Building and Rule of Law,* A Joint Venture of the United Nations Association of the United States of America and the Project on Justice in the Times of Transition of Harvard University (New York: UNA-USA, 2003), 8. SHU Archives, box 12.

10

Track II Diplomacy: The US-Iran Dialogue, 2001–2009

Diplomacy is not usually a public act. But when diplomacy is conducted independent of a government, it becomes even more obscured from public view. This type of negotiation has come to be called Track II diplomacy. In a 2010 report on the effectiveness of such work, Randa M. Slim of the Rockefeller Brothers Fund described Track II diplomacy as "all nongovernmental, unofficial and informal dialogues between non-state actors including business contacts, citizen exchange programs, advocacy work, and/or religious contacts. Track II diplomacy has become an increasingly important part of the evolving international political landscape."[1] In the first decade of the twenty-first century, UNA-USA launched a Track II initiative to overcome obstacles in the relations between the United States and Iran—an effort financed by the Rockefeller Brothers Fund.

In his September 21, 1998, General Assembly address, President Mohammad Khatami of Iran, who had been elected the year before as a reformer, introduced his proposal for a "Dialogue of Civilizations." In a rejoinder to Samuel P. Huntington's influential article, "Clash of Civilizations" (which argued that post–Cold War conflicts would be clashes based on people's religions and cultures, not on political or economic systems), the Iran leader proposed that the UN designate 2001 as the United Nations Year of Dialogue Among Civilizations. "The structure of power in our contemporary world must be reformed," Khatami said. "In a global society—whose constituents, much like equal individuals within nation-states, are nations of equal right and dignity—diverse cultures and civilizations can and should work collectively to build a moral and humane world with liberty and progress for all."

The General Assembly unanimously agreed to the proposal. Secretary-General Kofi Annan appointed Assistant Secretary General Giandomenico Picco as his personal representative. Picco was well positioned to handle this assignment. In his nearly twenty years at the UN (1973–1992), he played a central role in sensitive Middle East issues, including negotiating the release of Western hostages in Lebanon and representing the UN in the negotiations over the Soviet withdrawal from Afghanistan and the Iran-Iraq cease-fire.

Panels were held, and the dialogue was likely to be a focal point of the General Assembly when it convened in September 2001. But then Al Qaeda attacked the United States on September 11, 2001. The dialogue participants accelerated their work, publishing their report in November 2001, in the hopes, as Picco wrote in it, that the idea would not be seen as a "luxury" but rather "an idea whose time has now come" in light of the "brutality of those who do not believe in a dialogue."[2] Khatami and Annan introduced the book in the General Assembly. In his remarks, Khatami stunned at least some of his US listeners by declaring that "Osama bin Laden does not represent Islam; we're opposed to him," as William Luers, a former UNA-USA president, recalled in an interview for this book. The statement went almost unnoticed in the US media, which was preoccupied with the war in Afghanistan. "By then, nobody wanted to talk to Iran," Luers added. Khatami wanted to make another speech on the theme but away from the UN and in "a religious environment," Luers said. "So we went to Seton Hall," a Roman Catholic university in South Orange, New Jersey, as its School of Diplomacy and International Relations had served as the secretariat of the dialogue commission. In a speech on November 9, Khatami said of the 9/11 attacks,

> [The] tragedy caused by the terrorists must have awakened us to the necessity of finding a way to save humanity, and to engender hope for the future. Our world yearns for peace, and true peace can only come about through changing ourselves and our world. . . . Our world is weary of war and violence and longs for a coalition aimed at establishing peace, a peace based upon justice. We should strive to base our coalition upon compassion and justice as opposed to violence and terror. Only through such an effort can we hope to eradicate terrorism.[3]

Soon after, Suzanne DiMaggio, a policy executive at UNA, reached out to Mostafa Zahrani, an attaché at the Iranian mission to the UN, which led to conversations with Iran's ambassador to the UN, Javad Zarif. Luers recalled, "Suzanne got to know Javad Zarif during that period, and she said, 'You've got to go meet him.' So I went to talk to him. He and I hit it off very well, so we started to think about a Track II diplomacy thing with Iran. Javad put it together." Zarif had studied for his doctorate in international affairs under Madeleine Albright's father, Josef Korbel, at the University of Denver, and was well informed about the United States. Zarif, who would eventually be appointed foreign minister by President Hassan Rouhani in 2013, was central to the multilateral negotiations over Iran's nuclear program. Luers and his colleagues in the project lined up financial support from US foundations—most notably, the Rockefeller Brothers Fund—which allowed them to move ahead with talks with Iranians. "So we began planning it in late 2001–2002, and we finally had our first meeting near Stockholm later in 2002," Luers said, noting that the trip was kept secret, out of the public view, and entailed staying at an inn outside Stockholm.

Because the Dialogue of Civilizations was a multilateral initiative under the UN umbrella, a different structure needed to be created as the secretariat. The role was taken on by UNA-USA and Seton Hall's School of Diplomacy and International Relations. DiMaggio, who was the executive director of the UNA Global Policy Program during much of this time, said in an interview for this book, "It seemed like a natural progression from the UNA's Parallel Studies Program" with the "same sort of objectives and methodologies." She saw it as "a continuation of a UNA tradition of serving as a forum for representatives of those countries that normally would not have opportunities to meet." Luers agreed: "The model of Iran was taken directly" from Toby Gati's work on the Parallel Studies Program. In talks with US government officials, he said, "I kept drawing the parallels to Toby Gati, because it gives you access at very high levels. It gives UNA a distinction that it wouldn't have otherwise."

Slim's analysis from the Rockefeller Brothers Fund also noted this important point: "This dialogue was established when there was no formal US relationship with Iran and there had not been since diplomatic relations were severed in April 1980 after the Islamic Revolution and the taking of hostages at the US embassy in Tehran. This made the effort particularly challenging but also of greater potential significance."[4]

Both sides recognized the need for an impartial third party. That role was filled by Stockholm International Peace Research Institute (SIPRI), then chaired by Rolf Ekéus, a former Swedish diplomat and the first head of the UN weapons inspection team in Iraq. Most meetings took place in or just outside Stockholm, which avoided practical problems since it was questionable whether the United States and the Iranian participants could travel to each other's countries.

Formally called the Dialogue on Multilateral Diplomacy and the Management of Global Issues, the first meeting was held in Stockholm on December 13–14, 2002. The summaries of the meetings began on this note: "In the absence of official diplomatic relations between the two countries, the program seeks to bring together American and Iranian participants on an informal track to examine multilateral issues and the cooperative management of global concerns."[5]

The themes of the first session mirrored the key concerns of both governments and set the template for all later meetings: weapons of mass destruction (WMD), terrorism, international security after 9/11, Israel/Palestine, Iraq, Afghanistan, and bilateral concerns. The session report prepared by UNA identified the two most significant roadblocks as WMD and Hezbollah. Iranians argued that Iran condemned the 9/11 attacks and helped the United States in Afghanistan by providing intelligence on Al Qaeda, and yet President Bush had delivered his January 29, 2002, speech on the "axis of evil." According to the summary, Iranians felt "a sense of disappointment and betrayal." The Bush administration, they said, had "emboldened conservatives and angered Khatami."

The Iranian delegation was often organized by the Institute for Political and International Studies (IPIS), the foreign ministry's think tank. The Center for Strategic Research (CSR), a policy institute affiliated with the Iranian Expediency Council, which advises the supreme leader's office, also played a convening role. In *The Iran Primer*, an analysis of the Iran program for a publication by the US Institute for Peace, DiMaggio described the Iranian participants as "a core group of reform-minded diplomats, policy advisors and scholars" who "remained fairly consistent during the Khatami presidency." They "shared the view that rapprochement in US-Iran relations offered a way to advance Iranian interests over time."[6]

UNA participants usually included Luers and DiMaggio. Stephen Heintz represented the Rockefeller Brothers Fund. Other US participants were generally private citizens who had been (or would later be) in the government, such as Robert Einhorn, a nuclear weapons expert who held several positions in the Arms Control and Disarmament Agency under President Bill Clinton and would become a special adviser to Secretary of State Hillary Clinton; Vali Nasr, an Iranian American expert on the Islamic world who had held positions in the US State Department, Harvard, and the Council on Foreign Relations and is currently at the Johns Hopkins School of Advanced International Studies; Trita Parsi, the Iranian-born and Swedish-raised scholar who served on the Swedish delegation to the UN and founded the National Iranian American Council; former US ambassador to the UN Thomas Pickering; and Gary Sick, an Iran expert who served on the National Security

Council under Presidents Ford, Carter, and Reagan. Other foundations and think tanks, including the Open Society Foundations and the Carnegie Endowment for International Peace, were also often represented. (Concerned that the Iranians—even though they had the blessing of their government—might still face retributions for their participation in the dialogue, the former UNA participants requested that the Iranians not be named in this book.)

Occasionally, congressional leaders participated, such as Representative Bob Ney (R-Ohio), who chaired the House Oversight Committee, and Senator Dianne Feinstein (D-California), the chair of the Intelligence Committee, whom Luers called "a big supporter."

Luers described the talks in detail in an interview, saying, "We would talk, constantly. We got to know them so well and they became good friends, which is important with a country you don't know. There were a lot of other Track II efforts, but I don't know anybody who ran a Track II program like we ran with Iran." In an interview for this book as well, Pickering said, "We were all nonofficials. There was no official representation. Our pattern was to have conversations in Washington as often as we could beforehand." Pickering added,

> So generally speaking, our process was one, that we didn't speak for the United States; two, that we kept the United States briefed both ahead of time and after our meetings; and three, that we attempted to not reflect views that we knew were not going to be acceptable to the United States, even though we didn't speak for the United States. We attempted to keep the United States fully informed, particularly on what the Iranians were thinking and saying.

After his retirement from the Foreign Service, Pickering was recruited by Luers to serve on the UNA board; that led to Pickering's involvement in the Iranian dialogue (see Box 10.1).

Slim, the senior program adviser for the Rockefeller Brothers Fund, wrote,

> Because of the lack of a sustained diplomatic dialogue between the United States and Iran for the better part of the past 30 years, this unofficial dialogue gave US participants an inside look at Iranian politics and Iranian society. It provided a unique opportunity to gain insight about the Iranian decision-making process and the different power centers in the Islamic republic. They learned that the Iranian regime is not monolithic; that different power centers hold different views on various policy issues.[7]

Box 10.1 Thomas Pickering

As a US career diplomat, Thomas Pickering was engaged in some of the most dramatic events in Central America, Europe, and the Middle East. For over four decades in the Foreign Service, he was ambassador to El Salvador, Jordan, India, Israel, Nigeria, and Russia. He was the UN ambassador from 1989 to 1992; his tenure there was marked by the watershed developments of the end of the Cold War and the 1990 Gulf War. His last government assignment was as undersecretary of state for political affairs, from 1997 to 2000. After his retirement, the State Department's Foreign Affairs Fellowship Program was renamed the Thomas R. Pickering Foreign Affairs Fellowship Program. He moved into the private sector, where he was senior vice president of the Boeing Company from 2001 until 2006, after which he was named vice chair of Hills & Company, an international consulting firm headed by former US trade negotiator Carla Hills.

In 2013, Secretary of State Hillary Clinton named Pickering chair of the Accountability Review Board, which investigated the attack on a US diplomatic compound in Benghazi, Libya, in 2012, which killed US ambassador J. Christopher Stevens. In addition to UNA, Pickering has participated in the work of other organizations, including the Council on Foreign Relations, the American Iranian Council, and the Project on National Security Reform.

Bill Luers, a president and chair of the board of UNA, asked Pickering, who was at Boeing, to join the UNA board in 2001. After Luers stepped down as chair that year, Pickering and William McDonough were named cochairs. Pickering's tenure on the board matched the launch of the US-Iran Dialogue. His chairmanship also coincided with the initial move toward the alliance between UNA and the UN Foundation (see Chapter 18). After the alliance was concluded, he became chair of the UNA-USA Strategy Council under the UNF umbrella.

—J. W.

Thirteen dialogues were held from October 2002 to November 2007. The summary records of the sessions offered a snapshot of the state of play in each country, giving insights into the strengths and weaknesses of the respective leaders' trains of thought about the issues on the dialogue's agenda and the internal politics of each country. (The leaders of the countries were Bush and Khatami and then Mahmoud Ahmadinejad.) "The Iranians were interesting in the sense that in the discussions, they would often begin talking in exactly the same way about what was happening in Iran and how things were developing,"

Pickering said. "Before they were finished, each one of them had an entirely different view of the situation. So we got what was the line, and then we got what were the individual points of view."

By late 2002, most of the world was beginning to suspect that the Bush administration was set to invade Iraq, regardless of concessions by Saddam Hussein or the results of the UN weapons inspections. The US news media openly reported that the invasion would occur in February or March 2003, because after that, weather conditions in the desert would worsen. Against this backdrop, the summary of the March 7–8, 2003, session (also held in Stockholm) reported "the Iranians were more emphatic in conveying that Iran was ready to engage in talks with the US at some official level" and that these dialogues were supported by both Foreign Minister Kamal Kharrazi and Zarif. Iran believed that Hussein must go but was concerned as to what the United States would do next.

The dialogue dedicated a session to a "Post-Saddam Iraq?," accounting for a possible invasion of the country. The panel examined two scenarios: (1) inspections success and (2) military action removes Hussein. Successful inspections "might increase pressure for military action against Iran." Participants saw military action as a "mixed picture," with quick victory followed by "a situation of postwar chaos that would inhibit the [Bush] administration from moving on to other countries or targets." Even Iranian conservatives did not want an Islamic Iraq, with Iranian participants saying, "The best neighbors are secular."

On March 17, 2003, the United States warned the UN weapons inspectors to leave Iraq. The invasion of Iraq by the United States and its allies began with airstrikes on March 19. Baghdad fell on April 9. Bush delivered his "Mission Accomplished" speech on the deck of the USS *Abraham Lincoln* on May 1. The summary of the May 21–22, 2003, dialogue session noted that although the Iranians said they were "encouraged by the comments" of superiors when they reported on the dialogue, the parties were now dealing with the uncertainties of a post-Saddam Iraq. What does the United States want? More regime changes? Does that mean Iran? If so, then "there is no way of talking." As for Iraq, there was an Iranian consensus between reformists and conservatives: "Stay out of it. . . . No one in Iran is interested in establishing an Islamic state in Iraq," one participant said.

Unknown to most of the world, an opportunity for a thaw in US-Iranian relations occurred later in 2003. The Iranian government sent the Bush administration a memo in May 2003, outlining a "grand bargain" that put all issues, including the Iranian nuclear program and recognition of Israel, on the table. As reported in the *Washington Post,* the memo was transmitted to the US government by the Swiss ambassador to Iran, Tim Guldimann. "I got the clear impression that there is a strong will of the regime to tackle the problem with the US now and to try it with this initiative," Guldimann wrote in a cover letter.[8] The memo did not become public until 2007, and it is still not clear who in the administration had control over the memo, whether Bush had seen it, or why Washington never responded. DiMaggio said it "was a serious proposal and it was a missed opportunity that it was never pursued." DiMaggio, who saw the memo before it was transmitted, said, "I can't say for sure who was the original author, but I'm fairly certain that it was put forward by the Iranians with the right level of authorization." Luers said he thought Zarif had drafted it. UNA had thus become involved in one of the few serious attempts at rapprochement between the United States and Iran before the opening in 2013 of formal governmental talks over Iran's nuclear program.

In the summaries from the 2002–2005 sessions, postconference comments from Zarif were incorporated, in which he elaborated the government's official position on the topic under discussion. Pickering said, "It was always useful to get his views because he could give us a more official take. He was very knowledgeable and extremely helpful in conveying thoughts. I think the United States appreciated that . . . we [UNA] were seeing Zarif, where they had less or no capacity to officially see him." It was Luers who briefed Zarif. He and Pickering also briefed the US State Department, usually the undersecretary of state for political affairs. "I would brief each of them equally on what we were doing. We didn't have any secrets," Luers said. This information increased the UNA's access to the State Department. That access wasn't related to "all the people I knew," Luers said; "it was because I had things that they didn't know. This was during the dark era of [George W. Bush's administration], so what I did was I would go to the National Security Council, I would go to the State Department, and it was always portrayed as a UNA-USA initiative." Luers said that a group of Americans and Iranians produced

> an analysis of the problems between our two countries. We never published it. We may publish it one day, but we did give it to the State Department, and a group of us went to the State Department and the White House, and met with senior people on what we'd written. . . . They were fascinated, but they disagreed with us.

Iran's controversial nuclear program was an obvious topic throughout the dialogues. While recognizing self-defense imperatives, US participants (including some nuclear weapons experts) pressed the Iranians for clarity on Tehran's intentions as to the potential for developing nuclear weapons under the program. The Iranians stressed that Iran faced myriad security concerns but was not a partner in any "security umbrella." Although not explicitly linking these concerns to the desire for nuclear weapons, they regularly pointed out that Iran's enrichment program was within the letter of the law, meaning the uranium enrichment was pure enough for fuel but not for manufacturing nuclear weapons. US attitudes fluctuated with each new UN International Atomic Energy Agency report that said either there were questions about the program or Iran was cooperating.

An Iranian at the June 2005 dialogue said, "It now looks as if the public has come together and has accepted the establishment line that Iran is entitled to a nuclear program and does not want the bomb. There is a large element of high tech nationalism." Since Iran would never completely abandon the enrichment program, US participants floated alternatives such as an International Fuel Consortium, with Russia enriching and Iran accepting comprehensive IAEA inspections. The Iranians said that their government was willing to negotiate and that a small group of officials "had been given clear authority to resolve the nuclear issue." This group included Hassan Rouhani, who was Iran's authority on the nuclear issue (and has been Iran's president since 2013).

The pattern of dialogues alternated with four round-table discussions in May 2004, February 2005, January 2006, and November 2007. These more public events were held in New York City and dealt with some of the same issues explored in the dialogues: domestic developments in both countries, Iran's nuclear program, Iraq and the Middle East in general, and possible areas of cooperation. But the recurring theme was how to bring the two countries together for an official, Track I dialogue.

The only joint statement prepared by the dialogue participants was called "The US-Iran Relationship: Breaking the Stalemate." The October 11, 2005, paper called for a US/Iran "diplomatic framework," similar to the 1972 Shanghai Declaration between the United States and China, that "would allow our governments to 'agree to disagree' on many issues while committing themselves to frank, wide-ranging, and unconditional dialogue at the highest levels." The conclusion stated, "With courageous and visionary leadership, and a framework for direct engagement, we have a chance of making progress on the issues that divide us and the objectives that we share." The causes of the impasse were by now the familiar problems discussed openly: mutual hostility, Iran's nuclear ambitions, tensions over each country's role in Iraq, lack of a common strategy to combat terrorism, and differences over the Israeli-Palestinian conflict. The paper encouraged the two sides to begin a process of engagement directly and not through intermediaries.[9]

From Khatami to Ahmadinejad

The June 9–11, 2005, dialogue was held during the run-up to the Iranian presidential elections. An Iranian participant predicted that Hashemi Rafsanjani and Mostafa Moeen would face off in the second round of the elections, since no one would get 50 percent of the vote. He was right about the need for a run-off but wrong about the candidates themselves. Rafsanjani received 21 percent of the vote, while Mahmoud Ahmadinejad got 19.5 percent in the first round. In the second round, Ahmadinejad topped Rafsanjani, 61.7 percent to 35.9 percent.

The Iranian Dialogue participants regularly commented on Ahmadinejad's policies and personalities. At the October 29–30, 2005, dialogue, Iranians said Ahmadinejad lacked foreign policy knowledge: "His views are guided by his basic ideology. . . . He does not take into account the international implications of his words." In April 2006, he was called "a transitional conservative," meaning combining "elements of conservatism with a more pragmatic outlook." The participants also noted that Ahmadinejad's cabinet, which wanted him to focus on national rather than local issues, questioned Ahmadinejad's unprecedented trips to provinces, but the Supreme Leader, Ali Hosseini Khamenei, supported it, "calling it a productive move that the country needs to support."

By the July 2006 dialogue, the Iranians said Ahmadinejad was losing support, from the public and the Supreme Leader. The public was blaming the president for the West's sanctions and their impact on the economy. One participant said that Ahmadinejad has been a "disaster," not only because of his statements denying the Holocaust, but also because he "managed to worsen Iran's relations with everyone." At first, they said, Khamenei supported Ahmadinejad as "an atypical politician— not corrupt and not rich," but he was now distancing himself from Ahmadinejad as the latter's policies proved unpopular with the public.

Luers called Ahmadinejad "an interesting character." He added,

> He became more and more supportive of the secret police, and they grew in authority, which affected us, because the work we did, they tried to undermine all the time. Yet he did want ownership of US relationships and tried to communicate that to Obama . . . so he could take credit for breaking the [impasse]. But his overriding problem was that

he was a demigod, and I think he thought he could probably become more powerful than the Supreme Leader, which, in Iran, is bad news.

Pickering said that "Ahmadinejad followed a peculiar set of policies." He continued:

He put himself in the front of the Great Satan movement, the denial of Holocaust, and criticism of Israel. But behind the scenes, he was the first guy to reach out to see if he could get credit for reopening relations with the United States. Because he knew the latter was very popular with the Iranian public. So he played the hard right in public first but opened the door to him moving the other way. I think a lot of Iranians saw that it was a double game and that he wasn't going to get away with it. The US government in particular didn't want to play his game.

Eventually, the Ahmadinejad presidency put a chill on the dialogues. Under his government, DiMaggio said, "It was clear that this channel would be coming to an end in a year or two and the team would change or cease altogether." Since the Iranians were closer to Khatami or Rafsanjani, and Ahmadinejad declined to provide new participants, "we saw a real curtailing on the Iranian side of interacting in these sorts of Track II events." Another blow came in December 2006, when the IPIS hosted the International Conference to Review the Global Vision of the Holocaust, which featured Holocaust deniers. As a result, numerous policy institutes in the West severed relations with the Iranian IPIS.

In her US Institute of Peace paper, DiMaggio wrote,

By early 2008, hard-line elements in the Iranian government began to charge members of this group with a pro-US agenda. Most have since faced censure; some faced prosecution. Pressure on them increased after the disputed 2009 presidential election. Their ability to participate in international conferences and travel abroad has since been restricted. Some professors at Iranian universities have been subjected to downgrading of positions or altogether stripped of their teaching duties.[10]

Luers noted that "all the people we had contact with began to sort of disappear. I mean, they began to go into their own cubbyholes, and some of them lost their jobs in universities," including Zarif. "Some of them got into trouble with Ahmadinejad. I mean Zarif was sidelined for a long time, and we worried the worst, that he might end up in jail or worse," Pickering said. When Ahmadinejad had come into the picture, Luers said, he had "wanted to get rid of all those people who we knew." Luers continued:

So, the network of people who had worked with us, and with other Track II groups who had an interest in making a deal with the West on their nuclear program, that network was broken up deliberately by Ahmadinejad. He wanted control of it. He had nobody who really knew how to handle this complicated relationship with the West, and he kept not wanting to get back the old guard that had been under Khatami.

In contrast to what was happening to the Iranian participants, when Ahmadinejad attended the UN General Assembly, nearly all US dialogue participants were invited to meet with him, according to Slim.

The last dialogue took place in November 2007, but UNA-USA continued to work on other Iran-focused initiatives. "At that time, Iran turned inward; a lot of the people who were engaging in this work were no longer able to," DiMaggio said. "It took a turn to a darker period in Iran's political history, and it became much more difficult to engage in these kinds of dialogues. So I think UNA's response to that was to say how can we take what we've gleaned over these years and start releasing that information." Luers and Pickering had several meetings with Mohammad Khazaee, who succeeded Zarif as UN ambassador in 2007 but was replaced in 2015. "We wanted to continue to keep our contacts, to see what they were thinking, to talk to them about ideas. Whatever way we could be useful," Pickering said.

Pickering saw two "important aspects" to this style of Track II diplomacy. First, the "exchange of information and ideas focused heavily on the nuclear, but involving other questions and issues," which permitted the "continued ability to talk with Iranians." Those talks developed a plan for Iran's nuclear enrichment "based on some continuation of enrichment, but hedged in with a very strong firewall of inspection and control—which essentially is what has emerged in the joint plan of action" issued by the two governments in 2013. The second aspect was that the nuclear talks opened the door to dealing with other issues of common concern, Pickering said, including Afghanistan, Iraq, and Syria. Even seemingly mundane ideas—Pickering cited the proposal that direct flights be set up between the United States and Iran—took on heft because of the tense relationship. The flights themselves could be handled simply by relying on a third-party airline, but passengers would need visas, and visas needed to be issued by interest sections, which are government offices lower than embassies used when nations do not have diplomatic relations. Thus the visa procedure could be considered a step toward formal relations.

Opposition came from members of the UNA board and chapters that did not think the Iran Dialogues fell within the UNA mandate. Luers said,

> When the argument is made, why is the UNA the least bit interested in Iran?, I point out the depth of the involvement of the IAEA, the Security Council, and several other agencies in Iran as part of the thesis of don't spend your time talking about the UN; spend your time talking about the functions of the UN. This helps people understand what the UN's role is in the world today—by dealing with pieces, not dealing with the UN. And that's the whole strategy I had.

The program entered a period of flux between 2007 and 2009. In addition to the internal dynamics in Iran, there were changes on the US side. In 2007, DiMaggio left UNA and joined the Asia Society, where she organized dialogues on US-Iran relations. In 2008, when Luers invited Pickering to be the cochair of UNA's board, Luers said, "Tom and I began to become more public, and we wrote a lot of op-eds, and we wrote three articles in the *New York Review of Books*. So we've been very active publicly and on the Hill, and we've sort of been outspoken about our support for diplomacy—not support for Iran, but support for a deal to avoid war." These two initiatives operated separately but cooperatively. DiMaggio said, "A lot of the same people were involved in both," while Pickering noted, "There was some cross-fertilization."

The next year, Luers left UNA and worked on what is now called the Iran Project, under the auspices of the Foundation for a Civil Society, a nonprofit founded by Luers's wife, Wendy W. Luers. The Rockefeller Brothers Fund continues to be a major supporter and took on the Iran Project in 2011. After DiMaggio left the Asia Society in 2014, she continued working on Iran issues at New America, a New York–based think tank.

The articles Luers and Pickering wrote for the *New York Review of Books*, written with Jim Walsh, an expert on nuclear weapons and international security at the Massachusetts Institute of Technology, relied on insights learned from the dialogues. DiMaggio described the articles as "efforts that spun out into the Iran Project that have really played an important role in educating the broader public about these issues, about the potential benefit of reaching some sort of political, diplomatic solution with Iran."

The last UNA-USA report on Iran was the May 2009 working paper, "US-Iranian Engagement: Toward a Grand Agenda?," published with the

United States Institute of Peace (USIP). Based on a February 2009 round table cosponsored by UNA-USA, USIP, and Rockefeller Brothers Fund, and drawing largely from the *New York Review of Books* articles, the paper said that US overtures to Iran must be based on consensus in the US government "as to the strategic direction and purpose of US-Iranian talks." The paper, drafted by Daniel Brumberg of USIP and Eriks Berzins, a policy associate of UNA-USA, recommended that talks be pursued both bilaterally and multilaterally; also, "if the US wants to imbue the above multilateral initiatives with sufficient strategic meaning to attract a positive and sustained response from Iran, Washington must be prepared to engage Tehran directly and bilaterally."[11]

That year, 2009, was also when the alliance between UNA and the UN Foundation was being formulated. The key players in the Iran Project had already left UNA, so the project was not an element in the merger discussions. Pickering, a cochair of the UNA-USA board during the merger, said,

> It played out very well because I think over a period of time people thought the UNA needed to go back and focus more centrally on the UN questions it was engaged with. Negotiating the relationship with the UN Foundation solidified that, and it made it very clear that the Iran Project, as good as it was, was now a separable venture. So I think we all supported moving it over there to the organization that Bill [Luers] had put together to deal with it.

As of 2016, the Iran Project, still under the auspices of the Rockefeller Brothers Fund, operates with Luers as the chair and with the continued involvement of Pickering, DiMaggio, and other participants from the dialogues. Luers, Pickering, and Walsh continue to write reports and op-eds promoting the case for greater US-Iranian cooperation. Pickering said, "The focus of the Iran Project now remains what it always was, which was to promote contact and dialogue between the United States and Iran to resolve problems, leading, hopefully, to a resumption of relations and the settlement of the issues."

Notes

1. Randa M. Slim, *The U.S.-Iran Track II Dialogue (2002–2008): Lessons Learned and Implications for the Rockefeller Brothers Fund's Grantmaking Strategy* (New York: Rockefeller Brothers Fund, August 3, 2010).

2. Giandomenico Picco, A. Kamal Aboulmagd, Lourdes Arizpe, Hanan Ashrawi, Ruth Cardoso, Jacques Delors, Leslie Gelb, et al., *Crossing the Divide: Dialogue Among Civilizations* (South Orange, NJ: School of Diplomacy and International Relations, Seton Hall University), 2001.

3. *Seton Hall Journal of Diplomacy and International Relations* (South Orange, NJ: School of Diplomacy and International Relations, Seton Hall University), Winter/Spring 2002.

4. Slim, *The U.S.-Iran Track II Dialogue.*

5. All quotations from the dialogue documents are from internal reports prepared by UNA for the dialogue. Seton Hall University (SHU Archives), The Msgr. William Noé Field Archives and Special Collections Center, South Orange, NJ, boxes 23–25.

6. Suzanne DiMaggio, *The Iran Primer* (Washington, DC: United States Institute of Peace, December 2010) http://iranprimer.usip.org/resource/track-ii -diplomacy.

7. Slim, *The U.S.-Iran Track II Dialogue.*

8. Glenn Kessler, "2003 Memo Says Iranian Leaders Backed Talks," *Washington Post,* February 14, 2007.

9. SHU Archives, box 25.

10. DiMaggio, *The Iran Primer.*

11. Daniel Brumberg and Eriks Berzins, "US-Iranian Engagement: Toward a Grand Agenda?" (working paper, United States Institute of Peace, Washington, DC, June 2009).

11

UNA in the New Millennium, 1989–2010

Until the late 1980s, virtually every issue on the international agenda was refracted through a Cold War lens, impeding substantive cooperation not only in the UN's economic and social spheres but also in security. With the end of the Cold War, that distorting prism disappeared, allowing a reinvigorated interest in addressing these concerns. From the UN side, the world body was more vigorously engaged in peacekeeping missions (in mandates and number of missions) than any time since Congo in the 1960s. It worked to coordinate integrated responses to international concerns, including the environment, the rights of women and children, development, and human rights, as well as peace and security in the developing world's numerous interstate and intrastate conflicts. The drive for coordinated responses led to organizing megaconferences, or summits, that took a broad view of security—development, environmental, human rights—rather than exclusively military approaches.

From the NGO side, this meant that UNA continued its focus but with a wider vision. In addition, more NGOs than ever before became active at the UN, gaining formal participatory status and influencing policy more openly. Ed Elmendorf, a former president of UNA, attributed this greater visibility to UN agencies becoming more welcoming to NGOs and to Secretary-General Kofi Annan, who viewed these organizations as allies in helping promote his agenda with governments.

This period of large international conferences with sweeping themes and an inclusive roster of participants included the World Summit for Children (1990), UN Conference on Environment and Development (UNCED, 1992), World Conference on Human Rights (Vienna, 1993), International Conference on Population and Development (ICPD, 1994), World Summit for Social Development (1995), Fourth World Conference on Women (Beijing, 1995), the Habitat II Conference on Human Settlements (Istanbul, 1996), and the World Food Summit (1996).

As Steve Dimoff, a longtime UNA policy expert, said in an interview for this book, "This was also an evolution of NGO involvement in the UN. UNA was the only game in town for a number of years, but after those megaconferences in the 1990s, other NGOs sought their own representation in various UN bodies. That kind of exploded, so you had all kinds of American NGOs who all of a sudden had a seat at the table. It wasn't just UNA."

As discussed in Chapter 9, the end of the Cold War made it possible to promote innovative thinking on global issues without worrying that the ideas would become immediate victims of the superpower rivalry. The UNA-USA International Dialogue on the Enforcement of Security Council Resolutions was formed, issuing reports on revitalizing council mandates. The occasional papers series enhanced UNA's annual briefing books and reports. These papers also provided sophisticated examinations of current events (see below).

Leadership

The autobiography of John C. Whitehead is called *A Life in Leadership: From D-Day to Ground Zero*. The title is not an exaggeration. Born in 1922, Whitehead joined the US Navy in 1943 and participated in the Normandy landing and the battles of Iwo Jima and Okinawa. He joined Goldman Sachs in 1947, was named a partner in 1956 and a cochair in 1976. He retired after thirty-seven years and joined the US State Department. After leaving government, he held numerous leadership roles in civil, educational, and arts institutions, including UNA-USA. He died at age ninety-two on February 7, 2015.

In an interview for this book a year before his death, Whitehead recalled, "I've always dreamed of world peace ever since I can remember." As a senior in high school in 1939, he was a delegate to a high school peace conference in Washington, DC, where Eleanor Roosevelt was the principal figure. He said, "Mrs. Roosevelt introduced us to a lot of speakers who were leaders in the administration. . . . Foreign policy was an important part of it." At the end of the conference, the students went to the White House for a reception. They arrived in the reception room:

> There at the top of the stairs was a man in a wheelchair and Mrs. Roosevelt. I didn't for a minute recognize who in the world could that be in the wheelchair. It was the president. He had been president since 1933, and it was the first time I had seen him even in a picture in a wheelchair. . . . I was shocked to see him in the wheelchair. I shook

hands with him as everybody did when they arrived. He said a few nice words and then he disappeared. Mrs. Roosevelt took over the chairmanship of the group.

Whitehead recalled that a book was featured at the conference "about the dream of world peace and an organization—no mention of the United Nations—that would bring together all the nations of the world, and there would never again be a war like World War I."

Serving in the Navy in World War II, he piloted a small boat in the first wave in Normandy as well as at landings in the Pacific.[1] "I saw myself the ravages of war," he said in the interview. "I saw a lot of people being killed and wounded. I always thought that we needed to find a way to avoid this in the future." After the war, he re-enrolled in Harvard Business School, where the Navy had sent him to learn Navy accounting, and was then hired by Goldman Sachs in 1947. During his decades at the company, he said, "I was involved with various foreign policy activities. [I] met a lot of foreign leaders, presidents of foreign countries, and so on." In its obituary of Whitehead, *Bloomberg Business* credited him with beginning Goldman Sachs's international outreach, saying, "Whitehead developed a sales team to market the firm's services, laid out a code of ethics and spearheaded international growth."[2]

One leader he met was George Shultz, who was President Reagan's secretary of state from 1982 to 1989. When Whitehead retired from Goldman Sachs in 1984, Shultz offered Whitehead the post of deputy secretary of state. His official brief was Eastern Europe, but he was also regularly involved in jousting with Senator Jesse Helms (see Chapter 6). At the end of the Reagan administration, when Whitehead left government in 1989, "one of the things that happened more or less immediately after my term was up" was that Cyrus Vance and Elliot Richardson, the cochairs of UNA, asked if he wanted to become the chair. Whitehead recalled, "They had done it for quite a long time. Both wanted to retire, and they asked me if I would take it over."

He was ready for the change. "I felt I had done all the business career that I wanted to do. I had been on the boards of a lot of companies. I didn't want to go on boards. I had worked for the government," he said. "So the only thing left for me to do was be involved with a lot of worthy nonprofit organizations. UNA was one of the organizations that I became chairman of. . . . Ever since then and up to now, I have been involved with a whole variety of nonprofit organizations." These nonprofit organizations included the International Rescue Committee, the Andrew W. Mellon Foundation, the Harvard Board of Overseers,

Asia Society, the EastWest Institute, Brookings Institution, the Nature Conservancy, the Greater New York Councils of the Boy Scouts, the Eisenhower Exchange Fellowships, the Rockefeller University, Lincoln Center Theater, J. Paul Getty Trust, Outward Bound, the National Gallery of Art, the National Humanities Center, and Goldman Sachs Foundation.[3]

Whitehead also stayed involved in business, serving on the boards of numerous companies, as well as serving as director of the New York Stock Exchange, chair of the board of the Federal Reserve Bank of New York, and chair of the Securities Industry Association.

He served as chair of UNA-USA from 1989 to 1998, as vice chair from 1998 to 2010, and then as a member of the UNA-USA Strategy Council after the merger between UNA and the UN Foundation. "I was interested in UNA because I felt that . . . the UN was important and that we deserved an organization of people that was separate from the UN," Whitehead said. "We thought that the UN should be changed. We were free and had the responsibility of representing UN supporters all over America. We were free to make recommendations of changes that we American fans of the UN felt they should make. And so we did that from time to time."

Concerning the UNA chapters, he said,

> I had good personal relations with the chapters. Friendly with them. Trying to be supportive. We sent to all our members a quarterly bulletin about UN activities. That was sort of touting the benefits of the UN to the world. Try to remind them that peacekeeping is not the only thing they did. That they did a great many good things.

However, there were also tensions. As Whitehead recollected, "Right from the beginning, this was a difficult organization to be chairman of because the members were not eager or willing to finance headquarters: 'Who was this organization in New York that was trying to organize them?'" Thus, Whitehead saw increasing membership as a priority. In his first speech as chair, he said he was "ashamed" that membership was only 30,000, and he wanted to increase that to 100,000.

> It was a silly speech because I realized very quickly that there was no way that was going to happen. And if I could keep it at 30,000 I was lucky. We found that about a third of the members didn't pay their dues in the second year of their membership. So we got the full national dues of $35 the first year, and then $17 from each of the 30,000 people. That was it. That was our total gift.

Whitehead began to look for new sources of revenue. One method was to create a Chairman's Council and an Ambassadors' Council. "One of my main things was to go to people who were interested in foreign policy and active in political affairs [and ask them] to give. There are a lot of rich people in New York. We established a Chairman's Council [in 1992] that you had to pay $10,000 to join," Whitehead explained. Monthly meetings of the council afforded members access to "national speakers [and] important diplomatic figures to talk about foreign relations." He added, "That was an effective thing. One time, we had maybe twenty members of the Chairman's Council."

The Ambassadors' Council was established in 1993 and, like the Chairman's Council, was designed "to provide a regular and intimate venue for policy makers and business executives to discuss various international political and economic issues," a UNA fact sheet said. The Ambassadors' Council arranged events with UN ambassadors and senior UN personnel.

Seton Hall University created the School of Diplomacy and International Relations in 1997. Whitehead endowed the school, and it was renamed the John C. Whitehead School of Diplomacy and International Relations at Seton Hall University in 2002 (see below). The school built a strong partnership with UNA-USA and featured special training on the UN for students.

After the 9/11 terrorist attacks, Whitehead was appointed chair of the board of the Lower Manhattan Development Corporation, the organization responsible for rebuilding downtown Manhattan. He also served as the chair of the World Trade Center Memorial Foundation.

Arthur Ross was an investment banker and philanthropist who made UNA one of his many causes. Born in 1910, he was a salesman in his youth and began his business career at a Wall Street brokerage firm in 1932. As a lieutenant commander in the US Navy during World War II, he was stationed in Panama and Ecuador. After the war, through advancements and mergers, he eventually became the vice president of Central National-Gottesman, a papermaking company, in 1974. His combined success as an investment manager and at Gottesman made him a wealthy man.

Ross got involved in international affairs at the urging of Senator Jacob Javits (R–New York) in 1961. During the 1970s, Ross was part of the US delegation to the UN as a public member of the delegation to the General Assembly, UNESCO, and other conferences. When Ross left the US delegation, he became the chair of UNA-USA. In a

2004 interview, Ross recalled, "It really captivated my imagination to have a grassroots operation in touch with people across the country, and so I gave it whatever time I was able to." Noting the "ongoing tug-of-war" between the United States and the UN, he said UNA was "one of the main opportunities one had of improving and cementing the integration of US public opinion and the organization."[4]

Over the decades, Ross served in various capacities at UNA until his death in 2007. UNA named its conference room in his honor. After the merger with the UN Foundation, the remodeled offices retained the Ross name.

In a 2005 speech, Ross said he grew up "in a time of hope and disillusion about international institutions. . . . The United Nations was the effort by my generation to bring an end to 'the scourge of war' that had brutalized the twentieth century." He added, "I developed a sense of how the UN could serve our national interest."[5]

As William Luers said of Whitehead and Ross, "John and Arthur were exceptional people who carried the dream. They were old enough. They remembered. . . . The two of them shared this original dream, the Eleanor Roosevelt idea, [of] what the world could be like." That older generation "retained a residual respect for, and admiration for, and hope for the UN, and that kept them in there, no matter what happened."

In a 2001 speech accepting the Eleanor Roosevelt Award from UNA-USA, Ross said the US Constitution and the UN Charter were the most important documents for governance, since both "stand for the rule of law, a principle that is the final, civilizing instrument of a free society. The United Nations is the indispensable instrument in helping to achieve these objectives globally."[6]

Whitehead called Ross "one of our most generous contributors," regularly donating $100,000 every year, making his total contributions a million dollars "once or twice over." On his death, UNA received a $3.5 million bequest from Ross for the maintenance of the Ross conference room and for any "exceptional circumstances." Michael McMahon, UNA-USA's final financial director before the merger with the UN Foundation, said, "Due to financial difficulties during 2009 and 2010, $1,500,000 and $1,000,000 respectively were released from the [Ross] endowment. The remaining $1,000,000 was transferred to UNF."

Ross was also a champion of the World Federation of United Nations Associations. In his 2001 speech, Ross said WFUNA was "building on its newfound strength and creative energy, . . . spreading the message of the United Nations to every corner of the Earth. It is the one organization that speaks to all nations and to all peoples. That is why its revitalization has captured our imagination."[7] That newfound strength was mostly Ross's work. He spent "a decade reviving [WFUNA], which he call[ed] 'a very important element in the global structure in support of the United Nations.'"[8] The WFUNA website acknowledged the support of Arthur and Janet Ross, his wife, noting that Arthur "founded the Friends of WFUNA in 2001 and was a key supporter of WFUNA in the years following. In 2007, Mr. Ross bequeathed a generous endowment to WFUNA."[9]

In an interview for this book, Janet Ross said her husband found WFUNA compelling because "there were so many great possibilities to involve people in the United Nations. He thought it could become a world movement in support of the United Nations." Since he was so engaged with UNA-USA, "he wanted other countries to be equally involved." The UNAs were "the people's voice," she added.

The *New York Times* obituary on Ross focused on his arboreal philanthropy. "To many New Yorkers, the Arthur Ross Pinetum, adjacent to the northwest edge of the Great Lawn in Central Park, became a peaceful refuge. Begun in 1971, it covers four acres and comprises twenty-five species of conifers, including domestic pines as well as those of more exotic species from around the world."[10] Ross also endowed arboretums and greenhouses to the New York Botanical Garden and Barnard College. He lent his art collection to the University of Pennsylvania and to the Council on Foreign Relations. He was a trustee of the American Museum of Natural History, where he endowed the Hall of Meteorites and the terrace next to the planetarium. He gave $5 million to the Asia Society to establish the Center on US-China Relations. At the Council on Foreign Relations, he endowed the Arthur Ross Book Award to "recognize books that make an outstanding contribution to the understanding of foreign policy or international relations."[11]

The driving passion of William vanden Heuvel's public work has been the legacy of Franklin and Eleanor Roosevelt. He has been the president of the Franklin and Eleanor Roosevelt Institute since it opened in 1987. More recently, he was the main force behind establishing the Four Freedoms Park Conservancy on Roosevelt Island, across from the UN in the East River in New York.

"I never made a speech without pointing out that Roosevelt's dream was not a dream but a practical concern with an organization that could preserve the peace and prevent war and that's the United Nations," vanden Heuvel said in an interview for this book in 2014. "I never give a speech without pointing out the Universal Declaration for Human

Rights by Mrs. Roosevelt is the greatest document in international history emerging from an organization. It centered around the four freedoms and the Charter of the UN." Vanden Heuvel added: "I'm constantly doing battle with people to get them to understand that every generation has got to interpret this commitment separately. This is the foundation commitment of our nation, to build an organization that can preserve peace and prevent violence and at the same time do so many other things, like promote human rights and state development."

Vanden Heuvel held many leadership roles in UNA, including chair of the Board of Governors from 1992 to 1994. He was also the president of the Friends of WFUNA until 2014. He regularly argued for Roosevelt-style assertiveness in working with the UN and against its critics. He attended a luncheon in 1995 hosted by President Bill Clinton, commemorating the fiftieth anniversary of FDR's death. "Knowing how [Clinton] operated, I had prepared a memorandum to him on the UN, saying how important this was to the United States and how the president could do certain things and make things happen," he said. The memo to Clinton said the president should be more assertive in promoting the UN. According to vanden Heuvel, "The UN framework advances many of our goals better—much better—than a bilateral sledgehammer." He added, "The

Cyrus Vance, former secretary of state (left), and UNA-USA cochairman of the National Council, John C. Whitehead, with William vanden Heuvel at the 1988 UNA Gala.
(Photo courtesy of the Seton Hall University UNA-USA archives.)

UN bashers, led by the Heritage Foundation, have had an uninterrupted decade of faulting the UN, holding it to standards that few if any governments could themselves meet. The Congress has deliberately bankrupted the UN, making efficiency and forward planning almost impossible."

Writing one year after the 1994 elections that gave the Republicans control of Congress, vanden Heuvel wrote, "The attacks from Congress on the UN say more about the attackers than about the real difficulties confronting the organization. Behind it all lies the notion that American foreign relations involve no more than incessant lectures to an ignorant world interlaced with occasional unilateral forays."[12]

In the interview for this book, vanden Heuvel said he regularly made the case that polls show that 70 percent of Americans want the UN to succeed. When he said this to Clinton, he said the president responded, "Yes, but 15 percent don't want [it] to exist and that 15 percent votes on that issue while the 70 percent do not." Vanden Heuvel's counterargument was that if the president led, he would "get a big base of support that will say yes to you." That 15 percent "is powerful and they paralyze," vanden Heuvel said.

Beyond his UNA and Roosevelt work, vanden Heuvel was deputy US permanent representative to the UN from 1979 until 1981 and US permanent representative to the Geneva office of the UN from 1977 to 1979. He was also a special assistant to Attorney General Robert F. Kennedy from 1961 to 1964, special counsel to New York governor W. Averell Harriman, and vice president of the New York State Constitutional Convention in 1967. He has served on the New York City Board of Corrections, the Council on Foreign Relations, the International Rescue Committee, International League for Human Rights, the Office of Economic Opportunity (President Johnson's antipoverty program in the War on Poverty), and the Robert F. Kennedy Memorial Foundation. Well into his eighties as this book was written, vanden Heuvel continues to serve UNA-USA as a member of its Leo Nevas Human Rights Task Force.

Like many UNA board members, Ruth Hinerfeld came to the association from the League of Women Voters. In 1967, she was named the second alternate to the league's UN observer mission. After she became its observer in 1973, she was asked to join the UNA Board of Directors. "At that point, I was in a position where I had reached what they considered the proper stature to be asked on the board," she said in an interview for this book. She served on it until 2007—longer than anyone except for Arthur Ross. As the league's representative at the UN, her agenda had matched that of UNA. As she recalled, "We were concerned with public support [for] the UN. We were concerned with US funding for the UN. The issues of funding are ongoing and everlasting."

She was president of the League of Women Voters from 1978 to 1982. One of the favorite things she did with UNA during this time, she said, was to serve on the Economic Policy Council (see Chapter 15). She also worked with Peggy Carlin, a UNA staff member (see Chapter 4) on producing a joint UNA/League of Women Voters publication on the UN's twenty-fifth anniversary, as well as one on environmental issues leading up to the UN Conference on the Human Environment, held in Stockholm in 1972. Hinerfeld saw that conference as a turning point in NGO relationships with the UN. She said Stockholm was "about how NGOs can be effective, which was a model for many NGO gatherings thereafter. It really functioned as an organizing device to institutionalize a role for NGOs."

After Ed Luck left UNA as president, Hinerfeld said control of UNA was mainly in the hands of "sort of an old boys' club. They knew one another well. A lot of decisions were being made within a relatively small group, not being shared with the board." She mentioned Whitehead and Ross in this context, with the two of them making the decisions on hiring key staff, including some to "bring in young money," Hinerfeld said. She added,

> You had the old guard and the young guard, and they were both sort of vying. Who gets left out when these guys are competing a little bit? It's the members. The chapters. There was always tension between the national level and the grassroots. It was always in play. There were always things going on to make it better, or make it worse. It was constant. . . . Here are the members who really care and do the work of advocacy and educating the public. All you guys up there care about is money and fund-raising and bringing in board members who have big bucks.

But from the national level, she said, "People think that they don't know what we do for them. They run the organization. Without the office and internal staff and financial backing, there is no organization. I guess there was this, I wouldn't call it mutual respect, but understanding."

In addition to being on the League of Women Voters, Hinerfeld was a member of the Women's Foreign Policy Group, served on the White House advisory committee for trade negotiations, and was a vice chair of UNICEF. She was also a delegate to the 1980 International Women's Conference in Copenhagen.[13]

William McDonough, who was cochair of UNA from 2006 to 2010, came to the UNA board by an unusual route: former Secretary-General Kofi Annan asked him. McDonough, in an interview for this book, called Annan "a dear friend of mine" who told him the UNA-USA needed a new chair; he asked whether McDonough would be willing to serve: "So I said yes." He said Annan "was trying to be helpful to UNA. I had been president of the Federal Reserve Bank of New York since 1993, and John Whitehead and several other seniors at the UNA establishment thought that would be a good background. And I'm a former Foreign Service officer."

McDonough was the eighth president and chief executive of the Federal Reserve Bank of New York from 1993 to 2003, after which he became chair for two years of the Public Company Accounting Oversight Board at the US Securities and Exchange Commission; the board's mandate is to oversee the audits of public company financial statements. He also served on other financial institutions, such as the Federal Open Market Committee and the Bank for International Settlements. His move to the Fed came after a twenty-two-year career at the First National Bank of Chicago. From 2006 to 2009, he worked for both Merrill Lynch and as chair of the Investments Committee for the UN Joint Staff Pension Fund. Thus, "my perspective is much larger than the average businessperson," he said.

When McDonough joined the UNA board, Luers was president, and Thomas Pickering was McDonough's cochair. McDonough said Luers "was doing an effective job" and "the chapters were running along very well. The board of directors needed some pulling together." He said he often called the chapters "the crown jewel" of UNA.

"A bunch of people in New York were not going to help the United States have a great active interest in the United Nations," he said. "We're a fifty-state country, and if you don't have all the chapters, you're not really supporting the UN very well. So I was a very big fan of the chapters, and always attended their [annual] meeting and made a speech there." Public support also had to translate into governmental support. "You had to have congressional support for the UN, or it just doesn't work."

The Seton Hall Alliance

Seton Hall University (SHU), a Catholic university in South Orange, New Jersey, is known for its theology and law schools, as well as its basketball team. In 1997, the university began a partnership with UNA to create the School of Diplomacy and International Relations.

The idea for the school originated with the university's board of regents around Christmas 1996. John Shannon, who at the time was dean of the business school, said in an interview for this book that some alumni at first thought the business school could do "some executive education at the UN," but soon "we realized we had an opportunity to do something bigger than that." So Shannon and others raised the possibility of a school of international affairs with the president of Seton Hall, who approved the idea. Contact was made with UNA, as it "had substantial standing with the UN, [so] it made sense from a strategic perspective," Shannon said. Preliminary talks started with UNA staffer Ralph Cwerman in January 1997; by June, both the Seton Hall Board of Regents and the UNA board approved the initiative. The School of Diplomacy and International Relations accepted its first undergraduate students in September 1997, with a law professor as acting dean and a faculty drawn from the schools of international business and law and the college of arts and sciences. "We did not have much of a chance to recruit," Shannon noted.

Despite the short time it took to become a school, there were concerns, Shannon said. The primary question was, "Did we even need another school of international relations? The market was saturated." Seton Hall did some research, he said, and they determined there was room because, in the post–Cold War environment, interest in international affairs was increasing. In addition, "one of the key differences and the point of the whole exercise was that ours, from the beginning, meant to take a UN focus," whereas most schools were US-focused. According to Shannon, it was "pretty clear that the UN focus was the right thing to do" and that the work with UNA "was integral." Shannon called the school "a great success. [It was] a long-standing vision of what the UNA wanted to get done, and for us, it was an opportunity to build something we did not have."

Courtney B. Smith, who was one of the first faculty members recruited for the school in 1999, said that during the 1998–1999 academic year, the school was still developing the curriculum and using adjuncts to teach. Smith, now the senior associate dean at the school, said in an interview for this book that some adjuncts "were arranged through UNA and the UN community. [The school] also used professors on loan from other departments at the university to test the curriculum." For the 1999–2000 academic year, the school had four full-time faculty members, including Smith.

As chair of the UNA board then, Whitehead was already involved in the Seton Hall alliance, but his participation took a new dimension in 2002. In 1999, Seton Hall began holding a Global Leadership Gala, honoring business and labor leaders. In 2002, the university honored Whitehead. That year's gala, Smith said, "happened to be the naming event [for the school]. It was the biggest gala in terms of size and attendance and fund-raising." It also resulted in Whitehead's deciding to contribute endowment funds to the school, so it became known as the John C. Whitehead School for Diplomacy and International Relations. That relationship ended abruptly in 2013 when Whitehead withdrew his support over disagreements stemming from management decisions that did not include consultations with Whitehead. The school returned to its original name: the School of Diplomacy and International Relations. (The school is also the institutional home for this book, including plans to establish a web archive on the UNA-USA History Project.)

In addition to the traditional bachelor's and master's degrees, studies abroad, and internships (including interns who assisted in writing and researching this book), the school offers a graduate certificate in Post-Conflict State Reconstruction and Sustainability (including courses on justice, truth, and reconciliation in postconflict societies and civil conflict and development), a certificate in UN Studies, and the United Nations Intensive Summer Study Program. This last program, organized with UNA-USA, familiarizes students with the inner workings of the UN. The school's biannual publication is the *Journal of Diplomacy and International Relations*. The school also sponsors the annual World Leaders Forum, featuring international figures such as UN Secretaries-General Kofi Annan and Ban Ki-moon, former Soviet president Mikhail Gorbachev, former Israeli president Shimon Peres, Iranian president Mohammad Khatami, and Liberian Nobelist Leymah Gbowee.

The alliance has continued since UNA merged with the UN Foundation. The Walsh Library at Seton Hall welcomed the opportunity to serve as home for the UNA-USA archives, which contributes to the university's research presence. Smith described some "enhancements" resulting from the UNA/UNF merger—in particular, "the greater presence" in Washington. "The school has a program where we help students get internships in DC by offering classes to keep them as full-time students while in DC. Those classes are offered at UNF space," Smith said. "They have hosted our students as interns in that space. Additionally, a lot of the things UNA was willing to do, like helping us at recruitment events and marketing, have become easier at UNF. The relationship has not diminished in any way. It has persisted and grown through the transition, which is very rewarding to us."

UNA-USA's delegation to the second Sino-US Dialogue on
Global Security, Beijing 2005. From left: Ken Miller, Jeffrey Bader,
Richard Williamson, Toby Gati, Brent Scowcroft,
Suzanne DiMaggio, William Luers, and Kenneth Lieberthal.
(Photo courtesy of the Seton Hall University UNA-USA archives.)

Humanitarian Campaigns

In the international community, an important insight in garnering support on governmental and public opinion regarding politically sensitive issues, such as arms control and international law, has been to frame them in terms of their humanitarian impact. Rather than talk about the Nuremberg precedent, for example, or the shortcomings of the International Court of Justice, arguing in favor of an International Criminal Court focuses on ending impunity and delivering justice to powerless victims. This brings the debate on international issues out of the esoteric "high priest" realm and into the layperson's comfort zone.

When the Cold War ended and greater opportunities became apparent for nongovernment involvement in humanitarian efforts, UNA-USA's combination of political expertise and grassroots gave it a unique position to contribute to the dialogue and activities on many issues on the ground. The UN was not only allowed but also encouraged to take on responsibilities that Cold War paralysis had prevented it from addressing (see Chapter 9). Sometimes independently or concurrently, the UN, governments, and NGOs launched initiatives in the 1990s that framed international problems as humanitarian imperatives, drawing positive results.

Land Mines and Adopt-A-Minefield

The global campaign against land mines was a triumph of governmental and nongovernmental cooperation. Presenting it as a humanitarian catastrophe, rather than as a military or diplomatic problem, made the issue tangible, as it affected real people—invariably, civilians. This strategy also allowed average citizens to believe, correctly, that they could do something about land mines. Popular engagement was key to the rapid success of the campaign against land mines and the convention to ban them worldwide.

UNA-USA began its engagement on the issue in a familiar style: drawing on experts to inform and mobilize the chapters, students, and general public about the horrific human costs of mines and how the problem could be solved. In 1996, UNA-USA began its Landmine Awareness Campaign with the board of directors committing the organization to "securing the support of the United States government for the immediate negotiation of a complete ban on the production, use, export, and storage of anti-personnel landmines." UNA also joined the US and international campaigns to ban land mines. UNA organized a national speaking tour with land-mine victims and deminers, released land-mine awareness kits to its 177 chapters and divisions, and sponsored a national high-school essay contest on "The United Nations and the Elimination of Landmines."

In 1999, when the Landmines Convention/Mine Ban Treaty entered into force, UNA-USA launched an innovative campaign to reach out to the general public. Adopt-A-Minefield (AAM) was an example of traditional UNA activism that encouraged individuals and organizations—religious groups, schools, corporations, and local governments—to "adopt" active minefields by raising the funds to clear mines from designated communities across the world, with the cash raised by AAM sponsors earmarked for identifiable locations. The donations were channeled and administered through the UN Development Programme (UNDP) and used in its demining operations; financial support also came from the Better World Fund, part of the UN Foundation and the US State Department. In AAM's first two years, $3 million was raised for fifty-four "adopted" minefields in Afghanistan, Bosnia and Herzegovina, Cambodia, Croatia, and Mozambique, with 292,000 square meters of land cleared.

In 2000, AAM began partnerships with UNA-UK and UNA-Canada with their own AAM initiatives. AAM also established an advisory board, with goodwill ambassadors Paul McCartney and Heather Mills as cochairs. Mills, then married to McCartney, was an amputee and had worked with refugees in the former Yugoslavia.

AAM was a classic example of the national offices and chapters working together. Individual chapters "adopted" specific fields in specific towns. For example, Minneapolis adopted a minefield in Sarposa, Afghanistan; Port Washington, New York, adopted a field in Boeng Krosal, Cambodia; and Atlanta adopted a field in Aldeia, Mozambique. The typical grant was $20,000 to $40,000. In later years, minefields were adopted in the territory of Abkhazia, Angola, Colombia, Ethiopia, Iraq, Laos, Lebanon, Nepal, and Vietnam.

A number of UNA's active chapters elected to participate in the program. The Denver chapter leader, Gloria Dogan, saw it as a prototype for membership building by "localizing" the UN's work. She also found that fund-raising for clearing a minefield in Mozambique—to which she and other Denver chapter members made a site visit as the clearance proceeded—inspired in her a new passion for her UNA involvement. A dozen years after the fact, Seattle chapter leaders recalled AAM as a successful means for achieving impact in a way that circumvented the policy blockages of Washington, DC.

UNA members in Wisconsin raised $10,000 for mine clearance, and Lawrence Levine, a local leader in California, pointed with pride to Monterey Bay's becoming, in his words, "the first to successfully conclude an Adopt-A-Minefield campaign to raise $35,000 to sponsor mine clearance" in a Bosnian village in 1999. Participation in the minefield clearance program energized UNA participants in Monterey; after the collapse of the Taliban regime in Afghanistan, the chapter signed up to conduct a similar campaign to clear an Afghan minefield, which it concluded in 2004. Monterey's performance, however, was exceptional. In contrast to the year-in and year-out predictability of fund-raising for a publicly recognizable UN "brand," such as UNICEF, the majority of local chapters found intimidating the entrepreneurship required to understand and market a new campaign and the financial responsibility they would assume in "adopting" and having to clear a minefield.

Nahela Hadi began her UNA career as a consultant for AAM, becoming the deputy director of AAM in 1999 and executive director in 2002. In 2006, she was named vice president for humanitarian campaigns, and in 2007, she became the chief operating officer until a radical downsizing at UNA-USA occurred due to serious financial and organizational challenges. In an interview for this book, Hadi said AAM was successful in gaining support from many chapters and from young people. Chapters "were able to keep [young people] if they had interesting programs that were interesting to young people." She said AAM "developed this whole outreach campaign in towns and cities," in which she would speak to chapters. As she recounted,

We would work with them and promote partnership with other organizations. I would go and speak. Chapters that were really organized would have me busy for hours at a time. Doing interviews and appearing on TV at events and luncheons and dinners. The chapters that really cared about [AAM] would find new members as a result of it. After the campaign a lot of those people became involved.

In succeeding years, AAM became increasingly ambitious. Night of a Thousand Dinners began in 2001 as a joint venture by AAM and the Canadian Landmine Foundation. This series of dinners, lunches, wine tastings, and brunches was held in more than fifty countries, taking place in homes, restaurants, churches, schools, and the UN. In its second year, nearly 1,500 events were held. The first Night of a Thousand Dinners in Washington, DC, was hosted by Secretary of State Colin Powell—despite the United States not being a party to the Mine Ban Treaty—with members of the political and business communities attending, including Queen Noor of Jordan and Senator Patrick Leahy, a leading advocate for the ban. "We gather tonight to honor the wonderful work that has been done through public/private partnerships for mine action, and to recommit ourselves to this lifesaving work," Powell said.

AAM and its gala benefits and other social events also drew support from media luminaries and celebrities (journalist Walter Cronkite, actor Michael Douglas, *Saturday Night Live* producer Lorne Michaels, actress Julia Ormond), the private sector (Jamie Dimon of JPMorgan Chase and attorneys Ben Brafman and Edward Hayes), and other public figures (former UN undersecretary-general Maurice Strong and the former executive director of the UN Population Fund Nafis Sadik). In 2001 and 2002, gala concerts in Los Angeles featured McCartney and were hosted by *Tonight Show* host Jay Leno. The events attracted such singers as Paul Simon, Tony Bennett, and Juanes.

Like other campaigns seeking to mobilize public opinion, celebrities played key roles in promoting AAM. While in Moscow for a concert, McCartney and Mills met Vladimir Putin on May 24, 2003, in his first term as president, to urge him to reconsider the country's landmine policy. McCartney publicly repeated this plea at his concert in Red Square. (The country has yet to join the Mine Ban Treaty.) In 2003, actress Angelina Jolie, a goodwill ambassador for the UN's refugee agency, accompanied British schoolchildren to a Mines Advisory Group demining training center in Cheshire, England, where they combed a mock minefield as a training exercise.

A dedicated survivor-assistance program began in September 2002 and supported the work of specialized UN agencies providing services to land-mine survivors. AAM raised $200,000 the first year, including

$100,000 for the UNDP's Comprehensive Disabled Afghans' Programme, which helped nearly 20,000 victims. The American Chamber of Commerce in Bosnia-Herzegovina raised $100,000 from its Night of a Thousand Dinners in 2004; the dinner in 2008 raised $294,000, earning matching funds from the US State Department. UNA worked with Rotary International to create Rotarians for Mine Action, with more than 100 groups in the United States and Canada.

The campaign continued to spread. By 2006, UNA's annual report said it was "the largest private funder of mine action worldwide, raising more than $4 million in 2006 for mine clearance, survivor assistance and mine risk education projects in eleven program countries." That brought the total raised since AAM's beginning to $17 million, used for survivors' assistance and clearance of more than twenty-one million square meters of land. Also in 2006, AAM held its first New York gala, honoring Secretary-General Annan and featuring actors Michael Douglas and Catherine Zeta-Jones; Rachael Ray, the cooking-show entrepreneur; and Moby, the musician. The 2007 gala honored Ted Turner, the outgoing AAM chair Nancy Rubin, and restaurateur Daniel Boulud. That year, AAM joined the international campaign to support the Oslo Conference on Cluster Munitions, where forty-six governments (not including the United States) committed to concluding a ban on cluster munitions.

The UNA-USA board concluded the campaign in December 2009. It had raised more than $25 million, cleared more than a thousand minefields, aided thousands of survivors, and raised UNA's profile.

HERO

A short-lived UNA program meant to meet the educational needs of children orphaned and made vulnerable by HIV/AIDS in Africa began in 2004 and was dubbed HERO, or Help Educate At-Risk Orphans and Vulnerable Children.

One of the most heart-wrenching effects of the AIDS pandemic has been the enormous number of children orphaned when the adults in their lives have died from the disease. UNICEF and other international agencies have long identified education as a means of assisting these children and their communities, with schools being the focal points for meeting some of their basic needs.

HERO was another effort to involve chapters and the general public in a hands-on approach to solving international problems by raising funds to support villages and schools. HERO identified thirty-nine pilot schools in Ethiopia, Namibia, South Africa, and Zambia. The program attracted a wide range of players offering expertise and financing, including UNICEF, UNESCO, Procter & Gamble, *CosmoGirl* magazine, the Rockefeller Brothers Fund, and the US Agency for International Development. Regional partners included CARE Zambia, South Africa's Media in Education Fund, South Africa's Valley Trust, and the Urban Trust Namibia.

Hadi said HERO followed the model of the land-mines project: "You work with organizations that were already delivering services on the ground, so we're not reinventing anything. What we are doing here is raising funds and creating more partnerships."

From the start, teenagers were a principal audience for HERO, but within a few years that focus dominated. The Youth Ambassador Program began in 2006 to bring US teens to Africa under the HERO umbrella. The youth ambassadors spent about four weeks in the HIV/AIDS-affected communities and worked at HERO-sponsored schools. The teens tackled such basic problems as lack of water, food insecurity, and crumbling school buildings. Eleven teens enrolled in the program in 2006, growing to twenty in 2007. In 2008, twenty-one teens participated, expanding to include Canadians. The 2008 team worked in the KwaZulu-Natal province of South Africa, renovating HERO-supported schools by building playgrounds and security fencing and participating in recreational programs for the children. In Namibia, they helped build twenty houses, fences, and wash stations for the San people in the Eenhana region.

As the Youth Ambassador Program grew, the actress Eva Amurri, daughter of UNICEF goodwill ambassador Susan Sarandon, was named UNA-USA's goodwill ambassador for HERO in 2007.

The program was never fully embraced by the chapters, however, and support soon dwindled, with Hadi estimating that only twenty to thirty chapters participated. By the time discussions started over the alliance between UNA and the UN Foundation in 2009, HERO was no longer operating.

The opposite fates of AAM and HERO demonstrated how much these UNA initiatives depended on the support of the membership and wide resonance in US society.

Notes

1. John C. Whitehead, *A Life in Leadership: From D-Day to Ground Zero* (New York: A New America Book, Basic Books, 2005), 49, 54–56, 61–63.

2. Christine Harper, "John Whitehead, Who Took Goldman Global, Dies at 92," *Bloomberg Business,* February 7, 2015, http://www.bloomberg.com/news

/articles/2015-02-07/john-c-whitehead-who-began-goldman-s-global-growth
-dies-at-92.

3. Whitehead, *A Life in Leadership*, 219–226.

4. Barbara Crossette, "Global Visionaries," *The InterDependent,* Fall 2004,
7–10.

5. Arthur Ross, private collection.

6. Ibid.

7. Ibid.

8. Crossette, "Global Visionaries."

9. WFUNA, "Contributors," http://www.wfuna.org/contributors.

10. Douglas Martin, "Arthur Ross, Investor and Philanthropist Who Left
Mark on the Park, Dies at 96," *New York Times*, September 11, 2007.

11. Council on Foreign Relations, "Arthur Ross Book Award," http://www
.cfr.org/about/arthur_ross.html.

12. William vanden Heuvel, private collection.

13. Crossette, "Global Visionaries."

12

Leadership Dynamics
Across the Decades

Defining the mission of UNA-USA and its predecessors is straightforward: the promotion of internationalism under the rule of law in the United States, with the United Nations as a primary vehicle for the country's foreign relations. Or, as stated in numerous UNA publications, "UNA is dedicated to strengthening the UN system and to enhancing US participation in that system." It is the execution of that mission that has been complicated. During the days of the League of Nations Association (LNA), trying to engage a traditionally isolationist country to view itself as part of a global community was a thankless task. With the rejection of the League of Nations, internationalists were presented with a double bind by suggesting that Washington should be involved in a peaceful international structure. Then, a single day—December 7, 1941—instantly flipped the elite and popular opinion of the United States against isolationism. Again, it was war that drove opinion, but the LNA was there to work with like-minded leaders in building a postwar order.

Creating the UN turned out to be the easy part; sustaining US support was a struggle almost from the start. Running any large organization is a challenge, but UNA presidents—all of them have been men, from diverse backgrounds—had to strike a balance among national, local (the chapters), and international constituencies. And, of course, most of them had to raise money.

The UNA, through its incarnations and up to today, has been part of the public landscape since 1923. An extraordinary roster of people has held leadership positions in UNA. Naturally, academics and diplomats would be drawn to such an organization, but over the decades UNA also counted on the support of business leaders, Wall Street millionaires, labor leaders, scientists, patrons of the arts, movie stars, journalists and editors, novelists and playwrights, medical innovators, former US presidents, and former US first ladies.

In the years leading up to World War II, the president of the LNA was Frank G. Boudreau. A native of Quebec, he was a medical doctor who received his degree from McGill University in Montreal. Boudreau wrote often on global health concerns and was the director of the Health Organization of the League of Nations in the 1930s. He replaced James T. Shotwell as president of LNA in 1938. In 1945, he stepped down as president to become the executive director of the Milbank Memorial Fund, a New York foundation specializing in health care and population, a position he held for twenty-five years.[1]

Boudreau was succeeded by William Emerson, a grandnephew of Ralph Waldo Emerson and an architect. As the latter, he was largely identified with the design of bank buildings. He joined the faculty of MIT in 1919, advancing from professor to chair of the faculty to the dean of the School of Architecture. He was also an advisory architect to Radcliffe College. During World War I, Emerson was the director of the Bureau of Construction of the American Red Cross (based in Paris) and was awarded the Chevalier Legion of Honour by France. After the war, he worked for the LNA and served as chair of the Committee to Defend America by Aiding the Allies (CDAAA) in 1940, becoming president of LNA in 1945. He was also chair of the Unitarian Universalist Service Committee from 1940 to 1948.[2]

Emerson, who served until 1953, was followed by Charles W. Mayo, a member of the family that founded the Mayo Clinic in Rochester, Minnesota. His parents, Charles Horace Mayo and Edith Graham Mayo, and Charles H. Mayo's brother William James Mayo began a collective medical practice in the 1880s. In 1919, the elder Mayos and other partners turned the practice into a nonprofit organization called the Mayo Properties Association, the first such medical group practice in history. This later led to the creation of the foundation known as the Mayo Clinic. Charles W. Mayo became a surgeon in 1927, served as a consultant to the Mayo Clinic in 1931, and joined the board of governors in 1933 until his retirement in 1964. During World War II, he ran a Mayo Clinic military unit in the South Pacific. Over the years, he served on various medical, civil, and educational boards and was a US delegate to World Health Organization assemblies.

Mayo stepped down from LNA in 1957 and Oscar A. de Lima became acting president until the election of Herman W. Steinkraus in 1958. De Lima had held various AAUN positions, including chair of the Executive Committee. A businessman, he was the president of the Roger Smith hotel chain, including the one still operating near Grand Central Terminal in New York. Steinkraus, as a first lieutenant in the US

Army during World War I, won the Distinguished Service Cross for heroism in battle in 1918. He was the owner and president of the Bridgeport Brass Company in Connecticut, and was a leading advocate of labor-management committees during World War II. These committees were set up to ensure smooth labor-management relations to avoid disrupting war production. In a speech to the Kiwanis Club of Bridgeport on August 19, 1943 (in which he was described as "Colonel Herman W. Steinkraus"), he advocated for the committees: "Basically, the war has forced us to realize all over again that the spirit of good relations among all classes of people is essential to a winning war effort, and is fundamentally the key to a happy world." He added, "I believe those companies who, in the midst of what seemed impossible production requirements for war purposes, have discovered and used this great force of cooperative effort in Labor-Management Committees, will continue to use this same force when peace returns."[3] In addition to serving on AAUN, Steinkraus advised the Federal Mediation and Conciliation Service, the national YMCA, and the Twentieth Century Fund. He was president of the US Chamber of Commerce in 1949.

Steinkraus served until 1964, when the AAUN merged with the US Committee for the United Nations to become the United Nations Association of the USA. During that transition year, Robert S. Benjamin, a cochair of United Artists, became the transitional president of both the US Committee and AAUN, the only person to hold both posts (see Chapter 15).

Porter McKeever became the first president of the new UNA in 1964 and served until his retirement in 1972. McKeever was best known as an adviser and biographer of Adlai Stevenson II, the Illinois governor who ran and lost twice against Dwight Eisenhower for US president and who later became UN ambassador under President John F. Kennedy. A native of South Dakota, McKeever was a journalist in Washington in the 1930s, a psychological warfare officer during World War II, and a member of the State Department starting in 1946. Also in 1946, he was appointed press officer of the US mission to the UN. In 1947, he was named director of information at the mission, but he resigned in 1952, while "attacking the Truman Administration for bypassing the United Nations and reducing what had been a cornerstone of United States policy to 'the size of a pebble.'"[4] He went to work for the Chicago Council on Foreign Relations, and in 1953, he was named director of public information for the Ford Foundation. McKeever had also worked as a volunteer in Stevenson's 1952 presidential campaign. His biography, *Adlai Stevenson: His Life and Legacy,* was published in

1989. After UNA, he served on the John D. Rockefeller III Foundation, the Asia Society, and the Japan Society.

McKeever's successor, Edward Korry, served less than two years before being replaced by James Leonard in 1973. Korry's tenure was not only brief but also tumultuous. A career foreign service officer, he was US ambassador to Chile in the run-up to the CIA-engineered coup against President Salvador Allende in 1973. Korry was retired in 1972 when the UNA board hired him as the new president. But after the September 1973 coup, charges by Chilean exiles and human rights activists were leveled at Korry, accusing him of playing a role in the overthrow and of installing a military dictatorship. The critics cited cables sent to the embassy from Washington. In addition, Korry's public disdain for Allende was used against him.[5] In a 1993 interview, Leonard, who was hired by Korry to be vice president, said, "By the time I arrived he had begun to go off the deep end. He had become convinced that he was being persecuted for a series of actions in Chile which he was not guilty of. He thought he was being blamed for disasters down there connected with Allende and the coup d'état." As a result, "he was spending all of his time defending himself against these charges . . . and not doing his job as president. So the board of governors bought him out."[6] After leaving UNA, Korry taught at Connecticut College and was a visiting scholar at Harvard's Center for International Studies as he continued to defend himself against the charges related to Allende. It was not until 1981 that a *New York Times* investigation vindicated Korry by showing that the Nixon White House and the CIA had kept Korry in the dark about their plans.

Leonard became UNA president in 1973, just as US elite and popular opinion was turning against the UN and, subsequently, against the UNA. As detailed in Chapter 7, the increasing number of new member states from the global south ended the assurance of a US-friendly majority in the General Assembly. Soon, the GA voted to give the Beijing government the Chinese seat in the UN, ousting the Taipei government that had held the seat since the UN's founding; it adopted the notorious Zionism-as-racism resolution; and it promoted economic reforms that US conservatives deemed hostile to capitalism. Members of Congress denounced the UN, public opinion declined, and UNA chapters lost membership just as Leonard took the helm of UNA.

A career foreign service officer, Leonard's specialty was arms control and disarmament. From 1969 to 1973, he was assistant director of international relations in the US Arms Control and Disarmament Agency (ACDA) in the Nixon administration. In an interview for this book, Leonard said that, in 1973, there was a "purge" targeting the arms control bureaucracy both in ACDA and in related offices in the State Department. Because Leonard had tenure in the Foreign Service, the State Department was obligated to provide him an assignment of some kind. According to Leonard, Henry Kissinger "had been a major factor in purging the arms control community. . . . I really didn't want to work for Kissinger, who was moving from the White House to become Secretary of State at that time." Charles Yost, the US ambassador to the UN, suggested Leonard look for work at UNA. Korry had just been hired as president, and in the spring of 1973, UNA offered Leonard the vice presidency for policy studies. Leonard said, "The UNA offer appeared attractive," so he took that job.

He said the post was particularly appealing because the board had decided that East-West tensions were the most urgent foreign policy issues and since Leonard had served in Moscow, this agenda fit his interests and skills. The job also dealt solely with policy and not with fund-raising. The fund-raising task fell to another vice president, Robert M. Ratner, "an effective fund-raiser who was already on staff," Leonard said. Ratner succeeded Leonard as UNA president in 1977.

After Korry left abruptly, the board persuaded Leonard to take the top job. He became president just as the Zionism resolution was going through the UN committees in the General Assembly. Opposing the resolution and addressing US Jewish concerns about the UN and UNA became "the principal task" of his administration. In addition, the East-West Policy Studies program at UNA was launched. Now-retired Charles Yost was the first chair of the program, with future secretary of state Cyrus Vance as vice chair. The staff work was done by Leonard and researchers Edward C. Luck (who would become UNA president) and Toby Gati (who led the Parallel Studies Programs; see Chapter 8).

Another intense item on Leonard's agenda was lobbying Congress to pay US dues to the UN, defending foreign aid in general and the UN Development Programme (UNDP) specifically. UNDP came under criticism despite being led at the time by F. Bradford Morse, a former Republican congressman. A key ally, Leonard said, was Senator Charles Percy (R-Illinois), who was involved in both the Chicago UNA chapter and the Chicago Council on Foreign Relations. Percy was "very instrumental in bringing along some Republicans and wavering Democrats on foreign aid and UNDP," Leonard said. Percy also ended up with the unexpected role of explaining to UN diplomats—the Russians, mostly—what the Watergate scandal was all about. He said the Russians were concerned that it was a setup by right-wingers angry with Nixon for his willingness to negotiate with Moscow.

When the Carter administration took office in 1977, Leonard was nominated as deputy permanent representative to the UN; so he left UNA. He served at the UN mission until 1979 and then came out of retirement to serve as acting president of UNA in 1994.

From the perspective of working in government and in the UNA, Leonard saw that UNA "had a standing unlike any other NGO in New York. Not just the UNA-USA president but also sometimes its vice presidents were invited to diplomatic dinners and were consulted by members of foreign delegations." He added, "The UNA was almost a part of the diplomatic corps. I don't think the diplomats were concerned about what our membership was. They looked on us as a source of intelligence."

After Leonard left in 1977, Robert M. Ratner served as president until 1984. He was already at UNA as vice president in charge of fundraising after having worked for the United Jewish Appeal Federation of Greater New York. By all accounts, he was a proficient fund-raiser.

In an interview for this book, John Lange, who was a staff member when Ratner was president, called him "a brilliant fundraiser. He had a way with dealing with the rainmakers, he brought them into the concept of UNA, he was creative in linking business, labor, and academics." After UNA, Lange joined the US foreign service until his retirement in 2009. He then worked for the Bill and Melinda Gates Foundation from 2009 to 2013, before taking up his current post as senior fellow for Global Health Diplomacy at the UN Foundation. Lange credited Ratner with helping to create the Economic Policy Council (see Chapter 15).

Ratner, however, had no policy expertise. Steve Dimoff said, "I do recall that he was very proud of having assumed the presidency of the organization, but I did not have the impression that he was all that interested in the substance. He was a fund-raiser first and foremost—a good public speaker and personable." Lange said Ratner brought in a retired foreign service friend, Arthur "Pete" Day, as policy expert.

Compliments for Ratner did not extend beyond praise for his fundraising abilities. Leonard said Ratner's presidency "met with no success." Luck said of Ratner, "I can't complain, but he wasn't really the figure to head the organization. He was not a substantive guy and never pretended to be." Both Gati and Luck, in interviews for this book, were critical of the financial management at the time by both the board and Ratner. UNA was "in terrible, terrible financial trouble," Luck said. Gati said that, in general, UNA "went into decline because the books were— I don't want to say 'cooked,' but, you know—nobody paid attention." Lange speculated that "when he became president, UNA lost its best fund-raiser because once he became president, he had many other duties." Assuming the presidency just as the impact of the Zionism-as-racism resolution was being felt, Leonard found key funders—liberal Jewish New Yorkers—turning away from the UN. "He was likely too proud to admit that his sources were drying up, and so I wouldn't be surprised if he did not reveal financial problems until they were really serious," Dimoff said.

When Edward C. Luck took over the presidency in 1984, he was the youngest UNA president, at thirty-four. His first order of business was dealing with the financial problems of the association. He said Ratner was "a corporate fund-raiser . . . and he was good at that." But Ratner had a large staff. "We were lopsided. . . . We had too many people, I thought, in sort of fund-raising and administration and not enough doing the actual work. So that changed a bit," he said in an interview for this book. "When I took over, I knew it was in bad shape, but I didn't know how bad. We were nine months behind in payables."

According to Luck,

> Our basic structure was the issue. We had one-half that was funding itself and really working for itself and another half, which was grassroots-based, which couldn't be viable financially, certainly under the current circumstances. So I said, "Look, I'm going to start raising money for policy studies. If I'm going to stay in this, be on this one project, I'm going to really focus on fund-raising." And I spent a lot, a lot of time and effort with foundations in particular, some with individuals and corporations, but mostly foundations.

When he became president, Luck had been with UNA for ten years, starting as a researcher in 1974. He recalled the sequence of events: he had been a graduate student at Columbia University, working on his PhD in political science, when Leonard phoned and asked if he wanted a short-term job running a project on conventional arms control. Leonard—at the time the acting president—"called my adviser at Columbia, Marshall Shulman, who was director of the Russian Institute, and asked Marshall, Did he have any promising graduate students who might be candidates to become a project director of this project on conventional arms control? My work had been almost entirely on the nuclear side, and I was studying Soviet strategic doctrine," yet he ended up working on a project dealing with nonnuclear weapons. He recalls, "It was my first real job"; it was a two-year project, culminating in November 1976 with a report, "Controlling the Conventional Arms Race." Cyrus Vance, who was about to become secretary of state, was vice chair of the study. Luck said, "I think of that panel—and UNA always got these sort of blue-ribbon panels—seven of the members of that panel went into the Carter administration, in significant political positions."

He continued: "After that, there was a question whether I would stay with the association. . . . There were a couple of opportunities with the Carter administration. I actually wrote the transition paper for the incoming administration on arms transfer restraints." Instead, at the request of Toby Gati, he stayed at UNA to run the Soviet program temporarily while she was on maternity leave. Luck and Gati had been students together at the Russian Institute at Columbia. When Gati returned, Luck was hired full time to work on policy studies. Still in his twenties, Luck found himself working on the projects and raising money for them. The studies were a source of "good, steady money," he recalled.

Once he became president, "My responsibilities shifted; I began to look at ways to raise money for the organization as a whole," rather than on his projects only. Like Leonard and Gati, Luck was a policy expert, so it was natural that this would be his focus. The Parallel Studies Program under Gati had expanded while Luck was on staff. This program was favored by the leadership, membership, and financiers. Chapters had an ownership role because when Soviet participants came to the United States, visits to chapters were worked into the itineraries.

In general, however, although the emphasis on policy was good for UNA's national profile and for fund-raising, it also helped widen the divide between the chapters and the national office. According to Luck,

> The other half of the organization—the outreach part, public education part, the part that Eleanor Roosevelt had so much to do with, I guess the AAUN side—was not well integrated with the New York component and was not doing terribly well financially, and so you really had a two-faced organization. That, I don't think, was very healthy. So for the grassroots, they saw it as a membership organization, their organization, and they had good reason to think that. But the other part of the organization—sort of New York, Boston, Washington establishment, big business, money types—foreign policy wasn't really to be done by the masses. It was to be done by the few, the knowledge of a few sort of thing.

At this point, Luck said, there were 176 UNA chapters with 35,000 members, though that number was always the subject of "constant debate," with the number of dues-paying members more like 15,000, and the higher number resulting from family members being included in the count. Luck recalls,

This idea that we would only really function effectively as one integrated organization, that needed an elite piece, and that was important,
but it needed grassroots. And we needed to recognize that foreign policy and good ideas in foreign policy came from many places. . . . There
is no monopoly in New York or Washington or anywhere else on good
ideas, and so I made that one of my prime objectives. And oddly
enough, in fact, I said that every project, every policy studies project,
every parallel studies project must have a grassroots component. And
if the Soviets would come over or the Chinese would come over, they
would have to go visit one or more chapters. I think that worked rea-
sonably well.

Another initiative meant to partly bridge the gap between the chapters and the national office was the Multilateral Studies Program, which,
according to Luck, was "fundamentally an effort to bring different parts
of the organization together, bring up the level of work in a lot of the
chapters, to have the New York people recognize quality work, what was
going on in other parts of the country, and bringing money." Luck added,
"Those projects were well funded year after year" (see Chapter 9).

In his first speech as president, Luck noted,

I said: "We have two legs. If we don't walk on both legs, we are going
to fall over, and we have to make sure these legs are of equal length
and equal strength, and we need to integrate them." So that's why I
started that project; [it] was because it actually looked at all the chapters and divisions to come up with their own recommendations, their
own reports, and we would try to synthesize as well as they could with
the national. And it was quite successful. We got a lot of foundation
support for them, and some of those projects were quite good.

UNA funding was actually based on "three legs," Luck said, recount-
ing roughly the percentages:

One was foundation funding, which at points when I was there, it got
up to 40 percent of our overall income, which I thought was actually a
little too high. Then we had the corporate, which probably was running
25 to 30 percent. Then we had individual gifts, which, in the end,
probably closer to 40 percent, but in those days, probably closer to 25,
and we were trying to inch that up, also trying to get more legacies and
this kind of thing to leave us more significant funds. We got a couple
quite large gifts, but that takes a lot of time.

The political diversity of UNA helped, as did the Economic Policy
Council (EPC), which, according to Luck, "had big business and big

labor. It was an important forum and stayed for many, many years. But it was not cheap, so a lot of the EPC money really went into the EPC." According to an EPC pamphlet, the mission of the council, started in 1976, was to "orchestrate a systematic and constructive involvement in international economic problems by the American private sector" (see Chapter 15).

Another concern that plagued Luck echoed one that the organization had dealt with since the League of Nations Association: maintaining a bipartisan character. "I was just very uncomfortable being in an organization that basically felt it was a liberal Democratic organization," Luck said. "If the UNA was only going to be supported by liberal Democrats, it was never going to be really sustainable." As a liberal Democrat himself, "I just didn't feel comfortable without having a real bipartisan organization."

Referring again to his "two-leg" speech as UNA president, he said it was a priority to bring in "Republicans, bringing conservatives, bringing people with different viewpoints. If our values, our views, our reasoning has logic to it, we will bring other people aboard, and they will see this." When Luck started at UNA in the immediate post–Vietnam War period, Congress was becoming more assertive in foreign policy. The Zionism-as-racism resolution added to conservative distaste for the UN, while repelling one of the staunchest supporters of the UN and UNA: the US Jewish community.

When Luck became president, fresh troubles arose. The Heritage Foundation launched its UN Assessment Project in 1982, and the Reagan administration's foreign policy team was hostile to the UN. The Heritage project was designed to paint the UN and its specialized agencies as hostile to US-style capitalism. As Luck recalled,

> In . . . many ways, I think it was the end of the foreign policy establishment, and foreign policy changed. And people began to recognize that in a democracy, you actually should have strong public input, and the UN itself needed more civil society and more public input in the way it did its work. So I was very much a champion for bringing the two parts together.

It helped that this era was also a time of high-profile support for UNA from important figures in the Republican Party, including former US attorney general Elliot Richardson, the former Pennsylvania governor and ambassador William Scranton, and Senator Charles Percy of Illinois.

Ironically, the Reagan administration's discomfort toward the UN proved to be a boost for UNA. "I think the Republicans in some ways—in the Reagan administration, in particular—gave us more attention and readier access . . . because they didn't really know the organization as well," Luck said. "I think they were thinking what you don't know could be dangerous, and so I think they wanted to keep in touch. And they also knew, quite frankly, that they didn't have a lot [of] great depth of knowledge in the UN, and we happened to know the UN, so I think that made some sense."

A carry-over from the policy studies was the idea that UNA "should not just be cheerleaders for the UN," said Luck. He continued:

> The UN has a lot of real problems and also had artificial problems with US withholdings. My argument was that if you cared about the UN, you should want its money to be used well. You would want its people to be used well, and you'd want its programs to be as effective and efficient as possible. I didn't believe in sort of giving lip service to the UN. I said you should push to make it a stronger, better organization, and I said we should be constructive critics.

That philosophy was tested immediately, when the UN faced a financial crisis in 1985. As Luck described it, "I had just taken over my [first] year as president, but we had been working on a big project, which in part was to respond to some of the congressional objections to the UN and the Kassebaum-Solomon amendment, which had the first really large congressional mandate of withholdings." In response, UNA created a panel with Elliot Richardson as the chair (see Chapter 6), who convinced Nancy Kassebaum to join. "In the end, we were able to convince her and her people that, in fact, the objections, which had to do with weighted voting in the General Assembly on financial matters, had been met by this consensus-based formula, which we put forward, and then we very much helped to lobby and get it done in the UN"—a solid example, Luck said, of UNA influence on the UN. Luck concluded, "A week later, I think by consensus or very close to consensus, the General Assembly voted in favor of this measure. So, it was a radical turnaround in some ways, but it helped to seal a really, really horrific financial crisis in the UN."

Leonard said of Luck's presidency that he helped "restore the high respect that UNA-USA had previously earned." Moreover, the relationships among Luck, Gati, Joe Sills (vice president for field activities), and Fred Eckhard (who was chief editor) "were so close that their combined fount of knowledge gave UNA-USA a voice that continued as a serious factor in the thinking of the Secretary-General's office." Both Sills and Eckhard went on to serve as spokespeople for UN Secretaries-General (Sills for Boutros Boutros-Ghali and Eckhard for Kofi Annan).

Luck called 1993, the last year of his presidency, "difficult." The fiftieth anniversary of the UN was approaching. He said,

> Some people on the board said we should raise $50 million for UN50. That because it's 50, it was doable. And I said: "I'm sorry. The rule of thumb in any major campaign is that the board itself, the inside should contribute a third before I get started. . . . If there's $17 million around this table to get it started, I would take it as far as I can."

The problem, according to Luck, was that "there was no one in the history of UNA-USA that ever raised anything close to that." He said UNA was "in a better financial position than we had been" and was starting to build reserves, but he told the board he couldn't get them to fifty million. He added, "There was some back-and-forth among different members of the board and some competing about who should chair and who should do this and that," though he declined to identify the board members.

This disagreement was compounded by Luck's sense that he had stayed on long enough:

> I had a certain sense of déjà vu. Every time an issue would come up, I would remember the way we handled it five years ago or ten years ago or fifteen years ago, and I said, "You know, that's too long. . . . I should start thinking about doing other things." But I had made no other plans. I was probably naïve. I had never worked anywhere else in my life. I had never looked for a job. This job came to me. In every promotion, UNA just came to me, and I never even thought of being in the job market.

At the same time, he said, New York University approached him "about either coming to NYU myself or bringing the Policy Studies Program to NYU." He added: "They thought they could raise a lot of money. . . . So I did talk to some of the . . . top people on the board at UNA about . . . any possibility of looking at some kind of merger, where some of the work would be with NYU, so we'd have more of an academic base." Some people "thought I was bailing, but I was not bailing. It was just an option that had come up," he said.

"The transition wasn't handled well, but I didn't want to stay and be president forever," he said. "I had several big projects going that I didn't want to just drop, and we were beholden to foundations to do them." Luck stayed on as president emeritus from 1994 to 1998 to complete those projects.

How the board handled Ed Luck's termination, Leonard said, was a "disgrace." Leonard continued, "He was pushed out. . . . Politics within the board led to that. At any rate, the board fired Luck without any plan for how to replace him." Gati, who by that time had left UNA for a position in the Clinton State Department, said that after Luck, "they had a series of very unfortunate presidential choices, which didn't work at all. I really can't explain it." After Luck left, UNA went through a rapid succession of acting presidents and presidents. Leonard said he wanted William Maynes to be UNA president. Maynes was assistant secretary of state for international organization affairs in the Carter administration, later becoming editor of *Foreign Policy* magazine. However, "By then, the board of UNA was not in good shape," Leonard stated. "They didn't conduct a good search."

As Luck stayed on as president emeritus to complete UNA's commitments to some long-running programs, he also worked as a special adviser to the UN Secretary-General on UN reform, including the Security Council, from 1995 to 1997. The recommendations his study made included the creation of the post of deputy secretary-general—a proposal the General Assembly accepted when it created the post in 1997. After the UN, Luck held positions at Columbia University, was briefly dean of the Joan B. Kroc School of Peace Studies at the University of San Diego, and then returned to Columbia.

Luck was replaced at UNA by George Langdon, who was president for only eight months in 1993 and 1994 before being dismissed. Langdon had been president of the American Museum of Natural History, in New York, from 1988 to 1993. Before that, he was the president of Colgate University from 1978 to 1988. Ruth Hinerfeld, a long-serving member of the board of directors and UN representative of the League of Women Voters, recalled in an interview for this book that Langdon "came in and locked himself in the office. Never saw him. He was the president who wasn't there." As a history scholar, "he was not really interested in the chapters," she said.

The board then selected Thomas B. Morgan, a leading figure in New York journalism and politics. As a journalist in the 1950s and 1960s, Morgan wrote for *Esquire, Life,* and *Harpers* and was an editor of *The Village Voice.* He also worked on political campaigns, such as for Adlai Stevenson and Eugene McCarthy. Morgan had also been press secretary for New York Mayor John Lindsay and worked on his unsuccessful run for the Democratic presidential nomination in 1972. Morgan served as the president of the WNYC Communications Group, including public radio station WNYC, from 1990 to 1994. Upon his retirement from WNYC, he was named president and chief executive of UNA in July 1994, but left at the end of 1995.

"That's how I returned," Leonard said. "They were desperate. UNA's decline was due to poor leadership. There was a rather acerbic atmosphere within the board." Leonard came back as acting president for a few months in 1996. In September 1996, the board selected Alvin P. Adams Jr., who had just retired from the Foreign Service after a thirty-year career that included serving as ambassador to Djibouti, Haiti, and Peru. In an interview for this book, Adams said,

> I spent a good deal of my time visiting [chapters] . . . to go there and give them an idea that New York was not bad, that we cared about them. There was always this tension between the chapters and the big money people in New York. I tried to build that bridge by going out there a lot and showing concern for these people and helping with their morale.

John C. Whitehead, the chair of the UNA board at the time, approached Adams on the recommendation of Undersecretary of State Lawrence Eagleburger and offered him the presidency. "I was winding down my career in the State Department and was available. I spent a good part of my life growing up in NYC. So that was kind of familiar to me. The UN, I knew, was a challenge," Adams said. "I had a sense the board was a challenge, given the nature of it [with] activists from around the country and the financial people from Wall Street. I thought it would be interesting."

Financing UNA was the chronic problem. At the time, Whitehead and Arthur Ross were the most prominent board members and the major fund-raisers (including their own money). "We had some real significant financial issues. I think three or four members of the board pledged a million-plus dollars each to keep it up and running," Adams said. "We kept that up, but there wasn't a lot of money there." Despite his lack of experience in raising money, Adams said the board expected it of him. "They wanted me to do a lot of fund-raising," he said, despite "not having spent recent years in New York with a big Rolodex of funders. Whitehead could go to people and ask for support. Sometimes we would get it, and sometimes we would not." He added, "The UN was not an easy sell in those days." As a result, most of the funds for UNA came from the board members themselves. At the end of 1997, "Whitehead asked me to leave. I think there was a major concern about raising money basically," Adams said.

Finally, William H. Luers was appointed both president and chair of the UNA Board of Directors in 1999 and served for ten years. (He was president until 2009 but relinquished chairmanship of the board in 2001.) Luers became president as the world and the UN entered a tumultuous period: the aftermath of the 9/11 terror attacks and the Bush administration's subsequent "war on terror" and invasion of Iraq. When the UN refused to support the invasion, US officials derided the relevance of the UN Security Council and worked to drive Secretary-General Kofi Annan from office over the "Oil for Food" controversy.

Although he had spent thirty-one years as a diplomat, serving mostly in Eastern Europe and the Soviet Union, Luers came to the UNA via the Metropolitan Museum of Art. In late 1998, he was ending his tenure as president of the Met after thirteen years. Arthur Ross and John Whitehead, who was the chair of the UNA board, approached him to take over the chairmanship of the board. Luers recalled the moment, in an interview for this book: "I said: 'Why do I have to be chairman? My thing is to be president. My thing is not to be chairman, because I don't have any money. You two have a lot of money.' They said, 'Well, we'll help you, for a while.' So I thought about it and thought maybe this would help get me back into the international arena."

Luers attended his first board meeting in early 1999, where he was offered the presidency as well as the chairmanship of the board. "So I did it," he said. William vanden Heuvel, a member of the board, a prominent New York lawyer, and a former diplomat with the US mission to the UN, said Luers "was the right person in that he could combine it all. Most ambassadors couldn't do that. . . . But Bill had Metropolitan experience and raised hundreds of millions. He was articulate, and he knew everyone."

Luers's tenure was defined by three major internal issues: restoring UNA's fund-raising; new programs; and constant tensions with the chapters. When he took over, he realized that UNA was in trouble: "When I looked at the numbers, it was over. . . . They couldn't fund it." He said he rebuilt UNA on the strength of its programs. "I did it around programs. I raised a lot of money. I mean, I moved it up to $10 million within two years," he said, largely on the strength of Global Classrooms (which was financed mainly by Merrill Lynch) and Adopt-A-Minefield (which was started by staffer Ralph Cwerman before Luers arrived). Luers said neither project was fully embraced by the chapters: "They thought it was a headquarters-run thing, and I thought it was a natural. But I was looking for things—how do you get chapters involved? I thought Global Classrooms was a natural, just an absolute natural, working with high schools and the local government, and I thought that Adopt-A-Minefield was a natural." Jim Olson, who held numerous chapter and national UNA posts over the decades, saw chapter receptiveness differently. "While Global Classrooms and Adopt-A-Minefield were not universally implemented by chapters, there were many local units that were enthusiastic about these programs," Olson said in an interview for this book. "Global Classrooms was initially created by the Boston Chapter, after all. Adopt-A-Minefield required significant fundraising ability, which many chapters lacked."

Adopt-A-Minefield was a fund-raising success, with luminaries such as Michael Douglas and Jay Leno lending support. "Paul McCartney was our patron," Luers said. "I remember I was passing through London, and I had lunch with him, and after lunch he gave me a check for $1 million." HERO was another program that Luers thought "had great potential." While he was able to secure funding from Procter & Gamble, the chapters were not interested in this either (see Chapter 11).

Yet these programs and the Global Studies Program continued. Luck and Gati were both gone from UNA by Luers's arrival (after leaving government, Gati joined the UNA board). Luers said the programs under his tenure followed their model of substantive policy that was also funder-friendly. "What we had to do was start creating programs which grabbed people's ideas about the role of the UN [but] at the same time allowed us to get large contributions from people who were excited about what we were doing," Luers said. "So that was my strategy the whole time. It was how you create programs that draw interest, not just to the UN, but to the issues that the UN was dealing with. And it was a quite conscious program. . . . Try to get people who had money to come and be involved in something that they found interesting."

The chapters felt that the national office needed to do more to help finance them and that most of the projects were elitist. Chapter leaders also felt the national leadership did not listen enough to their concerns. "I guess the tension was, they felt I didn't spend as much time as I should have with them. When we'd get to board meetings, and I wanted to talk about substance and help them understand what's going on at the UN, they wanted to talk about me or the headquarters' failure to satisfy their needs," he said. "By and large, the board was made up of people who were interested in what the UNA was doing and what the UNA could do in its programs. I had a pretty distinguished group of people I got on the board." But this "distinguished group of people" was also a source of complaints.

The program that raised the most objections from both the chapters and members of the board was the US-Iran dialogue (see Chapter 10). "I think I can understand why they wouldn't be attracted by the work we did with Iran, but they forget that during the Ed Luck period, most of their money came from Toby Gati, who ran one of the best dialogues with the Soviet Union," Luers said. He added that the model for the Iran project "was taken directly from Toby." The Iran dialogue was well financed, mostly by the Rockefeller Brothers Fund. An important difference between the Soviet and Iran projects was that the Soviet participants traveled around the United States, meeting with chapters. This was impossible to replicate with the Iranians; so, the membership lacked participation.

Chapters and some board members also objected to the Iran project arguing that it was outside the UNA mandate. Faye Wattleton, the former president of Planned Parenthood who served on the UNA board when Luers was president, said in an interview for the book that she "could never understand" why Luers so heavily promoted the Iran project. Wattleton added that UNA "should see itself as a vigorous machinery to build support of what the value of the UN is among Americans." However, Iran was "a very different tacking"; she criticized Luers's "very strong drive to turn this into a foreign policy organization. . . . I couldn't see the connection to UNA." Luers rejected this point of view: "The Iran project was one of the most successful programs ever mounted by UNA, and rather than grouse about it, it should be a source of credit and pride for the organization because today, with this new [nuclear] agreement with Iran, I think UNA can take some credit for having foreseen it and built for it."

Luers's tenure closely matched the run of the George W. Bush administration, which led to some strange divergences between the official government positions and private relationships. Luers and Paul McCartney once toured the US State Department, advocating for the Mine Ban Treaty. While there, they met Secretary of State Colin Powell. As Luers recounts,

> Before we walked in, he [Powell] called Paul and me aside. . . . He looked at Paul, and almost in tears, he said: "I want you to know that I served two tours in Vietnam. Not the happiest days of my life. Some terrible days. And the only happy moments I ever had was singing Beatles songs." It was touching. And then we went in and sat down, we had our little discussion about why the US government will not sign the treaty.

Condoleezza Rice, who was national security adviser and Powell's successor as secretary of state, was a fan of Global Classrooms. "Condi Rice loved Global Classrooms. She would come and speak to our Washington event," Luers said.

> As a matter of fact, the most respect I ever gained for her was when she stood up there, with this group of largely black kids, and told them about how they can do it, how it's possible for a person from a modest background to overcome, through education and through learning. I mean, she's a forceful speaker. I didn't agree with a lot of her point of view on foreign affairs, but, boy, she's a moving speaker when it comes to these kids.

During Luers's last years as president, UNA's finances were near exhaustion. UNA and the UN Foundation made their first attempt at a merger. "The only way" the UNA could fund itself, he said, "was to have a foundation like the UN Foundation to pay for it. The chapters were never going to get funded unless there was an organization that saw some interest in it. Tim [Wirth, the president of UNF] and I talked about this for years, and it was the only way I could see it happening." Board members Thomas Pickering, John C. Whitehead, and Josh Weston worked with Luers on proposals for a year and half. "We had a couple of false starts at it," Luers said. "Then I finally just left" in the spring of 2009. Luers became a fellow at the Rockefeller Brothers Fund, where he continued working on the Iran project.

After Luers, the UNA focus was on designing and gaining constituent support for an alliance with UNF. The last two presidents of UNA served a combined three years: Thomas J. Miller (2009–2010) and A. Edward Elmendorf (2010–2011). Miller was a Foreign Service officer from 1976 to 2005, first concentrating on Southeast Asia and then on the Middle East and North Africa. His postings included Thailand, Greece, Cyprus, and Bosnia and Herzegovina. Upon retiring from the Foreign Service, he was named the chief executive of Plan International, a London-based nonprofit group focusing on improving the lives of children in the developing world. In an interview for this book, Miller, who now lives in the Washington metro area, said that during his tenure (2005–2009) at Plan, revenues increased from $400 million to $700 million. "I kind of got branded as a successful NGO person," he said. "There was a headhunter who contacted me and asked if I was interested in the UNA job."

Miller said he did not know much about UNA, but he did know Pickering, who was then a cochair of the association. Miller was hired for his policy work and for his interest in working with the chapters. Despite his success at Plan, he said fund-raising was not a major part of the hiring discussions. At Plan, Miller said the fund-raising was done by the organization's national chapters. "My focus was on the programs," he said. "I would facilitate and coordinate, but I cannot take credit for raising the money. I made it clear when they hired me. We had done well as an organization, but it wasn't exclusively through my efforts." Once he got to UNA, "They were in bad shape, and I didn't realize how bad of shape they were in. When I was offered the job, I probably didn't probe as much as I should have."

His two priorities became money and relations with the chapters. "My predecessor had done a lot of good things, but he was interested in what he was interested in, and he lost interest in the rest of the organization," Miller said of Luers. "I came into this and had to deal with it as best I can. You've got a situation with this decline in revenues. The losses that occurred were not something that happened overnight. This had been coming on for years." He raised money from the board members and hired a development director. Miller saw the UNA annual gala in October 2009 as a last chance to raise significant funds. It "was a last big hope to try and save us financially. It wasn't a boom or a bust," he explained, leaving UNA in increasingly serious financial straits.

Regarding the chapters, he said,

> I think the heart and soul of UNA has always been the chapters. I don't think Bill felt that way, because the chapters felt kind of ignored and abused. I spent a lot of time traveling to the chapters and speaking. That was a serious part of my activities. . . . The strength was the chapters and the grassroots people who would get involved.

Miller had a US map on a wall in his office, with pins showing the locations of the chapters that he had visited.

Miller resigned in March 2010, having been offered a post with Independent Diplomat, an organization run by Carne Ross, a former British diplomat to the UN. "I really tried, but after a period of time, given the competition, and the hole we were in, the best course for us [UNA] was the merger" with the UN Foundation, Miller said.

Elmendorf, a former World Bank official, was hired as president and chief executive specifically to oversee the negotiations on the alliance between the UNA and UN Foundation and gain the support of the multiple UNA constituencies needed to make the alliance possible (see Chapter 18). Elmendorf was recruited by Pickering. "I had a mandate from the very beginning to work out an alliance between UNA-

USA and UNF," Elmendorf said in an interview for this book. "It wasn't a standard continuing job of indefinite term as president and CEO. The expectation from the very beginning was that I would make the merger happen and then, by my own volition, step down."

With long international experience through the World Bank and UNA experience at the national and chapter levels, Elmendorf was seen by his predecessor as the ideal person to build support for the UNA-UNF alliance with the many UNA-USA constituencies. Elmendorf (who is also the primary sponsor and fund-raiser for this book) had been involved with the UN and UNA in various roles since the 1960s, including serving at the US mission to the UN as assistant to Adlai Stevenson, in the UN Secretariat, and leading the Washington, DC, chapter of UNA. He joined the UNA board in 2009.

Elmendorf joined the Foreign Service in 1963, after working as a teacher in Ghana. He was posted at the UN from 1963 to 1969. In 1970, he began a thirty-year career at the World Bank, where he focused on health strategy, policy, and projects in developing countries, especially in Africa. After he retired in 2000, he continued as a consultant for the World Bank, as well as for the World Health Organization, UNDP, the US Institute of Medicine, and the African Development Bank.

Notes

1. Milbank Memorial Fund, *Centennial Report: Informing Policy for Health Care and Population Health*, 20–22, http://www.milbank.org/uploads /documents/centennialreport.pdf.

2. Herbert Vetter, ed., *Notable American Unitarians: 1936–1961* (Cambridge, MA: Harvard Square Library, 2005), 91.

3. *Vital Speeches of the Day*, vol. IX, 726–728, http://www.ibiblio.org/pha /policy/1943/1943-08-19b.html.

4. Marvin Howe, "Porter McKeever, 76, U.N. Backer and Adlai Stevenson Biographer," *New York Times*, March 4, 1992.

5. David Stout, "Edward Korry, 81, Is Dead; Falsely Tied to Chile Coup," *New York Times*, January 30, 2003.

6. James Leonard, "The Association for Diplomatic Studies and Training Foreign Affairs Oral History Project: Interview with James Leonard," by Warren Unna, March 10, 1993, http://www.adst.org/OH%20TOCs/Leonard,%20 James%20.toc.pdf.

13

UNA's National Constituency: Members and Allies

Jeffrey Laurenti, with Tino Calabia

From the early twentieth century, along with the Progressive Era's middle-class movements for civic and social reform, a parallel movement seeking a new global international order arose, embodied first in the League of Nations Association (LNA) after World War I and then in the American Association for the United Nations (AAUN) as World War II ended. From its start, UNA was a nationwide membership organization.

The lopsided Senate vote for ratification of the UN Charter in 1945 did not signal the end of the struggle over support for the UN. A generation that had witnessed Washington's rejection of the League of Nations and, two decades later, the persistent grip of isolationism in the face of Fascist aggression could not be confident that the wheel would not turn again. America's fragile commitment to the new global system would have to be sustained at America's grassroots by a network of well-informed civic activists.

Challenges to the new international regime indeed arrived, starting in Cold War divisions mocking the internationalist promise of a new order based on law and international cooperation. Yet for all the decades of Cold War, the UNA membership continued to raise the UN flag at town halls and state houses every UN Day, sponsored Model United Nations simulations and educational programs, dispatched letters to local newspapers, called into local radio programs, and pressed their states' politicians to support the UN and the web of treaty law being spun around it.

Indeed, UNA's broad national membership, dedicated to a core organizing principle of international relations, has marked it as unique in that debate. Its forerunner, the League of Nations Association, built a membership network despite the gale-force isolationist headwinds of the interwar era. Other organizations in that period that also sought to

215

sustain the interest and engagement of US citizens in the international community included the Foreign Policy Association (1918), devoted to informing the broader public about foreign affairs, and the elite-minded Council on Foreign Relations (1921). But these organizations were not focused on the institutional scaffolding of a sustainable international order, did not recruit a broad national membership to press for a concrete internationalist vision, and did not see their mission as advocacy of such an order, though they readily joined the national coalition of the AAUN when World War II reawakened US political interest in effective international organization.

Americans who wanted to change how the world worked, who hoped at last to realize a genuine international community that could save succeeding generations from the scourge of war, enlisted in the cause of the UN. Astonishingly, they still do.

As with most civic-minded national membership organizations, the visibility and impact of UNA's chapters have varied widely based on the energy, commitment, and local prominence of their leaders. Unlike most civic organizations, the focus of UNA members' activism was not normally a local problem or issue; rather, it was a more distant and perhaps abstract one—one that they might be hard-pressed to affect directly. Long before the phrase "think globally, act locally" caught on, UNA local leaders sought to do just that: bringing local visibility to a faraway global institution through events garnering the attention of local media and officials; promoting young people's understanding of global politics through Model UN simulations; fund-raising for UN causes, especially UNICEF; and calling on fellow citizens and political leaders to see the UN as a more viable pathway for resolving international problems than reflexive reliance on US dominance.

Early on, UNA leaders confronted the challenge of making global concerns meaningful for local audiences. They had to ponder what could motivate citizens to expend energy in local chapters to support a universal political institution controlled by national governments. They needed their grassroots members to be advocates of the UN, without becoming tainted as political partisans.

They also had to consider whether and how local UNA leaders nationwide could help shape the issue stances and priorities that the association would advance nationally. Many national membership organizations have struggled with balancing grassroots interests with national perspectives in their governance. But it proved to be a particularly tricky task for an association addressing international affairs, a sector in which the policy conversation was traditionally among elites.

Would citizen internationalists follow the lead of a foreign policy hierarchy of experts and practitioners, or would they see themselves as a priesthood of all believers, speaking in their own voice on US foreign policy and the UN?

Another War Approaching

Loyalists of the LNA, increasingly despondent in the 1930s as the world lurched toward another global war, were energized as America's forced entry into the second war prompted public and elite reassessments of the country's failure to embrace international organization over the previous two decades. Irene Armstrong, executive director of the association's Massachusetts branch, wrote a letter to national director Clark Eichelberger, shortly after US troops first landed in North Africa in 1942. She urged the national office to embark on a nationwide "educational" campaign to take advantage of the new mood. "Get a slogan that will tell the story," she urged, "a story that will be as convincing not only to Americans but to the peoples of the United Nations and to the momentarily quiescent isolationists that it is an all-out and lasting peace effort . . . : 'This time the United States sees it through.'" Her observation about nativist isolationism being only "momentarily quiescent" proved prescient.

LNA activists were already adopting the new nomenclature pioneered by President Franklin Roosevelt, organizing "United Nations committees" in their regions. By 1943, the national office was actively pressing the creation of United Nations committees in every state, exhorting its local supporters to enlist influential community leaders in the cause: "Find some important person and write to him (or her), explaining what we have in mind. Send the printed plan and program of organization. Inquire about the situation and also ask for suggestions— names in the community where it is proposed to form the United Nations Committees." Even at this early stage, the memo added an admonition: "Remember it is easy to form committees—but they must be fed or they will die."

The new regional committees had an early advocacy target: seek support for a wartime congressional resolution supporting a postwar international organization. In April 1943, the allied affiliate in California, calling itself Citizens for Victory, implored its local committees to "get as many people as you can to write the members of the State Senate and Assembly in Sacramento from your district" to approve a state resolution memorializing Congress to approve such a statement of intent. The LNA national office then raised funds to send bipartisan teams of congressmen on a tour in major cities to build backing for the idea.

In April 1944, Citizens for Victory chapters sent to all candidates for the US Senate and House of Representatives a questionnaire asking their position on US membership in a postwar world organization to prevent aggression and preserve peace, including US participation "in joint military measures necessary to prevent aggression and preserve peace." In May, California Citizens for Victory chair Chester Rowell reached out to Governor Earl Warren, a member of the Republican national convention's platform committee, to help secure language supporting a world organization in the GOP's platform. After he also met the head of the California delegation to the Democratic national convention, Rowell telegrammed Eichelberger, the Citizens for Victory national director, saying, "We hope for uniform planks in both platforms." (The Democratic Party platform called for the establishment of "an international organization," while the Republican platform rejected "a World State" but supported "responsible participation" in a "post-war co-operative organization.")

Roosevelt's longtime secretary of state, Cordell Hull, a former Tennessee senator, was a principal driver inside the US government in planning for a postwar world organization (for which he won the Nobel Peace Prize in 1945). His supporters in Tennessee were among the first in the South to organize an AAUN branch, naming it after him and pressing the state's senators in Washington to commit to the embryonic organization. Seventy years later, one of the chapter's original members, Louise Baird Short, by that point 108 years old, recalled in an interview for this book that even as the world war was reaching its climax, skeptics were warning that Hull's pet project was a stalking horse for a one-world government. Chapter organizers rebutted by asserting that the United Nations would create the machinery needed to enforce what had just been an empty promise in the Kellogg-Briand Pact—that is, the abolition of war—Short reported: "It would be far better to talk it out than fight it out."

By early 1945, the new American Association for the United Nations coordinated a grand, nationwide debut for the new United Nations. Collaborating with local affiliates of fifty other national organizations, AAUN's branches would organize town meetings and local media campaigns on the proposals that had emerged at Dumbarton Oaks for a new international organization. Roosevelt himself embraced the Dumbarton Oaks Week planned for the eve of the San Francisco Con-

At age 104, Louise Baird Short, a UNA Nashville (TN) chapter member, was presented with a Lifetime Achievement Award in 2010 from the Nashville Cordell Hull Chapter by Karl Dean, Nashville's mayor. Short, a member of UNA since January 1946, turned 110 in January 2016. (Photo courtesy of the Nashville chapter of UNA-USA.)

ference. After the San Francisco Conference voted to approve the final text of a charter for the proposed United Nations, AAUN launched a large campaign to a wider network of national organizations than had taken part in the Dumbarton Oaks campaign.

As a historian of the conference, Stephen C. Schlesinger, marveled, writing in *Act of Creation: The Founding of the United Nations*,

> On June 23, the American Association for the United Nations brought together over seven hundred organizations for a day meeting at the Hotel Commodore in New York titled "What Happened at San Francisco." By now, the Lions Club, with its 4,700 clubs, had enlisted; so, too, the League of Women Voters, which also published a booklet; the National Grange; the American Farm Bureau; the American Veterans Committee; the Brotherhood of Railroad Trainmen; the National Congress of Parents and Teachers; the General Federation of Women's Clubs; the National Education Association, which had more than 50,000 members; the Woodrow Wilson Foundation; the American Legion; the American Federation of Labor (AFL); the Congress of Industrial Organizations (CIO); the US Chamber of Commerce; the National Association of Manufacturers; the American Bar Association; the National Maritime Union; and others.[1]

To build a firewall against isolationist resurgence, AAUN leaders believed it needed to sustain the interest of all the supporting national organizations and to grow its own grassroots presence. Four days after the Senate's overwhelming vote to join the United Nations organization, Eichelberger wrote to AAUN chapters:

> Now that the United States has joined, we should be able to build a large membership throughout the country. This is necessary for several reasons: that we have people throughout the country who are receiving our literature and know of our program; that we have people who are supporting our ideals; and that we have this consistent financial support which can only come from a steady mass membership.

To continue the citizen engagement and the political momentum would be the organization's lasting challenge well into the next century.

UN Bridges for America's Grassroots

The support system that AAUN created for building membership and deepening grassroots understanding of the infant United Nations began with thirteen regional offices, all outside the Northeast, to provide printed materials and assistance with speakers for volunteer-run local chapters. National headquarters called the nascent chapter network "the field," and in late 1945, "two field men," according to the organization's first annual report, "visited the field." By the end of 1945, the association counted fifty-five local and statewide chapters, which it said were animated by "the spirit of the beginning of the work to be done by the organization, rather than the end of a job." That work was aimed at "educating American public opinion to the people's responsibility in the United Nations."

The reincarnated UNA of Massachusetts issued its own pamphlet that fall to attract new members. Although many people in Washington were convinced that the nuclear monopoly of the United States would give it the upper hand in managing the postwar world, UNA-Massachusetts insisted that, to the contrary, "With the development of the techniques of atomic warfare *and the certainty of their spread to all major countries*, the *United Nations* and supporting associations have become vitally important to the survival of civilized mankind" (emphasis added). The organization tempted prospective adherents with its plans for an active presence in the print media and in radio debates and interviews, public events featuring knowledgeable speakers, a "publicity and 'rebuttal service' to prevent issues from becoming crises," and educational programs in schools and colleges.

Before 1945 was out, chapters in Maryland, Minnesota, New Jersey, Connecticut, and Southern California established "United Nations Youth" programs to acquaint high school students with the world, hoping to inculcate "citizenship in the United Nations" alongside the well-established loyalties of national citizenship. Over coming years, as the UN itself developed procedures of debate and decision taking—debates that in its first decades drew ample US media attention—Model United Nations conferences became a main vehicle for youth-outreach programs.

By 1948, however, harsh new geopolitical realities were dramatically diminishing the public's expectations of the UN. For many Americans, their government's exclusive control of nuclear weapons would more reliably deliver on the UN's promises of peace than the rickety organization hamstrung by Joseph Stalin's Soviet Union. As the storm clouds of the Cold War darkened the national mood, despondency set in among idealistic internationalists.

The head of the Santa Barbara chapter, Will Hayes, a dean at the University of California campus there, confided to Eichelberger that "the fortunes of AAUN here at Santa Barbara are at a very low ebb. Apathy and disinterest are much more in evidence than any conscious concern for the future of the United Nations." A discouraged Eichelberger, hoping for "some kind of program that will revitalize the Santa Barbara group," acknowledged the changing climate: "The apathy and disinterest you find in Santa Barbara is somewhat true in some other places, too. In my years of experience in this field, I find that the American people can rise up to the heights in their enthusiasm, and the next week will find them losing interest completely or becoming deeply discouraged."

Yet, as the UN itself survived the paralyzing confrontations of the Cold War, so did the AAUN—including its Santa Barbara chapter. For the next forty years of East-West antagonism, UNA chapters would keep the liberal internationalist flame alive and contest charges of UN irrelevance through activities based on templates set in the association's first three years. James Olson—who would serve as a chapter president in Jacksonville, Florida; as field director and vice president for national programs in UNA-USA's national headquarters; and as president of the Iowa division—summarized the core activities of the average local chapter, continuing from those earliest years:

> First, organizing an observance for UN Day, or in the earlier years UN Week. This was always the bare minimum for a chapter to do. Second, education or Model UN. There has always been the belief that we had to get the UN into the schools, especially because a lot of our members are educators. Third, host speakers and organize events, especially

around the themes of UN "years" [as designated by the UN General Assembly] or in later decades of UN global conferences. Fourth, raise money for UNICEF. Many chapters have been very active and very committed to raising funds for UNICEF. It was something "hands on" for people to do. Issues could be abstract and distant; selling UNICEF cards was tangible.

The association marked the first anniversary of the entry into force of the UN Charter by exhorting its affiliates to organize celebratory events during UN Week—the seven days bracketing the actual October 24 anniversary. NBC sponsored the initiative with the National Education Association, broadening the appeal of participating in the events. Chapters sought citizens' signatures to a message of fraternity and support for the UN. The national headquarters presented the 105,000 signatures to Paul-Henri Spaak, the first president of the UN General Assembly. From that year on, UN Day became a vital sign of life in a UNA chapter. UN Day observances in smaller communities typically featured remarks by a sympathetic elected official or distinguished local professor, the raising of the UN flag over the city hall or State House, a cameo role for students, and—most important—a photo opportunity for the local newspaper.

Sometimes merely organizing a UN Day observance could stir furious controversy. In 1950, when Los Angeles County supervisors took up a request ahead of UN Day to fly the UN flag at the Hall of Records, a crowd of fierce UN opponents descended on the meeting to challenge the Los Angeles UNA representative; they charged, as the *Los Angeles Times* reported on the front page, that the role of Alger Hiss, "a convicted perjurer," as "a moving figure" behind the creation of the UN was proof enough that the UN was a cover for Americans' stealth enslavement by the Communists. After emotional debate, the supervisors voted 3 to 2 to grant permission to fly the UN flag.

Over ensuing decades, the commemoration of UN Day would be less likely to trigger bilious resistance than indifference. In organizing UN Day events, perhaps especially in communities far from the nation's metropolitan centers, UNA chapters hoped to chip away at that indifference for a day. The media circus around the unprecedented participation of many national leaders at the opening debate of the UN General Assembly in 1960—including Soviet premier Nikita Khrushchev and his newfound Cuban ally, Fidel Castro—spurred "more intense programming across the country than in recent years," AAUN staffer Estelle Linzer reported. In 1965, governors in forty-four states appointed UN Day chairs to prepare their states' observance of the UN's

twentieth anniversary, and UNA reported that mayors in 1,600 communities had established observance committees. The number of states and
towns observing UN Day declined, however, as new conflicts bypassed
the UN and new controversies swirled around it; yet, UNA members
tenaciously continued to organize its observance.

The UNA chapter in Scranton, in Pennsylvania's coal country, was
an example. UNA-Scranton ran only the most skeletal program of activities. The chapter president, Marion Odell Carr, a faculty member at the
University of Scranton, asked Olson's help in obtaining a UN Day
speaker. Olson asked a colleague (the author of this chapter), then head
of policy studies who had organized a new chapter in New Jersey's
Princeton-Trenton area, if he would do the honors. "I drove the two-plus
hours up to Scranton, expecting to be speaking to a dozen UNA true
believers," Laurenti recalled twenty years later. "I get to the luncheon
and find Dr. Carr has a crowd of eighty people, including Scranton's
mayor, several councilmen, a county commissioner, and two members of
the legislature. 'Marion *is* the United Nations in Scranton,' the mayor
told me. 'All of us here, when she calls, we come!' I was awestruck."

In some places, UNA-allied organizations picked up the slack if
there was no functioning chapter. Local chapters of Zonta International,
an organization devoted to advancing women, have long supported their
area UNA chapters' commemorations of UN Day. In Boulder, Colorado,
the Zonta chapter organized the observance in the years before a UNA
chapter was finally able to do so in the mid-1990s.

Many communities made a bigger production out of UN Day. In
Wisconsin, a Governor's Commission on the United Nations organized
the observance with what Milwaukee chapter president Gary Shellman
remembered as "impressive UN Day programs in both Milwaukee and
Green Bay." The state commission became a victim of more ideologi-
cally combative politics when a new governor, Scott Walker, terminated
it in 2011. The Jacksonville, Florida, chapter brought a UN ambassador
from New York to be the guest speaker each year, and while Olson was
its president, their ranks included the permanent representatives of
India, Australia, and Liberia. In 1975, designated as International
Women's Year, the appearance of Ashraf Pahlavi, Iran's delegate and
the twin sister of the then-reigning shah, drew an unprecedented 500
people to the Jacksonville chapter's UN Day observance. Seattle too has
drawn UN Day speakers of distinction, including UN Secretary-General
Ban Ki-moon in 2009.

Redolent of its region's tormented history was the UN Day celebration in Birmingham, Alabama, in 1998. "Many local organizations helped

our chapter lead the city in an unforgettable celebration of the fiftieth anniversary of the Universal Declaration on Human Rights," then-chapter president Dorothy Baker recalled. That was also the year marking the thirty-fifth anniversary of the city's violent suppression of civil rights demonstrations and a lethal church bombing. Baker added, "The prominent people who had been directly involved in civil rights were honored with plaques from our chapter. The *Anniston Star* sent a reporter and a photographer to cover it and used the article and the photo as their front-page story."

If organizing a UN Day observance was a chapter's essential duty, fostering international awareness—and, by extension, awareness of the UN—in *the schools* was the outreach that most engaged UNA members. (See Chapter 16 for a discussion of educational outreach, including the Model UN.)

The third among the four core activities that Olson enumerated has been the organizing of public events to promote US citizens' discussion of issues on the UN agenda, especially relating to social and developmental themes that UN bodies have made the subject of UN observances or of global policy conferences. Such issues have not often attracted much interest among senior US policymakers and therefore in the media. Active UNA chapters would often see it as their mission to take such issues and organize programs around them.

In the first post–World War II years, human rights was such an issue. With much of the country still complacent about racial segregation, human rights triggered some of the first congressional efforts to roll back the UN—famously, in the Bricker amendment controversy early in President Dwight Eisenhower's administration. Yet in 1958, AAUN marked the looming tenth anniversary of the General Assembly's adoption of the United Nations Declaration on Human Rights, led nationally by a committee chaired by Baltimore industrialist Jacob Blaustein, with the American Jewish Committee "prominent in the preparation and production of publications for the observance," national staffer Estelle Linzer recalled. The honorary cochairs of the national observance were Lebanon's Charles Malik, who, as his country's UN ambassador, had been a lead sponsor of the declaration (even as the first Arab-Israeli war raged); France's René Cassin; and the widely admired Eleanor Roosevelt herself. Local chapters organized parallel celebrations. Since then, the most widespread UNA chapter event nationwide, aside from UN Day, has been the December 10 commemoration of Human Rights Day.

Numerous local UNA groups have convened public events over the years around anniversaries of landmark UN decisions, starting with or around the theme of "years" designated by the General Assembly. No other issue has been as galvanizing as the environment, which became a defining national issue with the first Earth Day in 1969. Soon after, the global dimensions of many Americans' embrace of the new environmentalism arose, with the first UN global conference on the environment in Stockholm in 1972. A global policy project in the run-up to the Rio conference twenty years later led many UNA chapters to organize public events on the issue—as a continuing theme for some. Michigan UNA organized and funded a conference after the Rio conference, titled "The Citizens Respond: The Earth Summit and Beyond." Iowa UNA conducted public hearings and community forums to produce an "Earth Charter and Agenda 21 for Iowa" in 1994, followed by more activities on the challenges of climate change in 1999. It also tapped students at the state's colleges to put a report, *Sustainable Futures for Iowa,* on the state agenda in Des Moines. UNA San Francisco joined in organizing an observance of the UN's World Environment Day, which lasted five days in 2005, and worked with the mayor, Gavin Newsom, in launching a citywide "Green Cities Expo," featuring best practices in sustainability by businesses and communities.

When the UN declared 1979 as the International Year of the Child, twenty years after the General Assembly adopted a declaration on the rights of the child, the Jacksonville chapter in Florida sought to arrange an event to draw public attention to the issue. Olson recalled "striking the jackpot," when the chapter landed for its launch the nation's (arguably) most famous mother at the time—Lillian Carter, mother of president Jimmy Carter who had gained international recognition as a Peace Corps volunteer nurse working in India in her late sixties.

Some chapters claimed seigniorial rights to unique anniversary observances. To honor the leading role of Cordell Hull in establishing the UN, Nashville UNA president Pearl Bradley marked America's 1976 bicentennial and the UN's thirtieth anniversary by inviting all UN ambassadors and the Secretary-General to the Tennessee capital. More than a hundred ambassadors and Secretary-General Kurt Waldheim participated on June 7, 1976. Waldheim was presented with a Cordell Hull peace medal, and the dignitaries were fêted at the Grand Ole Opry House by Dolly Parton, Roy Acuff, and other luminaries of American country music.

Patricia DiGiorgio of UNA San Francisco initiated an even more audacious event: a ceremonial session of the UN General Assembly in

San Francisco for the UN's fiftieth anniversary, which both UN Secretary-General Boutros Boutros-Ghali and President Bill Clinton addressed. Done in collaboration with the Commonwealth Club, the World Affairs Council of Northern California, the San Francisco Convention and Visitors Bureau, and the mayor's office, they organized a ceremonial event at the San Francisco Opera House, an interfaith service at Grace Cathedral, and a civic luncheon. Jim Olson noted that UNA-USA, for the first time in its history, held its convention outside New York City, in San Francisco to coincide with the UN50 observance. A decade later, San Francisco's chapter president, Nancy Peterson, organized another milestone event, featuring the former UN high commissioner for human rights Mary Robinson and UN undersecretary-general Shashi Tharoor.

Some chapters, led by Stanford University film lecturer Jasmina Bojic, of the Mid-Peninsula (Palo Alto) chapter and Lawrence Levine's Monterey Bay, undertook annual film festivals screening international documentaries. The UNA Film Festival aimed, Levine explained, "to educate and inspire our diverse community about global social, environmental, and security issues, bringing together our internationalist community in a great spirit."

Finally, the core activities of many chapters included fund-raising for international aid programs sponsored by the UN, for which governments could never make sufficient voluntary contributions to meet the need. The agency that became the poster child for citizen philanthropy was, of course, the UN Children's Fund. UNA members embraced UNICEF early on because it involved a cause—aiding innocent children—that transcended the political animosities quickly emerging at war's end between the Soviet Union and its wartime Western allies. UNA chapters helped mobilize schoolchildren to seek something greater than chocolate bars on Halloween, by soliciting small contributions for UNICEF to help address the needs of children caught in war or preindustrial poverty worldwide.

More than a dozen chapters raised funds to operate UNICEF gift shops and storefront offices in their downtowns that became mini information centers about the UN and UNICEF—East Bay (Berkeley-Oakland), Greater Lansing, Los Angeles, Mid-Peninsula (Palo Alto and vicinity), Minnesota, Monterey, National Capital Area (Washington, DC), Orange County, Pasadena, St. Louis, San Diego, Santa Barbara, and Santa Cruz. The UNA storefronts "provided visibility and a source of income for chapters and divisions," recalled Olson, generating "more money for UNICEF than did any other NGO." But in the 1990s—as the end of the

Cold War put the UN back on the front pages regarding international security—most storefronts closed as volunteers available to run them dwindled in number, as rents rose faster than UNA chapters' income, and after the US Committee for UNICEF shifted to a new marketing strategy of selling UNICEF cards only through commercial outlets.

Other UN agencies have tried to develop similar grassroots fund-raising appeals, such as the UN Population Fund, the Office of the UN High Commissioner for Refugees, and the UN Development Program. Some found an occasional UNA chapter leader willing to take up the cause. As fund-raising for UNICEF passed into the hands of more "professional" operators, however, UNA's national headquarters proposed to channel grassroots philanthropic energy in a different direction, such as the Adopt-A-Minefield program, which involved membership chapters "adopting" a particular minefield and energetically pursuing donations in their communities to draw a matching contribution from the US government. (See Chapter 11.)

Motivation and Membership

The reason that people wanted to join UNA in its first years was, quite literally, to change the world. Nashville's Louise Baird Short recalled the excitement of taking part as a citizen in the founding of the UN, taking the idea of democracy and rule of law to the whole world, and thus bringing "an end to wars." After the charter's ratification, what sustained Americans' commitment to UNA was the realization that UN institutions would never deliver on the charter promise if powerful national governments failed to work through them, as well as the concern that those "momentarily quiescent isolationists" were not converted but were only lying low. As a nativist backlash to the UN surged at midcentury—often closely linked to the militant anticommunism of the period and to fears of upsetting entrenched racial hierarchies—internationally minded citizens felt a moral imperative to stay engaged in the UN to prevent the rollback of the US commitment to the charter.

The urgency of sustaining that engagement waned during the grinding Cold War years, as the UN increasingly appeared quite permanent—yet, to many, ineffectual and deeply flawed. The global political battles playing out in the UN after the Vietnam War and the Arab-Israeli wars of 1967 and 1973 alienated many onetime US supporters, and UNA membership fell dramatically. By the UN's fortieth anniversary in 1985, facing the first US administration openly adversarial to the UN—refusing payment of UN assessments, withdrawing from UNESCO, and repudiating America's 1946 subscription to the compulsory jurisdiction of the World Court—the ranks of active UNA members ready to defend the charter had fallen by more than half since 1965.

Membership numbers might not be completely comparable across the years because of vagaries of counting units and local chapters sometimes keeping their own membership rolls, but there was no hiding the trend. In 1965, the executive vice president, Porter McKeever, reported to UNA-USA's first postmerger convention that national headquarters counted 48,370 members on its lists, plus another 7,090 contributors "not on any chapter's membership lists," for a total, he said, of 55,761 members and contributors.

After the UN General Assembly's hotly contested vote in 1975 for an Arab-sponsored resolution lumping Zionism with racism, US Jewish opinion of the organization curdled, and a mass exodus from the association ensued. In 1989, UNA reported to the Ford Foundation "a national membership of about 20,000 distributed in a network of 165 local chapters and divisions." That year was also when the Soviet Union terminated its forceful sponsorship of Communist regimes across Eastern Europe. One result was a reactivation of UN security machinery—most notably, in reversing Iraq's conquest of Kuwait. President George H. W. Bush's success in working through the Security Council on Iraq and then on many far-reaching peace operations refuted the canard that the United Nations worked only to thwart US power and purposes or that the UN was a failure and an irrelevance.

Yet the UN's renewed salience did not lead to resurgence in UNA's membership. As with global disarmament movements, the demise of the Cold War seemed, ironically, to induce complacency rather than new citizen energy. For two decades after 1990, UNA's asserted membership levels fluctuated between 9,000 and 15,000. In 2014, after UNA-USA became part of the UN Foundation, a precise count was again reported: 18,341, about half of whom were nonpaying student members.

Why, when the world organization already was more active in more places on more issues and more evidently indispensable than ever, would people think it necessary to devote energy to an association to defend the UN idea?

For many members outside the biggest metropolitan areas, UNA was a way to celebrate international understanding and friendship, being respectful of other peoples' cultures and traditions. Critics with more robust notions of national interest and power might deride "kumbaya internationalism," but UNA members in many communities felt that welcoming the foreigner as an equal was a political statement in itself—a people-to-people version of the "sovereign equality of states" that was quietly subversive of prevailing assumptions of national superiority.

Most leaders of chapters—especially those involved in UNA's regional and national structures—became active in the association to challenge nationalist assumptions more directly. They came by different routes to their conviction that their active involvement was a concrete way to uphold their belief in a better world, where "the acceptance of principles and institution of methods" outlined in the charter would advance tolerance, prosperity, freedom, and justice, thus curtailing and finally eliminating war—even when their government acted otherwise.

The Rochester (New York) Association for the United Nations, Olson recalled, was, for decades, one of UNA's largest chapters, thanks to the pioneering commitment to the UN cause of Joseph C. Wilson, founder of the Xerox Corporation. "It had thousands of members," Olson remembered. "It was *the* organization socially to be part of. In terms of social prominence, they were a really big deal, and per capita [based on an area's total population], they were the largest UNA local organization." In Iowa, Dorothy Schramm, the wife of a wealthy department store heir with strong Republican connections, early on embraced the UN cause, invited Eleanor Roosevelt to Iowa as her first road trip for AAUN, and capitalized on that visit to secure funding for a statewide Iowa affiliate.

Some were conjoined to UNA at birth. In the case of Edison Dick, who led UNA's National Capital Area division in the 1990s, his mother, Jane Warner Dick, who had chaired Adlai Stevenson's successful campaign for governor of Illinois in 1948, joined him in New York as President Kennedy's representative to the UN Economic and Social Council's social commission. The father of Shirley Sabin Quisenberry in North Carolina was one of the officials who led UNICEF in its infancy, aiding war-displaced children in Europe. Joan Roberts Robertson of UNA Milwaukee was brought into UNA by her mother, Annette, a suffragette at the start of the twentieth century, whose restless energy for civic improvement led her into UNA in the 1940s. Joan was active until her death at 102 in 1986. Joan's own daughter Annette and then granddaughter Carol Alexander followed in becoming "active advocates for a peaceful world through the UN." Instead of reaching audiences through mimeographed mailings as her great-grandmother had done, Carol established an online presence for chapter outreach.

Other UNA local leaders found the association a way to give practical and meaningful extension to a formative stint in their youth or a lifelong career in public service internationally. Iowa's Katy Hansen and Monterey's Larry Levine had been Peace Corps volunteers. Westchester's Philip Reynolds, likewise a onetime Peace Corps volunteer, made his career in the UN Development Programme, as did California East Bay's Herbert Behrstock. Rita Maran, also in Berkeley, was a Fulbright scholar in Indonesia. Nashville's Mary Pat Silveira worked for the UN in Mozambique, Kosovo, and Geneva. Boulder's Bill Kellogg was an army medic in the Korean War, did sabbaticals abroad, and engaged in a summer archaeological dig with Palestinians. Westchester's Molly Bruce joined the UN Secretariat in the late 1940s and worked on the UN's landmark human rights conferences. Princeton-Trenton's John Vincent retired from a Foreign Service career in Africa. Asheville's longtime leader John "Jack" Fobes spent his career at UNESCO, ending as deputy director general before retiring to North Carolina. Dorothy Watson in Sarasota, Florida, worked in the UN mission in New York. Connecticut's Willard Hass worked in public information at UN headquarters.

Some came to UNA through their educational experiences. Seattle's Matthew Metz studied for a year at the Sorbonne and, after law school, worked with a nonprofit organization in Mexico City, helping small-scale farmers with technical expertise and credit. Milwaukee's Gary Shellman, sent by the US Army to study German before posting to Frankfurt, became assistant director of the Institute of World Affairs at the University of Wisconsin. Anne Fouts of Lansing, Michigan, who became chair of UNA-USA's council of chapters and divisions in the late 1980s and a member of UNA's Board of Governors, was a schoolteacher. Denver's Gloria Dogan joined the international relations club in college and taught in schools operated by the US Defense Department (including in Turkey, where she married a Turk and taught at a Turkish university). Dogan, in fact, insisted that what kept her committed to UNA "during the tedious and sometimes bleak work of keeping a faltering chapter afloat" were her memories of "sitting in on a General Assembly meeting, walking through areas cleared of minefields in Mozambique, and witnessing a UNICEF vaccination session."

Other UNA leaders got their internationalism from a higher calling. Nebraska's John Krejci and Wisconsin's Sam Romano were laicized Catholic priests, and Dallas's Bill Matthews and Hans Holborn of Whittier, California, were both Methodist ministers. The longtime UNA president in Riverdale (Bronx), David Cockcroft, was a minister in the Presbyterian Church, and Southern California's Richard Harris, in the United Church of Christ. Oregon's Leonard Hunting was a Unitarian Universalist minister.

Not quite as ordained was the path of Mary Taussig Hall of St. Louis, daughter of a nationally renowned specialist in gynecology. After working with Jane Addams in settlement houses in Chicago in the 1930s, she returned to St. Louis to lead efforts for desegregation in the city. By dint of elite contacts and personal indefatigability, she then built UNA's St. Louis chapter into one of the largest in the country. Other UNA leaders came directly from politics: Frank P. Zeidler, mayor of Milwaukee from 1948 to 1960, then led the UNA chapter there for twenty-five years; New Haven's Irving Stolberg was speaker of the Connecticut House of Representatives; and William Miller, a onetime Peace Corps volunteer, headed the research office of the Kentucky legislature.

Some UNA leaders arrived at internationalism the old-fashioned way—by being born internationally. Denver's Ved Nanda, past president of the World Jurist Association, national board member of UNA-USA, and professor of international law at the University of Denver, was raised and educated in India. Ilse Diasio, president of UNA Birmingham (Alabama), grew up in Austria. Southern California's Kam Leung came to the United States from China. Miami's Santiago León was from Cuba; Boston's Lena Granberg, from Sweden; Palo Alto's Sally Kiester, from the Philippines; Sarasota's (Florida) Daniel Lu, from Vietnam; Pomona's Ardi Rashidi, a Kurd from Iran; and Minnesota's Zehra Keye, from Turkey. "We have much more diversity in terms of national origin than we did, say, thirty years ago," recalled Jim Olson, who has more than four decades of involvement with the association.

Starting in the 1990s, UNA's national office sought to stem the decline in UNA members by such initiatives as "phone-a-thons" and direct-mail prospecting, just as other long-established national membership organizations faced with declining membership rolls were doing. A 2005 review for the membership committee of the UNA-USA Board of Directors found, however, that UNA was spending a staggering $100 for each new member acquired through the direct-mail campaign. George Garland, the Washington, DC, area UNA chapter executive director who was lured to New York City in 2004 to direct national membership development, observed that because retention rates "were so low, we did not make up that cost over time as projected by the direct-mail firm." Direct-mail prospecting was abandoned, and staff members focused on UNA's own lists of lapsed members. Garland's team discovered that when they contacted lapsed members, those members expressed "no major complaints; they just felt they hadn't heard from us."

As Olson noted, "The most spectacular membership growth occurred in those chapters where one person worked tirelessly day in and day out on membership." Starting in 1988, UNA presented awards to the chapters and divisions with biennial membership growth of 10 percent or more. The infectious conviction of a local chapter leader unembarrassed to ask people to join a good cause proved the single-biggest factor in attracting new members. A handful of local leaders stood out at the turn of the century for their evangelization and rising membership rolls: Pasadena's Rene Wilson, Cedar Rapids (Iowa)'s Mary Alice Erickson, and Monterey's Levine. UNA Monterey Bay raised its membership from slightly more than 100 dues-paying members to more than 800; at chapter events, as many as 85 new members joined on the spot.

Yet, the recruitment energies of a few could not offset the shyness of scores more chapter leaders about pressing friends and coworkers to enlist in UNA's mission. There were growing doubts about whether the cause of global peace would even seem relevant to generations that had no experience of global war. Moreover, models of nonpartisan grassroots civic engagement that had sustained volunteer organizations from the League of Women Voters to Common Cause to UNA seemed less and less viable in a world of two-earner households, Internet communication, Robert Putnam's *Bowling Alone,* and intense partisan polarization.

A Hip Generation Meets a Septuagenarian Institution

In one respect, calling on younger people to actively support the United Nations in the post–Cold War era was pushing on an open door. Survey research, including that undertaken by UNA in the 1990s and the United Nations Foundation thereafter, consistently found that the hard nut of hostility toward the UN in the US public was concentrated among white male conservatives over age fifty-five, whereas people under thirty were the most supportive. "The generation that has grown up since the end of the Cold War is quite positive about the UN," noted Jeffrey Laurenti, who had worked on UNA's polling studies before the mid-Atlantic region chapters elected him to the national board of directors. "The problem with mobilizing this swelling age cohort to stand up for the UN is that most young adults take the UN for granted. It's there. You obviously have to work with it. 'So, what's the big deal?'"

UNA's biggest outreach to younger people—through its Model UN programs—consistently disappointed advocates who thought that role-playing at international politics would lead students and their families to become members of an organization dedicated to cementing US cooperation on the UN. "Model UN is wonderful in teaching public speaking, research, leadership, learning about other countries, putting yourself in someone else's shoes," Olson observed. "But it does not attract large numbers of young people to join or become active in UNA-USA."

In the 1990s, UNA began exploring parallel formations, such as Student Alliance groups to attract youths in high schools and colleges and Young Professionals in International Cooperation, aimed at engaging recent college graduates in UN-supportive activities. The challenge, Olson noted, was, "How do we link or integrate these student and young professional groups with our chapters, most of whose members were one or two generations older than the youth?"

Elizabeth Latham, who helped pioneer the new Young Professionals (YP) format in Washington, DC, at the turn of the century, observed that UNA's longtime members wanted young people in their ranks but were "often stifling because they brought their own notions of how young professionals should be engaged." Too often, she thought, UNA veterans saw the junior joiners as well adapted to "do logistical work at big meetings and host an occasional happy hour" but not up to the division's policy work.

Latham's youthful nucleus organized receptions and topical events at the end of the workday, when UNA's older and middle-aged members were returning home to their families. "This kind of parallel structure," Latham said, "allowed YP members to benefit from the expertise and experience of the older members without taking over the established committees. It was attractive to YP members because they could include policy-related activities on their résumés." Career-oriented events were much more important to YP adults in an era of relentless networking for jobs than they would be to the more settled adults who dominated the National Capital Area division.

George Garland helped navigate the Washington-YP affiliate's way with the established chapter leaders, some of whom, he recalled, imagined the parallel group "as a bunch of rowdy drinkers and date seekers." Shortly after Latham became president of the YP affiliate in 2000, the National Capital Area division asked her to be its vice president for programs. In 2003, she became the first YP representative to take a newly dedicated seat for Young Professionals on the national board of directors in 2003.

For his part, Garland sought to replicate nationally the YP success in Washington after moving to national headquarters in 2004. A three-year Ford Foundation grant to develop a nationwide YP program "eventually yielded 665 new dues-paying members in New York alone," he recalled. In his 2006 report to the Ford Foundation on the grant's progress, he wrote that the program "is the fastest growing membership segment of UNA-USA." This was certainly also true in Nashville, where the chapter found that the Young Professionals affiliate successfully managed three events a year, earning it seats on the chapter board. San Francisco chapter president Pablo Castro reported that the YP affiliate drew young recruits to the chapter's committees on human rights and on women's advancement. Although Denver's Young Professionals group initially struggled, chapter leader Dogan acknowledged, it eventually established itself. The YP group in Seattle managed to build a membership of fifty, growing the entire chapter's membership rolls by a quarter, and held its numbers by sponsoring career networking opportunities and film screenings.

By March 2007, Garland's program had trained twelve Young Professionals to seed YP programs in their cities. That same month, however, he and some other national programs staff were terminated due to funding shortfalls. "Though the original Ford Foundation support did not end," Garland observed, "the grant was then needed to support the general membership program."

Liuba Grechen was hired as an assistant for the national membership programs in March 2007. In her first week, she found herself the only staffer left in the department and suddenly charged with overseeing all its programs. The Student Alliance outreach to students currently in school had been relegated to UNA's back burner because it had proved to be, Garland said, "a high-maintenance and labor-intensive segment with a renewal rate of only around 10 percent." Even with annual churning, however, the 2,000 Student Alliance members made up the second fastest-growing component of national membership; Grechen said in an interview for this book that she sought to revive the program and drafted a student handbook to guide its participants.

Perhaps the real metric for assessing the impact of the Student Alliance investment would not be knowable for decades. Would those who had taken part in UNA's Student Alliance end up, as adults a quarter century later, embracing the UN as a cause worth their time and advocacy at a higher rate than do others in the public at large?

Headquarters Support for Those on the Front Lines

From the heady days of the UN's founding, the national office of AAUN and then UNA recognized the importance of its members around the country and sought to equip them with tools to help them carry the day in the public debates. Local energy and local funding propelled the committees for the UN that were forming around the country. Those committees needed a depth of information about the new institution taking shape that they could not glean from the national news media, and they sought expertise and celebrity from outside their own communities to energize their members and impress their local media. Over the arc of nearly seven decades, materials and messengers became members' two major "asks" of national headquarters.

From the start, Eichelberger wrote a steady stream of mimeographed updates to local chapter leaders to encourage their outreach and inform their arguments in the run-up to the UN Charter ratification vote in the Senate. More than three million pieces of printed matter were distributed to the field. "Letters of information and instruction are sent periodically to the local chapters and groups working with the Association," Eichelberger reported in AAUN's first annual report in January 1946. Concomitantly, chapters would send reports on their activities to the national office for inclusion in the "branch news section" of AAUN's newly launched monthly publication, *Changing World*. "Thus the branches feel that they are playing an integral part in the national office," the report breezily concluded.

In time, *Changing World* itself was changed, first after the 1964 merger (into a magazine named *Vista*), and again a decade later, as the association sought to rebrand its membership publication to reflect a new rationale for US participation in global institutions—that is, the notion of nations' growing "interdependence," which dominated internationalist discourse in the 1970s. UNA relaunched its membership magazine in 1973 as *The InterDependent*. "*The InterDependent* magazine was a real and tangible membership benefit and may have helped sustain membership," asserted Seattle leader Metz. By the 1990s, however, its frequency was reduced to save on printing and postage costs, first to every two months and then to quarterly. It was reformatted again in 2003 to be visually more appealing, and in 2010, it became a strictly online publication, quickly fading from many members' consciousness. (For more information on UNA publications, see Chapter 17.)

Of course, a live person from headquarters could have far more impact on energizing grassroots support for the UN than a decade's worth of newsletters or mailings to UNA chapter leaders. Traveling to the emerging chapter network became a priority for Eichelberger early on. Given the keen interest in much of the country in the conflict brewing between Arabs and immigrant Jews in Palestine in the UN's first years, AAUN organized a 1949 speaking tour to Chicago, Seattle, Los Angeles, and Dallas for UN mediator Ralph Bunche, an African American originally from Detroit. Bunche had just negotiated the armistice agreements that shut down the war between the new Israeli state and the Arab countries, whose armies had fought to prevent Palestine's partition. Bunche's efforts earned him the Nobel Peace Prize the following year, even as the United States had not yet come to grips with widespread racial segregation. Bunche's AAUN appearances as spokesperson for the UN had a revelatory resonance.

When Eleanor Roosevelt became AAUN's most celebrated volunteer in 1953, she readily agreed to travel to membership chapters nationwide. As the best-known US delegate to the UN, who had wrangled with the Soviets over human rights, she drew crowds and new members for UNA chapters. Her speaking tour in 1954 took her to California, Oregon, Montana, and Wyoming; the next year, she traveled to nearly a dozen cities in the South and Midwest. After her death in 1962, UNA had no one of her stature to put on the road. Four decades later, Gillian Martin Sorensen, a former UN assistant secretary-general who had worked briefly in the UNA national programs and constituencies office in 1990, would reprise Roosevelt's evangelizing role. From 2003, Sorensen worked for the UN Foundation, which financed her travel to UNA chapters. (See Box 13.1.)

Box 13.1 Gillian Sorensen: Speaking to the Grassroots

While never officially on the board of UNA, Gillian Sorensen's work in spreading the word about the UN across the United States had a significant impact on UNA's work. Decades of public service began in 1978, when Sorensen was named New York City commissioner for the United Nations and Consular Corps, a position she held for twelve years. This work "almost immediately" made her aware of "an active United Nations Association presence in New York. There were some very distinguished people involved." In an interview for this book, she said, "I also came to understand quickly that the UNA was not just a policy group, but it was also the grassroots effort to . . . build support and understanding for the United Nations."

She added that the "many chapters across the country, in towns large and small, . . . were comprised of some civic leaders, some regular citizens, some people from academia or the business world or whatever who simply cared about the UN." She attended UNA events such as the annual meeting, with hundreds of members attending. She said, "I began to get a better sense of the activity and to meet some of the leaders from across the country. And they were great. They were informed, they were the kind of people that see across borders."

That involvement with UNA intensified when she moved to the UN itself. From 1993 to 1996, she served as special adviser for political affairs to Secretary-General Boutros Boutros-Ghali. Part of her responsibilities included directing the events marking the fiftieth anniversary of the UN in 1995. When Kofi Annan became Secretary-General in 1997, he named Sorensen assistant secretary-general for external relations. This meant liaising with parliamentarians, academia, religious groups, and civil society. In this post, she traveled around the United States, working to strengthen public support for the UN. In all, she spoke at more than 700 events.

As she recalled,

> At that point, the UN was becoming, at various times, a target of criticism and, particularly from the right, a sort of dismissive attitude about "we didn't need it" or "it was imposing on our sovereignty" and all kinds of nonsense like that. . . . And I began to feel more strongly that if we didn't have voices from the field, that members of Congress, most of whom knew very little about the UN, would just think it didn't matter.

This led to more trips around the country, often (but not always) to UNA groups. The trips were meant "to speak about the UN, what's at stake, why does it matter, what is the real cost, how do we contribute, and how do we benefit by serving as an active leader." Sorensen said, "Through this work, I came, little by little, to know the UNA folks very well." She added, "I enjoyed it a lot. I saw America in a whole new way." UNA chapter leaders and members, who enjoyed the speeches she made to UNA audiences, always welcomed her.

Since 2003, Sorensen has been a senior adviser to the UN Foundation as the national advocate.

—James Wurst

In general, though, chapters financed the costs of national speakers from their own resources, turning to the national headquarters "speakers' bureau" for help in securing a UN speaker if they could pay the speaker's traveling expenses. National program staff had "a very limited travel budget—less than $10,000 per year," Olson recalled, which "was stretched with very generous home hospitality and meals provided by chapter people." In these visits, he or a national programs colleague "did everything—meetings with chapter boards, division annual meetings, public events, school and college events, media contacts."

In 1998, a new UNA president, Alvin Adams Jr., proposed an alternative outreach to UNA members: a Members' Day inside UN headquarters, with a program of discussion panels on issues of the day, to

Gillian Sorensen (in a 2004
photo), a longtime UNA
member who helped to
promote its work nationally.
(Photo courtesy of the Seton Hall
University UNA-USA archives.)

which all UNA members were invited to participate. The first Members'
Day drew a few hundred participants, including many dues-paying supporters of UNA who had not been active in local chapters. To the surprise of UNA headquarters staff, the annual Members' Day program
would also draw growing numbers of members from far beyond the
New York metropolitan area.

Members' Day was not particularly costly; however, as a financial
noose tightened around the national office, it announced in 2008 that
Members' Day would be discontinued. Based on the success of the nine-
state Mountain West region and the Northern California region in organizing regional conferences across their sprawling areas, could not the
much-more compact Mid-Atlantic region pull off a Members' Day–style
event on its own at the UN, filling the void left by national headquarters?

UNA Southern New York State agreed to assume primary financial
responsibility for Members' Day, with contributions and a planning committee drawn from UNA's New York and New Jersey chapters. The
national office agreed to dispatch an electronic invitation to all UNA
members, and the Mid-Atlantic chapters opened the event to area colleges and any interested people, hoping to garner new members. When
the regional assembly convened in February 2009, the 500-person capacity of the UN conference hall was filled to overflowing. Each year thereafter, they continued to organize the regional assembly, which "morphed
into a combination Mid-Atlantic region and national Members' Day,"

Garland said. "Now we have members from DC, Philly, Boston, and, remarkably, from California." Surveys of participants at the end of each assembly found high levels of satisfaction overall, and new members were enrolled from student ranks. Garland would, in fact, count the Mid-Atlantic chapters' rescue and expansion of Members' Day as one of his greatest gratifications in decades of volunteer and staff work with UNA.

The success of UNA chapter leaders in expanding the Members' Day program was, however, also evidence of the growing distance between the national office and the pro-UN constituency in the field. Grechen, the program assistant who joined the national programs staff in 2007 and became its head a week later, quickly discovered that she had stepped into "a decade-long feud," she said, between the field and a national office that "all but ignored the chapters."

Chapter leaders and their representatives on the board of directors were distressed by what they saw as the national headquarters' timidity in challenging the George W. Bush administration's invasion of Iraq; were dismayed by its failure to defend Secretary-General Kofi Annan against mendacious accusations of "corruption" in the UN's administration of the Oil-for-Food exception to Iraqi sanctions; and despaired at its refusal to oppose the nomination of UN foe John Bolton to represent the United States at the UN. Far from receiving support from the national headquarters in the contentious early twenty-first-century political battles over core UN values, they wondered whether the national office had abandoned the cause in the interest of keeping access to senior US government officials. For their part, UNA's top officers believed that open confrontation with the US administration would not alter government policy and might jeopardize other association interests.

In the end, it was the national office and its elite-focused programs that disappeared when the UN Foundation agreed to a merger with UNA, as the membership chapters were the principal asset of UNA that the foundation sought to sustain. For the foundation, which already had a Better World Campaign affiliate undertaking advocacy for the UN in Washington as a program of the Better World Fund, UNA's membership was the irreplaceable network of citizens that could give grassroots resonance to the US public's support for the UN idea.

Advocating for the UN in Post-Isolationist America

Except where economic interests or ethnic identities are at stake, Washington debates on international policy tend to be perceived as an inside-the-Beltway affair. The wider public is assumed to be disengaged from foreign policy unless young people are being dispatched to foreign wars or drivers cannot find gasoline. The capital is crowded with policy institutes pleading for political attention to their foreign policy ideas, hoping to break through the wall of indifference and, with the right slogan, ideological niche, or media marketing, to find traction with an influential member of Congress or a persuadable senior administration official. UNA was an anomaly on the cluttered Washington foreign policy stage.

As Steven Dimoff, who headed UNA-USA's Washington office for its last three decades, observed,

> I can't tell you how much Washington foreign policy research and advocacy groups envy UNA-USA for having chapters and members nationwide. They all wish they had members around the country that could give some political resonance out in the States and congressional districts to their issues. Even if our membership is relatively small, just having voters back home who raise these issues makes every congressional office pay at least enough attention to respond to those constituents. We can get a hearing in offices where so many of these other foreign policy groups cannot. UNA really is unique in that regard.

UNA was born as an advocacy organization, pressing the bipartisan cause of chartering a new international order to "save" future generations from war. But with US adherence to the UN achieved, grassroots advocacy atrophied. Just after the 1952 election, AAUN wrote of its concern "with the intensified attacks on the United Nations in some areas of the country" and convened a meeting of allied organizations to gauge "the public opinion they had found within their own organizations and the sentiment about the United Nations they had heard in their own trips throughout the country." Alarmed by the erosion in support, AAUN's Linzer wrote to chapters at the end of November, asking them to work with local leaders of partner organizations to undertake "intensified programs on the UN that will be 'fact-finding' projects to bring the correct information to the public."

In the heyday of Wisconsin Senator Joseph McCarthy, however, genteel "citizen education" efforts back home were pathetically insufficient to cope with the raw Washington politics of a conservative resurgence. In the spring of 1953, empowered conservatives eyed two UN bêtes noires—the United Nations Educational, Scientific, and Cultural Organization (UNESCO) and the emerging corpus of human rights treaty law. They sought to slash funding for the first and derail the threat of the second by a constitutional amendment. Sponsor of the constitutional amendment was Ohio Senator John Bricker, the Republican candidate for vice president against Harry Truman in the 1944 election, described by journalist Robert A. Caro as "a fervent hater of foreign aid, the United Nations, and all those he lumped with Eleanor Roosevelt under the contemptuous designation of One Worlders" (a label understood to include the entire AAUN).[2]

Eichelberger wrote urgently to AAUN members, warning that "a strident, violent isolationist minority has hammered at UNESCO harder than any other part of United Nations activities" and beseeching them "to write letters to the members of the Senate [Appropriations] Committee letting them know that there is support for UNESCO's activities." To stiffen resistance to the Bricker amendment among the Senate's small band of liberal and moderate members, Eichelberger reached out to AAUN's allied organizations to stitch together a coalition including the League of Women Voters, the New York State Bar Association, the American Jewish Congress, the American Federation of Labor, B'nai B'rith, and the American Association of University Women. Although they faced a seemingly unbeatable combination of all the nation's leading war veteran organizations, the Chamber of Commerce, the Daughters of the American Revolution, the American Medical Association, and the National Association of Evangelicals, the AAUN coalition needed simply to deny the Bricker amendment a two-thirds majority in the Senate. The amendment failed by a single vote—60 to 31. UNESCO escaped the ax in 1953, but would be felled thirty years later. (For more details on the series of Bricker amendments, see Chapter 4.)

It was the crisis of the 1980s that finally shook UNA's membership out of political detachment. "There was always an emphasis on involving public officials in events but not asking for votes on specific legislation," Olson recalled of the long tradition among UNA chapters. "Members and volunteers attached much less importance to political advocacy," he added. In the 1970s, even as the storm clouds gathered over a UN whose growing membership was becoming independent of Washington—transferring China's seat to Beijing, pressing a new international economic order, and denying the legitimacy of Israel's Zionist raison d'être—"we didn't do any political advocacy in Jacksonville," Olson said. "[US representative] Charlie Bennett was there, he knew we were there, and we didn't feel we had to show him there was a constituency," he continued. The advent of a Carter administration actively supportive of the UN, constructively engaged with the developing countries on which UN majorities now hinged, and successful in beating back the rising attacks on it in Congress permitted UNA chapters to continue in their complacency—but not for long.

The assault of 1953 could be blunted because President Eisenhower was himself a Republican internationalist. Together with his impeccably anticommunist secretary of state, John Foster Dulles (conservative yet internationalist), Eisenhower could hold his party's isolationists at bay. In 1981, President Reagan and Secretary of State Alexander Haig Jr. brought the isolationists into the administration, often in influential positions. Dimoff recalled the transformations that prodded reluctant UNA members into political activism:

> I think that the importance of UNA grassroots input into the policy-making process became apparent in the early 1980s, after the Reagan administration decided to withdraw from UNESCO and the Kassebaum amendment [restricting US dues payments to the UN] was enacted into law. Until that time, my impression is that UNA had relied on its leadership and like-minded experts to make its case for US engagement in the UN to a largely sympathetic White House and State Department.
>
> By 1980, Congress was already becoming a difficult audience due to the General Assembly's 1975 adoption of the Zionism-as-racism resolution. By the mid-1980s, it became clear that the ideological battles within the Reagan administration, growing US-UN arrears, and growing skittishness about the UN on Capitol Hill required our chapters and members to mobilize beyond what they had previously done—both in terms of building support for the UN within their communities and interacting with elected officials beyond the organizing of the annual UN Day observances.

Local opponents were nativist networks brimming with hostility not only to international engagement but also to a UN that incarnated to them everything foreign. The San Fernando Valley chapter office in Encino, California, had been bombed in 1963, and by the early 1990s, these isolationist networks were girding for battle against the "UN black helicopters" said to be descending to subjugate US citizens to the jackboot of UN peacekeepers. Some of UNA's members in Michigan reported to the national office their anxiety when muscle-bound, self-styled "militiamen" began stalking their events.

Although these opponents had to be taken seriously, in some ways they were actually a desirable foil for UNA advocates. If a congressperson or staff might caricature constituents from UNA as naïve and doddering, albeit educated and informed about world affairs, the UN's fiercest foes back in the district could seem rabid or simply nuts. The more insidious opponents were inside the Beltway—conservative "realists" dismissive of UN ineffectuality and neoconservatives determined to keep the world body from "thwarting" US power and policy, especially in the Middle East. Their stints in government during the Reagan years gave them access and credibility in mainstream media and political circles.

As US policymakers maneuvered the UN into an ever-deeper financial crisis by multiplying pretexts for nonpayment of assessed dues, UNA turned to its members and pleaded with them to communicate to members of Congress the urgency of paying US dues, "in full, on time, and without conditions." Although national leaders of a number of UNA's allied organizations sent letters endorsing payment of UN dues, they could not interest their own members in so technical an issue distant from their organizations' normal concerns. Unlike the celebrated battle over the Bricker amendment in 1953 three decades earlier, UNA's members took up the cudgels for paying UN dues virtually alone: nobody else back home was asking members of Congress to honor the treaty obligation to the rest of the international community. Nor would it be decided in a single up or down vote; the arrears issue dragged on, sapping members' morale for more than two decades.

After several years of providing sample letters to chapter leaders that their members could send to congressional representatives and of asking them to arrange meetings with those representatives in district offices, UNA attempted to orchestrate a single day of meetings in Washington in 1993, with congressional members or their staffs. The meetings were to be held in conjunction with the annual meeting of the Council of Chapter and Division Presidents. "Hill staff were always intrigued by the fact that we had chapters, and I think much of our credibility as an organization on the Hill was based on that fact," Dimoff reiterated; so it was time for them to actually see UNA members blitzing their offices. A number of members of UNA-USA's Board of Governors and the chair, John Whitehead, came to Washington for this first effort, Dimoff recalled. Members were instructed in some of the arcane details of UN funding before visiting their legislators' offices.

"Lambs amid wolves, I remember thinking as I watched our members trek down the corridors," said Laurenti, who would accompany teams on their rounds first as a policy staffer and later as the Mid-Atlantic chapters' national director. "You saw million-member organizations' contingents marching smartly through the halls, pressing agendas that invariably promoted their economic interests, and you saw our little groups, and you swelled up with pride because our homespun citizens were asking only to make a better world."

The Day on the Hill exercise had impact, Dimoff said. He added, "This did not escape the notice of other foreign policy related groups, who faced their own funding and policy issues in the context of intensifying pressures on the federal budget. For these organizations, UNA-USA's grassroots membership structure looked like a 'prescient' response to the 'all politics is local' maxim." The Day on the Hill became an annual event.

The top "asks" in 1993 were full payment of UN dues and Senate approval of several pending UN human rights treaties. Two of those treaties won ratification during that session of Congress, but the arrears issue worsened after the 1994 midterm elections. The demographic profile of UNA membership—better educated, white, older, and more liberal and Democratic-leaning politically than the electorate as a whole—had difficulty communicating with the leaders taking control of the chokepoints in Congress, such as the implacable new chair of the Senate Foreign Relations Committee—North Carolina's Jesse Helms. The Democratic skew to UNA's membership had troubled the national leadership since the early days of the Reagan administration; UNA chair Elliot Richardson and president Edward Luck invested considerable effort in trying to bring moderate Republicans into the organization; that effort was more successful at top levels than at the grassroots, where the few moderate Republicans willing to give local chapters a try often found little in common with the do-gooders whom they saw running them. UNA had to go into the political wars with the citizen army it had, not the army its leaders wished it had.

Members' annual trek to Capitol Hill nonetheless made an impression: there was *somebody* back home who did care about what the UN did and represented. "I do think our friends on the Hill appreciated our efforts," Dimoff said. In addition, UNA was developing a more elaborate support structure for the new emphasis on advocacy. The national board of directors established an advocacy committee in 2000, chaired by Edison Dick, past president of the Washington, DC, division of UNA; the committee surveyed chapter leaders in compiling each year's advocacy agenda, ensuring greater buy-in among those doing the selling.

Dimoff also launched an e-action alert system when UN-related issues appeared on the congressional voting horizon, explaining the issue and proposing a sample text that UNA subscribers could adapt and e-mail to their senators and representatives. Friendly staffers on Capitol Hill would occasionally let him know that a trickle of e-mails had been logged exhorting the lawmaker to act on a UN matter—often the only constituent input they would hear on such subjects.

At one level, the e-action alert system did not make the grade on Capitol Hill. Despite repeated efforts to promote the service among UNA supporters, "I don't believe we ever got beyond 7,000 subscribers," Dimoff recalled. "The response to action alerts was usually disappointing, with no more than 2,000 to 2,500 responding in individual cases," though a 30 percent response rate to appeals to contact public officials would be considered remarkably high in almost any membership organization.

The Chapters and Divisions Steering Committee underscored the new priority on advocacy by creating its own committee on advocacy, with one representative from each of UNA's nine regions and one from the Young Professionals network. Each advocacy committee member served as the focal point to prod all of his or her region's chapters to respond to Dimoff's appeals. Chief among these was a plea for designation of an advocacy chair or contact in every chapter to arrange an annual visit to the district or in-state office of each lawmaker representing some or all of the chapter's members. With the committee's help, Dimoff said, "We did make good progress in encouraging chapters to name advocacy chairs on local boards." The advocacy chair—New Jersey's Laurenti after 2003 and California's Behrstock after 2011—sent e-alerts to each region's representative on the advocacy committee for him or her to forward to local chapters' leaders and advocacy chairs.

This e-alert system was also used for substantive issue resolutions adopted by the national convention, which traditionally the Washington office had sent en bloc to members of the foreign affairs committees of both houses. The advocacy committee reasoned that if a constituent sent in a nationally approved convention resolution, the congressional office would have to assign a staffer to read it and compose a reply. Laurenti estimated that, on average, barely half of the advocacy committee representatives forwarded the ready-made cover message and resolution to the chapter in their regions, and maybe a quarter of the recipient chapters dispatched them to their congressional representatives. "There was a lot of attrition at each step," he observed. "But, based on the letters of response that lawmakers sent in reply to the chapter leaders in their state, it was clear that some underling in one or two dozen congressional offices had had to read the issue statement and pass it up the food chain. That was probably more attention than these statements had gotten before."

For many chapters, the new mandate for advocacy proved a welcome tonic, and they forged close working relationships with sympathetic representatives. Phil Reynolds, former president of the Westchester, New York, chapter, called the Day on the Hill "a win-win which supports the UN while providing a great experience for participants"; Democratic representative Nita Lowey, "a great fan of the UN," was always supportive. Until his retirement in 2003, Republican representative Ben Gilman in Orange County, New York, was also as helpful as his caucus

Monterey, California, UNA member Larry Levine (left) with
Representative Sam Farr (D-California) at the Day on the Hill, June 10,
2008. Levine was also chair of the Council of Chapters and Divisions at
the time. Farr is also a member of UNA. (Photo courtesy of Larry Levine.)

would allow. UNA's Iowa division maintained a close and supportive
relationship with Republican representative Jim Leach and then with his
replacement, David Loebsack, an actual card-carrying member of UNA.
Levine's Monterey Bay chapter worked closely with representative Sam
Farr. Rita Maran's East Bay chapter had an open door to fiercely antiwar
representative Barbara Lee and took pride in persuading her to seek
appointment as one of the two congressional members of the US delegation to the General Assembly in 2013—and then in her being unusu-
ally active as a public delegate there.

Elsewhere, however, advocacy could be a much harder slog. "Living in a 'red' state, our chapter has been ignored by the politicians,"
lamented Ilse Diasio, chapter president in Birmingham, Alabama. "At
in-district and on-the-Hill meetings, aides listened politely to our suggestions re: advocating for UN issues, but our legislators took no positive action. Oh, well, such is life in Dixie."

Democratizing the UNA Voice

The belief that an organized pro-UN presence was needed in every state
to counter political backsliding in Washington lay behind Eichelberger's
emphasis on expanding AAUN's grassroots membership after the 1945
victory on charter ratification. But that membership did not have much

voice in directing the organization. When the association was incorporated in 1943, its first bylaws created a two-tier membership: charter members and general members. The charter members were constituted as a self-perpetuating group, choosing the organization's board of directors; to be admitted as a charter member, an applicant had to be "proposed by a Director or Charter Member" and approved by the board of directors. The general members would be people "who declare their support of the program of the Corporation and their desire to become affiliated with it."

The distinction between an elite governing membership and a supportive citizen membership was not unusual. The Council on Foreign Relations created local committees on foreign relations in major metropolitan centers in 1938, without even a notional role in the elite institution's governance; it ultimately cut them loose in 1995, and as the "American committees on foreign relations," the orphaned local chapters continued to exist, "dedicated to serving the national security interests of the US by enhancing citizen knowledge and understanding of foreign policy" in the "American heartland." UNA would take a different direction than the council.

Eichelberger, in fact, invested heavily in sustaining the engagement of leaders of other nationwide organizations in the UN cause. A broad coalition of organizations, arguably representing millions of Americans, was the crucial demonstration of the public's postwar rejection of isolationism. But once the core institutional question was resolved with the charter's ratification, subsequent controversies that seemed fundamental tests of practical internationalism to some, including Eichelberger, turned out not to interest the leaders or membership of many of AAUN's allied organizations. During the UN's first half dozen years, AAUN struggled to hold its partner organizations—and some of its own members—together on two issues in particular: (1) the UN plan for partition of Palestine and then unilateral US recognition of Jews' proclamation of an independent Israel and (2) the representation of China at the UN after the Communist victory in the Chinese civil war.

AAUN's national directors were still comfortably blue chip in 1950, even with the resignation of the organization's treasurer over the issue of Chinese representation. They included a sitting US senator, Herbert Lehman of New York; a sitting big-state governor, Adlai Stevenson of Illinois; a US delegate to the UN, Eleanor Roosevelt; and former undersecretary of state Sumner Welles. But the leaders of local AAUN chapters were increasingly chafing at their vassal status in the national office, for which articles in *Changing Times* about their activities hardly compensated. That year, the board of directors yielded to chapters' demands for a more integral role in AAUN's affairs by amending the bylaws to create a board of governors that would, to the extent practicable, "be representative of the membership of the Association's branches and the regions of the United States."

In a further concession to the general membership, the board also agreed, in 1950, to convene a three-day national conference in Chicago—the first such meeting of representatives of allied organizations since the planning conference five years earlier for securing Senate consent to ratification of the UN Charter. The 1951 conference and a successive 1953 national conference would also include delegates from AAUN chapters and allied local cooperating groups.

AAUN general members who felt a strong commitment to the cause found a champion on the national board of directors in Frank Porter Graham, a former president of the University of North Carolina. (Graham's appointment to a vacancy in the US Senate in 1949 had inspired a furious primary challenge from a Red-baiting segregationist, whose victorious campaign was masterminded by a young Jesse Helms.) In 1954, Graham called on the board to take steps to "democratize" AAUN, supported by Eleanor Roosevelt. Roosevelt had proposed a plan of organization the year before, calling for the membership chapters to be grouped into multistate regions, with the designation of one regional chair for each.

In 1956, Graham was named the head of a board committee to make recommendations on AAUN's "democratization," which advanced a plan to strengthen the role of AAUN chapters. Among the recommendations accepted by AAUN's board of directors was a mandate for a biennial convention of AAUN, with representation from both the local and state membership branches and the national organizations with an institutional membership in the association. The first biennial convention was held in 1958 and achieved enough progress on "how representation shall be assured on a more democratic basis on the board of directors" as to satisfy Eleanor Roosevelt, who noted in a "My Day" column in 1958, "For the first time I feel convinced that there is real vitality in the chapters of the AAUN and that as they learn how to achieve their purposes they are going to be more and more effective in their localities."

The arrival of national conventions presented an awkward question for the association: what was to be the status of resolutions they adopted? Several national membership organizations were concerned they might be tarred by—and their own members might be irate over—stances endorsed at an AAUN convention that might prove too far out front of public opinion. The lightning-rod issue on which many allied national organizations had no interest in taking a stand continued to be the representation of China at the UN. The Kuomintang Party regime, beloved of the influential "China lobby" but ruling no Chinese territory except the island of Taiwan and associated islets, still represented China at the UN; the new Communist regime that actually controlled China only hardened US antipathy by its intervention against US-led forces in the Korean War. But once the fighting ended and expectations of the unraveling of Mao's government proved illusory, its exclusion posed a basic question about the world organization: should it embrace all countries' governments or be restricted to like-minded ones?

At their 1960 biennial convention, AAUN members pressed for a resolution text that they hoped could break the Cold War taboo. National leadership came back with a nuanced policy statement, which the membership adopted; this statement underscored the principle of "universality" in the UN membership and warned that resisting universality would alienate "the new states" flooding into the UN after decolonization. Although the wording was guarded, it was understood to be a tacit endorsement of including the regime that ruled the world's most populous nation. The incoming Kennedy administration moved gingerly on the subject, opening a discreet diplomatic dialogue with Beijing through the two countries' respective embassies in Warsaw and lifting the US veto on UN membership for Mongolia; but it did not change course on the UN seat before the president's assassination.

In 1965, the first national convention of the postmerger United Nations Association accommodated members' desire for a bolder call to change a dead-end policy. It made a calibrated appeal to the Johnson administration "to state clearly the conditions under which it would be prepared to see the representatives of Peking take a seat in the United Nations," while simultaneously endorsing continued UN membership for the Chinese republic on Taiwan (see Chapter 3).

In fact, the chapter leaders' assertion of a right to take positions on major policy issues at the national conventions was a sticking point in the 1964 merger negotiations. Iowa's Dorothy Schramm, one of the few prominent chapter people to gain a seat on the new UNA's board of directors, reported to the board's committee on chapter relations, "The problem of chapter position-taking, to no one's surprise since this has been the contentious issue of the merger on all levels, has posed the greatest difficulties." Acknowledging that UNA's "primary function" is the dissemination to the US public information about the UN, she insisted, "An important element in the discharge of that function is the formulation and dissemination of policy views."

The bylaws of the US Committee for the United Nations, the junior partner in the merger, had prohibited taking positions on "controversial issues"; AAUN bylaws obviously had not. McKeever, the reconstituted association's first executive head, in his opening address to its first national convention, made clear his desire to rein in chapter leaders' enthusiasm for position taking: "Far too often such resolutions are born to blush unseen by any but their creators . . . and whose main result, therefore, is to make association with UNA [by affiliated national organizations] incompatible with the charters of their own organizations." He left unspoken the fear in headquarters that a runaway convention might stake out positions so at odds with current government policy that UNA's leadership could lose its access to senior officials, and thus its space to affect policy where it was formulated—that is, in private meetings with policymakers.

The US entry into direct combat in Vietnam that year was a case in point. Just a week after the first US Marines went ashore at Da Nang in March 1965, the Rochester, Michigan, chapter was the first to plead with the national headquarters for a UNA statement on escalating US military involvement. The chapter was organizing a public program on the UN and Vietnam and sought a clear alternative to propose. As chapter anguish mounted, Eichelberger—still the point man on policy—sent a congratulatory telegram to President Johnson after his April 7 speech on Vietnam at Johns Hopkins University—a speech that called for a political settlement premised on "the independence of South Viet-Nam" and that urged the UN Secretary-General to "use the prestige of his great office" merely to help launch "a plan for cooperation in increased development."

The apparent shunting aside of Secretary-General U Thant from any role in ending the political and military conflict did not reassure chapter leaders. Their consternation mounted, especially after Johnson announced a major increase in US troop levels in July 1965. With no guidance coming from national headquarters, the Manatee County (Florida) chapter filed a request for a meeting of a "national assembly" of UNA officers to define a more resolute stance. Eichelberger responded promptly on behalf of the national office, asserting that he detected "a decided improvement in the position of the government towards the United Nations," citing a letter that the newly arrived US ambassador Arthur Goldberg had sent to the Secretary-General. In Eichelberger's reading, that letter "urged the Security Council to do everything possible to get negotiations going," which, Eichelberger wrote, "would indicate a considerable change in the situation" within the administration. (What Eichelberger did not say was that UNA leaders were working feverishly to press the administration to reach a compromise end to the UN's financial and constitutional crisis over the Soviets' refusal to pay assessments for Congo peacekeeping, a crisis that threatened the UN's very survival.) When delegates pressed for a declaration on Vietnam at the November convention, the New York office wrote an artful statement that won adoption by a vote of 154–0 with 13 abstentions: "We support the United States Government's call for a ceasefire and unconditional discussions in Vietnam and we call upon all parties simultaneously to stop military action and immediately come to the peace table."

The 1965 convention also set significant precedents for the governance of the remade association. It took up "minimum standards for chapter programming," approved a new dues structure, and approved the "election" of 100 members to the new board of directors for staggered terms—all on a slate that included two chapter leaders, Iowa's Dorothy Schramm and Oregon UNA president Thomas Young, a Portland businessman. As New York chapter leader James Sheldon protested from the floor, the slate's tilt toward "extremely distinguished people" meant "the chapters who vote here and who *are* the organization for the most part are not represented." The chair of the nominating committee politely explained the criteria behind the slate: geography, NGO affiliations, youth, "the amount of influence that the individual has in the community," and, frankly, "whether they might be of some help in raising money."

Connecticut's Herman Steinkraus, the titular president of the association presiding over the convention, told chapter leaders that the new UNA would "have the dual character of a citizens' voluntary movement and a federation of member organizations." Since, notionally at least, the convention would approve the selection of the board of directors, it acquiesced to the bylaw provision that the board "shall have the power to establish and declare the policies of the Association and to manage its affairs," while the biennial convention "may make recommendations and take positions with respect thereto."

The 1965 convention was deemed successful, ushering in a strengthened association dedicated to deepening US commitment to the UN. The "charter members" of the original bylaws were no more, as the organization had formally adopted a more democratic governing structure. Membership debates on some of the most contentious foreign policy issues roiling US politics at the time had been successfully managed, with the new UNA staking out carefully worded positions that were out in front of the Johnson administration, though not so much that the administration would freeze out the association on UN issues that were its core concern. There was a danger, however, that what Washington viewed as "UN issues" might become more marginal. Moreover, despite the lovefest at the 1965 convention, there emanated from the national office a festering sense of "a negativism and a deprecating of any action which might be taken by the convention other than a rubber stamp of approval" of statements from the national office, as Mrs. Dana Converse Backus, a prominent New York chapter member, wrote in a letter to headquarters. For the next half-century, the tensions between an activist-inclined grassroots membership and the national office waxed and waned, despite periodic fixes intended to bridge the gap.

"The policy/New York versus grassroots gulf was prominently on display at our national conventions," Olson acknowledged. "The UNA-USA bylaws gave the convention the ability to adopt substantive and business resolutions and to elect the board. Some national staffers and board members viewed this event as something like the arrival of the barbarians at the gates of Rome. The convention was described as a 'circus,' and the delegates had to be 'managed'—by me." Aside from perennial squabbles over the levels of UNA membership dues, it was indeed over UN policy issues that the gap between the field and the New York office could be glaring. As Olson recalled, "There were usually contentious resolutions that, in theory, would become official UNA-USA policy if adopted—for example, resolutions supporting Palestinian rights. Much time and energy were spent in committee and on the floor of the convention trying to find middle ground on these resolutions."

In Olson's view, the president of UNA, Ed Luck, enjoyed confidence among the membership and showed that he took their views on policy seriously by pioneering the Multilateral Project (later dubbed Global Policy Project, discussed in Chapter 9), which presented weighty issues on the global agenda for citizen debate and policy recommendations. Luck frequently did speaking appearances for chapters and seemed to treat them as central to the organization. So, "despite the divisions that surfaced during the conventions," Olson observed, delegates "were nevertheless excited and inspired to be in New York to visit UN headquarters. During the debates on resolutions Luck would often stand up and be the quiet, extraordinarily well-informed and articulate voice of moderation and reason, and advocates on all sides would listen and follow his suggestions."

Laurenti recalled Luck turning the tide when antiwar delegates came to the January 1991 convention, determined to pass a resolution of opposition to the impending Gulf War:

Ed rose on the convention floor to challenge them, saying this was a test of credibility for the UN—and for UNA. The US government is playing by the UN rules here, the Charter exists to stop aggression, the Security Council has authorized sanctions and now military action, so how can UNA say we should look the other way? He got them to overcome their own visceral antiwar instincts and reject by a large majority the hand-wringing language calling for more negotiations with Saddam. The delegates trusted him. In fact, our convention delegates were almost always sensible and realistic, when you laid out the facts.

Despite some chapter leaders' feelings of powerlessness in the organization, they steadily gained representation on the association's governing board. Two decades after the 1964 merger, six chapter leaders were part of the slimmed-down board, which also included representatives of religious, civil rights, and labor organizations, as well as the person chairing the council of UNA-affiliated organizations' UN representatives. But the board's nominating committee still controlled the selection of even these board members. As Olson recalled, "The nominating committee would present a slate of candidates for the board of directors and the national council. Delegates could vote yes or no, so the elections were something of a joke—like a Stalinist regime in Eastern Europe, as one chapter wag observed."

The chapter leaders on the board were reminded of how marginal they really were when an inner circle of New York–based board members decided to oust Luck from UNA's presidency. As UNA went through four successor chief executives in as many years, chapter leaders agitated for further democratization in the association's governance. Betty Sandford of Pasadena, who had served on the UNA board in the 1970s and returned to the board two decades later, helped broker a 1997 agreement on bylaws revision with one of the financially supportive younger New York board members, Michael Sonnenfeldt. A revamped forty-five-member board of directors would include nine directors elected by the chapters and divisions in each region, plus two working-level representatives of the Council of Organizations—the one chairing the representatives of UNA's allied national organizations at the UN, and the other chairing their representatives in Washington. Term limits were introduced for all directors, except for the UNA officers.

It became clear the next year that the new system had not changed the fiduciary reality that the major donors, whose generosity kept the headquarters open, effectively led it. The appointment of William Luers to replace Alvin Adams, without board directors having been polled to discuss the changes, revived old concerns among chapter leaders. Luers, a former ambassador who had just stepped down as president of the

Metropolitan Museum of Art, was credited with good entrée to Manhattan's wealthiest donors. He quickly demonstrated skill at fund-raising, which helped assuage some of the distress in the chapter network about the circumstances of his appointment.

But the replacement of the last labor and religious organization representatives on the board by wealthy individuals whom Luers was wooing as donors fanned UNA members' concerns about national headquarters becoming more elitist and focused on access to senior officials in government, and more disconnected from the UN's constituencies in the US public. The regionally elected directors became increasingly cohesive, caucusing among themselves on the eve of each board meeting. They protested the termination of membership-oriented programs and staff, warned against launching "grassroots" fund-raising campaigns that had no buy-in from chapters, questioned the accounting that disguised deficits in headquarters programs, and pressed for a vigorous defense of the UN and its principles as the nation's top political leaders were openly challenging the UN's "relevance."

The 2008 financial crash helped sweep away UNA-USA's national office. When the headquarters staff lacked the money (or staff) to convene the biennial national convention in early 2009, the chapter network itself took on the burden. In organizing the national convention and a Members' Day on their own, UNA's membership chapters demonstrated their determination to carry on the task of mobilizing public support for the UN. Before his retirement that spring, Luers began discussions with the United Nations Foundation on a possible merger, which two years later would lead to the foundation's adoption of the membership chapters, the Council of Organizations, the Business Council for the United Nations, Global Classrooms, and related programs. Thus UNA survived an existential crisis, with its "crown jewels"—that is, its membership network—intact.

Notes

1. Stephen C. Schlesinger, *Act of Creation: The Founding of the United Nations* (Boulder, CO: Westview Press, 2003), 268.

2. Robert A. Caro, *Master of the Senate* (New York: Random House, 2002), 528.

14

Advocating for Human Rights and International Justice

The strongest way to combat the rise of dictatorships and their suppression of human rights, the League of Nations Association/AAUN deemed, was to push for strong human rights components in the UN Charter and later initiatives and covenants—most famously, the Universal Declaration of Human Rights.[1] As detailed earlier in the book, the association advocated for the most holistic approach to peace and security, thinking that ending war would never be accomplished solely by military means. The association saw human rights, democracy, and decolonization as parts of the same whole. For example, in *UN: The First Ten Years*, Eichelberger wrote, "The Charter of the United Nations places human rights and the dignity and worth of the human person as one of its first objectives." Furthermore, he wrote, "No part of the Charter better illustrates the obligations that members undertake for both individual and collective action than the human rights provisions."[2] Eichelberger had been urging that the charter "provide for a commission on human rights" because he "was afraid that otherwise postwar reactions might prevent creating such a commission."[3]

This view of human rights was incorporated into the UN Charter, largely through the work of civil society led by AAUN (see Chapter 3), and continued to advance after the charter was ratified.

The Universal Declaration of Human Rights

Regularly referred to as the most important international document of the twentieth century after the UN Charter itself, the Universal Declaration of Human Rights is the taproot of all human rights declarations and conventions thereafter. Adopted unanimously, with the Soviet Union and its allies abstaining, by the UN General Assembly in Paris on December 10, 1948, it acts "as a common standard of achievement for all peoples and all nations." It sets out, for the first time, "fundamental human rights to be universally protected."[4] The declaration was the first step in the long process of creating an International Bill of Human Rights, with legally binding conventions on specific human rights issues to follow.

The declaration, however, is not a treaty, was never ratified by any country, and is not binding international law. Nigel S. Rodley, an analyst for Amnesty International, called the declaration, "The moral touchstone for all claims at the international level that justice has not been done at the national level." But because it does not include any enforcement mechanisms, he added, "This was the beginning of the emergence of the practice whereby states were to prove themselves more willing to enunciate desirable standards as long as this did not involve direct legal obligation."[5] In other words, it is easier to get states to agree to broad principles than to get them to agree to precise and possibly enforceable legal obligations.

The declaration is based on the US Bill of Rights and France's Declaration of the Rights of Man and of the Citizen. Of a more modern vintage, the Atlantic Charter and FDR's Four Freedoms speech in his 1941 State of the Union address (freedom of speech and religion, freedom from want and fear) provided additional concepts for the declaration.

An important figure from the San Francisco Conference who was focused on founding the UN was also involved in laying the groundwork for the declaration. Virginia Gildersleeve, the dean of Barnard College and a native New Yorker, was the only female US representative to the conference and helped shape the human rights language of the charter and its preamble. She added the language to the latter calling for "higher standards of living, full employment, and conditions of economic and social progress and development" and "universal respect for human rights and fundamental freedoms for all without distinction as to race, sex, language, or religion." Her advocacy extended beyond the rhetorical. Gildersleeve was also a forceful voice in insisting that the UN Economic and Social Council use its powers to create commissions and establish a Human Rights Commission.

Rosalind Rosenberg, an American historian who teaches at Barnard, wrote, "To carry out its work, the council was given the power to appoint whatever commissions it deemed necessary, but Gildersleeve successfully insisted that the charter require the appointment of one in particular: the Commission on Human Rights."[6] It was this commission, under the leadership of Eleanor Roosevelt, that wrote the declaration.

One of Roosevelt's most important achievements after the White House years was her role in creating the declaration. Over the two years it took to draft the document, Roosevelt chaired both the Commission on Human Rights and the commission's drafting (see Chapter 5). Immediately upon the adoption of the declaration, Roosevelt began work on the covenants that would make up the second segment of the International Bill of Human Rights. However, US domestic politics intervened—Dwight Eisenhower, a Republican, became president—and she left the Commission in 1952. A memorial to her stands on the North Lawn of the UN campus, commemorating her contributions to the declaration. It is only one of two UN memorials dedicated to an individual who was not a Secretary-General or head of state. (The other such memorial is of Count Folke Bernadotte, a Swede and UN mediator assassinated in Jerusalem in 1948.)

The need for a declaration was so essential to the AAUN's vision that it drafted its own Bill of Human Rights.[7] Written by the Commission on the Study of Peace's Committee on Human Rights, the July 1946 paper drew on the founding documents of the United States and on the UN Charter. The AAUN/CSOP document was more ambitious than the final UN declaration, but it did include many elements that found their way into the UN's version. Although cause and effect cannot be unequivocally demonstrated, it is known that Roosevelt and other delegates did see the draft bill. Of course, the drafters drew on the same sources of inspiration as the AAUN.

Ideals in the AAUN draft that were also in the declaration included freedom of belief, expression, assembly, and association, as well as the rights to a fair trial, freedom from arbitrary arrest, and education. It calls for the "freedom of petition for redress of grievance," "the privileges of citizenship," and "the right to protection against arbitrary discrimination regarding property." But there were also important differences. The most essential was that the AAUN envisioned a legal document, whereas the declaration was voluntary. The AAUN draft is also more state-centric, focusing on the responsibilities of the state, saying "the state has a duty to enforce the rights" detailed in the document, as well as the responsibility "to prohibit actions that deny the rights outlined," whereas the declaration places no such obligations on the state. Further, the AAUN draft envisioned the bill as international law, with violations handled by the International Court of Justice. Because the declaration is not a legal commitment, however, it cannot be enforced in a court of law, as is the case for many UN resolutions passed in the Security Council. Although they are legally binding, the only "enforcement" tools are sanctions and censures, among other indirect and direct measures, though a resolution written under a Chapter VII (in the UN Charter) mandate can entail military action. Resolutions passed in the General Assembly—other than for personnel and budget matters—are not legally binding. "The nations stopped short," Eichelberger wrote, "of taking an obligation to give the United Nations itself authority to enforce human rights and fundamental freedoms. . . . Nevertheless, it has come to be a source of law because of the way in which it has been implemented."[8]

A good indication of how important the declaration became to public opinion was an event that marked the first anniversary of its adoption. Held at Carnegie Hall in New York on December 10, 1949, the celebration featured speeches by Eleanor Roosevelt, Secretary-General Trygve Lie, and General Assembly President Carlos Rómulo; Leonard Bernstein conducted the Boston Symphony Orchestra; Laurence Olivier hosted and read the preamble to the declaration; Bernstein and violinist Yehudi Menuhin performed solos; and the evening concluded with the Collegiate Chorale performing Beethoven's "Ode to Joy."[9]

Creating a Body of International Law

The declaration was the start of a long process in forging human rights obligations. The UN, with AAUN's enthusiastic support, continued to create human rights instruments covering a range of issues. The key difference at this point was that the new instruments would be treaties, or binding international law.

The AAUN saw the drive for human rights as a complicated, lengthy initiative. An Executive Committee statement from August 31, 1950, recommended that the General Assembly adopt the Covenant on Human Rights. "[AAUN] is aware of the fact that the Covenant is of a more limited nature than the Declaration," but "it has always been understood that the Declaration should contain the highest aspirations for human rights and . . . the Covenant should contain those rights which could be defined in multilateral agreement to be ratified and to become part of international law." Furthermore, the AAUN urged the General Assembly to "explicitly" authorize the Commission on Human Rights to begin "the drafting of additional covenants and measures dealing with economic, social, cultural, political and other categories of human rights not contained in the draft First Covenant."[10] This was not a unique tactic. Rodley noted that nongovernment organizations were "committed to working for the widest possible ratification of the

Covenants" and that "campaigning for respect for human rights is essentially a technique of step-by-step application of the pressure of international public opinion." This was the approach adopted by the UN itself. "The UN has promoted the adoption of a large number of instruments, both legally binding treaties and resolutions of debatable and varying legal force on specific areas of human rights," Rodley wrote.[11]

The declaration, followed by the International Covenant on Civil and Political Rights and the International Covenant on Economic, Social and Cultural Rights, represented early efforts to establish a legal basis for the protection of human rights worldwide. Over the decades, nine core treaties became the International Bill of Human Rights.[12] Here is a list of those treaties, with the US position noted (ratification in the United States requires a two-thirds majority vote in the Senate):

- International Covenant on Civil and Political Rights, 1966. US ratified in 1992.
- International Covenant on Economic, Social and Cultural Rights, 1966. US has not ratified.
- International Convention on the Elimination of All Forms of Racial Discrimination, 1965. US ratified in 1994.
- Convention on the Elimination of All Forms of Discrimination Against Women (CEDAW), 1979. US has not ratified.
- Convention Against Torture and Other Cruel, Inhuman or Degrading Treatment, 1984. US ratified in 1994.
- Convention on the Rights of the Child, 1989. US has not ratified.
- International Convention on the Protection of the Rights of All Migrant Workers and Members of Their Families, 1990. US has not signed the convention, the first step to ratification.
- International Convention on the Rights of Persons with Disabilities, 2006. US has not ratified.
- International Convention for the Protection of All Persons from Enforced Disappearance, 2006. US has not signed.

As is apparent by comparing the years the treaties were written and when the US took action on them (or took no action), the momentum that propelled the creation of the declaration quickly dissipated. For reasons detailed in this chapter, the quest for an international set of human rights dropped as a priority issue for the United States after 1952. The AAUN continued, however, to promote the covenant. Although some human rights treaty negotiations took place in the 1970s and 1980s, they dropped down on the agendas of the UN, the United States, and the

UNA as Cold War issues dominated. In an interview for this book, Felice Gaer, a human rights expert, said,

> You have to appreciate what the UNA was trying to do and what [the] broader context was. The UN didn't do very much except draft instruments in the late 1940s and 1950s. We had the Bricker amendment, and with that the opposition to human rights treaties and the like. They not only kicked [Mrs.] Roosevelt off of the Human Rights Commission when the Eisenhower administration came in, but they just didn't do anything really in the human rights area except bilaterally or rhetorically.

The UNA, she added, "reflected the fact that there was nothing going on." Slowly but surely, however, progress was made. Ed Elmendorf, who later became UNA chief executive officer and had served at the US Mission to the UN in the 1960s, said in an interview that Arthur Goldberg, who came off the Supreme Court to serve as US ambassador to the UN at the request of President Johnson, overcame resistance in Washington and convinced Johnson to sign the UN's human rights covenants when they were adopted by the General Assembly.

Gaer has worked for numerous organizations and entities, including UNA and the Ford Foundation. She was nominated and renominated to human rights posts over the years by the Bush, Clinton, and Obama administrations, and she was the first American to serve as an independent expert on the UN Committee Against Torture, where she had been the vice chair. Gaer is now director of the Jacob Blaustein Institute for the Advancement of Human Rights of the American Jewish Committee. She has also served as chair of the UNA-USA Leo Nevas Task Force on Human Rights (see below). "In the human rights area," Gaer said, the Cold War divide was between the Soviet bloc, which "did not accept the human rights paradigm and the Western countries, which insisted on it." She continued: "One of the goals of the Soviet bloc countries was to make it as obscure as possible and use procedure as a shield whenever possible to keep things from being discussed, summarized; it would be a decision, not a resolution; it would be in a presidential statement, which doesn't then get reproduced in the official documents."

Although human rights remained on the UNA agenda, it was not a priority at the national level, despite the interest of members in the matter. It was not the subject of any occasional paper or of the Global Policy Project studies in the 1970s and 1980s or of any conferences. In Washington, however, President Jimmy Carter kicked the ball forward by making clear that a country's domestic human rights record could be a factor in US relations with the country. The only time human rights were the focus of the association occurred in 1979, when UNA produced a volume called *United States Foreign Policy and Human Rights: Principles, Priorities, Practice.* Coinciding with the return of human rights concerns on the international agenda through the Carter administration, the report was produced by the National Policy Panel of the UNA (Robert V. Roosa was the chair of the Policy Studies Committee). It argued why human rights should play a role in US foreign policy. "Reasons of morality, humanitarianism, the furtherance of peace and world order, and international obligations, both global and regional, require it," the report said. Its list of prescriptions—ratification of human rights covenants, strengthening the human rights component of the specialized agencies, creation of the post of UN High Commissioner—highlighted how little progress had been made on the issue for nearly three decades.[13]

With the Cold War's demise and the deadlock it had caused at the UN, human rights concerns were among the issues granted a new lease on life. UNA produced three papers on the subject and became a prominent proponent for the creation of the post of the High Commissioner for Human Rights, the revamping of the Human Rights Commission, and the creation of the International Criminal Court (ICC). All these initiatives were also priorities for advocates outside UNA. Jacob Blaustein, for example, called for creating the high commissioner post in a Columbia University speech in 1963.[14]

The UNA reports that took on the subject were *Promises to Keep: Securing Human Rights in a Changing World,* by Shareen Hertel (1994); *Inalienable Rights, Fundamental Freedoms: A UN Agenda for Advancing Human Rights in the World Community,* no author (1996); and *Bringing New Life to UN Human Rights Operations,* by Eric G. Berman (1998). All three promoted strengthening the framework by ratifying the human rights conventions, creating the ICC and war crimes tribunals, establishing the Office of the High Commissioner for Human Rights, and encouraging greater involvement of civil society in securing these rights—all leading the way for action by the UN World Conference on Human Rights held in Vienna in 1993. In addition, the Washington office of UNA tried to get Congress to focus on ratifying the treaties that had been neglected for years—notably, CEDAW and the Rights of the Child—with no success.

UNA contributed to honoring human rights champions with the inception of the Leo Nevas Program on Human Rights in 2007. The program—one of the last initiated before the UNA alliance with the UN Foundation and the only New York–based policy program to have continued after the alliance—"aims to impact policy, educate UNA chapters and members, and foster new and innovative thinking that encourages constructive U.S. engagement through the UN's human rights bodies."[15] The program is managed by the Leo Nevas Human Rights Task Force, which chooses the Leo Nevas Human Rights Fellow and bestows annual human rights awards (one for lifetime achievement and one youth awardee). Nevas received the first award in 2007; other lifetime achievement awardees include author Kati Marton (and widow of US ambassador Richard Holbrooke); Paulo Sérgio Pinheiro, the chair of the Independent International Commission of Inquiry for Syria; and US ambassador to the UN Samantha Power (who in her 2013 acceptance speech said, "From Leo Nevas we see two things: an insistence on tending to the needs of the less fortunate and a determination to oppose bigotry and discrimination"). UNA's Global Classroom's curriculum on human rights was also updated through a grant from Newman's Own Foundation.

Leo Nevas, a lawyer and human rights champion, served on the UNA-USA Board of Directors for forty years. As the lawyer for Paul Newman and Joanne Woodward, who all lived in Westport, Connecticut, these three commitments merged when Newman, through the Newman's Own Foundation, agreed to fund the program. An obituary of Nevas, who died in 2009 at age ninety-seven, quoted Nevas as saying, "I have represented Paul Newman in business, charitable and personal matters for over 40 years. About 20 years ago, he became interested in doing something significant to help little kids facing life-threatening illness. I was involved from the beginning." The project became Newman's Hole in the Wall Gang Camp, based in Connecticut. Newman established the human rights program at UNA "in gratitude" for Nevas's work.[16] (See Box 14.1.)

One of UNA's last occasional papers, published in March 2010, was aimed at re-engaging the US government in promoting international law. Called "Renewing America's Commitment to International Law," it was written by Lawrence C. Moss, a member of the UNA-USA Leo Nevas Task Force and a Human Rights Watch specialist at the time. Moss wrote of the United States:

> [It] now has the opportunity to advance international norms from which it has long stood apart. To secure agreement and cooperation on issues central to American security, the US needs to lead by example and ratify and implement existing arms control and environmental

Box 14.1 Leo Nevas

There was nothing conventional about Leo Nevas. He dedicated his life to challenging dogma and defended human rights when it wasn't fashionable to do so. What better way to honor his memory than to nurture a new generation of leaders who would do just that? With that idea in mind, under the leadership of UNA-USA board members Bob Rifkind and Ed Elmendorf, as well as with Felice Gaer, the UNA-USA Task Force on Human Rights found resources to establish a fellowship to award individuals who questioned conventional wisdom with the combined skills of a storyteller, an academic, and an activist.

UNA-USA was well situated to make a difference, given its support by thousands of members nationwide. Pursuing human rights through the UN requires a tangle of questions with no ready answers. What role do UN bodies play in integrating human rights policies and practices into its peacekeeping and development activities, for example? How do UN treaties and conventions contribute to the protection and promotion of human rights, and how can they advance US interests? How could the United States promote the universality of women's rights and political and religious freedoms in alignment with its broader foreign policy goals? Traditional human rights groups have provided a valuable service by holding governments accountable and speaking truth to power when pushing for action on specific human rights issues; yet these groups can have unrealistic expectations. UNA-USA wanted to fill an important gap by putting forward realistic recommendations and streamlining human rights into the broader foreign policy priorities of the United States. The Leo Nevas Fellow would pursue bold but practical ideas for US participation and mobilize support through making such ideas accessible to UNA-USA members.

"Don't let UNA-USA put human rights on the back burner," Leo Nevas once told me over the phone. Although he was more than fifty years my senior and a board member, he talked to me as if I were a peer. He called and wrote letters regularly to me and others at UNA. He listened. He cared. He was aware of the organization's competing priorities and that resources were scarce for even maintaining daily operations. When everyone saw crises, he saw an opportunity and elevated human rights to the top of UNA-USA's research and advocacy agenda by making funds and expertise available to us in the right way.

When we met a few months before his death at age ninety-seven, he was dressed in his usual three-piece suit. He was still the sharpest mind in the room.

—Ayca Ariyoruk

treaties. To promote democracy and respect for principles of human rights, the US should join and implement human rights treaties that many of our friends and allies have endorsed.[17]

The goal of Moss's paper, said Ayca Ariyoruk, a senior policy associate for UNA at the time, "was to have a reference which the chapters could use as a quick guide on US standing on international treaties and assess the Obama administration's track record thus far." The paper was distributed to chapters to encourage grassroots advocacy, but "we weren't around long after that to make a new push for ratification," Ariyoruk said in an interview for this book. Treaties have been a UNA-USA advocacy matter for decades. She added,

> Treaties are process oriented, so the outcome is hidden in the process—which is to get countries to have a dialogue about standards. . . . I think UNA's most important policy achievement was not really about making huge improvements but was damage control most of the time. As long as there was considerable support in the grassroots, the [US] administrations paid attention. UNA-USA probably was more effective in preventing downgrading of the UN than promoting an upgrade.

Ariyoruk continued: "UNA-USA was good at having an impact on UN's bureaucracy and gathered small victories here and there." The Leo Nevas Human Rights Task Force, however, has given increasing attention to the UN's special procedures, special rapporteurs, and commissions of inquiry, such as the 2012 and 2014 Commissions of Inquiry on Syria and on North Korea, respectively.

US Domestic Politics and Human Rights

Despite the pivotal role of the US government and US private citizens in embedding human rights into the UN Charter and writing the Universal Declaration, human rights issues dropped off the government's agenda as the 1950s wore on and the Human Rights Commission drafted binding covenants. This turned out to be a glass-house phenomenon—as the civil rights movement grew and became more vocal and visible, it became harder for the United States to pretend that human rights on US soil were universal. In addition, as detailed in Chapter 4, the Bricker amendment and other anti-internationalist initiatives put the US government on the defensive. To placate the isolationists, the Eisenhower administration announced that it would not submit to the Senate for ratification any human rights treaties or covenants that might be negotiated at the UN, thus undercutting the government's own negotiating position.

There was also pressure from the other side of the debate. Human rights was one area where the AAUN pressed much further than the US government was willing to go. The AAUN's 1952 policy statement reflects this disenchantment with Washington. As usual, the statement looked at the range of issues on the UN agenda—peaceful settlement of disputes, disarmament, and economic development—and promoted the most UN-based solutions. But when it came to human rights, the statement took an uncharacteristically inward approach. It naturally supported the declaration and the covenants. However, the statement began, "The American people have the heavy task of improving the practices of human rights within their own borders." The AAUN said it was "humiliated" that the US government had not ratified the Genocide Convention. In paragraphs clearly aimed at the anticommunist witch hunts, the statement said: "The right to dissent is the birthright of every American. We deplore those growing apprehensions which have promoted both measures and attacks aimed at dissident opinion." Furthermore, "The safety of the country can be more imperiled than assured if measures directed against an alleged conspiracy take on the attributes of a police state."[18] Ten years later, the statement from the Third Biennial Convention dedicated more space to general human rights concerns and was no longer talking about a police state at home, but it still led off advising the United States that it "should contribute to the advancement of the cause of human rights and fundamental freedoms as envisaged in the Charter by setting its own domestic house in order."[19] In a statement to the Democratic National Committee's platform hearing in 1960, Eichelberger said that the human rights "picture is not an encouraging one." The country's "refusal to ratify the Genocide Convention and other human rights conventions and to participate in the completion of the human rights covenants has served to delay the advancement of human rights through the United Nations."[20]

AAUN was only one of many US organizations advocating for human rights at home. To bring attention to the plight of minorities, the National Negro Congress and the National Association for the Advancement of Colored People (NAACP) lodged a complaint to the UN Economic and Social Council, demanding an investigation into the US treatment of its minorities. W. E. B. Du Bois detailed for the council the "panoply of human rights violations against blacks."[21] Even though the great civil rights legislation of the 1960s brought the United States more in line (at least theoretically) with the International Bill of Rights, the United States still refused to take up the covenants. The Soviet Union ratified both the International Covenant on Civil and Political Rights and the International Covenant on Economic, Social and Cultural Rights in 1968—two years after they were adopted. But the United States continued to refuse to take them up. (The United States did not ratify the Civil and Political Rights covenant until 1992 and has not ratified the Economic, Social and Cultural Rights covenant.)

It was not until 1976, under President Carter, that the United States reintroduced the language and concept of human rights into policy. He signed the Covenant on Civil and Political Rights; the Covenant on Economic, Social and Cultural Rights; and CEDAW. He used the rhetoric of human rights in defining US relationships with other countries. But under the Reagan administration, which was notably influenced by the hard-line UN ambassador Jeane Kirkpatrick, human rights became a situational issue; this was understandable when allies violated human rights, but awful when the violator was an enemy. By then, human rights were back on the UNA agenda, with the association supporting the creation of a High Commissioner for Human Rights and reorganizing the Human Rights Commission.

The International Criminal Court and the American NGO Coalition for the ICC

In the diplomatic history of unintended consequences, a General Assembly resolution introduced by Trinidad and Tobago in 1989 ranks high. Like most Caribbean nations, drug running and money laundering were corrupting their societies. So Trinidad resurrected a GA resolution from 1948 that had invited the International Law Commission (ILC), a UN body consisting of thirty-four experts under the General Assembly to develop and codify international law, "to study the desirability and possibility of establishing an international judicial organ for the trials of persons charged with genocide." An analysis by the Coalition for the International Criminal Court (a collection of international NGOs promoting the ICC) noted that "while the ILC drafted such a statute in the early 1950s, the Cold War stymied these efforts and the General Assembly effectively abandoned the effort pending agreement on a definition for the crime of aggression and an international Code of Crimes."[22]

Although Trinidad's original intent was to enlist international support for a regional concern, once the negotiations started, it did not take long for governments, nongovernment experts, academics, and activists to push for a comprehensive draft convention. In 1994, the ILC presented its final draft statute for an International Criminal Court to the General Assembly and recommended that a diplomatic conference be convened to negotiate a treaty and enact the statute. As a result, the GA established the Ad Hoc Committee on the Establishment of an International Criminal Court, which met twice in 1995. The committee recommended setting up a preparatory committee to write a draft convention. Six sessions, from 1996 to 1998, produced the text, which was used by the GA to create the UN Diplomatic Conference of Plenipotentiaries on the Establishment of an ICC.

Meeting in Rome for five weeks in June and July 1998, 160 countries participated in the conference. After tense negotiations, 120 countries voted to adopt the Rome Statute of the ICC, with 7 nations voting against the treaty (including the United States, China, Israel, and Iraq) and 21 states abstaining. On April 11, 2002, the sixtieth ratification necessary to trigger the entry into force was deposited, and the treaty became official on July 1, 2002. The ICC Assembly of States Parties held its first meeting in September that year.

Compared with other treaty negotiations, this happened fast, but it was not painless. The Clinton administration actively participated in the negotiations. David Scheffer served as Clinton's ambassador to the talks. Scheffer had written policy papers for UNA-USA in the 1980s and became a UNA vice president in 2003. In an interview for this book, Scheffer said that as the ambassador-at-large for war crimes, his contacts with UNA were "constant," and he called Steve Dimoff "a fantastic resource." According to Scheffer, UNA

fulfilled a useful function during those eight years, because I could always go to those people like Steve Dimoff and say, "Look, I need the latest factual information about this issue with the UN or this budgetary issue." He would know, too, where the UN budget in Capitol Hill was progressing. . . . As an NGO, UNA was fulfilling that really critical function of helping policymakers do their job. . . . I don't think there was anything major other than [UNA] in those years.

Conservative opposition was intense—as was always the case regarding international law. It centered on the claim that the ICC could be used for politically motivated prosecutions of US citizens—particularly, military personnel. It was clear that the ICC's ratification would not get through the Senate, even if Clinton submitted it. Finally, in one of his last official acts as president, Clinton signed the Rome Statute on December 31, 2000, the last day it was open for signature.

Soon after, the George W. Bush administration launched a global campaign to undermine the court, including enacting legislation in 2002 to shield the United States from ICC reach. The laws were the American Servicemembers' Protection Act (ASPA) and the bilateral immunity agreements (BIAs) with other countries to prevent the transfer of US nationals and others to the ICC. Then, in an unprecedented step, President Bush withdrew the US signature on May 6, 2002, saying that the United States would no longer be involved in the court and that the US did not have any legal obligations under the Rome Statute. The ICC does not recognize the "unsigning" of the statute.

The US rejection of both the Rome Statute and later the Mine Ban Treaty led UNA-USA to work not only to support the campaigns but also to try to sway the US government in favor of the treaties. The crucial difference between the two treaties was that although the United States did respect certain features of the Landmines Convention (notably on export, mine clearance, and survivor assistance), the Bush administration and allies in Congress actively worked to undermine the ICC. The opposition was based on several factors, notably the fear that the court would, again, launch politically motivated prosecutions of US citizens and the desire to have the land-mines option available (especially on the border between North and South Korea).

As a result, NGOs promoting the ICC formed the American Non-governmental Organizations Coalition for the ICC (AMICC) in 2001, which became a program of UNA. The initiative, led by John Washburn, a former UN official and alumnus of Harvard Law School, and Matthew Heaphy as deputy convener and also a lawyer, worked to raise awareness of the issue among the public, while attempting to overcome outright hostility to the court. AMICC, with the support of the Ford Foundation and Planethood Foundation, arranged visits to Washington, DC, for the ICC president at the time, Judge Philippe Kirsch, a Canadian, and other ICC judges. The James H. Ottaway Revocable Trust and other foundations also contributed funds to AMICC.

Before his post at the UN, Washburn had been a career Foreign Service officer in Iran, India, and Indonesia. When he was posted in Washington, he worked on issues relating to international organizations. He retired in 1987 and took a job in the Executive Office of the UN Secretary-General in the Representation Unit, which "had to do basically with the Secretary-General's interaction with all manner of organizations in civil society," he said in an interview for this book. "When my contract there was up, I got involved with the international NGO coalition for the ICC in 1995," he added. "I participated in their founding meeting" as a representative of the Unitarian Universalist UN office and ended up participating "in almost all of the negotiations to create the court's governing treaty, including the diplomatic conference in Rome in 1998 that adopted the statute." Washburn said,

> After the diplomatic conference, it became clear that there were going to be problems with the United States. . . . I was asked by the head of the international NGO coalition [William Pace], with whom by this time I had become a close colleague, to see if we could organize a national network in the United States to promote the cause of the ICC there.

The informal Washington Working Group on the ICC (WICC) was founded in 2000 to educate legislators and senior government officials on the court. Steven Dimoff, a UNA-USA vice president, was cochair. According to the UNA annual report that year, "A major WICC achievement during the year was its leadership in the successful effort to prevent final action in the House of Representatives on the American Service-members' Protection Act (ASPA), a bill seriously hostile to the ICC." This was when the UNA became deeply instrumental. "I succeeded in establishing that network and . . . brought the idea of the network and funding to the UNA," Washburn said. In June 2002, "we established it as a UNA project." Washburn described AMICC as a nationwide organization, whereas WICC, hosted by the Bahá'ís of the USA, "works inside the Beltway exclusively." But they both operate as "sister organizations," said Washburn.

"We interacted with people in Congress who felt this legislation was unwise," he said, referring to ASPA. "Some of the people weren't particularly keen on the ICC but still thought the legislation didn't make much sense." In addition, Washburn explained, "these people in the administration were concerned for the constitutional foreign affairs powers of the president. . . . Washington is a place where, through individual contact, you can do a great deal and learn a great deal, even if official postures are unsympathetic and hostile."

By the second George W. Bush term, there was "considerable softening toward the court," Washburn noted, such as increasingly extending waivers to the ASPA and exemptions for BIAs, so that states parties to the ICC would not have their US military and economic aid cut. "I don't credit [WICC] with turning it around, but I do credit it with having a significant role in a very large process that many were engaged in," Washburn said.

> WICC takes credit for having continually pushed the Bush administration to get to that point. We have a pattern in which the people maybe have severe reservations about the court but find it useful and wish to

encourage it in the context of specific cases and situations. And that is, of course, what we had with the referrals from the Security Council. . . . The Bush administration, for example, abstained on the first referral [on Darfur] by the UN Security Council of a case to the ICC. There were statements made at that time by [Secretary of State] Condoleezza Rice and others about the usefulness of the ICC in certain situations.

The United States abstaining on the Darfur referral meant the referral could go forward; thus, it was a victory for ICC supporters.

Anticipating the 2008 presidential and congressional elections, AMICC "approved a new strategy" in 2007 that included "outreach to foreign policy advisers to presidential candidates, dissemination of electronic resources on the candidates and the ICC, and questioning candidates about the ICC," Washburn added. The WICC aimed to remove some of the punitive anti-ICC laws—most notably, the removal from the ASPA restrictions on military funds for nations unwilling to sign BIAs with the United States to shield US nationals from ICC jurisdiction.

The Obama administration further lowered the rhetoric but did not fully embrace the ICC. During her confirmation hearings as secretary of state in January 2009, Hillary Clinton said, "We will end hostility towards the ICC and look for opportunities to encourage effective ICC action in ways that promote US interests by bringing war criminals to justice." Later that year, the United States sent a delegation to the court's Assembly of States Parties for the first time, and in 2010, it participated in the Review Conference for the ICC. In 2012, Susan Rice, US ambassador to the UN, said, "We have actively engaged with the ICC Prosecutor and Registrar to consider how we can support specific prosecutions already underway, and we've responded positively to informal requests for assistance."[23] An ambassador-at-large for war crimes issues, Stephen Rapp, attended ICC meetings, but he resigned the post in 2015 out of frustration for failing to set up a tribunal to investigate and try atrocity crimes by the Syrian government in its civil war. On the other hand, because the United States is not a party to the ICC, laws bar the nation from directly funding the ICC, and the ASPA and BIAs remain law, with the sanctions provisions repealed. Moreover, the United States has provided some technical support to the court and financed a fund to reward people who provide valid tips, for example, on the whereabouts of Joseph Kony, the Ugandan warlord wanted by the ICC for war crimes and crimes against humanity.

"When UNF decided to acquire the assets of UNA, they were not at all interested in acquiring AMICC," said Jeffrey Laurenti, a former policy analyst for UNA who later worked for the Century Foundation think tank in New York. Laurenti added, "Their work was too controversial. Because the United States is not a party to the treaty and there are a lot of controversies around the ICC in certain political circles in the United States, it was not palatable for the UN Foundation."

Washburn agreed that the UN Foundation "felt that our issue was politically toxic." But he added,

> There also were other reasons, which I respect. First of all, the International Criminal Court is not in the UN system. It's an autonomous international organization that has a relationship with the UN and works closely with it, but is not part of the UN system in any way. So I think that that also influenced their attitudes. I also think the UN Foundation is not particularly interested in the international law or legal categories of the UN's activities.

According to Peter Yeo, who was vice president for advocacy at the UN Foundation at the time of the merger and was involved in that work, the ICC campaign was not picked up because "it wasn't core to what we wanted. . . . We don't really do advocacy for the International Criminal Court because it's not a UN body."

After UNA-USA provided a transitional subsidy that made it possible for AMICC to be accepted as part of Columbia University's Institute for the Study of Human Rights and allowed AMICC to continue, Washburn moved from UNA to the campus. According to Washburn, "It turned out we were a fit because it turned out they were looking for a program like this."

Notes

1. Jared A. Daly and Mariah G. Ross contributed research to this chapter.

2. Clark Eichelberger, *UN: The First Ten Years* (New York: Harper & Brothers, 1955), 70–71.

3. Clark Eichelberger, *UN: The First Twenty Years* (New York: Harper & Row, 1965), 69–71.

4. Office of the High Commissioner for Human Rights, "About the Universal Declaration of Human Rights Translation Project," http://www.ohchr.org /en/udhr/pages/introduction.aspx.

5. Nigel S. Rodley, "The Development of United Nations Activities in the Field of Human Rights and the Role of Non-Governmental Organizations," in *The US, the UN, and the Management of Global Change* (A UNA-USA Publication), ed. Toby Trister Gati (New York and London: New York University Press, 1983), 264.

6. Rosalind Rosenberg, "Virginia Gildersleeve: Opening the Gates," *Columbia University Alumni Magazine*, 2001, http://www.columbia.edu/cu /alumni/Magazine/Summer2001/Gildersleeve.html.

7. The Clark M. Eichelberger Papers, Manuscripts and Archives Division, New York Public Library. Astor, Lenox, and Tilden Foundations (NYPL Archives), box 64.

8. Eichelberger, *UN: The First Twenty Years,* 69–71.

9. NYPL Archives, box 114.

10. Seton Hall University (SHU Archives), The Msgr. William Noé Field Archives and Special Collections Center, South Orange, NJ, box 908.

11. Rodley, "The Development of United Nations Activities," 267–268.

12. Office of the High Commissioner for Human Rights, "Fact Sheet No. 2 (Rev. 1): The International Bill of Human Rights" (Geneva: United Nations, June 1996), http://www.ohchr.org/Documents/Publications/FactSheet2Rev.1en.pdf.

13. UNA-USA, *United States Foreign Policy and Human Rights: Principles, Priorities, Practice* (New York: UNA-USA, 1979).

14. AJC: Global Jewish Advocacy, "UN High Commissioner for Human Rights Salutes AJC's Jacob Blaustein Institute," http://www.ajc.org/site/apps/nlnet/content2.aspx?c=7oJILSPwFfJSG&b=8479733&ct=12483551.

15. UNA-USA, "Leo Nevas Program on Human Rights," http://www.unausa.org/programs/leo-nevas-program-on-human-rights.

16. "Leo Nevas, Westport Legal Icon, Dies at 97," *Westport Now,* August 27, 2009.

17. Lawrence C. Moss, "Renewing America's Commitment to International Law" (occasional paper, UNA-USA, New York, March 2010).

18. NYPL Archives, box 121.

19. Ibid., box 117.

20. Ibid.

21. Carol Anderson, "A 'Hollow Mockery': African Americans, White Supremacy, and the Development of Human Rights in the United States," in *Bringing Human Rights Home: A History of Human Rights in the United States,* ed. Cynthia Soohoo, Catherine Albisa, and Martha F. Davis (Philadelphia: University of Pennsylvania Press, 2009).

22. Coalition for the International Criminal Court, "History of the ICC," http://www.iccnow.org/?mod=icchistory.

23. http://www.amicc.org/usicc/administration.

15

Engaging
the Private Sector

Reflecting the US society at large, the League of Nations Association, leading up to and during World War II, benefited from broad support of private and public figures. For their own distinct reasons, big business and big labor tended to be internationalist: business grew by expanding overseas, and labor saw itself as part of a worldwide struggle for workers' rights. So though they were antagonistic in nearly every other field, these forces in the isolationist America of the 1930s found common ground in opposing Hitler and, in the 1940s, in supporting a world organization. Continued backing by business and labor could be viewed as a natural continuation of the collaboration among business, labor, and traditional foreign policy organizations after the San Francisco Conference — the ABLE coalition at the San Francisco Conference is an example. During those decades, the internationalist groups boasted a who's who in industry and labor, including Thomas Watson of IBM; Robert Benjamin of United Artists; United Auto Workers president Walter Reuther; and A. Philip Randolph, the civil rights leader and union organizer who founded the Brotherhood of Sleeping Car Porters.

For decades, these people and their business connections lent their vocal and financial backing to AAUN and then UNA-USA. Commitments went well beyond allowing their names to be placed on a letterhead or buying an ad in a program. They and their affiliations were engaged in the association's daily work. Benjamin and Reuther, for example, served on the committee stewarding the merger of AAUN and the US Committee for the United Nations. Benjamin served as chair of the newly formed UNA in its first year. Labor was rallied by Eleanor Roosevelt, whose friendship and politics matched labor's own focus on rights of workers and moderate socialism, espoused by her husband, Franklin Roosevelt, while he was in the White House. (See Box 15.1.)

273

Box 15.1 The Economic Policy Council

Before merging with the Business Council for the UN (BCUN), UNA's primary vehicle for reaching out to the business community was the Economic Policy Council (EPC). Started in 1976, the EPC forged an understanding between labor and management on international economic issues. According to an EPC pamphlet from 1982, the council worked through seminars and studies "to orchestrate a systematic and constructive involvement in international economic problems by the American private sector." The council members, "in collaboration with economists and professionals, are able to come to policy recommendations that have special legitimacy because management and labor represent the two most important elements in the US domestic economy," the pamphlet said.

The chair was Robert O. Anderson, the head of Atlantic Richfield. The cochairs came from businesses and labor unions. Bipartisan meetings with the executive and legislatives branches were also part of the council strategy. A series of conferences, called "How to Do Business with the United Nations," was run by a UNA staffer, Ralph Cwerman, who later developed the Adopt-A-Minefield program (see Chapter 11).

Richard Seifman, the executive director of the EPC from 1978 to 1982, said in an interview for this book that the council was "a very special body in that it was created to bring together business, labor, and think tanks to deal with the cutting-edge issues of the time." As an example, he cited one of its first reports, titled "Mutual Gains from Expanded Trade," with authors who included the banker and former US secretary of commerce, Pete Peterson, and the international aid expert and future head of UNICEF, Jim Grant.

Ruth Hinerfeld, a longtime member of the UNA board, said the EPC was "one of my favorite things I did at UNA. . . . That was a really well-run show during its high point," with "a sterling list of businesspeople." In an interview for this book, she said that what the council was "trying to do, because it was concerned primarily with international economic policy, was to forge a coalition or common stance, even if it was the lowest common denominator on international issues of concern, in the economic sphere."

Although Seifman said the council was "an example of the kind of leadership . . . that has an impact on the national debate," he added that they did not try to quantify EPC's impact. "Its impact was more about how it was embedded in the people in the process," he added.

The EPC papers included *The Productivity Problem: U.S. Labor-Management Relations, US Trade, and Economic Relations with Japan and Mexico* (1983); *Parents and Work: Family Policy in a Comparative Perspective* (1984); *The Productivity Problem: US Labor-Management Relations* (1984); and *Third World Debt: A Reexamination of Long-Term Management* (1988). The council lasted until 1986. Seifman, looking back at the reports after thirty-five years, said, "They have weathered very well."

—*J. W.*

Ample evidence exists to explain why business and labor leaders put such a premium on the style of internationalism embodied in the UN and UNA. In 2014, John C. Whitehead, a former chair of Goldman Sachs and chair of the UNA Board of Directors, said in an interview for this book, "It was in the interest of companies—as it was in the interest of individuals—that the UN be a stronger organization; a company should express their interest and CEOs should express their interest in cooperating with the UN in every possible way." Whitehead himself was a profound example of this interest—a business leader of a large, well-respected investment firm who also dedicated years of his life to civil society, including the UNA (see Chapter 11). Like other US business executives in the immediate post–World War II era who championed the UN, Whitehead had fought in the war, having commanded a landing craft at Omaha Beach in the D-Day invasion of Normandy, among other roles.

On the labor side, support for the UN and AAUN can be traced to Franklin and Eleanor Roosevelt's close relationship with unions. In Eleanor Roosevelt's newspaper column, "My Day," she often praised labor leaders, including Reuther and Randolph, and supported unions domestically and internationally. A December 21, 1936, column, for example, defended the rights of the Women's Trade Union League and the rights of migrant workers. A December 19, 1955, column praised Reuther and George Meany, the leader of the American Federation of Labor, on the newly merged AFL-CIO. "I have the greatest respect for both these men and recognize that they have well earned any award that comes to them," she wrote. When Senator John Bricker (of the Bricker amendment fame) attacked the International Labour Organization, saying it aims "to become economic overseer of all humanity," Roosevelt leaped to its defense in a February 21, 1953, column, saying, "The ILO is trying only to equalize standards throughout the world. And this is a laudable effort, which we who have high standards should certainly stand by, since it will lessen the competition against us in the low-standard areas." The ILO was part of the Third Committee agenda when Eleanor Roosevelt was a delegate to the UN.[1]

Reuther was not only the most prominent labor supporter for the AAUN but also one of the most important in the history of the US labor movement. He served on various AAUN committees, including the one overseeing the merger of AAUN and the US Committee for the United Nations (see Chapter 4), and he often spoke at AAUN events. In his address to the fourteenth biennial conference on May 10, 1964, he spoke in favor of the UN's Decade of Development and of the arms control negotiations between the United States and Soviet Union. Obviously, his main focus was on economic issues and workers' rights in the United States and abroad. Noting that there was full employment during the war, which was not the case in 1964, Reuther said,

> We need to harness this unused economic potential represented by millions of unemployed workers in idle factories and lack of economic growth, and we need to relate the economic abundance that that economic potential will make possible to two basic areas. First we have to improve the quality of American society itself and secondly we need to raise our sights on what contribution we need to make.

Taking the same approach as Henry Ford's view that "a rich world means good business," Reuther explained the vision in labor's terminology. He added, "This is both an economic and a moral obligation to the emerging peoples of the world who live in poverty and ignorance and disease because their problems are our problems."[2]

Thomas J. Watson Jr. was a major figure in business and politics for decades, developing the technology that led to mainframe computers as standard equipment. The son of the founder of IBM, Watson Jr. was the second president of IBM (1952–1971) and US ambassador to the Soviet Union (1979–1981), among other achievements. Throughout the 1950s and 1960s, he served on various AAUN/UNA boards, including the Board of Governors. Watson provided insight in a December 2, 1959, speech that combined a business perspective with internationalism. Without mentioning the UN, he called for greater US engagement with the rest of the world. "We've had our way for so long that perhaps we conclude we can continue to win on international issues without real knowledge and effort," he said. "It's imperative that we understand our need for friends and allies abroad. We simply can't exist without them." Domestically, he said, this meant "we must elect government leaders who understand that partisan politics at home must be balanced by effective international leadership."[3]

Watson continued to say that in the "great ideological contest of our times"—that is, democracy versus Communism—"uncommitted nations will play a strategic part; indeed, as they grow in power and strength, their weight may be great enough to shift again the entire world balance of power." For the West to win this contest, he explained, it was "imperative that all Americans know more about these nations and that we in the United States exert the kind of bold and imaginative leadership essential to win the large majority of these nations towards western orientation." Central to this strategy was robust foreign aid. Watson cited the obvious example of the Marshall Plan as a precedent: "Foreign aid is aimed at building up the economies of our allies and friends throughout the world. Developing nations need capital just as we needed foreign capital here at home to aid in developing our own economy years ago."[4]

While Watson lauded the Marshall Plan, another business leader administered it. In the 1940s and early 1950s, Paul G. Hoffman was the president of the Studebaker Corporation; as noted in Chapter 4, he was also president of the Pasadena chapter of the AAUN when he criticized the Bricker amendment, saying it would "impair if not destroy the independence of the Executive Branch" in concluding international agreements. This was a small part of his internationalism.

In a biography, *Paul G. Hoffman: Architect of Foreign Aid,* Alan R. Raucher identified Hoffman as a "business progressive," which Raucher defined as business leaders "seeking to prevent the harmful consequences of the business cycle, including heightened class conflict. They wanted economic growth with rational order and stability."[5] Hoffman was an opponent of the New Deal and the National Recovery Administration, in particular (in 1936, he called FDR "the absolute dictator"), even as he called prolonged unemployment a threat to democracy.[6] "Thus the survival of democracy depended on the reduction of poverty and unemployment," Raucher noted. Continuing into World War II and the postwar period, Hoffman argued for workers' rights and a strong free market system to ensure that democracy thrived. A firm believer in the role that international trade should play in driving the US economy, Hoffman accepted President Truman's invitation in 1947 to serve on the Special Committee on Foreign Aid, which was charged with implementing the Marshall Plan. Hoffman "promoted the foreign aid program as an economic weapon in the ideological Cold War and a cheap way to prevent a hot war."[7] The next year, Truman appointed Hoffman as the Marshall Plan administrator. Given that Hoffman was a Republican popular with the party leadership but was appointed by a Democratic president meant a smooth confirmation hearing for Hoffman.

Raucher wrote, "Although the Marshall Plan started with a broad base of support, no one had drawn up a blueprint for putting the concept into operation. That task fell to Hoffman."[8] Hoffman hired a staff heavy with business leaders and veterans of the Special Committee on Foreign Aid. He was based in Washington, with an office of the special representative in Paris to facilitate Marshall Plan programs as joint endeavors of the United States and the recipients. (This office was the forerunner of the Organization for Economic Co-operation and Development, or OECD.)

Hoffman resigned in September 1950 and took over the presidency of the Ford Foundation from Henry Ford II. In 1956, President Eisenhower appointed Hoffman a delegate to the UN General Assembly with a brief focusing on aid issues. As part of a campaign to create a UN International Development Association, Hoffman traveled to Europe, where he attended a meeting of the World Federation of UNA (WFUNA) in Brussels and met with delegates of the Soviet UN Association in Moscow.[9] In December 1957, the UN created the UN Special Fund, an agency that would "concentrate on helping poor and underdeveloped countries survey their resources and build their infrastructures." Hammarskjöld, the UN Secretary-General, promised Eisenhower that the managing director would be a US citizen; Eisenhower selected Hoffman, who assumed the post in January 1959. Enjoying the backing of Eisenhower and Hammarskjöld, Hoffman's main challenge was defending the fund before Congress. Although the United States provided 40 percent of the fund's finances, conservatives attacked the program as a "multibillion dollar giveaway carnival," said Representative H. R. Gross (R-Iowa).[10] The General Assembly reappointed Hoffman to the post in 1962.

In his 1961 General Assembly address, President Kennedy urged the UN to declare the 1960s the Decade of Development, putting aid higher on the international agenda. The UN Special Fund's mandate was to provide money for feasibility studies for projects to be implemented by much larger and more established UN agencies, such as the World Health Organization and UNESCO. Hoffman saw aid for economic development as "a new practical humanism on a world scale" designed to "meet human needs, to give each individual among the hundreds of millions of the poor a chance to build a life that is really worth living."[11] After the Decade of Development was declared, there was a push to consolidate the fund with the UN Technical Assistance Board. The United States wanted the merger "in order to make the Decade of Development more effective," and Secretary-General U Thant wanted greater centralization in the UN's administration. In January 1966, Hoffman became the first administrator of the UN Development Programme, a post he held until 1972.[12] (See Box 15.2.)

Robert S. Benjamin, a lawyer and Hollywood studio executive, was another successful entrepreneur who dedicated much of his time to UNA and UN-related activities. Benjamin was chair of the US Committee for the United Nations under Presidents Kennedy and Johnson from 1961 to 1964, marking the only time a chair served more than one year. In that role, he helped engineer the merger of the US Committee and the AAUN to form the UNA-USA in 1964 (see Chapter 4).

Benjamin's greatest business achievement was as cochair of United Artists from 1951 to 1978. He was a partner in the movie litigation law firm of Phillips, Nizer, Benjamin, Krim & Ballon from 1938 to 1978. His role in United Artists began when he and a partner at the law firm, Arthur Krim, struck a management deal with movie stars and United Artists' co-owners at the time, Charles Chaplin and Mary Pickford, in which Benjamin and Krim would run the struggling studio. Their proposal was that "if they could turn the troubled organization around in five years, they would earn an option to buy it. The aging stars agreed, and so began the busiest and richest period in the company's history."[13] In 1955, Benjamin and Krim bought out Chaplin and Pickford and became cochairs of the studio. Under Benjamin and Krim, United Artists produced classic films such as John Huston's *African Queen,* Billy Wilder's *Some Like It Hot,* Woody Allen's *Annie Hall,* and Martin Scorsese's *Raging Bull,* in addition to *Midnight Cowboy, One Flew Over the Cuckoo's Nest,* and *Rocky.* United Artists merged with the Transamerica Corporation insurance entity in 1967. It was a friendly

---

Box 15.2 Sutton Place

UNA and Paul Hoffman had a role in securing the Sutton Place townhouse that serves as the official residence of the UN Secretary-General. The townhouse, at 3 Sutton Place, is only a few blocks north of the UN. J. P. Morgan built the house for his daughter Ann in 1921. After she died in 1952, it was bought by Arthur A. Houghton Jr., the president of Steuben Glass. In the early 1970s, Houghton offered the mansion as a residence for the US ambassador to the UN, but Washington preferred to keep its residence at the Waldorf-Astoria. At this point Hoffman, who had just retired as the head of UNDP, suggested that the house could become the permanent residence of the Secretary-General (up until then, each Secretary-General had lived at different locations).

Hoffman, who was a friend and neighbor of Houghton's, also had the idea that Houghton should present the mansion as a gift to UNA, so the owner could receive a tax deduction.* UNA then sold the house to the United Nations, with the money going to UN-related programs. The townhouse, which has been the Secretary-General's permanent residence since 1972, is now valued at $48 to $52 million.

---

* Kathleen Teltsch, "Town House Offered to UN," *New York Times,* July 15, 1972.

takeover, and Benjamin and Krim as cochairs continued to produce profitable films. However, in January 1978, Benjamin, Krim, and other top executives resigned from the company.

Throughout those years, Benjamin was also a strong supporter of the UN and the AAUN/UNA, as well as other philanthropic institutions, often focusing on religious tolerance. In a speech to the American Jewish Committee on November 6, 1963, upon receiving an award for his work on human dignity and equality, Benjamin said, "The great religions could reach into the churches, synagogues, mosques, and temples of every town and village on earth to raise a spiritual umbrella for the protection of men and women everywhere from the storms of bigotry and hate, handmaidens of world suicide."[14] He saw the UN as an organization dedicated to bettering the people of the world, where domestic politics might be set aside. "The United Nations organization was one such institution with its avowed goal of a brotherhood of nations," he said in a 1975 speech. "We know that the UN will reach this goal only if it follows the principles of its Charter—which are the same principles established by far more ancient institutions, I refer of course to the world's great religions."[15]

After the creation of UNA-USA in 1964, Benjamin served as the interim president of both the US Committee and AAUN until a new president, Porter McKeever, was named. Afterward, Benjamin continued to serve in various capacities, including as chair of the Board of Governors. In 1975, he was a senior adviser to the US delegation to the UN; and in 1977, he was appointed chairman of the board of directors of New York City's UN Development Corporation, established to manage the construction of UN-related buildings.

Benjamin died in 1979. In 1980, UNA published a biography and a collection of his speeches in *Robert S. Benjamin, A Citizen's Citizen*. The same year, the UN issued commemorative stationery "In Memory of Robert S. Benjamin, Founding Chairman of the United Nations Association of the United States of America."

James S. McDonnell, the aviation pioneer, earned a master's degree in aeronautical engineering from Massachusetts Institute of Technology in 1925. After the Great Depression ruined his first attempt to start an aircraft company in 1929, he worked for other aircraft manufacturers. He went solo again and launched McDonnell Aircraft Corporation in 1939. The company provided missiles, fighter planes, and airplane parts to the US government during World War II and the Korean War. The company remained a major producer of military aircraft and missiles for the United States. McDonnell Aircraft and Douglas Aircraft Company merged to form McDonnell Douglas in 1967. The company produced commercial aircraft (the DC-8, 9, and 10), military aircraft (the Phantom and Skyhawk jet fighters and the Apache helicopter), and spacecraft (the Gemini capsule, Skylab). At the UNA's 1965 biennial, Benjamin introduced McDonnell as "the manufacturing father of Mercury and Gemini." In 1997, McDonnell Douglas merged with Boeing, with the Boeing name alone representing the company.

In 1950, McDonnell established the McDonnell Foundation to fund his goals of "supporting scientific, educational and charitable causes," as the foundation's website says. McDonnell died in 1980; in 1984, the charity was renamed the James S. McDonnell Foundation.

Widely known as Mr. Mac, McDonnell served in many positions in AAUN and UNA, including chair of the board of directors. He was also one of the association's most generous benefactors. In December 1976, McDonnell created an endowment fund totaling $1 million. In 1978, the fund was renamed the James S. McDonnell Permanent Reserve Fund. The fund fluctuated over the decades as UNA borrowed against it and as more money was added. In 2010, that money, once again totaling $1 million, was used to smooth the way for the alliance between UNA and the UN Foundation (see Chapter 18).

Involvement of well-known business leaders in the AAUN and later in the UNA often resulted in "fascinating connections," as Ed Luck, a former president of UNA, said in an interview for this book. Luck recalled a 1985 UNA mission to the Soviet Union as part of the Parallel Studies Program in which McDonnell participated. Luck and McDonnell flew on an Aeroflot plane, which was a copy of a McDonnell design. Bad weather was preventing the plane from landing in Moscow, and McDonnell was "very worried as we got near Moscow because the flight was going on for a long time, and he had the [flight] plans. He kept looking at the plans, with his wife sitting next to him, and you could see he was unhappy. By his calculations, we were going on fumes," Luck said. The plane finally landed safely. It was McDonnell's "first and only time" in the Soviet Union, Luck said. "You couldn't buy this kind of experience."

In a 1965 article, "Only the United Nations Can," McDonnell wrote, "The destiny of our planet, the development of its human and material resources, the spread of scientific knowledge, the population-explosion and the evolving world community—these are the subjects which should make up the continuing dialogue between heads of governments." He concluded, "If the United Nations is to fulfill the hopes of all men, the parochial concerns of the moment must be subdued in favor of the long-term universal concerns that ultimately will determine Humanity's future."

The irony that one man could be an avid supporter of the UN and a leading arms manufacturer was not lost on McDonnell. As his son, James F. McDonnell, noted in a 1999 speech, "In the area of global and complex systems he had two complementary, but seemingly contradictory, interests. He was a great supporter of both NATO, a military alliance, and the United Nations, a global institution to preserve peace."[16] Quoting a 1967 speech by his father, James McDonnell said, "As I have said many times, the waging of peace must be achieved from a foundation of great strength. Our mission at McDonnell Aircraft is to contribute to the building and maintaining of that strength." NATO represented the foundation of strength, and the United Nations represented, the younger McDonnell said, again quoting his father, "Man's most noble effort to achieve international peace."[17]

McDonnell Douglas was apparently the only organization in the world where all employees were given paid holidays on NATO Day (April 4) and UN Day (October 24).[18]

UN We Believe

Not many people's résumés can include both negotiating with Dag Hammarskjöld and using an airplane flight to lobby diplomats, but those acts helped define Charles Dent, a founder of UN We Believe, the first civil society initiative designed to organize business support for the UN. Dent and Richard Munger, both veterans of the Korean War, were piloting a commercial flight in 1956 and started talking about world affairs. Munger, in an interview for this book, recalled that the two were talking about the Hungarian revolution (in 1956) and the nuclear arms race and thought, "Here we go again. We just cannot afford to have another world war." The pair continued discussing this line of thought, about a possible war in Hungary and worse, with Roger P. Enloe (Dent's brother-in-law and a Presbyterian minister) and Al Teichmeier, a business executive from North Carolina. Then in 1957, Dent, as a pilot for United Airlines, averted a disaster by successfully landing a malfunctioning plane, for which he received a $5,500 bonus. He used his bonus as seed money for UN We Believe. The group had two purposes: "To persuade industry, business and organizations in the United States to make it their policy to support publicly the principles and purposes of the United Nations and to provide specific ways in which this support can be expressed."[19]

UN We Believe was launched on October 6, 1959, with Dent, Munger, Enloe, and Teichmeier as its founders. Enloe was named its first director. Munger, the last surviving member of the quartet behind UN We Believe, described Dent as "the idea man. A good pilot and self-educated . . . happy and wanting to do something." It turned out that UN We Believe would be Dent's first "something."

Munger described himself as a "one day veteran of World War II"—deployed the day Japan surrendered; he went on to serve in the Korean War, where he was "not anywhere getting shot at." He started working for United Airlines in 1952 and met Dent a few years later. Enloe was a Presbyterian minister with a degree from the Princeton Theological Seminary. He was a Marine Corps chaplain in the Pacific theater during World War II, and in the 1950s, he worked with Protestant churches in Spain. He returned to the United States in 1965 to study at Columbia University, where he got involved with Dent and Munger's project. Teichmeier was an executive of a plywood manufacturing company in North Carolina. Munger described Teichmeier as much more conservative than the other three—an executive who "brought some business stability to our organization" in the early years, when it needed to get established and raise funds.

"We decided we were going to call this thing UN We Believe. It was not an easy thing to sell because people say these guys sound like religious zealots," Munger said. "But basically, when we had a chance to explain, we said, 'Hey we're identifying the UN and we're expressing support and belief in the principles of the preamble of the charter.' . . . The key was to use the same tactics used in World War II in the corporate world to support the war effort, through public advertising and support of corporations." Munger added, "It's not that we believed in everything the UN did. . . . But we believed in the principles embodied in the preamble to the UN Charter to save succeeding generations from the scourge of war, and it was the scourge of war brought to our attention again by the Hungarian revolution and the Soviet troops going into Hungary."

Dent wrote regularly to Hammarskjöld, requesting a meeting with the Secretary-General to discuss his idea. After multiple requests, Hammarskjöld met with Dent, endorsed the idea, and gave permission for Dent to include the UN symbol in the UN We Believe logo. This was the only time the symbol (as opposed to some modification) was allowed to be used by a non-UN entity. The Business Council for the UN (BCUN), the successor organization that became a project of the UN Foundation, incorporates the logo in the original UN We Believe symbol.

Initially, UN We Believe was a program of the US Committee for the United Nations, which provided office space to the organization. At an AAUN conference in 1958, Stanley Rumbough Jr., president of the US Committee, described UN We Believe as part of its agenda.[20] When the US Committee and AAUN merged to form the UNA-USA in 1964, UN We Believe became an independent group. In the beginning, it focused on sponsoring luncheon conferences—small gatherings where UN ambassadors and business executives mingled. It was at such a luncheon that UN We Believe made a cameo appearance during a national tragedy. Eisenhower was a guest of honor at a UN We Believe luncheon on November 23, 1963. Enloe interrupted the meeting to announce that President John F. Kennedy had been assassinated. A photo taken at that moment caught the former president's numb expression on hearing the news.

In 1967, UN We Believe started its annual UN Ambassadors Dinners at the Waldorf-Astoria. A blend of networking, entertainment, and fund-raising, the dinners drew leading political and business leaders with ensuing media attention. The dinners continued when the organization became the BCUN but ended in 2000 when BCUN and UNA merged. Former Presidents Eisenhower, Truman, Reagan (who could not attend), and George H. W. Bush, as well as former British prime minister Margaret Thatcher, Mikhail Gorbachev, and Nelson Mandela were among the honorees.

Dent mixed aviation and diplomacy again in 1971. It was an era of airplane hijacking, and the UN had negotiated three draft treaties to help address the threat. Dent led a team that included other pilots in a campaign dubbed T+ (the "T" representing Tokyo, where the first treaty was negotiated, and the "+" standing for all three treaties). The campaign aimed at promoting the ratification of the treaties. Dent chartered a passenger plane on November 6, 1971, to fly 153 members of the UN General Assembly and their guests (including US Ambassador George H. W. Bush) to Montreal, the home of the International Civil Aviation Organization, where the final negotiations and signing of the treaties were to take place. Guests on that flight included thirty crewmembers who had been hijacked and who "vividly depicted their horror stories and spoke forcefully of the need for these treaties to provide no sanctuary," wrote Dent's nephew, Peter C. Dent. "The flight and tales of hijacked crews left deep impressions on the participants and UN delegates. They vowed to obtain swift ratification from their home countries."[21] The protocols were signed, and the treaty, the Convention for the Suppression of Unlawful Acts against the Safety of Civil Aviation, entered into force in January 1973.

During this period, UNA had limited outreach to the business community, though the association had strong business supporters such as McDonnell and Benjamin. In the 1970s, the association sponsored annual events at the UN called The World Is Our Business, a series of workshops and lectures on common interests between US businesses and the UN. The 1976 program listed McDonnell as the chair of UNA and Benjamin as the chair of the UNA Board of Governors. Supporters listed in the 1978 program included David Rockefeller of Chase Manhattan Bank and Lee Iacocca of Ford, as well as such companies as McDonnell Douglas, Goldman Sachs, IBM, American Express, General Foods, and Time Inc. In August 1974, a special issue of *The InterDependent* magazine, UNA's publication for members and general readers, commemorated the thirtieth anniversary of the UN, listing McDonnell as the national chair of the UN30 committee and including ads from the likes of National Steel Corporation, Swissair, United Technologies, Atlantic Richfield, Gulf Oil, Salomon Brothers, Beechcraft, General Dynamics, Teamsters, Rockwell International, Northrop, Continental Airlines, and, naturally, McDonnell Douglas.

The Business Council for the United Nations

In 1984, the trustees of UN We Believe changed the group's name to the Business Council for the United Nations. Munger said the change reflected the board's thinking that new corporations needed to be added and that a name change "would do the job." He added that although the founders and other board members "retained emotional connections to the UN We Believe concept of support for the UN and the dedication to its principles, [in order] to have more corporate contributions and participation, . . . Business Council for the UN would do the job." He added, however, "We did keep our logo, and I'm happy to see it's still on the letterhead."

Leadership also changed. Enloe retired as president and was succeeded by Samuel Brookfield in 1984. In 1986, Richard A. Voell, a trustee and president of the Rockefeller Group, was named chair. In an interview for this book, Brookfield said the name change meant "it would be easier to go to a corporate person and say, 'Would you become a member of the Business Council for the United Nations?' than it was to say, 'Would you become a member of UN We Believe?'"

Brookfield, who was BCUN president from 1984 to 2001, was an academic, mostly in the administration of boarding schools. "At one point, one of the families I was associated with asked if I ever thought about working for the UN in the business community," Brookfield said. "It wasn't very hard to sell."

At the time, forty businesses were affiliated with BCUN (a number that stayed steady over the years, though members changed), but it had a budget deficit of approximately $90,000. Voell, who used his connections to the banking world "and supported us generously because of the Rockefeller connection," told Brookfield that his primary instruction was to not allow deficits. "He said to me, Sam your first commandment is 'Thou shall not have a deficit.'" Brookfield said the council never ran a deficit again.

BCUN kept its original structure and program after the name change. The New York City luncheon conferences and the UN Ambassadors Dinner continued, with the dinner continuing to be the council's highest-profile event of the year. Brookfield said the strategy, started by Enloe, was to use personal connections to get a business executive to become the dinner chair. The chair would donate something in the range of $50,000 and encourage other leaders to donate the minimum $5,000. The next year, the old chair would help recruit the new chair, and the cycle continued. What the donors got for that money was personal time with world leaders, business executives, UN officials, and ambassadors.

Brookfield came into the job with "very little knowledge of the enormous criticism" the UN faced from the US public. As he recalled, "I really was unaware of that. I was pretty well educated but I was still unaware. . . . I suddenly realized that the political support for the UN in this country was very thin." Therefore, his strategy became one of "approaching the leaders of the business community and convincing them that the UN was important." He added, "The idea that the UN could help serve business in some way was new to a lot of the businesspeople we were talking to." Improving understanding turned out to be a two-way street. He added, "At the same time, we were trying to educate the UN community that the private sector was a valuable asset to them."

An initiative created under Brookfield's tenure was the National Conference Program. The founding trustees felt the luncheon program was working well, so "why not take it out of the city?" Brookfield devised itineraries by which a UN ambassador would spend a week visiting four or five US cities for events with local business leaders. It was a shoestring operation, with only the ambassador and spouse and Brookfield traveling. "In each city, we would have a dinner arranged by our hosts—the movers and shakers of around ten or fifteen people around the dinner table in a private home or private room of a restaurant," Brookfield said. "The next morning, we would have a private breakfast, press conference, luncheon, and mad dash to the airport to get on a plane to fly to the next city and repeat that over five times."

Although the public and donor perceptions of UNA and BCUN saw the two organizations as similar, Brookfield said "the real difference" between the two was that BCUN avoided the "we're saving the world kind of image," which he ascribed to UNA-USA; it instead focused on advancing business. According to Brookfield,

> I tried to say we are here to do business. This is a business operation. It's going to be run as a business. We are going to get people together for business not just because we love the UN. I purposely tried to avoid people who had sort of stars in their eyes and thought the UN was the greatest thing since sliced bread.

William Paul Underwood started as the vice president for programs in 1995 and became executive director in 2000, after the BCUN merger with UNA. He served in that position until 2005. As vice president, Underwood handled all BCUN programs, including the luncheons and Ambassadors Dinners. In an interview for this book, Underwood said that, before coming to BCUN, he had worked as the head of advertising at the Council on Foreign Relations and then on a startup magazine focusing on emerging markets.

In the late 1990s, BCUN added a World Congress program modeled on the Davos World Economic Forum. Underwood said the idea was to "get a group of really senior businesspeople [and] invite your diplomatic friends and the Secretariat people." After an evening lecture, "We break everybody up into groups of ten, and we would send them to an ambassador's residence for a dinner." He added, "That's our World Congress. It was a rather expansive name for a program that might have continued to grow." At that point, Underwood said, BCUN membership consisted mostly of "large American corporations with a multinational presence or primarily US corporations with a foreign-born CEO. They got it. Or foreign corporations who realized it wasn't such a bad thing to be on paper with the UN. There were a few who did it just for the dinner. They were trying to do business with the ambassador of the country they represented."

When the UN launched the Financing for Development initiative in the early 2000s, BCUN created a role for itself, Underwood said. He met with the UN Secretariat staff working on the project that would lead to the UN International Conference on Financing for Development in Monterrey, Mexico, in 2002, and said, "Let me try to facilitate a process where you engage with Wall Street. . . . We did, and the BCUN chaired the private-sector working group on infrastructure finance. We pulled together a series of working meetings in UN conference rooms that brought together both sides of the equation." From the government sector, that meant ministers of finance and industry and heads of the investment promotion authorities. From the private sector, he said,

> We brought in the heads of the international projects of infrastructure and finance for the major banks, investment and insurance companies, rating agencies. The question to everybody was, "What are the impediments to financing infrastructure?" The immediate response from everybody was, it wasn't a lack of money; it was risk. So we embarked on this process of working to extract some of the ideas presented at those meeting and work with the people who came up with them into a series of white papers that shared the risk between private and public sectors.

By the end of the 1990s, Enloe had retired, and Dent had died in 1994. Munger said, "A lot of our trustees had served long years, and we didn't see another generation coming along, so we were engaged in talks with the UNA" about a merger of the two organizations. Brookfield had reservations about doing so with UNA: "We are totally different organizations. We are structured, managed, and perceived differently. We are not bleeding hearts for the UN. We are hard-nosed, practical businesspeople working on behalf of the UN because it is a good institution that deserves our support. It is a whole different attitude at UNA." But Voell was getting ready to retire from the BCUN board, and John Whitehead was retiring from the UNA board, so "they both decided that it was time to put the two organizations together," Brookfield said.

Voell persuaded Brookfield that the merger would be beneficial. Voell also suggested that with the merger, Brookfield would be in line to be the next president of UNA. As Brookfield recalled, "Dick came to me and said, this is a real opportunity for the BCUN. You are going to go in for a year and work. Then become president of UNA. To my own ego, that was attractive." However, after Alvin Adams left the presidency in 1999, William Luers was selected as UNA president instead. Brookfield left BCUN the next year, and Underwood became the council's executive director.

Although *merger* was the commonly used word, Brookfield insisted that it was legally incorrect: "There was never a vote, as I remember. It just happened. BCUN was dissolved technically and became a program of UNA." The BCUN Board of Trustees' report is titled *Plan of Disso-*

lution. Dated July 29, 1998, the document said the condition was that the UNA would create "a new division to carry on activities now conducted by [BCUN] to be called . . . BCUN Division." The board voted to "dissolve the absolute charter" of BCUN on February 3, 1999.[22] "We had put in a reserve fund of a million and a half dollars, which was technically property of the UNA. We brought our staff and programs and money," Brookfield said. He added, "There was also a push from the Secretary-General [Kofi Annan], who saw it as unnecessary competition in the NGO marketplace for organizations competing to raise money for the benefit of the UN. The question was: 'Why aren't you guys working together?'" Since Voell and Whitehead were retiring, "The idea was that it made sense to bring these two organizations together. It was going to be easier to find one chairman than two," Underwood said.

Under UNA, the lunches continued, Underwood explained, but "the ambassadors' travel program was cut immediately. It's not a program that UNA was keen to spend money on. They didn't consider it a program. They considered a program to be something more substantive." The Ambassadors Dinner was folded into UNA's own annual gala.

Allison MacEachron came to BCUN after more than twenty years in advertising. She also had an interest in international relations and was a member of the Foreign Policy Association. So, when she arrived, as she said in an interview for the book,

> I was leveraging my background in client relationship management. . . . The product is different; the product is related to international relations. As you know, what we do is we bring the business community together with the UN community—whether the missions or the permanent representatives or the UN agencies. It's my job to build awareness of the organization and the mission and to get new companies to join the fold and get engaged with the UN and UN members.

She started in 2008 as a staff member and served as the executive director from 2009 until her death in March 2015.

There was a gap between the time Underwood left in 2005 and MacEachron was hired in 2008. During that time, MacEachron said, "BCUN closed its doors, in effect. Paul Underwood left. I think the whole staff left. I don't know exactly why. And then they really didn't start up again. Not officially closed . . . but in effect closed." Brookfield objected to that characterization, saying BCUN continued to function. Bill Luers, the UNA president at the time, called the council "quite inactive," except for the annual dinner. Underwood said the two BCUN staffers left shortly after he did, but he did not know why they were not replaced. He surmised, "Probably the UNA, knowing they had financial stresses, was happy not to spend money on the business council rather than use it as the cash cow for the dinner fund-raising."

Although the mission of BCUN has remained constant, the businesses interested in building relationships with the UN have changed. Globalization, the 2002 International Conference on Financing for Development, and the Millennium Development Goals (MDGs) were responsible for much of the shift in the kinds of businesses wanting to work with the UN, MacEachron said. "Fifteen years ago, when the MDGs came out, companies were looking for what role they might play in the MDGs," she said. "Pharmaceutical and agricultural issues were key to the goals, and furthering the MDGs and pharm and food and agricultural issues . . . were very much a part of the MDGs." Even with the shift, however, the membership of BCUN stayed steady at around twenty businesses, she said.

The UN's Global Compact, an internal effort to engage corporations and encourage them to follow good practices, also affected BCUN's work. "I would say we kind of complement each other," MacEachron said. "First of all, they are the UN, and we're not. [The compact] encourages responsible corporate business practices, from pollution to trafficking. . . . That's not what we do." Most Global Compact members are "from abroad," whereas most BCUN members are based in the United States, she said.

With the merger of UNA and the UN Foundation, BCUN once again became its own program, with both UNA and BCUN becoming programs of the UN Foundation with their own executive directors. As to why the BCUN was carried over into UNF, MacEachron said, "I think UNF found lots of reasons," including that "it found value in the UNA because it has grassroots citizen support, business support, and engagement with the UN." After MacEachron's death in 2015, UNA hired an interim coordinator and has convened sessions with the international financial sector promoting the UN's new Global Goals for Sustainable Development.

Notes

1. Eleanor Roosevelt, "My Day," various entries.
2. The Clark M. Eichelberger Papers, Manuscripts and Archives Division, New York Public Library. Astor, Lenox, and Tilden Foundations (NYPL Archives), box 118.
3. Thomas J. Watson, "Achieving a Peaceful and Prosperous World: It Will

Take Sacrifices, Courage, and Hard Work" (speech), 64th Congress of American Industry, sponsored by the National Association of Manufacturers, New York, December 2, 1959, as reproduced in *Vital Speeches of the Day.*

4. Ibid.

5. Alan R. Raucher, *Paul G. Hoffman: Architect of Foreign Aid* (Lexington: The University Press of Kentucky, 1984), 42.

6. Ibid., 45, 48.

7. Ibid., 60.

8. Ibid., 65.

9. Ibid., 128.

10. Ibid., 135.

11. Ibid., 137.

12. Ibid., 143.

13. Dave Kehr, "Four Stars' Bright Idea Still Shines 90 Years On," *New York Times,* March 27, 2008.

14. UNA-USA, *Robert S. Benjamin: A Citizen's Citizen* (New York: United Nations Association of the United States of America, 1980), 80–81.

15. Ibid., 114.

16. John F. McDonnell, "Tribute to James S. McDonnell" (tribute), National Academy of Sciences, Washington, DC, April 8, 1999, https://www.jsmf.org /about/tribute.pdf.

17. Ibid.

18. Ibid.

19. "World Federalist Report," 1964.

20. NYPL Archives, box 115.

21. Peter C. Dent, "Allentown Pilot Charles C. Dent Helped Fight Growing Hijack Threat," *The Morning Call,* November 6, 2001, http://articles.mcall.com /2001-11-06/news/3383465_1_air-piracy-hijackings-treaties.

22. Seton Hall University, The Msgr. William Noé Field Archives and Special Collections Center, South Orange, NJ, box 886.

16

Reaching Out:
UNA-USA and Education

Doug Garr, with Tino Calabia

From its earliest days, UNA-USA dedicated a major part of its mission to educating the public—especially in schools—on the critical role that the United States played in forming and perpetuating the United Nations. Clark Eichelberger knew that studying "the problem of world organization for peace" was most likely a never-ending quest. In general and early on through public relations efforts—mainly through media and lectures—the organization created a message and ensured that it was spread as far as possible, nationally and globally. Eichelberger was canny in this respect. He knew that Eleanor Roosevelt made news and that professionals like Edward Bernays (who built a reputation as the "father of public relations") could help keep UNA-USA ingrained in the thinking public. Eichelberger enlisted both of them to contribute to the organization's monthly publications. More formally, UNA-USA has relied on programs such as Model UN, Global Classrooms, public lectures, seminars, and workshops, as well as various publications aimed at young professionals and people established in the work of the UN.

AAUN faced the challenge of promoting new political institutions and history in school curricula that had been largely focused on national, state, and local narratives. Its goal was to ensure that schools would teach the younger generation how to understand the changing world and the emerging institutions for managing those shifts. The challenge was especially difficult because of deep suspicions of so-called "One Worlders" and the prominent narrative of Cold War struggle. AAUN and later UNA efforts to include the UN in schools encountered fierce opposition in a number of places. Even as recently as 2010, while approving the history curriculum standards for that year's round of new books, conservatives on the Texas State Board of Education required that students evaluate whether the UN undermines US sovereignty.

According to the informal history of AAUN, written by its manager, Estelle Linzer, and covering the twenty-year period up to its merger when it became UNA-USA, the "AAUN was strong in its basic belief . . . that the youth of our nation could be the training ground for future leadership in the association."[1] The Collegiate Council for UN and the annual National High School Essay Contest on the UN were two major projects that arose from this belief. The Collegiate Council was a formative experience for many, including Stephen Schwebel, who later became a State Department official with UN responsibilities and then a judge on the International Court of Justice.

The postwar advocates of the UN were painfully aware of the failure of the League of Nations, and Eichelberger understood that education was crucial to public support of the fledgling international coalition in order to achieve anything resembling a lasting world peace. In the October 1946 issue of AAUN's magazine *Changing World,* the first annual Intercollegiate Institute on the United Nations was announced, and student delegates to the institute established the Collegiate Council for the United Nations.[2]

The AAUN education director, Dorothy Robins-Mowry, said in an interview for this book, "Those early days were very exciting. We were part of building a new thing. Even after the Cold War broke out, the optimism continued. There was a kind of euphoria [based on] what the United Nations was going to be doing in helping to build a new world." Struggling to explain how conditions and public attitudes changed years later, Robins-Mowry speculated, "The initial euphoria was because it was all new. Things became routine. You can't be on a high forever."

Engaging the College Campuses

Two months after the Collegiate Council began in 1946, in an "Open Letter to College Students," Ryland Duke Miller, a Northwestern University student and chair of the council, wrote a heartfelt call to action to his peers. His letter started,

> If you are twenty now, in ten years you will be thirty. At the outset this statement sounds rather silly, but let's examine it. In ten years we collegians will have reached the age when serious thought and decisive action will be expected of us. In ten years we may be entrusted with grave responsibilities, perhaps with the destiny of the world. We have ten years to prepare for a grave undertaking which will have the collegians of ten years past at the helm. Will we be ready? . . . If we are to be ready for that job facing us in ten years, we must make every minute count. What are you doing to back the United Nations on your campus now?

It took only a moment of epiphany for Alys Brady, a senior at Antioch College, to change majors. She spent an internship in the AAUN education department in 1948. "When at the age of 17, I first arrived at Antioch College, I wanted to be a fashion designer," she wrote in *Changing World* in May that year. "Under the work-study plan of putting classroom-learned theory to . . . practical application, I tested that desire. A negative answer emerged. Would it matter very much what one was wearing on a day when an atom bomb fell? So I became an international relations major."[3]

Perhaps the longest-running effort in UNA-USA's history to increase awareness of the UN goes back to the annual student essay competitions, certainly as far back as when the group was called the AAUN. The League of Nations Association held contests as early as 1926. Although winners were noted, often with pictures, there was no news about the contents of winning entries.

In 1945, more than 1,400 public high schools had already enrolled in the contest. That year, the AAUN high school essay contest was expanded to include private and parochial schools. By 1947, some 1,730 schools competed in the UN student essay contest. Also in that year, the first college course undertaken through AAUN sponsorship was inaugurated at the State Teachers College in Oneonta, New York, and a teacher training contest was held.

The contests proved to be popular; by 1961, the high school essay challenge was sent to 40,000 students, of which 3,000 sent in entries. By 2004, Richard Rush, a former high school history and geography teacher in Colorado, had felt that the annual essay contests for high school and college (and artwork contest for students in middle school) were not enough. Eager to introduce an even younger audience to the UN, his chapter at UNA-USA developed art contests for children in kindergarten through fifth grade.

The contests were an important national initiative, with thousands of essays being submitted by chapters nationwide for years. The national winners received cash prizes and were invited to UNA-USA Members' Day at the UN, with their names and photos often noted in *Changing World*. But according to a 1989 Ford Foundation evaluation of UNA-USA, a high-school essay contest had been established four years earlier, which indicates there may have been gaps in continuity. One formidable challenge put to students in 1988 was asking them to write a US presidential speech to the UN General Assembly. The winners traveled to Morocco, Egypt, and Jamaica to visit UN development projects and also appeared on NBC's *Today* show.[4]

The program got a boost in 1986 with a $10,000 gift from Peter Daley, President Reagan's ambassador to Ireland. But that boost was short term, as interest in the program waned, surely as high school essay contests gradually fell out of favor. Prizewinners were still featured on Members' Day during the presidency of William Luers in the 2000s, but interest was declining. The national contests ended before UNA's merger with the UN Foundation, although local essay contests still occurred in some chapters.

Model UN: "Infinitely Worthwhile"

In addition to the essay contests, perhaps the two best-known education programs throughout the history of the AAUN and UNA-USA were the Model UN and UNA's trademark version, Global Classrooms. The Model UN's roots date back to the League of Nations. In 1927, Harvard University invited nine colleges to a simulation of the League of Nations—nearly a decade after that body's creation in the wake of World War I. Harvard's program continues to this day.[5] The programs grew rapidly after World War II, and most often, they were established and operated autonomously without formal links to the AAUN or UNA-USA. In 1961, the Eleventh College Model UN of the West was held at the University of Oregon. Nearly a thousand students from eighty-two schools in eleven Western states attended, making it the largest meeting of its kind.[6] Today, 100,000–200,000 high school and college students in the United States participate in Model UN activities each year.[7]

After Dorothy Robins-Mowry ran the UNA Model UN program, it was managed by Jordan Horvath, James P. Muldoon Jr., Fernando Flores, and then Lucia Rodriguez.

The concept of a Model UN is elegant in its simplicity. Participants gather at a scheduled meeting to authentically assume the roles of members of the Security Council, the General Assembly, or another multilateral body. They are expected to have studied the world issues they're about to debate, draft resolutions, and plan strategies to solve the problems that continually arise among governments. Generally, they employ rules of procedure adapted from the actual rules of the UN. In replicating the work of ambassadors and delegates in UN bodies, they should, by the end of a session, acquire a basic working knowledge of international diplomacy, public speaking, research, negotiation, and decisionmaking. The specific topics addressed in Model UN conferences have changed over the years, but the underlying themes of conflict, peace, and international cooperation remain, despite changes in the names of nations and the rise of new conflicts and the end of others. As the UNA-USA website says, "Model UN delegates learn how the international community acts on its concerns about peace and security, human rights, the environment, food and hunger, economic development, and globalization."[8]

AAUN chapters' youth outreach began in 1945, with chapters working to enlist high schools in the association's first student essay contest. The first intercollegiate institute on the UN, in 1946, formed a collegiate council for the United Nations, with ensuing Model UN conferences. Early on, chapter leaders began to reach out to social studies teachers in high schools, offering grade-appropriate UN publications on economic, social, and political issues; furnishing materials for students boning up to represent their assigned country in a Model United Nations conference; often underwriting (which they still do) participation of local schools' Model UN teams in regional or national conferences; and encouraging students to participate in the annual essay contest.

Support of Model UN programs has remained a core activity of many UNA chapters. The once widespread nativist suspicions of communizing intentions behind Model UN have all but disappeared. However, at the turn of this century, a local UNA chapter had to turn out its members to support the Jefferson County (Alabama) school superintendent, "harassed by the John Birch Society" for permitting a Model UN program, Dorothy Robins-Mowry wrote. The annual essay contest, however, atrophied amid high school students' increasingly crowded academic and extracurricular schedules, changing communications technology, and changing incentives related to their future.

The Model UN concept was never the province of a single organization, despite the monumental effort of UNA-USA to promote it. In recent decades, Model UN has spread to East and South Asia, the Middle East, North Africa, and sub-Saharan Africa. Major conference organizers, including The Hague International Model UN, have created conferences in these regions, thanks to a healthy demand. The Ivy League Model United Nations, an arm of the Model UN at the University of Pennsylvania, now hosts conferences for high school age delegates in India and China.

In May 1977, a national Model UN was held in New York City. About 1,200 students from colleges and universities around the country attended the six-day event. Brian Urquhart, the UN undersecretary-general for special political affairs at the time, gave the keynote address. He had just returned from Vienna, where UN representatives were discussing the uprising in Cyprus. Urquhart was so impressed with the young UN impersonators that he remarked that he wished they were the real negotiators and that his Vienna interlocutors were the models. "I admire you," he said. "Putting yourselves in the shoes of the world spectrum is labor that is infinitely worthwhile."[9]

At UNA-USA, its Model UN program's popularity varied with the efforts and budgets of different chapters. For example, there was robust interest in the program in California and in several other Western states. As is often the case in voluntary efforts of bodies like UNA, however, the success of a program could be measured by the enthusiasm and input of its facilitator. The San Fernando Valley's chapter had such a person to reach out to new audiences. Sondra Zeigler started college thinking that she would become a physician, but after stopping her studies to raise two children, she returned and switched to political science. She had been inspired by a professor who taught the Model UN class. She became the honor society's president, as well as the Model UN professor's student teacher. In the 1980s, Zeigler served as president of UNA San Fernando Valley and became the chapter's education committee chair in the 1990s. She also helped develop an intergenerational Model UN that encouraged all age groups to participate. Zeigler inaugurated Model UN West in 1992, which has comprised more than fifteen colleges.

During the 1980s and 1990s, the UNA published the annual *Guide to Delegate Preparation,* a manual on the preparation of Model UN resolutions. In addition, UNA hosted an annual Model United Nations Summit, which was a training and networking conference for Model UN leaders from around the country.

In Florida, the UNA Tampa Bay chapter was led by two well-educated, passionate women—Kelly Miliziano and Sara McMillan—both of whom emphasized the value of education and expanding the geography of their influence. Miliziano was born to a family active in civic organizations, such as the Lions and Rotary Clubs. After earning a social science degree from New York University, she taught at the American Community Schools in Athens. While living in Greece, she partnered with the UN Information Center in Athens in 1994 to organize the city's first Model UN conference of international schools, a program that still exists. There was also an initiative in the 1990s to expand Model UN into historically black colleges and universities. Funded by the Ford Foundation, James Muldoon started the project; and after his departure, Dorothy Watson, a Foreign Service officer who was seconded to UNA just before her retirement, coordinated the work.

Boston's Global Classrooms Program

The UNA-USA Greater Boston chapter is perhaps emblematic of some of the groundbreaking work that UNA-USA did in Global Classrooms over the years. As early as 1994, before the initiative of UNA-USA at the national level, the Greater Boston chapter launched the Bringing the World to Our Children program, the centerpiece of its outreach efforts. The chapter continues to offer one of the most successful student programs in the UNA fold.

The program relied on fifteen lesson plans about the UN that could be used in classrooms of approximately thirty students each. It was so successful, that in the spring of 1996, the curriculum was featured in the Massachusetts Corporation for Educational Telecommunication for a series of nationwide interactive broadcasts via satellite. Lena Granberg served from 2000 to 2014 as the Boston chapter's executive director, supervising five staffers and as many as ten interns from four local universities; six or more interns were dedicated to the chapter's education programs. Her chapter provided teacher-training workshops on the lesson plans and ensured that the training was applied toward professional development credits for teachers. She implemented a self-published, 200-page *Teacher's Guide,* which included an endorsement letter from then Secretary-General Kofi Annan, as well as student workbook.

The Boston chapter's Global Classrooms team offered the curriculum to the city's public schools at no cost. In 2001, the curriculum was updated, creating the present-day Global Classrooms program, which has been carried out in more than thirty-five schools in the Boston area.

Each year, the program reaches some 2,000 middle- and high school students through comprehensive Model UN activities, such as teacher training and in-classroom support, Model UN conferences, and "mini simulations." The chapter has featured many diplomats at its events, including its annual Consuls Ball and fund-raiser, where a member from each of the local consulates attends.

Granberg summarized the program's response:

> Walking into a classroom full of teenagers is always a special moment. I love their enthusiasm and am awed by their knowledge of both the issue being debated and their country's position, especially at the middle school level. I admire their poise when presenting arguments and responding to other delegates. Watching them deep in discussion, working together to devise solutions to a complex problem as delegates—it gives me hope. Raising a generation better informed on global issues is bound to strengthen support for the UN's work.

Since 2004 (and continuing since the merger with the UN Foundation), Global Classrooms has worked in twenty-four major cities worldwide, helping to bridge the gap in the Model UN community between experienced programs and traditionally underserved public schools or schools new to Model UN.

Luers Expands Education

Over the decades, an ambitious leap was made from the steady national programs of Model UNs and essay contests to a broader, deeper enterprise, which brought not only more attention to UNA-USA but also considerable new funding. When William Luers assumed the leadership of UNA-USA, one of his prime initiatives was to expand the reach of Model UN. One of the first people he hired was Lucia Rodriguez as director of education. As Rodriguez recalled in a 2015 interview for this book, "I really wanted to focus on the youth. I had not known of Model UN before I arrived at UNA-USA. I had gone to good schools [Columbia and Georgetown], so why didn't I hear about it? Any school that was a good school had a model UN team." But the roots remained in elite universities, especially Ivy League schools. Rodriguez knew that to enlarge and popularize Model UN, the association needed to fund-raise. She explained: "If we focused on Model UN, that was going to be a way to bring in and increase youth participating and raising awareness of the UN beyond these elite universities. . . . We needed money to do Model UN. And we needed to then expand it to the public schools."

Rodriguez updated the *Guide to Delegate Preparation* manual, which took the Model UN and broke it down for teachers who did not have any Model UN experience. UNA-USA connected that to the skills students should be learning. The program then trickled down not only to high schools but also, most important to a new cohort—middle schools.

Rodriguez enlisted chapter members to help with the training. For example, in both Houston and Tampa, each had a chapter member who was recruited specifically to lead Model UN programs in coordination with the local school administrators and teachers. This helped bring the program into the public schools. In New York, staff members did that work. The Chicago chapter was small at the time and had no coordinator to lead the Model UN, so Rodriguez enlisted an employee from the Chicago public schools. "We trained her with what we needed her to do," Rodriguez recalled. "That was the model, and we did that in all these cities. We were in thirty-one cities and around the world. Not just in the United States."

Lucia Rodriguez, UNA vice president of education, left, and William Luers, UNA president, right, with others on Members Day 2004 at the United Nations. (Photo courtesy of the Seton Hall University UNA-USA archives.)

In 2005, UNA-USA received a five-year $7.5 million grant from Merrill Lynch that enabled the organization to expand to urban public schools in areas not previously served by Model UN, as well as to take it to an international level. Eddy Bayardelle, who specialized in giving grant money to various organizations, represented the brokerage firm; the Model UN program especially appealed to him. Merrill's funding helped, as UNA-USA was always on the lookout for financial support. To the irritation of many chapter leaders, who thought the Global Classrooms grants should support UNA-USA education activities in the US, the grant enabled Rodriguez to travel to such places as Lebanon and Germany to introduce Model UN to foreign students. "I've been all over the world doing this," Rodriguez said. "It was bringing the world of the UN to these folks." At its peak, she said UNA had introduced at least 100,000 students to the program worldwide.

Bringing the World to Our Children

Luers, in his aim to enhance the Model UN program at UNA-USA, also set out to extend the education component into what he called Global Classrooms—even trademarking the name. He felt that UNA-USA could have a presence among a wider age group of students, and the program could be implemented all year long, not just as a onetime annual event like Model UN. His goal was to encompass less-privileged urban areas that had been ignored in the past to participate in extracurricular academics. Funds from the Merrill Lynch grant were made available to provide school districts with teaching materials and other support.

Rodriguez remembered when the program was first proposed: "Our board was excited," she said. "We were talking about global classrooms, and we were getting into these school systems and working with these kids. It wasn't exclusive. It wasn't just private schools." Luers understood that students in economically disadvantaged neighborhoods rarely had the opportunity to participate. Their parents might not have the money to send them to national Model UN meetings. Global Classrooms could go a long way to change that.

To get the program going, Luers stepped up his fund-raising effort. Aside from major donors like the Annenberg Foundation and Merrill Lynch, he tapped new sources whom he knew would support his idea— he was, after all, the former head of the Metropolitan Museum of Art, so he had a huge network of contacts in New York society. One stop Luers made was at the Manhattan apartment of Courtney Sale Ross. Ross was the widow of Steve Ross, the executive who built Warner Communications into a film and media conglomerate. She had founded a small school in the Hamptons in 1991 with an innovative philosophy of integrated learning and an emphasis on global outreach.

Rodriguez remembers accompanying Luers to a breakfast meeting at Ross's apartment and his artful pitch. Ross was intrigued with the potential of Global Classrooms, Rodriguez said—enough to ask, "'Would 500,000 dollars work?' And she took out her checkbook right there."

Global Classrooms in the District of Columbia

UNA-USA's other chapters participated in varying degrees in Global Classrooms, depending on resources and personnel. The effort to improve education is ongoing within the organization's local outlets. The Metro DC chapter appeared to be a microcosm of the challenges faced by Global Classrooms in large cities. It even evaluated its Global Classrooms DC (GCDC) program, which was inaugurated in 2003, with a study completed in 2009.[10] The evaluation team examined the three goals of the DC branch: (1) aiming to help students become global citizens, (2) developing their social science research skills, and (3) improving their communications skills. It found the program highly relevant to the needs of students in the area, reported progress on the specific learning objectives, and related the observation of an independent interviewer: "We had a winner—education that works!"

Among the recommendations from the final report were that a curriculum advisory group "should give particular attention to student motivation and [to] ensuring closer linkage between the chapter's objectives, evaluation tools, and program content." In addition, training conferences should be rethought to expand outreach. The curriculum could "include content on globalization, economic and financial issues, strengthening and reform of the United Nations and reproductive health issues." The program could be expanded to include charter schools and independent schools in the local suburbs. The sixty-three-page report also found that the chapter should develop better quantitative evaluation tools and metrics to assess the program's impact and should "actively participate in dialogue with current and potential partners on possibilities for a broader, more integrated program of global education enrichment for high school and, as appropriate, middle school students in the metropolitan area." Finally, the chapter "should enter into a new dialogue with UNA-USA, nationally and with other chapters, under which each participant would learn from the Global Classrooms experience of the others. Issues covered should include both programmatic and managerial questions, including financial resource mobilization, evaluation of program impact and partnership outreach and development."

So, what improvements did the GCDC program achieve five years after the report was done? The chapter team initiated successful new fund-raising activities, especially online. It attracted more support from family foundations, more recently via corporate sponsorships; and it received fees from private schools. Fund-raising, however, remained a challenge, as UNA-USA financial support, which initially covered all costs, had been reduced to zero.

The recommended curriculum advisory group morphed into a teacher advisory group focused on curriculum. The chapter continuously adapted curriculum to local needs, moving increasingly into social media, including webinars. New evaluation tools were also prepared.

Teacher testimonials and social media increased the chapter's visibility. UNA-USA distributed a new extensive curriculum on globalization and economic and financial matters, though its introduction into the DC curriculum was slowed by lack of time and resources to train users.

The program expanded greatly into public charter schools and independent and suburban schools in northern Virginia and Maryland. Washington, DC, public schools, however, remained the central focus.

More than 3,000 students participated in the chapter's Global Class-room in a recent academic year, with nearly 80 percent of those from the capital's public schools. UNA's National Capital Area has under-scored the intergenerational nature of the program, which engages col-lege students from local universities, as well as midcareer and senior members engaged in volunteer and mentoring opportunities.

In Washington and beyond, long-term evaluation of Global Class-rooms' effect on students is difficult, given the challenge of keeping in touch with former participants. In addition, lack of interest by potential partners and limited resources mean that little progress has been made toward setting up an integrated program of global education enrichment in the DC metro area. Increasing numbers of young professional volun-teers are enriching the chapter, but they do not generally have the pro-file or the time needed for a larger leadership role.

The discussion on education with UNA-USA and other chapters has grown—notably, between the DC and Boston chapters. Yet, a broad pro-gram of mutual enrichment among chapters has yet to be achieved, as UNA-USA lacks the resources to facilitate this. A Google group has been established, and informal contacts among those concerned with education regularly characterize the UNA-USA annual meeting in Washington, DC.[11]

Education at UNA-USA Endures

As the governments of UN member states continue to confront a grow-ing array of challenges and responsibilities in and beyond their borders, there is no greater tool than the teaching and training of the next gener-ation of leaders.

Gillian Sorensen, a longtime member of UNA-USA, surely under-stands the value of educating and preparing students to lead responsibly, professionally, and imaginatively in all walks of life. Sorensen, a former New York City commissioner for the UN and a former UN assistant secretary-general for public affairs, served for many years as national advocate for the UN in the UN Foundation.

In that last role, she gave literally countless speeches to UNA chapters nationwide. From about 1990 and continuing for about the next twenty-five years, she began traveling the globe as an "itinerant preacher," as she called it, extolling the work of the UN. Although much of the effort she made was rewarding, in an interview for this book, she said,

> In the course of all that, it became clear to me that as far as teaching the UN and schools, it had diminished to practically nothing. If it was

fifteen minutes in the American history class, then it was probably a lot. People used to celebrate UN Day in October, and that seems to have fallen away. Trick or treating for UNICEF doesn't seem to happen much anymore. This is a serious issue because the UN needs public support, not just from diplomats but general public support.

Despite the constant conflicts among many nations that dominate the news, world peace appears to be losing ground to other causes among the public. "The environment for education on the UN remains challenging," Sorensen said. "Sixty percent of the members of UNA are under the age of twenty-five. That's a very good sign," she noted. But UNA-USA has an uphill track to keep building its membership. Other NGOs have far more people participating in their causes.

Still, UN advocates are a dedicated group. The education of the millennial generation is lasting, which gave those like Sorensen hope. Despite her laments, she said, "Model UN is the one exception. That seems to thrive, and I really mean thrive. The kids love it, and the numbers have grown both at the high school and college level."

Notes

1. Estelle Linzer, "The Way We Were: An Informal History of the American Association for the United Nations from 1945 Through 1964 When It Merged with the United States Committee for the United Nations to Become the United Nations Association of the United States of America" (unpublished manuscript, 1995, pages unnumbered).

2. Clark Eichelberger, "At the First Annual Inter-Collegiate Institute on the United Nations," *Changing World*, October 1946.

3. Alys Brady, *Changing World*, May 1948.

4. UNA-USA, International Affairs Program, Ford Foundation, October 1989, 33–34.

5. The Model UN held its sixty-first session in February 2015, according to http://www.harvardmun.org/.

6. *AAUN News,* April 1961.

7. Anjli Parrin, "The Dog-Eat-Dog World of the Model UN," *The New York Times,* August 2, 2013.

8. UNA-USA, "About Us," http://www.unausa.org/about-us.

9. "Talk of the Town," *The New Yorker,* May 9, 1977, 35.

10. *United Nations Association of the National Capital Area Evaluation of Global Classrooms, 2006–2009* (Washington, DC: UNA National Capital Area, December 20, 2009).

11. UNA National Capital Area, "GCDC Evaluation Recommendations: Notes on Follow-Up" (three-page document), provided by A. Edward Elmendorf.

17

Vista, The InterDependent, and Other Prominent Publications of UNA-USA

Dulcie Leimbach

Long before Fred Eckhard landed his post as a spokesperson for UN Secretary-General Kofi Annan, he edited UNA's publications from 1973 to 1985—a job that set him on a trajectory toward the UN Secretariat. His editorial career in foreign affairs started with a publication called *Atlas Magazine,* where he worked from 1971 to 1973, at its base in New York. The magazine was started in the 1960s by a woman from the West Coast to "help Americans stay in touch with the rest of the world," Eckhard said in a 2014 interview for this book. A fan of *Atlas,* Richard Stanley, of the Stanley Foundation in Muscatine, Iowa, bought it and changed the name to *World Press Review.*

The *Review* became an important stepping-stone for Eckhard, who had heard that UNA-USA was looking for an editor to manage its publications, which included a magazine and an annual book on issues before the UN General Assembly. Eckhard joined UNA when Ed Korry was president. Korry was not overly enamored with the organization's magazine for members, called *Vista,* a bimonthly with liquor, airline, cigarette, and other luxury advertising that did not fit UNA's persona— even when it was interspersed with insightful articles, essays, and features on the UN, catering to an internationally minded audience. *Vista* had been too slick, Eckhard explained, for Korry's taste. (Korry was UNA president from 1972 to 1973.) By the time Eckhard actually joined UNA, *Vista* was shut down.

But before all that happened, *Vista* had developed an identity, first excerpting most of its content from other publications, hoping to appeal to UNA members across the country. Yet some of the magazine's elements were original. Its logo, designed by Richard Hess, an art director who became prominent in New York graphic design circles, portrayed a clean modernist sensibility with the "A" an upside-down "V." The magazine projected a suave tone to readers from coast to coast, who were eager to learn about the UN and its specialized agencies.

Vista also took its cues from the past—decades, in fact, when UNA was the AAUN and Clark Eichelberger wrote a stream of mimeographed updates to chapter leaders to encourage their promotional efforts and inform their arguments in the run-up to the 1945 UN Charter ratification vote in the Senate. Three million pieces of printed matter were distributed to the field. "Letters of information and instruction are sent periodically to the local chapters and groups working with the Association," Eichelberger noted in AAUN's first annual report in January 1946. Chapters then sent reports on their activities to the national office for inclusion in the "branch news section" of AAUN's newly launched monthly publication, *Changing World.* "Thus the branches feel that they are playing an integral part in the national office," the report concluded, according to papers in the Clark Eichelberger papers held by the New York Public Library.

In time, *Changing World* itself was changed—first, after the 1964 merger, when it transformed into *Vista*, and a decade later to *The Inter-Dependent,* when the association rebranded its membership publication to reflect a new rationale for US participation in global institutions. The rationale was the notion of nations' growing "interdependence," which came to dominate internationalist discourse in the 1970s, propelled by negotiations on international trade and environmental issues.

Vista made its debut with a July/August issue in 1965—a heyday for the US magazine industry. In its earliest form, *Vista* was digest size, with newsprint paper bound in a thick paper cover. The first issue was graced at the bottom with the UNA-USA logo and a bald eagle—a publication that declared its dual allegiances. The original issue offered a short list of hot topics, some of which continue to plague the world today: famine, the gap between rich and poor countries, cases in which the UN Charter was thought to have been abused (such as Russia's invasion of Hungary and the United States' presence in Vietnam). Yet it also zeroed in on stories more rooted in the era: the possibility of big game (elephants) being eaten at the dinner table and the danger of thalidomide. (Elephants are still on menus—say, in elite circles in Zimbabwe; thalidomide, no longer used in pregnancies to alleviate morning sickness, had led to serious birth defects.)

An excerpt from *The View from a Distant Star,* by Harlow Shapley, an astronomer looking at internationalism amid the cosmos, brought an air of intellectualism into the pages. A "Comment" section excerpted, among other pieces, a message that President Lyndon B. Johnson delivered to the Senate in which he said that the UN "has been near the heart of the United States foreign policy for two decades."

The UN: Running Out of "Gush"

Andrew Boyd, a writer for *The Economist,* became a regular contributor to *Vista.* In his first essay for the magazine, he wrote that the UN had "run out of gush" (steam) and that the "case for keeping it going— or for trying to enlarge its capacity—has to be argued as matter of factly as if it were a railway, an airline route, a mental hospital or a royal commission. It has something in common with all of these."

The table of contents reflected *Vista*'s attempts to appeal to a wide audience—UNA members and foreign affairs and policy experts—with headlines like, "UN in the U.S.—\$ and ¢," and an article about the UN joint staff pension fund investing more than \$100 million in US government bonds and stocks of US corporations. "Peking's Game at the UN," by K. V. Narain, excerpted from the *Hindu Weekly Review* and *Atlas Magazine,* discussed whether China was interested in membership in the UN. A reprint by C. L. Sulzberger of *The New York Times,* titled "Partition Is a Global Problem," contended that the principal threats to world peace "can be summed up in a single word—partition." He went on to say, "Soviet menaces to West Berlin only reminded us again that Germany as well as its former capital are still split in two." UNESCO, a favorite topic in *Vista* over its lifetime, got full treatment in a piece on its work "preserving mankind's heritage." Book reviews and "UN Notebook" tackled such pressing matters before the Security Council as Cyprus, Southern Rhodesia (now Zimbabwe), and the Dominican Republic.

Eichelberger joined the chorus of writers in a column that repeated its virtues twice—"Personal Opinion." In it, he wrote about delegates meeting in San Francisco to commemorate the twentieth anniversary of the signing of the UN Charter, convening in a "mood of considerable confusion resulting from the fact that the Nineteenth General Assembly is in limbo,[1] so to speak, and that military actions in Southeast Asia and the Dominican Republic are going on with the UN seemingly helpless to act."

Vista grew in influence and style, filling a niche of foreign affairs coverage through a UN lens, expanding to a more compelling 8.5 x 11 inch format, and adopting glossy paper. The magazine published a masthead, becoming more confident in its editorial voice: the January/February 1966 issue, in which the people behind the curtain were identified, listed Albert H. Farnsworth as editor; Marion Bijur, managing editor; Ruth L. Massey, assistant editor; and John Brodersen, art consultant.

Interviews with UN officials, such as Dr. Binay Ranjan Sen, director-general of the UN Food and Agriculture Organization, became more common, as did daring graphics, inspired by the New York school, with illustrations by such rising stars as Seymour Chwast, R. O. Blechman, Isadore Seltzer, Milton Glaser, and Saul Steinberg.

Boyd pontificated in the January/February 1966 issue on "competitive peacekeeping," and Walter H. Wheeler Jr., chair of the board of Pitney Bowes (also an advertiser), opined on Vietnam, Soviets in Europe, and other important UN topics. The end page brought readers into the UN's Meditation Room, with its Marc Chagall stained-glass artwork.

The UNA executives must have understood the value of publishing a magazine: they could make their presence known far beyond the New York office, reaching into the homes of UNA members, as well as other readers who sought information on UN issues in a readable format. They could also lure new members by offering *Vista* as a reason for joining the organization. The magazine reinforced the sense that UNA had a direct line to people in the know at the UN.

Robert S. Benjamin, chair of the UNA board (as well as cochair of United Artists), invested time in *Vista* by writing a column, "The World of the UN." Herman W. Steinkraus, president of UNA, wrote forewords for the magazine. Porter McKeever, an executive vice president and later president, reported on the organization's progress. In his write-up, McKeever echoed a message that UNA members heard through many permutations over decades—that UNA "is dedicated to strengthening our country's capacity for advancing peace, freedom and justice in the world through the development of the United Nations and other international organizations. It is independent, private, nonpartisan."

More photos edged into *Vista,* yet illustrations remained center stage. A sassy photo essay by Cindy Adams, a correspondent for ABC-TV (and later a gossip columnist for the *New York Post*), captured the period as she championed the female UN tour guides, calling them ambassadors. Yet it was an era when women were relegated, without shame or embarrassment, to sideline roles at the UN. Adams refused to overlook tour guides' true contribution. They were, she said, an "international corps of brains and beauty," who explained the "workings of the United Nations to over a million visitors a year" and who consisted of a "passel of guides (all ladies, from Pakistan, Denmark, Brazil, Israel, Canada, Taiwan, Russia, and points East)." They wore uniforms, she added, though some wore native dress, such as a kimono. During breaks, "they play bridge; they are apprised of the workings of the UN."

The magazine's big-name advertisers—Citroën, TWA, Virginia Slims, Western Union, Esso—might have covered the magazine's costs or at least helped defray the expenses of publishing a bimonthly, which was no small financial endeavor. By 1967, the masthead formally listed Richard Hess Inc. as art director. Hess gave the design of *Vista*—which his biography inaccurately describes as "a small ailing magazine published by the United Nations"—a clean look, with the logo its most outstanding feature.

Hess commissioned for *Vista* posterlike art from avant-garde graphic designers. When the art budget ran out, Hess began to make the artwork himself. By 1968, the masthead listed Dick Hess and Teresa Alfieri as the art directors; that was also when *Vista* moved from newsprint paper inside to glossy. (In 1968, the art directors changed to "Hess and/or Antupit and Teresa Alfieri," reflecting a short-lived merger of firms.)

Among the honorary chairs of UNA, now positioned near the masthead, were Harry S. Truman, Dwight D. Eisenhower, Ralph Bunche, and Robert Benjamin, president and board chair. Basic annual UNA membership dues were $7.00, which included a subscription to *Vista*. (An annual subscription to the magazine was $3.50 for nonmembers, and a single issue was $1.00.)

By 1970, with its waning years not visibly apparent, *Vista*'s efforts at self-promotion became more ambitious, proclaiming with a full-page ad that "Vista Readers Look at the World in a Different Way." Or that "Vista gives America's thought leaders a direct communication with the people who are trying to reshape the world," noting that it offers "corporate advertisers a direct communication with these readers"—more than 100,000 "opinion molders."

Through *Vista,* UNA offered travel ventures to "members and friends," with tours to Eastern Europe, the Caribbean, and Central America: "Delightful, modestly priced opportunities to visit with United Nations personnel in United Nations installations overseas."

VIP names graced the commemorative issue marking the UN's twenty-fifth anniversary in 1970, with comments published from such politicians and UN people as Nelson Rockefeller, the governor of New York; Charles Yost, the US ambassador to the UN; U Thant, the UN Secretary-General; and Mayor John Lindsay of New York. Even a statement from Richard Nixon, the US president, was featured. Subscription rates rose to $4 a year, entitling readers to receive *Vista* but not UNA membership (for the latter, it cost $7 a year with a one-year subscription). In 1972, a marketing director was added to the masthead (R. J.

Gouverneur), and circulation figures were posted: 64,000 to 65,000, of which 54,000 to 56,000 were paid.

Vista's demise came suddenly, however, with the February 1973 issue. The cover, featuring an illustration by Seymour Chwast, distracted readers from the news buried in the back pages, announcing the death of *Vista* with a cursory editor's note. Little explanation was provided in the note, though the costs of producing a magazine of *Vista*'s caliber could have contributed to its closing.

Issues Before the General Assembly

In 1972, a new supplement was inserted in *Vista,* focusing on Issues Before the 27th General Assembly and prepared with a grant from the Carnegie Endowment for International Peace. The supplement was the predecessor publication to *A Global Agenda,* UNA's annual stand-alone book about the major issues before the UN. *A Global Agenda*'s compendium of essays by international policy experts and academics became a must-read for diplomats, delegates, and students. It served as a reliable, objective source of information to guide these readers through the annual September topical debates in the opening of the General Assembly. But at least one academic who depended on the publication for his coursework in international organizations bemoaned, in a 1989 Ford Foundation evaluation on UNA, that UNA "does not aggressively promote the book among faculty members in international relations departments and law schools around the country."

Like *Vista,* the book endured erratic financing, even though it was in much demand at the UN bookstore every fall. Its publication lasted from 1973 to 2012, albeit with big gaps during that time. Its final three annual issues, designed by the graphic artist Laurie Baker, were paid for by grants from several Korean universities, which enjoyed being associated with UNA, especially because the Secretary-General of the UN at the time, Ban Ki-moon, was Korean and had a strong relationship with UNA.

The InterDependent Debut

Ed Korry first hired Fred Eckhard as assistant to John Roberts, a British editor. But Roberts found that he could not work with Korry and quit after six months. Under financial pressure, Korry gambled and made Eckhard editor.

Korry wanted Eckhard to edit the publication alone in order "to save money," according to Eckhard in the 2014 interview for this book.

Korry, a Democrat with ties to the Kennedys, had been US ambassador to Chile just before the coup ousting Salvador Allende. He told Eckhard to keep *The InterDependent*'s articles short, with compelling opening paragraphs. Most important, he wanted Eckhard to make *The InterDependent* "interesting to read" for the "average person."

By then, UNA had acquired a "bipolar" personality, as Eckhard described it, with both Republicans and Democrats as members and supporters and both a grassroots and a Washington policy staff. Yet Korry understood the value of educating UNA members through the magazine, however "average" he might have perceived them. He appears to have relished journalism, even helping to choose headlines and suggesting layouts. Nevertheless, editorial freedom prevailed, Eckhard said, thanks to board member Porter McKeever, who was also a former journalist and previously a spokesperson for the US mission to the UN. "I reminded everyone about it," Eckhard said about the publication's independence.

Eckhard described, for example, an article he wrote about the possible dangers to people's health by microwave radiation. Yet the presence of a board member, Jean Picker, whose husband operated an x-ray company, made some people nervous. (For more on Jean Picker, see Chapter 5.) Jim Leonard, the UNA president then, asked Eckhard to delay publication of *The InterDependent* for a few days while Leonard reviewed the article. Leonard then suggested a few minor changes before the article was published.

The magazine became known despite minimal financing. Eckhard hired Sam Antupit, a popular New York graphic artist, to create a design on a slim budget. Antupit had designed the *New York Review of Books,* and *The InterDependent* followed that format. (Antupit had also been part of the team "Hess and/or Antupit and Teresa Alfieri," behind *Vista* in the late 1960s, until the partnership ended.) Once again, the logo was given rightful consideration: Antupit split the name in two by capitalizing the "I" and the "D," a decision that signaled sophistication despite the publication's newsprint pages. Antupit also asked leading illustrators to do cartoons and drawings for nominal fees.

As the *ID,* as it was nicknamed, found its footing, Korry left—also suddenly. (Details of his departure are in Chapter 12.) Jim Leonard, second in command, stepped in as interim chief of UNA in 1973. More musical chairs ensued, and soon Robert Ratner became president, having been a major fund-raiser for the organization. His expertise at finding money, however, had begun to falter, even though he was "key to holding on to a few influential members of the board, like Benjamin,"

Eckhard noted. According to Eckhard, these vital members included Jewish supporters who stayed on despite the UN's Zionism-as-racism resolution, which had alienated a huge segment of US backers of the UN (see Chapter 7).

The InterDependent was growing in popularity, so Ratner offered Eckhard a budget of $25,000 to hire an assistant. "Hell," Eckhard told Ratner. "For $25,000, I can hire three." Eckhard placed an ad in *The New York Times,* seeking writers for the publication at a salary of $8,000 a year, enticing many young, eager reporters. These included Alan Tonelson, straight from Princeton (who became an influential economics writer); Michael Gordon, a son of a former UN spokesperson Matt Gordon and a graduate of the Columbia Journalism School (who now covers the State Department for *The New York Times*); and Betsy Sullivan, who landed at the *Cleveland Plain-Dealer,* covering foreign policy.

Yet disruptions continued, portending more difficult days for UNA and the *ID,* including Ratner's decision to temporarily suspend the publication at one point. The fate of the *ID* was hanging in the balance when Elliot Richardson, UNA chair, wrote Eckhard a letter of support. McKeever seconded it, enabling Eckhard to revive the publication. With McKeever's help, Eckhard asked for support from the deans of schools of international affairs—Columbia, Georgetown, Johns Hopkins, Tufts—and they responded by ordering bulk subscriptions for their students.

Eckhard savored his job. He recalled being taken to lunch regularly with an editor of *Pravda* at small restaurants in the UN neighborhood. He suspected the Russian journalist was a spy and asked Jim Leonard's advice. Leonard said, "You don't know any state secrets, right?" Eckhard nodded. "Then talk to him freely," Leonard answered—adding, "The better they know us, the better it will be for all of us."

Eckhard left UNA in 1985 to become editor of *UN Chronicle,* the UN's magazine. Although he was promised the job at first, it fell through at the last minute; so, instead, he worked as an information officer at the UN and eventually as spokesperson for Secretary-General Kofi Annan.

As Much Coverage of the UN as Americans Wanted

The InterDependent continued to course through as many ups and downs as the UN endured over the decades. By the 1990s, the magazine's frequency was reduced to save on printing and postage costs— first, to every two months and then to quarterly. In 2003, it was reformatted again to be more visually appealing; and in 2010, it became a strictly online publication, quickly fading from many older members' consciousness. Yet over the decades, editors spared no efforts to maintain the publication's relevance and vitality.

THE INTERDEPENDENT

Bringing Global Issues to the Local Level   A UNA-USA Publication   Vol 2 No 3 Fall 2004

New Ambassador
John Danforth Briefs
UNA-USA on His Plan for
U.S.-U.N. Relations

Senator Lugar on the
Ratification–or Lack
Thereof–of Treaties

PLUS:

Democracy Caucus:
Yay or Nay?

The Opening of the 59th
General Assembly

And the 10 Stories
the U.N. Wants Told

Global Visionaries
**ARTHUR ROSS AND
JOHN C. WHITEHEAD**
Determined to Keep the U.N.
Strong – Well into the Future
by Barbara Crossette

An *InterDependent* cover from 2004 featuring John C. Whitehead (right) and Arthur Ross. (Original photo by Lori Grinker; magazine cover courtesy of the Arthur Ross Archives.)

As head of communications for UNA-USA, John Tessitore took over the *ID* in 1985 and continued as its editor until 2001, he said. It was a quarterly publication by then, aimed straight at UNA members. During a 2015 interview for this book, Tessitore said that the *ID* was mailed to every dues-paying member. Each issue was eight pages, and it still reported on the work of the UN, as well as on US-UN relations, "which were particularly difficult during the Reagan years." It also reported "on the work of UNA-USA both at the national level and at the local chapter level." The *ID*, Tessitore added, "was a typical 'house organ' designed to keep its membership informed of the goings-on both at the UN and within UNA itself, and I think we accomplished that quite well."

One of his favorite roles as editor was interviewing interesting people who worked with or for the UN system. As he recalled, "My very first interview when I arrived at UNA in 1985 was with the then UN correspondent for CBS News, Richard C. Hottelet." (Hottelet, one of the London-based "Murrow boys" working for Edward R. Murrow during World War II, died in 2014 at age ninety-seven.) Tessitore wrote, "Richard was a sort of hero of mine, because as a young boy I would see him almost every evening on CBS news reporting directly from the UN." Hottelet would stand on the sidewalk of First Avenue in front of the row of flags at the UN and report to America on what happened at the world body that day, recalled Tessitore, adding, "There are not many Americans left who will remember this, or who would even believe that there was a time when the US news media actually thought the UN was so important that it deserved daily reporting." Tessitore continued:

> In those days [the 1960s] there were about 300 full-time US reporters covering the UN. At the time I interviewed Hottelet in 1985, that number was less than 50, and it continued to decline every year thereafter. I asked him about this decline in coverage, and I still recall his response. He said that the American people always had exactly as much coverage of the UN as they wanted at any given time. In other words, he felt that the decline in reporting was in direct relation to the decline in public interest in the institution, and not the other way around. And in my years at UNA, I discovered that he was exactly right.

Yet interest in the UN among other nations—especially in Europe and the developing nations—remained high, Tessitore said. "As such, the number of non-US correspondents remained large, which was a direct reflection of the importance that their government and citizens attributed to the world organization," he said.

The *ID*, meanwhile, continued to appeal to what Tessitore called "a definite audience and a definite purpose, and so it remained fairly constant." It did not encounter, he added, "any real challenges," and there was always plenty to report on—the UN and the organization itself—with only eight pages to fill. *"The InterDependent* magazine was a real and tangible membership benefit and may have helped sustain membership," said Matthew Metz, a leader of the Seattle chapter of UNA.

By the early 2000s, the *ID* had transformed into a glossy magazine again but with a broader mix of features and essays. Members joined UNA to receive the magazine, because few US publications offered such a full inside look at the UN as the *ID*. One important development for the magazine involved the editorial participation of Barbara Crossette, who had left *The New York Times* in 2002 as its UN correspondent and was invited by Bill Luers, the head of UNA-USA, to help brainstorm on how he could create a new look and attitude for the magazine. Soon, Crossette was actively involved in the magazine's evolution, bringing insight on the UN into the pages of the *ID*—and UNA readers appreciated her voice.

Crossette, in an e-mail from her home in Pennsylvania, described her role in the reinvigorated *ID* from the start: "I made a dummy copy with more pictures, a magazine layout, bigger headlines, and a cover that was designed to attract readers, and he [Luers] then worked with that." Luers, she said, "had especially wanted to kind of 'wall off' the more boring chapter reports and other UNA trivia, and make the *ID* a more general foreign/UN news magazine." He appointed Crossette editor in chief, with Angela Drakulich the daily staff editor. Crossette said that Luers authorized a "considerable expansion of the staff, taking in outsiders instead of UNA people."

Drakulich came not only with magazine experience but also a master's degree from the Seton Hall's John C. Whitehead School of Diplomacy and International Relations (now the School of Diplomacy and International Relations). She started at UNA in 2002—at about the same time Luers decided to revamp *The InterDependent* as a quarterly. She described the situation at first: "The magazine was published in a newsletter-type format and written primarily by UNA-USA staff members. The articles focused on UNA-USA programs, such as the Business Council for the UN, Global Classrooms, and Adopt-A-Minefield, with one to two editorial and analytical type pieces." The goal in relaunching the publication in fall 2003 "was not only to change the look and feel of *The InterDependent* but also to widen its reach in terms of authorship and audience," she said.

"We wanted to expand the impact of the articles by incorporating more policy, analysis, and insight into the world of UN-US relations and of the way the UN itself worked, while also keeping readers informed of UNA-USA chapters and their work across the country," Drakulich said in an e-mail. "In fact, we established a tagline for the magazine, appearing on every issue: Bringing Global Issues to the Local Level." She said that hiring Crossette, who was well connected with UN administrators, diplomats, and nonprofit programs worldwide, meant tapping her expertise of US-UN relations—a crucial asset in providing value and generating strong interest in the *ID*.

A new designer, John Tom Cohoe, was recruited. (His wife, Laurie Baker, had designed the final issues of *A Global Agenda*.) Cohoe had worked in the Manhattan magazine industry, including as a graphic designer for *The New York Times*. "We also eventually hired a professional freelance photographer, Lori Grinker, for photo essays about the UN's work worldwide, as well as a special cover featuring Tim Wirth, head of the UN Foundation, and Ted Turner," Drakulich recalled.

New editorial sections included "In the Know" (high-brow gossip about UN insiders and appointments); "UN Watch" (news briefs about UN programs and agencies); "UNA-USA at Work" (featuring the organization's chapters); and the cover story—always written by Crossette—on a major topic.

The debut issue of the relaunch featured an exclusive interview by Crossette with Secretary-General Kofi Annan. The new magazine also included a "Debate and Viewpoint" section, featuring two differing opinions on vital current events, written by current or former ambassadors, authors, or well-known international relations professors; an "Insight" column, representing a traditional opinion/editorial piece on controversial US-UN relations; and another column, "Of Relevance," spotlighting a different UN program or agency each issue. A light last page, titled "Did You Know?," offered curious facts about the UN and UNA-USA.

The new design, which increased the page count to forty, "Gave the *ID* a more consumer feel," Drakulich said, helping to expand its readership. The stable of authors grew quickly as UN staffers, diplomats, and university programs took notice of the magazine's heightened sophistication and relevance.

Each issue featured interviews with and articles written by notable professors, such as John Ruggie of Harvard and a former UN assistant secretary-general, Benjamin Barber of the University of Maryland, Jeffrey Sachs of Columbia, Mark Malloch-Brown of the UN Development Programme, Nobel Peace Prize winner Mohamed ElBaradei, Robert F. Kennedy Jr., and General Assembly president Jan Eliasson (who became the UN deputy secretary-general). US congressional members and Stephen Schlesinger, a longtime writer on the UN, also contributed articles.

Using the magazine as a forum for news on the UN and UNA, the content blended both angles, highlighting, for example, UNA's annual Global Humanitarian Action awardees, such as Bono, the Annenberg family, Oprah Winfrey, and Angelina Jolie. "We also took advantage of our policy experts at UNA-USA—in particular, Suzanne DiMaggio, on Iran policy and UN relations, and Steve Dimoff, on US-UN relations—to incorporate timely policy papers and key insights," Drakulich said. Drakulich also developed a relationship with the UN Bookstore and the UN communications people, enabling the *ID* to be available—at no charge—in the bookstore and offices throughout UN headquarters in New York. "The changes we made to *The InterDependent* throughout 2002 and 2007 were well received not only by UNA-USA chapters and members, but also by our organization's contacts in the US government, embassies, and within the UN itself," Drakulich said, adding that readership grew from a few thousand to a 22,000-print run four times a year.

But UNA's financial problems still wreaked havoc on the publications department. By 2010, with the organization foundering and the magazine industry in general decline, the *ID* stopped publishing a print version and went digital, hoping to stay alive with a tiny budget. The new online version aimed to keep its UNA readers engaged as much as the print publication had, while also drawing in others browsing the web for news on the UN and foreign affairs. But many older members did not even have a computer to read it on the Internet. As with other major newspapers and magazines in 2010, going digital meant going free; after much debate within UNA ranks, the *ID* followed that "open" sharing approach.

A design team from Chicago, which had created the Bulletin of the Atomic Scientists website, ushered the *ID* onto the Web with a look that resembled the format of the *New York Times* website. This was not surprising, as the author of this chapter [Dulcie Leimbach] was the *ID*'s editor by then and a former editor at *The Times*. But the graphic designers kept the *ID* aligned with the UN by matching the UN peacekeeping blue in the *ID*'s logo. In addition, articles kept up the publication's strong journalistic tradition, which had been imbued by Crossette and Drakulich—albeit mindfully avoiding criticism of the UN. Another goal was to veer from repeating UN jargon, even when writers in UNA defaulted to such language out of habit.

At first, UNA members found the loss of the print *ID* devastating and the digital format off-putting. New articles were posted weekly, and an army of interns from such schools as the City University of New

York Graduate School of Journalism, Columbia University, Seton Hall, Johns Hopkins, Hofstra, Vassar, State University of New York, Buffalo, and Bard wrote, reported, and photographed on topics related to the UN. International interns also found working on the *ID* exhilarating, with students from Sweden (two sisters), Belarus, Britain, Spain, Russia, Nigeria, Italy, Finland, Zimbabwe, and elsewhere diving into the editorial experience. Some professional writers, like Evelyn Leopold, formerly of Reuters, were paid from a budget that waxed and waned. Crossette remained an indelible presence as consulting editor and writer, rarely tiring of the UN as subject matter.

Yet the *ID*, even in its digital form, could not survive—perhaps more so after it became exclusively available to UNA members as a bonus for joining. A budget for an (freelance) editor grew meager, and paying writers became impossible. The *ID* ceased publishing new stories in early 2014 (its old content remains online). Digital magazines, like PassBlue, a project of the Ralph Bunche Institute for International Studies at the Graduate Center of the City University of New York, have taken its place. (PassBlue was founded by this author with Crossette in 2011. It is mainly financed by the Carnegie Corporation of New York.)

Many UNA members, especially among the older generation, still bemoan the loss of the print *ID*, keenly aware that it was a great perk for their dues. Where else could they find information on chapter meetings in Iowa while also reading—in the final print edition—about US ambassador to the UN Susan Rice and her top deputies, all rendered with that crucial "insider" point of view?

Note

1. The Nineteenth UN General Assembly was suspended for many months because of a dispute concerning payments due to the UN by the Soviet Union.

18

UNA, the UN Foundation, and the Ways Ahead

Like many other nonprofit groups, AAUN and UNA-USA faced financial challenges over many years. One advantage the organization had was a pool of benefactors and foundations. Those benefactors either donated from their own funds or could draw on wealthy colleagues— or both. Adjusted to 2014 dollars, UNA-USA's annual revenues and expenditures were steady with at least $9–10 million through the 1970s; but they declined gradually to just over $6 million in the 1980s, rising again in the 1990s and through the first decade of this century to a peak of $14 million. The figures then fell sharply in the final years before the alliance with the UN Foundation in 2010.[1] Support by major donors had collapsed, for a variety of reasons, including the death of many early supporters, waning interest of the older generation in the UN, and falling confidence in UNA financial management.

Membership fees were a stable but small part of the income. Most of the money came from wealthy individuals and foundations. Particularly during the presidencies of Edward Luck and William Luers, the strategy was to launch projects that foundations would support. UNA also benefited from two endowments set up by James S. McDonnell and Arthur Ross. McDonnell established the Endowment Fund in 1976; it was renamed in 1978 the James S. McDonnell Permanent Reserve Fund. The fund's goal was to reach $1 million by 1987, with permission to use $200,000 annually for general operations. In 1990, the McDonnell money was combined with other endowments to create a general endowment so the audited reports no longer listed the fund as a distinct item and instead combined it with other sources of income under the heading "Permanently Restricted Net Assets." By the end of 1991, the combined endowment totaled $1.025 million.[2] UNA's total assets in 1994 were $4.19 million. Arthur Ross, upon his death in 2007, left $3.5 million to UNA (see Chapter 11).

UNA-USA established the Eleanor Roosevelt Society to stimulate planned giving; it also held fund-raising campaigns in several years, such as a UN Fiftieth Anniversary Campaign in 1995. In the final years before the alliance with the UN Foundation, UNA-USA had to draw on its endowment fund assets for operations. After settling its final obligations, it transferred its remaining funds of just over $3 million to the Better World Fund of the UN Foundation.

Some saw a shift in funding priorities as furthering the decline of UNA finances. Larry Levine, from the Monterey (California) chapter, said national fund-raising efforts focused on "special programs" like Adopt-A-Minefield and Global Classrooms, "with a down-playing of fund-raising for what we considered the core mission of the organization—advocacy work, policy development, communications, and membership/chapter development." The result of this shift in fund-raising, he said, was the "successive downsizings of staff in those core areas." (Levine was a chapter representative on the UNA-USA national board of directors from 2001 to 2009 and national chair of the network of chapters and members from 2005 to 2009.) Minutes from the period reflect the deepening financial hole. For example, the UNA executive committee minutes of February 2, 2009, noted that Luers "expressed concern over the current financial crisis and noted that UNA would have to shrink its budget from the projected $7 million to that of $4+ million."[3]

Levine added, "Eventually it appeared to us that the general budget was being tapped to meet the deliverables of some of the program grants, especially Global Classrooms, accelerating the downsizing; then even the organization's modest long-term endowment funds were being tapped for basic operations—never a good sign." He explained, "It soon became apparent that the very viability and existence of UNA-USA was threatened, unless a savior appeared quickly. And fortunately, the United Nations Foundation was a possibility."

Ted Turner's $1 Billion and the Creation of the UN Foundation

By any measure, Ted Turner is an enormous public figure of his generation: founder of CNN, owner of other TV networks and stations, the former owner of the Atlanta Braves baseball team, champion of nuclear disarmament and buffalo ranching, film producer, sailor, one of the largest private landowners in the United States, and billionaire. Once known as "The Mouth of the South," because he had made his early fortune in Atlanta and has been outspoken on all issues that engage him. Those issues included the United Nations. His flair for the dramatic led to his historic gift of $1 billion to help the UN, which was then the largest single charitable donation in history.

The gift became legendary. Turner's commitment to the UN was well known. At a speech at the National Press Club in Washington, DC, on October 9, 2006, he recalled his thinking during the 1996–1997 period leading up to the donation:

> The United States had not paid its dues to the United Nations for approximately two years and were a billion dollars in arrears on their regular dues. . . . And the UN couldn't pay their bills, and that really concerned me. And so that's why I tried to—well, I tried at first to give the billion dollars to the UN, and my lawyers told me you can't do that because the UN could not receive donations at that time. They got all their revenue from member states.[4]

The announcement took place at the UNA's Global Leadership Award gala at the Marriott Marquis Hotel in New York on September 19, 1997. Turner was the keynote speaker. Beverly Sills was the mistress of ceremony. John Whitehead, as chair of UNA, hosted a VIP cocktail reception of only twenty-five people before the speech. As Whitehead recalled of Turner in an interview for this book,

> He took me aside and said, "John, I have something I want to talk to you about." He said, "I'm thinking about giving a billion dollars, announcing tonight at your dinner, that I am going to give a billion dollars to the UN." I thought he said a "million dollars." And I said, "Did you say a million dollars?" being quite impressed with that. And he said, "No, I said a billion dollars." And he said, "I haven't fully decided, but I have been thinking a lot about it. That I have all of this money now from my investments." And I think he said: "My wife and I, we have no children. So I want to give away my money. It's five billion dollars that I have, and I want to give it away."

Whitehead felt Turner was asking for "final advice, but he had mostly made up his mind." So the gala went on. "I gave him a laudatory introduction, which I lauded up a bit after that conversation," Whitehead said. He continued:

> Then he got on, and I didn't know if he was going to do this or not. The crowd thought he said million. And so there was a big pause. And he paused. All of a sudden, there was a beginning of clapping and then wild clapping with standing ovation, when they began to realize one by one that he had said a billion. He didn't say what it was for. He

went on to say about all the good things that the UN does and that "nobody appreciates them." He thought that this was his way of his making one grand gift. . . . It was a great speech.

When Turner took the stage, he said, "The stars came into alignment for me to make the decision only two nights ago, and I waivered several times and almost changed my mind when I found out this morning that the UN cannot accept the gift." He added, "We can't give the money to the UN, so we're going to create or find a UN foundation. That UN foundation I'm going to put a billion dollars of stock in." At the gala, he explained, "We're going to have a committee of this foundation and a committee of the United Nations to decide how it gets split up, but the money can only go to UN causes and go into the funds that make things better for people all over the world."

In response to the announcement, UNA president Alvin Adams wrote a letter to the chapter and division presidents on October 3, saying the national headquarters was "hard at work developing ideas for a UNA-USA role in Ted Turner's $1 billion gift to the United Nations." Adams explained: "We are convinced that UNA-USA can present itself positively to Mr. Turner. To this end, we are developing a set of ideas which we hope will help distinguish us from others and draw on our historic strengths—grassroots, advocacy, and policy studies."[5]

By November 1997, Turner had decided to create his own conduit; he established the UN Foundation, named former Colorado senator Tim Wirth as its president, and created a board of trustees. Turner said in his 2006 National Press Club speech,

> [The UNF] could work in parallel with the United Nations and make donations and help out in areas that the United Nations felt they needed additional financial assistance. And it turned out that it was a pretty good idea, because they did need financial assistance, and they didn't have a very strong lobbying operation, and they needed help with government relations, particularly with the United States. And so it's worked out, I think, quite well.

Why did Turner create a foundation for his $1 billion when the UNA existed? "I guess I criticize myself for not having spoken up more loudly because the combination of UN Foundation money and the UNA programs would have been a terrific one," Whitehead said. But despite promoting the idea of "your money and our programs," Whitehead said, Wirth and the board (which included numerous former foreign heads of state) took a more global view and looked at UNA as "just a US organization."

Once UNF was running, they "found out just how many things weren't getting done in the other areas," Turner said. "The thought occurred to me that maybe an NGO could help in the area of weapons of mass destruction—at least, perhaps help raise the profile." The Nuclear Threat Initiative, chaired by former senator Sam Nunn (D-Georgia), was created to focus on weapons of mass destruction.

Turner planned for $100 million disbursements to be paid out annually over ten years, channeled through the UN Office for Project Services (UNOPS). The billion dollars was in the form of Time Warner stock. In October 1996, Time Warner purchased Turner Broadcasting (which included CNN) for $7.5 billion. Turner's share of the deal was worth $2.2 billion but soared to $3.3 billion in less than a year. However, "Turner's wealth [was] tied overwhelmingly to the stock value of Time Warner," according to the *Washington Post*.[6] (Shortly after the announcement of the gift, the value of the stock dropped significantly.) "In the end he [Turner] paid it all. He had some troubles in the third and fourth year when his stock of AOL/Timer Warner went way down, but it's come back," Whitehead said. "There were lots of stories about maybe he wouldn't make the payments, but he did. He made all the payments right on time."

The UNA-USA Alliance with the UN Foundation

As the first decade of the twenty-first century waned, UNA-USA was continuously losing membership and funding. Some programs were unpopular with financers, membership, or both (see Chapter 11). Once the UN Foundation decided that it would continue beyond Ted Turner's original ten-year financial commitment, two NGOs with "United Nations" in their titles existed in the United States. Talk of a merger between the two UN-centric organizations began between William Luers, the president of UNA-USA, and Tim Wirth, the president of UNF. Describing Wirth as "a very close friend of mine," Luers said the two "worked pretty closely" when the idea first came up in 2007. As Luers recounted,

> The only way they [UNA-USA] could fund themselves was to have a foundation like the UN Foundation to pay for it. The chapters were never going to get funded unless there was an organization that saw some interest in it. Tim and I talked about this for years, and it was the only way I could see it happening. Otherwise, it would go south.

Luers said he, Tom Pickering, and Whitehead "had a couple of false starts. . . . Basically the three of us worked with Tim for almost a year and a half. Then I finally just left." Negotiations foundered on two issues flagged by the UN Foundation lawyers: the financial solvency of UNA-USA and a pending sexual discrimination lawsuit. Elmendorf said UNF was "unwilling to assume the potentially open-ended obligation" that the lawsuit could cause.

Luers resigned in spring 2009 and was succeeded by Thomas Miller. In an interview for this book, Miller said UNA was facing "a decline in revenues, . . . [which] had been coming on for years." He added, "I think there was a perception that I was the great white hope and I could turn things on a dime. I really tried, but after a period of time, given the competition and the hole we were in, the best course for us was the merger." When he took up the post, Miller said he was told that the first merger attempt had "ended very abruptly and it ended with a 'Hell, no, and don't come back to us ever again' . . . so that's not really an option." He added, "We considered other organizations. One thing I do recall was that we didn't want to take on a partner that had the same financial problems as us. We wanted someone who had financial resiliency, and UNF stood out in that respect."

He explained that the other organizations that were contacted were the Council on Foreign Relations, the Asia Society, and the Carnegie Endowment for International Peace. However, a UNA-UNF alliance was the only one that made sense: the UNF had the policy and advocacy programs and money, while UNA had the grassroots network. Miller said he mentioned the idea to Wirth. "He said, 'Don't bring this subject up ever again.' . . . I said okay, I heard loud and clear." However, Kathy Calvin, who was the chief operating officer at UNF at the time and a member of the UNA board, was more receptive. "So we started by Kathy and I having casual conversations, and we realized that it really made sense. We knew it was a good idea. We also knew we had some serious bad history to overcome," Miller said.

"I was in agreement with Tim's view the first time around," Calvin said in an interview for this book. She continued:

> I felt there were problems we just couldn't overcome at that time. Tim felt strongly that it could put the foundation at some risk, and he was right about that. I continued to think, however, . . . that I couldn't see any better options for UNA. I continued to worry that it would be a big black eye for the United States and for the UNA globally if it was unable to continue operating in the United States. I was eager to have this opportunity again, and I give a lot of credit to Tom for recognizing the moment was different and coming back with a somewhat different proposal.

Calvin is now president and chief executive officer of the UN Foundation.

One important difference in the second attempt was that the discrimination lawsuit was settled during the negotiations. That left the financial questions. "We put a somewhat different team together to begin doing a lot of the due diligence and exploration of some of the financial challenges, also looking at what we would realistically do with the organization if it became an initiative of the foundation," Calvin said. "The cash flow continued to be a very serious issue, and I think it is what brought [UNA] back to the table the second time. Because they realized they had to do something to preserve the brand and the name and the chapters, and we had a strong interest in doing that."

Calvin added that they really had to look at "what pieces would really support our ongoing advocacy, what we could do to strengthen chapters, how we would really make sure it had a chance of being successful," because, she explained, "our board still said that we could only take this step if it turned out to be revenue-neutral for the UN Foundation."

Peter Yeo was vice president for advocacy at UNF in 2009. In an interview for this book, he said, "I was asked to take a fresh look at it in light of the fact that they approached us again. I said, 'Well, we hate to say no just for the sake of saying no.' So I studied what the previous nature of the concerns were and looked at what the assets were that UNA had to offer." Yeo determined that "there was enough income stream that could potentially continue to come in that we felt that some sort of takeover could be financially viable, because the instruction I got from our board—or at least from our leadership—was it had to have no legal ramifications and it had to be cost neutral."

Miller said, "When I got to the point where I knew we could pull this off and everything was working, I bowed out. When you do a merger and you have two CEOs, there's always an odd man out. Early in the conversations with Kathy, I said just to make it easier, 'I'd love to continue, but I'm happy to be taken out of the equation.'" Ed Elmendorf was then named president, with the mandate to complete the merger. Elmendorf said, "I was asked very early on, before there was any public discussion, whether I thought an alliance would appeal to UNA-USA members and chapter leaders. My answer was unambiguously positive." He noted that Miller "brought me into the conversation quite early because, at that point, I was the chair of the Council of Chapters and Divisions—that is the head of the volunteer network and volunteer leadership within the UNA-USA. The chapters were the principal element attractive for the UNF in the discussions."

Elmendorf joined UNA-USA's board of directors in 2009. At the urging of Pickering, he took on the role of president and chief executive officer in 2010. "I had a mandate from the very beginning to work out an alliance between UNA-USA and UNF. It wasn't a standard continuing job of indefinite term. . . . From the very beginning it was that I will make the merger happen and then, by my own volition, step down."

Miller and Elmendorf also said the inclusion of a new actor during the second attempt was crucial to the success of the negotiations. SeaChange Capital Partners is a nonprofit consultancy firm that Elmendorf called "a very good and powerful dimension to the discussion." (SeaChange is a nonprofit merchant bank specializing in enabling nonprofit organizations to increase their impact through collaborations.) Two officials from the firm—John MacIntosh and Jerry Hirsch—worked with UNF and UNA, acting as mediators. "This was, to my mind, [an] outstanding example of facilitation by independent third parties," Elmendorf said.

MacIntosh, the SeaChange board member who oversaw the work with UNA and UNF, said he consulted Miller and Yeo and determined that "most of what they thought was irreconcilable was not," so it was "well worth seeing to try again." He said it was a "tricky issue" figuring out how to meld the "decentralized" UNA and the "centralized" UNF. In an interview for this book, MacIntosh said it was also important that the chapters "got comfortable" with the idea of an alliance.

MacIntosh added that the Lodestar Foundation was instrumental in the work. Lodestar is one of the few foundations focusing exclusively on helping nonprofits partner. In terms of the UNA-UNF negotiations, Lodestar financed the work, which included MacIntosh as the facilitator. Hirsch, the founder and chair of the foundation, said in an interview for this book that Lodestar's mission is "to leverage philanthropy within the limited resources we have." To do this, the foundation pursues two strategies: encourage nonprofits to collaborate and encourage more individual philanthropy. "I worked with Jerry on the transaction, which was only made possible because of Lodestar's financial support," MacIntosh said. Hirsch said that the negotiations needed "a tremendous amount of human effort to complete the transaction." The six months it took to complete it was "relatively rare," he added. Both said this project was one of their greatest successes. "Maybe it was not the best deal," MacIntosh said, but it was "one of the ones I will always remember."

In retrospect, Elmendorf said,

> I think the merger between UNA-USA [and UNF] in some form was inevitable once the UN Foundation had taken a decision to become a permanent institution rather than, as had initially been anticipated, to spend down Ted Turner's billion dollars over ten years and then go out

of existence. It didn't make any real sense in the American political and NGO landscape to have two organizations with such similar missions without some real close link between them.

Yeo, who came to the UN Foundation after serving on the staff of the House Foreign Affairs Committee, was first executive director of the Better World Campaign and then its president. The campaign is a sister organization of the UN Foundation. As Yeo explained, "It was actually created as a separate brand because the original board of the foundation wanted to make sure that we weren't using the UN name up on the Hill to advocate and lobby for the UN." The Better World Campaign "is focused on America's relationship with the United Nations," Yeo said, but "we didn't want it to be seen as somehow the UN was lobbying for itself. . . . That's why they created a separate brand." (The UN Foundation has six advocacy programs, including UNA and the Better World Campaign.)

Elmendorf also saw how the two organizations could complement each other. UNF and its Better World Campaign had "a strong presence in Washington, a strong staff advocacy capacity on Capitol Hill, and . . . an increasing presence at the UN in New York." Elmendorf went on to say, "But what the UN Foundation and Better World Campaign did not have is exactly what UNA-USA was able to bring to the table—namely, a nationwide presence on the ground, a hundred-plus chapters across the country, individual members, and a capacity through that network to speak publicly and to engage in advocacy with our elected representatives on UN issues."

The UNA chapters were the major selling point for the foundation. "It was a very wise investment from our perspective," Yeo said.

There were several different assets that the old UNA had, including BCUN, Global Classrooms, as well as the chapters. But from our perspective, the chapters were the most important asset because we have the Better World Campaign, which does DC-based advocacy and then does a lot of online organizing. But that sort of deeper level of advocacy, where you actually have trained, super-smart, educated champions who can talk to their policymakers and media about the power of the UN? You really get that with the chapters. . . . It has exceeded expectations.

The Council of Chapters and Regions (CCR) has continued to serve a "liaison role," bridging the chapters and the national office. Karen Mulhauser, the current chair of the council and an elected regional representative of the UNA-USA mid-east state chapters, said in an interview for this book, "I see the role as being the regional representative — what happens at the grassroots and what happens in the national office — as well as a resource for advice" for members to turn to. The focus of the new UNA, according to Mulhauser, "is to build grassroots capacity, to educate and advocate for the UN. While each chapter has a certain amount of autonomy — the ability to adopt certain resolutions and to advocate — the primary mission is to build support and awareness of the UN."

Since taking on UNA had to be revenue neutral, this condition guided the decisions by UNF when it decided which programs to retain. Yeo said the guiding principle was "don't take over initiatives without income stream." The chapters, BCUN, Global Classrooms, the Leo Nevas Human Rights Award, and the annual gala dinner all had their own sources of income. The Council of Organizations was also retained, even though it did not have an income, as it cost nothing. As to the other programs, Yeo said Adopt-A-Minefield had already been phased out, and HERO was "dead by the time we came" (see Chapter 11). The Iran Project, according to Yeo, "was a Luers thing . . . that was never on the table."

Chris Whatley, the executive director of UNA-USA, said in an interview for this book that, before the merger, UNA was, in many ways, "a think tank, with the chapter leadership as one small part of that organization." He added, "We are really a grassroots movement; so, for us, the decisions on how we allocate resources, where we invest our time and priorities are really defined by the chapter leaders who are represented through the [CCR]."

The NGO coalition for the International Criminal Court (AMICC) "was not core to what we wanted," Yeo said. It was based in New York and dealt with an international treaty, not a UN body. Yeo said it was not a political decision, even though "the ICC does not pop on the Hill." Not everyone saw it that way. (For more information on AMICC, see Chapter 14.)

Finally, there were legal issues regarding the alliance. "Within the UNA-USA, we had a number of important constituencies whose endorsement was required under the New York state nonprofit law," Elmendorf said. "The first was the UNA-USA board; hardly surprising, the first discussion in the full UNA-USA board gave rise to many, many skeptical questions. That was just at the point when Tom Miller was passing the baton to me." In addition, UNA-USA was incorporated in New York State, and most of the chapters received their tax-exempt status from the parent organization. Yeo said, "Our concern was for the existing organization to go away and be dissolved under their New York State law and for all the chapters to sign new affiliation agreements with us. And that's ultimately what we did. . . . It ended up not being much of a challenge." At that point, there were more than 100 chapters representing about 12,000 people. "It was worth the effort, and it has completely exceeded expectations as to what kind of impact it has had on our ability to be effective advocates," Yeo said. "Frankly, it should have happened years before it did because it's been incredibly helpful to us, and I think a lot of the long-standing UNA members are really pleased that this whole merger happened, because they feel that we're really servicing their needs. It's been good for us."

The makeup of UNA membership is changing. Whatley said that as "traditional" membership has remained constant, a concerted effort to increase youth membership has worked; he noted that roughly 60 percent of the current members (14,000) are younger than twenty-five years old. "It's creating opportunities for leadership at a chapter level where these young people reside and where they are cultivating their identity," Whatley said. "When you just think about activism within grassroots movements in the United States, they tend to happen with recent retirees and students." Mulhauser noted that "it's fairly dramatic," resulting in "expanded ideas for advocacy and education," such as Girl Up (a UNF campaign to address the needs of adolescent girls in developing countries) and Nothing But Nets (an antimalaria project of UNF).

According to Elmendorf,

> I think it would have made much more sense to work out an alliance between UNA-USA much earlier under the first attempt or even before that. Probably UNA-USA would have had more autonomy within the UN Foundation world and could conceivably even have remained a separate institution with [a] very close link to the UN Foundation. As time went on, the pressures within UNA-USA to move toward an alliance as a result of organizational and financial challenges rose that also inevitably reduced UNA-USA's room to maneuver in a negotiation for a merger.

Despite the smoothness of the second attempt, it was still bittersweet for UNA, especially for the long-standing board and chapter leaders. Miller said, "When I say merger, I really mean takeover, but merger makes it sound good." Felice Gaer was harsher: "I don't think it was a merger; I think it was a hostile takeover. I think the UNA suffered because it's now just a membership group."

On the other hand, Gillian Sorensen, who invented the term *alliance* to describe the new relationship, said,

> The coming together, and I do call it alliance, that's the correct term, . . . has turned out to be productive and has given added strength to both UNF and UNA. Naturally, there was a period of adjustment and some apprehension, particularly on the UNA side, but I think just about everyone in the chapters would now agree that it's been a very good outcome.

She added, "I very deliberately tried to become not just a supporter but a champion of this alliance. And I thought this can work, and it's very important that it work, because if not, UNA might sink. And that was unthinkable. So I felt the logistical questions, which were legal, financial, and personnel questions, could be resolved." Sorensen was also a member of the "quartet" that helped work out the details for the merger. The other three were Mike Beard (then deputy director of the Better World Campaign), Elmendorf, and Yeo.

Pickering, who was the cochair of the UNA-USA Board of Directors at the time, said, "It played out very well because I think over a period of time people thought the UNA needed to go back and focus more centrally on the UN questions it was engaged with. Negotiating the relationship with the UN Foundation solidified that." He added, "The United Nations Association has now a real opportunity to focus on bringing in new, younger membership. Becoming even more focused on a chapter-based organization. Supporting a number of continuing projects, which in effect either fill holes in what the UNF was doing or complemented the general direction of where UNF was going."

Looking Forward

Defining the mission of UNA-USA and its predecessors is easy: the promotion of internationalism in the United States, with the United Nations as a primary vehicle for the country's foreign relations. It is the execution of that mission that has been hard. During the days of the League of Nations Association (LNA), trying to engage a traditionally isolationist country to view itself as part of a global community was a thankless task. With the rejection of the League of Nations, suggesting that Washington should be involved in a peaceful international structure presented internationalists with a double bind. Yet the events of one day—December 7, 1941—instantly flipped the elite and popular opinion of the United States against isolationism. Again, it was war that drove opinion, but the LNA was there to work with like-minded leaders in building a postwar order.

Immediately after World War II, internationalism enjoyed tremendous popular support. In June 1945, more than 80 percent of Americans favored joining the United Nations and, in July, nearly two-thirds approved Senate ratification of the UN Charter, with only 3 percent opposed. The efforts by the AAUN, other NGOs, and political leaders to gain support for the United Nations and ratification of its charter (discussed in Chapter 3) clearly had a positive impact on public opinion, at least among people who knew about the UN.

Although there has been a consistent overall positive view of the UN in the United States, Americans' views of the world body have fluctuated over the seventy years of the UN's existence. In the 1970s, with the decline of the high levels of earlier popular support for the UN, a 1972 poll showed respect for the United Nations decreasing as the years went by. But, in the halcyon optimism of the post–Cold War period, a 1990 poll showed respect for the United Nations to be increasing. Americans' support for increasing US participation in the UN after the end of the Cold War is indicated by a nearly 20 percent growth in support from 1989 to 1991. In 1994, nearly 90 percent of Americans thought it extremely important or somewhat important that the United States cooperate with other countries by working through the UN.[7]

As Jeffrey Laurenti noted in Chapter 13: "Americans who wanted to change how the world worked, who hoped at last to realize a genuine international community that could save succeeding generations from the scourge of war, enlisted in the cause of the United Nations. Astonishingly, they still do."

This book has been a story of how an internationalist-minded, citizens-movement NGO helped drive a shift in a long-isolationist country to public and political acceptance of a new international order, through both grassroots and elite activism. LNA/AAUN and CSOP were pioneers in developing foreign policy positions that had public support, yet were designed for the governmental and international policymakers. As recounted in the first chapters, the UN and the AAUN-UNA never saw the responsibility to end "the scourge of war" as exclusively a military issue. Peace also involved creating the "conditions for stability and well-being." From the creation of UNESCO in 1945 to the Sustainable Development Goals of 2015, the UN and civil society, under the leadership of UNA-USA, have been advocates of peace throughout the history of both organizations.

Despite the overwhelming governmental and popular support for the UN at its founding, AAUN was almost always in a defensive position. When Porter McKeever, a future president of UNA, resigned from the US mission to the UN in 1952, he criticized the Truman administration for reducing the role of the UN in US policy to "the size of a pebble." The diminishment of the UN in the eyes of the US government has been a decades-long problem. In 1960, Eichelberger said at an AAUN conference that the UN was facing "a different kind of crisis, because it's not dramatic, it's the problem of interest slipping away from the United Nations." He added, "It has yet to be proven that to fragmentize the world's concerns and weaken the moral concern of the United Nations for peace problems will in any way lead to their solution in a more rapid way."[8] It is a commentary that still holds true.

US foreign policy stopped being an elitist pursuit decades ago. UNA and its emphasis on grassroots through its chapters helped promote an active, informed internationalist citizenry. According to Ed Luck, by the 1970s, "In many ways, I think it was the end of the foreign policy establishment, and foreign policy changed. And people began to recognize that in a democracy, you actually should have strong public input." UNA constantly adapted to this situation. It didn't hurt that this era was also a time of high-profile support for UNA from important figures in the Republican Party, including former US attorney general Elliot Richardson; William Scranton, the former Pennsylvania governor and ambassador; and Senators John Danforth of Missouri, Richard Lugar of Indiana, and Charles Percy of Illinois.

The fortunes of UNA have often been tied to the public perceptions of the UN itself. The UN had a central place in the post–World War II optimism. The AAUN (with the unique contributions of Eleanor Roosevelt) gained prestige and members accordingly. As a large segment of the US public soured on the UN and its work, UNA suffered as a result. Today, opposition to the UN ranges from the traditional unilateralists (John Bolton) to the truly paranoid (the belief that Agenda 21 will ban golf courses in the United States). Despite high-profile US advocates such as Ted Turner, the default setting of the current public mood is skepticism toward the UN.

A source of tension within UNA has been the divergent views of the fundamental role of UNA: whether it was primarily a vehicle for mobilizing US public support for the UN or whether it should also be an active participant in shaping foreign policy in general and toward the UN in particular. In fact, it has played both roles and gone beyond that to directly impact the UN itself. UNA's work developing policy strategies from the 1970s (the Parallel Studies Program) to the 1990s (the Multilateral Studies Program) to the 2000s (the Iran Dialogue) was not always popular with the membership and all board members, but the work broke new ground in dialogue and research that addressed ever-evolving challenges in international affairs. David Scheffer noted, "As an NGO, UNA was fulfilling that really critical function of helping policymakers do their job. . . . I don't think there was anything major other than [UNA] in those years" of the 1990s.

The growing diversity in UNA membership has been a positive trend over recent decades. Jim Olson pointed out the increasing ethnic diversity: "UNA-USA is much more diverse than it was, say, twenty-five years ago. American ethnic communities and new Americans have the potential to reenergize UNA and its local units." Peter Yeo noted that the stereotype of the UNA member as a retiree is outdated. Younger people are getting involved, he said, with 60 percent of members now under twenty-five years old. As Yeo explained, "We go around to Model UNs around the country and sign people up." Elmendorf also noted that under the UNF umbrella, UNA is working to expand its reach to new demographic groups, such as the Alpha Kappa Alpha sorority of African American women, with which it concluded a partnership several years ago.

As the UN dropped further out of the eye of the US public, "UNA becomes all the more important in the future to the United States as a responsible and collaborative global player but no longer the single dominant player," Elmendorf said. "Civil society now tends to mobilize more around specific issues (combatting poverty, banning land mines) than the more abstract notion of an international, or even global, community and this will continue to pose challenges to UNA as it identifies issues and opportunities that can motivate future generations to advocacy and action." Gillian Sorensen said, "What has changed is that the policy function . . . is now being done elsewhere. But the grassroots activity, which I think is very important, is growing and deepening. So it is different, but I think it's a good outcome." She added, "UNA is a very special organization, and it's very important that it survive and thrive. I'm confident that it will. The rough patch it has come through is now resolved. And the UNA/UNF relationship is here to stay."

Notes

1. Unless otherwise noted, financial figures in this section were derived from the annual audit reports of UNA-USA, as analyzed by A. Edward Elmendorf, with assistance from Bridget B. Brady and Brian Dolan.

2. "Financial Statements of UNA-USA, Report of Independent Auditors," Ernst & Young LLP, 1987–1991. Seton Hall University (SHU Archives), The Msgr. William Noé Field Archives and Special Collections Center, South Orange, NJ, box 124.

3. Minutes, Executive Committee Meeting, February 2, 2009, SHU Archives, box 124.

4. Ted Turner, National Press Club (speech), Washington, DC, October 9, 2006.

5. SHU Archives, box 003.

6. John Goshko, "Ted Turner to Give UN $1 Billion," *Washington Post,* September 9, 1997.

7. For a detailed analysis of public opinion polling on the UN and UNA, please see the UNA-USA History Project website: http://blogs.shu.edu/UNA -USA/.

8. The Clark M. Eichelberger Papers, Manuscripts and Archives Division, New York Public Library. Astor, Lenox, and Tilden Foundations (NYPL Archives), box 116.

Acronyms

AAM	Adopt-A-Minefield
AAUN	American Association for the United Nations
ABM	Anti-Ballistic Missile Treaty
ACDA	Arms Control and Disarmament Agency
AFL	American Federation of Labor
AMICC	American Nongovernmental Organizations Coalition for the International Criminal Court
APAJ	Asia Pacific Association of Japan
ASPA	American Servicemembers' Protection Act
BCUN	Business Council for the United Nations
BIA	Bilateral Immunity Agreement
CCR	Council of Chapters and Regions
CCUN	Collegiate Council for the UN
CDA	Committee to Defend America
CDAAA	Committee to Defend America by Aiding the Allies
CEDAW	Convention on the Elimination of All Forms of Discrimination Against Women
CIO	Congress of Industrial Organizations
CIS	Commonwealth of Independent States
CSD	Commission for Sustainable Development
CSOP	Commission to Study the Organization of Peace
CSR	Center for Strategic Research
DoD	Department of Defense
ECOSOC	Economic and Social Council (of the UN)
EPC	Economic Policy Council
FAO	Food and Agriculture Organization (of the UN)
FFF	Fight for Freedom
G77	Group of 77
GA	General Assembly

GCDC	Global Classrooms Washington, DC
HERO	Help Educate At-Risk Orphans and Vulnerable Children
IAEA	International Atomic Energy Agency
ICC	International Criminal Court
ICJ	International Court of Justice
ICPD	International Conference on Population and Development
ILC	International Law Commission
ILO	International Labour Organization
IPIS	Institute for Political and International Studies
LNA	League of Nations Association
MDG	Millennium Development Goals
NAACP	National Association for the Advancement of Colored People
NGO	Nongovernmental Organization
NIEO	New International Economic Order
NPT	Nuclear Nonproliferation Treaty
NSC	National Security Council
OECD	Organization for Economic Co-operation and Development
OMB	Office of Management and Budget
ONUC	Opération des Nations Unies au Congo
SIPRI	Stockholm International Peace Research Institute
UNA-USA/UNA	United Nations Association of the United States of America
UNCED	United Nations Conference on Environment and Development
UNCTAD	United Nations Conference on Trade and Development
UNDP	United Nations Development Programme
UNEF	United Nations Emergency Force
UNESCO	United Nations Educational, Scientific and Cultural Organization
UNF	United Nations Foundation
UNFPA	United Nations Population Fund
UNICEF	United Nations Children's Fund
UNIDO	United Nations Industrial Development Organization
UNOPS	United Nations Office for Project Services
UNSC/SC	United Nations Security Council
USIP	United States Institute of Peace
WFUNA	World Federation of United Nations Associations
WHO	World Health Organization
WICC	Washington Working Group on the International Criminal Court
WMD	Weapons of Mass Destruction

Bibliography

Adams, Alvin. Telephone interview with authors (April 17, 2015).

Arieff, Irwin, and Dulcie Leimbach, eds. *A Global Agenda: Issues Before the General Assembly*. New York: United Nations Association of the United States of America (various editions; 2009–2011).

Ariyoruk, Ayca. Telephone interview with authors (January 22, 2015).

Baillargeon, Patricia. Telephone interview with authors (Spring/Summer 2014).

Benjamin, Robert. "Franklin D. Roosevelt Oral History Program: Interview with Robert Benjamin." By Dr. Thomas Soapes, Hyde Park, NY.

Birenbaum, David E. Telephone interview with authors (August 26, 2014).

Boettiger, John Roosevelt. E-mail interview with authors (February 4, 2015).

Brookfield, Samuel L. In-person interview with authors (March 4, 2015).

Brumberg, Daniel, and Eriks Berzins. "US-Iranian Engagement: Toward a Grand Agenda?" USIP Working Paper, United States Institute of Peace, Washington, DC, June 2009. http://www.usip.org/publications/us-iranian -engagement.

Calvin, Kathy. Telephone interview with authors (May 11, 2015).

Carlin, Peggy. In-person interview with authors (December 2014).

Changing World magazine (various editions, 1941–1946).

Crossette, Barbara. E-mail interview with authors (Summer 2014).

Dallen, Russell M. Jr., ed. *A UN Revitalized: A Compilation of UNA-USA Recommendations on Strengthening the Role of the United Nations in Peacemaking, Peacekeeping, and Conflict Prevention*. New York: United Nations Association of the United States of America, May 1992.

Dick, Edison. In-person interview with authors (August 30, 2012).

DiMaggio, Suzanne. *The Iran Primer*. Washington, DC: United States Institute of Peace, 2010. http://iranprimer.usip.org/resource/track-ii-diplomacy.

———. In-person interview with authors (December 11, 2013).

Dimoff, Steven. In-person interviews with authors (November 12, 2012; July 22, 2014).

Dimoff, Steven, et al., eds. *Washington Weekly Report* (various editions; 1973–1998).

"Directions and Dilemmas in Collective Security: Reflections from a Global Roundtable." New York: United Nations Association of the United States of America, January 1992.

Drakulich, Angie. E-mail interview with authors (Summer 2014).

Eckhard, Fred. In-person interview with authors (May 2014).

Eichelberger, Clark M. *Organizing for Peace: A Personal History of the Founding of the United Nations*. New York: Harper & Row, 1977.

— — —. *The United Nations Charter: What Was Done at San Francisco*. New York: American Association for the United Nations and the Commission to Study the Organization of Peace, June 1945.

— — —. *UN: The First Fifteen Years*. New York: Harper & Brothers, 1960.

— — —. *UN: The First Ten Years*. New York: Harper & Brothers, 1955.

— — —. *UN: The First Twenty Years*. New York: Harper & Row, 1965.

— — —. *UN: The First Twenty-Five Years*. New York: Harper & Row, 1970.

The Clark M. Eichelberger Papers. Manuscripts and Archives Division. New York Public Library. Astor, Lenox, and Tilden Foundations.

Eliasson, Jan. In-person interview with authors (June 2013).

Elmendorf, A. Edward. In-person interview with authors (October 22, 2014).

Farnsworth, Albert H., ed. *Vista* (various editions; 1965–1973).

Fromuth, Peter, ed. *A Successor Vision: The United Nations of Tomorrow* (A UNA-USA Publication). Lanham, MD: University Press of America, 1988.

Gaer, Felice D. "American Association for the United Nations." *The Eleanor Roosevelt Encyclopedia*, 5–8. Westport, CT: Greenwood Press, 2001.

— — —. In-person interview with authors (July 25, 2014).

Gati, Toby Trister. In-person interview with authors (December 11, 2013).

— — —, ed. *The US, the UN and the Management of Global Change* (A UNA-USA Publication). New York: New York University Press, 1983.

Glendon, Mary Ann. *A World Made New: Eleanor Roosevelt and the Universal Declaration of Human Rights*. New York: Random House, 2001.

A Global Agenda: Issues Before the General Assembly (various editions; 1978–1986).

Hadi, Nahela. In-person interview with authors (February 5, 2015).

Hartley, Livingston, et al. *Washington Office Information Letter*. Washington, DC: Committee to Defend America by Aiding the Allies, 1941.

Hinerfeld, Ruth. In-person interview with authors (March 16, 2015).

Hirsch, Jerry. Telephone interview with authors (June 3, 2015).

Horvath, Jordan. In-person interview with authors (Winter 2014).

Hunt, Janice. Telephone interview with authors (March 3, 2013).

The InterDependent (2000–2009).

Johnstone, Andrew. *Dilemmas of Internationalism: The American Association for the United Nations and US Foreign Policy, 1941–1948*. Surry and Burlington, VT: Ashgate, 2009.

— — —. "To Mobilize a Nation: Citizens' Organizations and Intervention on the Eve of World War II." In *The US Public and American Foreign Policy* (Routledge Studies in US Foreign Policy), edited by Andrew Johnstone and Helen Laville. London: Taylor & Francis, 2010.

Josephson, Harold. *James T. Shotwell and the Rise of Internationalism in America*. Teaneck, NJ: Fairleigh Dickinson University Press, 1975.

Kennedy, Paul. *The Parliament of Man: The Past, Present, and Future of the United Nations*. New York: Random House, 2006.

Krasner, Stephen D. "The United Nations and Political Conflict Between the

North and the South," 210–226. In *The US, the UN, and the Management of Global Change* (A UNA-USA Publication), edited by Toby Trister Gati. New York and London: New York University Press, 1983.

Lange, John. Telephone interview with authors (December 18, 2015).

Laurenti, Jeffrey. *The Common Defense: Peace and Security in a Changing World* (A Report of the UNA-USA Global Policy Project). New York: United Nations Association of the United States of America, 1992.

———. In-person interview with authors (December 12, 2013).

———. *Partners for Peace: Strengthening Collective Security for the 21st Century* (A Report of the UNA-USA Global Policy Project). New York: United Nations Association of the United States of America, 1992.

———, ed. *The Preparedness Gap: Making Peace Operations Work in the 21st Century* (A UNA-USA Policy Report). New York: United Nations Association of the United States of America, 2001.

———. *Pulling Together: A Program for America in the United Nations* (A Report of the UNA-USA Multilateral Project). New York: United Nations Association of the United States of America, 1988.

———. *A Stronger Hand: Shaping an American Agenda for a More Effective United Nations* (A Report of the UNA-USA Multilateral Project). New York: United Nations Association of the United States of America, 1988.

Laurenti, Jeffrey, and Francesca Lyman. *One Earth, Many Nations: The International System and Problems of Global Environment* (A Briefing Book of the Multilateral Project). New York: UNA-USA and the Sierra Club, 1990.

Lenefsky, David. In-person interview with authors (November 17, 2014).

Leonard, James. "The Association for Diplomatic Studies and Training Foreign Affairs Oral History Project: Interview with James Leonard." By Warren Unna, March 10, 1993. http://www.adst.org/OH%20TOCs/Leonard,%20 James%20.toc.pdf.

———. In-person interview with authors (March 15, 2013).

Linzer, Estelle. "The Way We Were: An Informal History of the American Association for the United Nations from 1945 Through 1964 When It Merged with the United States Committee for the United Nations to Become the United Nations Association of the United States of America." Unpublished manuscript, 1995.

Luck, Edward C. "The Impact of the Zionism-Racism Resolution on the Standing of the United Nations in the United States." In *Israel Yearbook on Human Rights* (published under the Auspices of the Faculty of Law, Tel Aviv University). Dordrecht/Boston/London: Martinus Nijhoff Publishers, 1987.

———. In-person interview with authors (September 19, 2014).

———. *Mixed Messages: American Politics and International Organization, 1919–1999.* Washington, DC: Brookings Institution Press, 1999.

Luers, William. In-person interview with authors (September 30, 2014).

———. Telephone interview with authors (July 29, 2015).

Luers, William, Thomas R. Pickering, and Jim Walsh. "For a New Approach to Iran." *New York Review of Books,* August 15, 2013.

———. "How to Deal with Iran." *New York Review of Books,* February 12, 2009.

———. "A Solution for the US-Iran Nuclear Standoff." *New York Review of Books,* March 20, 2008.

MacEachron, Allison. In-person interview with authors (August 2, 2014).

MacIntosh, John. Telephone interview with authors (June 3, 2015).

Meagher, Robert F. "United States Financing of the United Nations." In *The US, the UN, and the Management of Global Change* (A UNA-USA Publication), edited by Toby Trister Gati. New York and London: New York University Press, 1983.

Meisler, Stanley. *United Nations: The First Fifty Years.* New York: The Atlantic Monthly Press, 1995.

Miller, Thomas. Telephone interview with authors (February 24, 2015).

Miller, William. In-person interview with authors (August 19, 2014).

Moss, Lawrence C. "Renewing America's Commitment to International Law." UNA-USA Occasional Paper, United Nations Association of the United States of America, New York, March 2010.

Mulhauser, Karen. Telephone interview with the authors (August 22, 2015).

Munger, Richard. Telephone interview with authors (December 8, 2014).

Murrow, Edward R. *Person to Person* (broadcasts). CBS News archives.

Olson, Jim. E-mail interviews with authors (March 2014; September 2014).

Piasecki, Edmund T., ed. "Curbing the Middle East Arms Race: Policy Options for the United States and the United Nations." UNA-USA Occasional Paper 8, New York, December 1992.

Picco, Giandomenico, A. Kamal Aboulmagd, Lourdes Arizpe, Hanan Ashrawi, Ruth Cardoso, Jacques Delors, Leslie Gelb, et al. *Crossing the Divide: Dialogue Among Civilizations.* South Orange, NJ: School of Diplomacy and International Relations, Seton Hall University, 2001.

Pickering, Thomas. In-person interview with authors (February 21, 2014).

Raucher, Alan R. *Paul G. Hoffman: Architect of Foreign Aid.* Lexington: The University Press of Kentucky, 1984.

Robert S. Benjamin: A Citizen's Citizen (anthology). New York: United Nations Association of the United States of America (no author or editor), 1980.

Robins-Mowry, Dorothy B. *Experiment in Democracy: The Story of US Citizen Organizations in Forging the Charter of the United Nations.* New York: Parkside Press, 1971.

———. In-person interview with authors (June 6, 2013).

Rodley, Nigel S. "The Development of United Nations Activities in the Field of Human Rights and the Role of Non-Governmental Organizations," 263–282. In *The US, the UN, and the Management of Global Change* (A UNA-USA Publication), edited by Toby Trister Gati. New York and London: New York University Press, 1983.

Rodriguez, Lucia. In-person interview with authors (February 2015).

"Roles for the United Nations After the Gulf War." New York: United Nations Association of the United States of America (no author or editor), February 1991.

Roosevelt, Eleanor. "My Day." A comprehensive, electronic edition of Eleanor Roosevelt's "My Day" newspaper columns, prepared by the Eleanor Roosevelt Papers Project, George Washington University, http://www.gwu.edu/~erpapers/myday/.

———. *This I Remember*. New York: Harper & Brothers, 1949.

Rosenberg, Rosalind. "Virginia Gildersleeve: Opening the Gates." *Living Legacies: Great Moments, and Leading Figures in the History of Columbia University*, 2001. http://www.columbia.edu/cu/alumni/Magazine/Summer2001 /Gildersleeve.html.

Ross, Arthur. Private collection, courtesy of Janet Ross.

Ross, Janet. In-person interview with authors (May 5, 2015).

Scheffer, David J. Telephone interview with authors (January 22, 2015).

———. "The United Nations in the Gulf Crisis and Options for U.S. Policy." Published by UNA-USA, October 1990.

Schlesinger, Stephen C. *Act of Creation: The Founding of the United Nations*. Boulder, CO: Westview, 2003.

Seton Hall University. The Msgr. William Noé Field Archives and Special Collections Center, South Orange, NJ.

Shannon, John. In-person interview with authors (April 21, 2015).

Slim, Randa M. *The U.S.-Iran Track II Dialogue (2002–2008): Lessons Learned and Implications for the Rockefeller Brothers Fund's Grantmaking Strategy*. New York: Rockefeller Brothers Fund, August 3, 2010.

Smith, Courtney B. In-person interview with authors (March 26, 2015).

Sorensen, Gillian. In-person interview with authors (January 16, 2014).

Tessitore, John. E-mail interview with authors (January 30, 2015).

UNA-USA Annual Reports, 1983–2009/2010.

UNA-USA. "Celebrating 70 Years." http://www.unausa.org/membership/70th -anniversary.

Underwood, William Paul. In-person interview with authors (March 24, 2015).

United Nations. "History of the United Nations." http://www.un.org/en/about un/history/index.shtml.

The US-Iran Relationship: Breaking the Stalemate. Unpublished UNA-USA report, October 11, 2005.

vanden Heuvel, William. In-person interview with authors (October 2, 2014).

———. Private archives.

Vital Speeches of the Day. https://www.vsotd.com.

Washburn, John. In-person interview with authors (September 17, 2014).

Wattleton, Faye. In-person interview with authors (February 26, 2015).

Weston, Josh. In-person interview with authors (February 3, 2015).

Whatley, Chris. In-person interview with authors (August 5, 2015).

Whitehead, John C. In-person interview with authors (January 21, 2014).

———. *A Life in Leadership: From D-Day to Ground Zero*. New York: A New America Book, Basic Books, 2005.

Yeo, Peter. In-person interview with authors (April 30, 2015).

Index

About the Book

Little known outside a small community of insiders, the United Nations Association–USA has had an impact on both the UN and the US-UN relationship far greater than its size would suggest. James Wurst explores that impact as he traces the sometimes tortuous history of the UNA-USA from its earliest days to the present.

Beginning with efforts in support of the creation of the United Nations—and covering the decades-long campaign to promote the UN to the US public, the role of Eleanor Roosevelt, the decline of popular support, Track II diplomacy with Iran and the Soviet Union, and much more—Wurst draws on a wealth of archival material and personal interviews to tell an honest, and long overdue, story of the UNA-USA's persistence, problems, and achievements.

James Wurst has been reporting on international affairs, and especially the United Nations, since 1977.